THE BRITISH CONTRIBUTION TO THE EUROPE OF THE TWENTY-FIRST CENTURY

THE CLIFFORD CHANCE LECTURES
VOLUME VI

The British Contribution to the Europe of the Twenty-First Century

The British Academy Centenary Lectures

Edited by

PROFESSOR BASIL MARKESINIS, QC, DCL, FBA

·HART·
PUBLISHING
OXFORD – PORTLAND OREGON
2002

Hart Publishing
Oxford and Portland, Oregon

Published in North America (US and Canada) by
Hart Publishing c/o
International Specialized Book Services
5804 NE Hassalo Street
Portland, Oregon
97213-3644
USA

Distributed in the Netherlands, Belgium and Luxembourg by
Intersentia, Churchillaan 108
B2900 Schoten
Antwerpen
Belgium

© The editor and contributors severally 2002

The editor and contributors to this work have asserted their right under the
Copyright, Designs and Patents Act 1988, to be identified as the authors of
this work

Hart Publishing is a specialist legal publisher based in Oxford, England.
To order further copies of this book or to request a list of other
publications please write to:

Hart Publishing, Salter's Boatyard, Folly Bridge,
Abingdon Road, Oxford OX1 4LB
Telephone: +44 (0)1865 245533 or Fax: +44 (0)1865 794882
e-mail: mail@hartpub.co.uk
WEBSITE: http//www.hartpub.co.uk

British Library Cataloguing in Publication Data
Data Available
ISBN 1–84113–276–4 (hardback)

Typeset by Hope Services (Abingdon) Ltd.
Printed and bound in Great Britain on acid-free paper by
TJ International Ltd, Padstow, Cornwall

Contents

	Preface and Acknowledgements	vii
	List of Contributors	ix
1	The Tides of Change *The Rt Hon The Lord Woolf*	1
2	Europe and English Commercial Law *Professor Sir Roy Goode*	15
3	The British Contribution to the Development of Law and Legal Process in the European Union *Judge David Edward*	25
4	The British Contribution to Italian Legal Thinking *Professor Dr Dr.h.c. Guido Alpa*	37
5	Tutorial and Repetitorium: Parallel and Different Techniques of Teaching Law in England and Germany *Professor Basil Markesinis*	63
6	Two-Way Traffic: the Warburg Institute as a Microcosm of Cultural Exchange between Britain and Europe *Professor Nicholas Mann*	93
7	Freedom of the Press and Intellectual Interchange *Baroness Onora O'Neill*	105
8	Insiders and Outsiders *Professor Sir John Elliott*	115
9	British Art, Art History and Aesthetic Criticism in a European Perspective *Professor Stephen Bann*	129
10	Political Culture: Renegotiating the Post-War Social Contract *Mr Frank Field*	139
11	Strategic Direction or Tactical Management? Doctrinal Constraints and Political Perceptions of Europe *Professor Kenneth Dyson*	151
12	After Keynes *Professor Giorgio La Malfa*	187

13	The British Contribution to European Union in the Twentieth Century: The Idea of Responsible Government *Professor Vernon Bogdanor*	199
14	The British Contribution to the Europe of the Twenty-first Century *The Rt Hon The Lord Hurd*	215
15	Great Britain and France, Driving Forces Behind a Benchmark Europe *M Laurent Fabius*	229
16	The Role of Britain in Europe of the Twenty-first Century: The International Law Firm Perspective *Mr Keith Clark*	241
17	The Impact of European Law in French Law: Lessons for England? *Mme Noelle Lenoir*	249

Preface and Acknowledgements

In the summer of 2000 the Overseas Committee of the British Academy of which I am a member was asked to put forward ideas about events that would suitably celebrate the Academy's forthcoming Centenary. I proposed a conference with the title of this book as its theme. As is so often the case with such proposals, the title did not do full justice to the broad interests of the Academy. But it was moderately manageable compared, at any rate, with other suggestions that were considered; and it indisputably dealt with a problem which, whether we like it or not, is one of the defining issues of our times: Europe. It was thus accepted by Council late in September 2000 and I found out what a mistake it can be to volunteer ideas and services.

Precisely because "Europe" is such a rich and controversial subject, we tried from the outset to approach our topic from different angles—the political, the legal, the economic, and one which, for lack of a better heading, could be called the "movement of ideas". We also tried to give it a slant that has not frequently been reflected in the current debates on the subject since most of these try to demonstrate how beneficial or disastrous our eventual joining of "Europe" will be. In the conference, however, we tried to discuss the reverse: what we have done or can do for Europe. Once again, the coverage is neither complete nor conclusive (and the guideline was not always strictly adhered to by all authors.) But given the numerous technical difficulties that confronted us, not least of which was the need to organise a conference that did not last beyond one day, this is as good as it could be. On its own, this conference (and this book which was born of it) cannot hope to do full justice to the important occasion which the Academy is celebrating. But taken together with the other events organised by the Academy, I believe it does demonstrate its wide interests, its keenness to encourage (where appropriate) interdisciplinary debate, and its firm commitment to an open mind.

Twenty-five speakers were invited to deliver brief keynote addresses to a selected audience of two hundred and fifty people from all walks of life and then spend most of the day debating their ideas with them. Twenty accepted our invitation. Two subsequently dropped out while a third withdrew his stimulating script, literally on the day we were going to the printers because his party embargoed all speeches on Europe. A bigger loss was that of the former French Prime Minister and, currently, Minister for Finance, M Laurent Fabius. Initially eager to join us, he later pulled out from the conference itself because the legislative elections in his country meant that he could not take time off from the fray to join us in London. With characteristic style, however, he offered a written contribution, which we were glad to include in this collection. Sixteen others, despite the many demands on their time, took full part in an event, which was as important to the Academy as it was enjoyable and, I hope, profitable for those who attended it. Our first debt of gratitude is thus to all of these busy speakers for the considerable time they devoted to our undertaking. We are also grateful to Madame Noelle Lenoir, until recently a Justice at the *Conseil Constitutionnel*, for allowing us to reprint as a postscript her recent Annual Clifford Chance lecture on "The Impact of European Law on French Law". This unpublished text was included not only because of a certain wit and frankness which is not typical of the pronouncements of high judges, but also because it shows how the European factor has worked in some countries to strengthen not weaken transparency and democratic accountability. For these reasons and also because it provides some interesting insights into the art of comparative law, it has been included as a kind of postscript to the proceedings. But by itself the time given to us by our various speakers would not have been sufficient. To stage such an important production a "χορηγὸς" is needed now as was in the times of Aeschylus and Sophocles. With us he took the form of Clifford Chance. I think I speak for the entire Academy when I stress our indebtedness to this firm and, in particular, its former Chairman Keith Clark and its current CEO Peter Cornell for making, through a magnificent gift, such a huge multinational event possible. Culture like business can do better when not confined by national borders.

To the Academy's debts I must add my own as one of the organisers of the conference and the (main) editor of the book. Professor Nicholas Mann CBE, FBA, supervised the entire project from "conception to safe delivery", sparing me and others many embarrassing mistakes and crucially helping me with the editing of one script. Peter Brown CBE, the omnipresent secretary of the Academy, likewise provided constant advice and support for which I am most grateful. Closer to the coalface were Jane Lyddon and Amy Brown. Jane's enormous experience with the Overseas Committee (among other things) was combined with a degree of dedication and an ability to meet the deadlines (and they were many) which, in my experience, is as unique as it is impressive. Amy, who is my Personal Assistant at UCL's Institute of Global Law, kindly volunteered her invaluable services *outside* normal office hours and (with Jane) handled everything from invitation lists to bookings and editorial work. Neither the conference nor the book would have been possible without their help and the least I can do is to make this debt public.

I can only conclude by saying that the customary phrase "I remain responsible for all remaining mistakes and misjudgements" has never been more sincerely meant.

Bentham's College Basil Markesinis QC, LL.D., DCL, FBA
London
28 October 2001

List of Contributors

Professor Dr Dr. L.c. Guido Alpa is Professor Civil and Commercial Law at the University of Rome, *La Sapienza*; Visiting Professor of Comparative Law at the University of Genoa; Doctor Iuris, honoris causa, University of Madrid (*la Compultense*) and Hon. Bencher of Gray's Inn, London. A prolific author on matters of civil, commercial and comparative law, he also practices law in Rome and Genoa.

Professor Stephen Bann is Professor of History of Art at the University of Bristol and has served as Visiting Professor at the Universities of Rennes, John Hopkins, and Bologna. He is a Fellow of the British Academy.

Professor Vernon Bogdanor CBE, FRSA, is Professor of Government and Fellow of Brasenose College, Oxford. He is a Fellow of the British Academy. Since 1988 he has served as a Special Adviser on Constitutional and Electoral matters to the Governments of the Czech Republic, Hungary and Israel.

Keith Clark, BCL, was Chairman of Clifford Chance LL.P. from 1990 to 2000 when he resigned his post to become Head of International General Counsel of Morgan Stanley. Last year, he was made a *Chevalier dans l'Ordre Nationale de la Légion d' Honneur* by President Jacques Chirac for services to Anglo-French relations.

Professor Kenneth Dyson is Professor of European Studies at the University of Bradford and Co-Director of the European Briefing Unit of the same University. He is a Fellow of the British Academy and the Royal Historical Society.

Judge David Edward has been a Judge of the Court of Justice of the European Communities since 1992. He was previously Salvesen Professor of European Institutions at the University of Edinburgh. He is a Companion of the Order of St Michael and St George and a Fellow of the Royal Society of Edinburgh. He is a member of the Faculty of Advocates in Scotland, an honorary Bencher of Gray's Inn and an honorary Fellow of University College, Oxford. He has been awarded honorary degrees in law by the Universities of Aberdeen, Edinburgh, Münster, Napier, and the Saarland.

Professor Sir John Elliott was Regius Professor of Modern History at the University of Oxford between 1990 and 1997 and Fellow (and now Hon. Fellow) of Oriel College, Oxford. He is a Fellow of the British Academy, the American Academy of Arts and Sciences and a Corresponding Member of the Hispanic Society of America, of the *Real Academia Sevillana de Buenas Letras*, the Royal Academy of Letters of Barcelona and The National Academy of History of Venezuela. He holds honorary doctorates from, among others, the Universities of Madrid, Genoa, Barcelona, Valencia, Portsmouth, and Warwick. Among his many civil honours are the Grand Cross of the Order of Alfonso X and the Grand Cross of the Order of Isabel la Católica.

M Laurent Fabius is a graduate of both the Ecole Nationale Supérieure and the Ecole Nationale d'Adminsitration and a Coseiller d' Etat. He was first elected to the Assemblée Nationale in 1978 and then again in 1981,1986,1988,199, and 1997. He served as Directeur du Cabinet of the late François Mitterand and then in various ministerial posts before becoming at thirty-eight (the youngest) Prime Minister of France. He served in that office until 1986 and was then elected President of the Assemblée Nationale where he served between 1988 and 1992 and 1997 and 2000 when he took over as Minister of Finance of the Economy, Finance, and Industry. He is the author of four books: *La France Inégale*, Le Cœur du Futur, C'est en allant vers la mer, and *Les Blessures de la Vérité*.

The Rt. Hon. Frank Field has been Member of Parliament for Birkenhead since 1979 and served as the Chairman of the Select Committee on Social Services between 1987 and 1990. He also served as Minister of State in the DSS between 1997 and 1998 when he was made a Privy Councillor. He has authored or co-authored many books on welfare reform and related matters.

Professor Sir Roy Goode QC, CBE, was Professor of Commercial Law at the University of London from 1973 to 1990 where he founded and Directed at Queen Mary and Westfield College the Centre for Commercial Law. Between 1990 and 1998 he held the Norton Rose Chair of English Law at the University of Oxford along with a Fellowship at St. John's College, Oxford. The author (or co-author) of numerous books, he is Fellow of the British Academy, an Honorary Bencher of the Inner Temple, and an honorary doctor of the University of London.

The Rt. Hon. The Lord Hurd of Westwell, CH, CBE was Member of Parliament from 1974 to 1997. He served as Secretary of State for Northern Ireland (1984–85), Home Department (1985–89), and as Foreign Secretary between 1989 and 1995. He is the author of many novels, short stories, and works on contemporary affairs.

Professor Giorgio La Malfa is Professor of Economic Policy at the University of Catania, and currently a Member of the Italian Parliament, and Chairman of its Finance Committee. He was previously Budget Minister (1989–92) and a Member of the European Parliament (1989–92, 1994–99).

Mme Noelle Lenoir is a member of the Conseil d' Etat. After working as a full time judge she was seconded to various Government posts (including the Senate and the Ministry of Justice) and was then appointed the first woman Member of the Conseil Constitutionnel. Her nine-year stint came to an end last year when she reverted to the Conseil d' Etat but decided to take sabbatical leave and serve for a year as Visiting Professor at the Yale Law School and University College London. A prolific author, especially on matters of biotechnology and bioethics, she is an Honorary Bencher of Gray's Inn and holds honorary doctorates from a number of Universities, including the University of London.

Professor Nicholas Mann CBE is Professor of the History of the Classical Tradition and Dean of the School of Advanced Study in the University of London, having served as Director of the Warburg Institute between 1990 and 2001. He is a Fellow of the British Academy and its Foreign Secretary since 1999.

Professor Basil Markesinis QC, LL.D. (Cantab.), DCL (Oxon.), is Professor of Common Law and Civil Law at University College London and Jamail Regents Chair at the University of Texas at Austin. Before taking up his present post he held the Chair of Comparative Law at the University of Oxford where he founded and Directed the Oxford Institute of European and Comparative Law (1995–2000). He is a Fellow of the British Academy, a Corresponding Fellow of the Academies of Athens, the Royal Belgian Academy and the Royal Netherlands Academy and a Member of the American Law Institute. He has been honoured with honorary degrees by the Universities of Ghent, Munich, and Paris I.

Baroness O'Neill of Bengarve, CBE, has been Principal of Newnham College, Cambridge since 1992. She is Fellow of the British Academy and a Foreign Hon. Member of the American Academy of Arts and Sciences and was a Fellow of the *Wissenschaftskollegium* of Berlin during 1989–90.

The Rt. Hon. The Lord Woolf of Barnes is the Lord of Chief Justice of England and Wales having previously served in the House of Lords as Lord of Appeal in Ordinary (1992–6) and then Master of the Rolls (1996–2000). He is an Honorary Fellow of the British Academy and holds honorary doctorates from (among others) the Universities of Buckingham, Bristol, and London. He has served as Pro-Chancellor of the University of London since 1994 and is the President of UCL's Institute of Global Law.

1

The Tides of Change

THE RT HON THE LORD WOOLF

INTRODUCTION

For at least 400 years the influence of the common law has spread round the globe from this country so that it provides the base for approximately a third of the world's legal systems. The global spread of the civil law system on which the legal systems of France, Germany and Holland are based has been equally impressive. It is, however, only in the last half, and more obviously over the last quarter, of a century that there has been increasing evidence that at least in Europe the common law and civil law systems are each having a profound influence on the other.

The catalyst for change has been the development of economic interdependence within Europe, coupled with the development of the global economy and the growth of human rights. The European Court of Justice and the European Court of Human Rights have played a central role in facilitating the process. From an historical perspective the critical events will probably prove to be the eventual decision that this country should become part of the European Community in 1972 and the belated decision in 1998 that the European Convention of Human Rights should become part of our domestic law.

Few lawyers and even fewer politicians anticipated that this country's membership of the Community would have a profound effect on our legal system. Twenty-seven years ago, Lord Denning MR prophetically anticipated the consequences for the English common law legal system of this country becoming a member of the European Communities in these famous words:

> "When we come to matters with a European element, the Treaty is like an incoming tide. It flows into the estuaries and up the rivers. It cannot be held back".[1]

But even Lord Denning could not anticipate the full effect of our becoming a member of the European Community. Just before making the remark which I have already cited, he said:

> "The first and fundamental point is that the Treaty concerns only those matters which have a European element, that is to say, matters which affect people or property in the

[1] *Bulmer Ltd* v. *Bollinger S.A.* [1974] Ch. 401, 418.

nine countries of the common market besides ourselves. The Treaty does not touch any of the matters which concern solely England and the people in it. These are still governed by English law."

Subsequent events have therefore not totally vindicated Lord Denning. While the first cited comment has proved to be profound, the consequences of our membership have been much broader then he anticipated. As a result of Community law becoming part of our law even the cornerstone of our constitution, the sovereignty of parliament, has been compromised: it is now subject to the superior force of Community legislation, which is of direct effect, and the decisions of the European Court.

The jurisprudence of the Community swept in with the tide deeply rooted principles from the legal systems of the founding Member States. Principles, which had been absorbed into Community law,[2] were then in turn sucked into our domestic case law and in course of time digested so completely that their ancestry has become of no significance. To take but two examples, the German principles of legitimate expectations and proportionality are now firmly rooted in English administrative law.

Tides do not flow in only one direction. While every river and estuary boasts an incoming tide, of equal importance is the outgoing tide. The effect of the outgoing tends to be overlooked. While it is trite that the contribution of European jurisprudence to the English legal tradition is now considerable, the picture would be grossly incomplete were we to ignore both the actual and the potential impact of the English common law on the legal orders of European institutions and the legal systems of the other European states. The legal systems of the continent are no longer cut off from the common law by fog in the channel. It is upon the result of this that I will primarily be focusing in this paper.

The evolution of both the common law and civil law traditions reveals that there has always been some measure of cross-fertilisation. When viewed over a relatively short time-span, this can be imperceptible. But the civil law and the common law systems are not antonyms. There is no clear dichotomy between the two legal systems. On the contrary, the dividing lines between the two systems are blurred and porous.

Legal historians have documented the ongoing relationship between the two systems which has sometimes waned and, at other times, thrived. But the relationship is documented:

> "The works of Grotius, Pufendorf, Domat and especially Pothier have all enjoyed a great deal of doctrinal ascendency in English law. In addition, English law and continental European law share sources which are identical: Roman law, canon law and custom. Even the trust, often considered to be a typical institution of the Anglo-American system, has its roots in continental ideas. For centuries, continental solutions have been transplanted to English law and vice versa. English academics

---

[2] JA Usher "The Influence of National Concepts on Decisions of the European Court" (1976) *European Law Review* 359.

cultivated knowledge of continental law and contacts with their continental counterparts" (footnotes omitted).[3]

"What we call the common law system did not, of course, spring fully armed into life. Many of its roots lay far in the past, and some of its seeds almost certainly germinated in foreign soil."[4]

This relationship has seen English law playing a more significant role in the development of civil jurisprudence over the three decades since this country joined the Community.

THE CONTRIBUTION TO THE EUROPEAN COURT OF JUSTICE

At the outset there was real concern in legal circles that the legal traditions of the United Kingdom based on the common law, would conflict with the proceedings before the ECJ, which were steeped in a continental (civil law) tradition. There was also considerable doubt as to whether new members of the Court coming from common law backgrounds would be able to have much influence on an established system premised on a legal tradition starkly different to theirs. The appointment of Lord Mackenzie-Stuart as a judge to the ECJ,[5] and his English colleague, J.-P. Warner QC, as one of the Advocates General, caused such doubts to evaporate rapidly. As stated by Professor Alan Dashwood:[6]

"The secrecy of the deliberation, and the collegiate nature of the Court's judgments, makes it hard, if not impossible, to measure the influence that individual Judges, drawing on their background and experience, may be able to exert on the development of substantive Community law. However, the impact on the Court's judicial style, of the members who joined it in 1973, was dramatic. The syllogistic form of judgment, based on the practice of courts in France, was abandoned in favour of more discursive reasoning. Also abandoned was the Bench's habit of listening quietly and politely while counsel made long speeches. Judges and Advocates General began to interrupt counsel with questions, to the consternation of some who were unused to such rough treatment."

The sturdy foundation laid by these great legal pioneers has been built upon. There have subsequently been a number of outstanding British Advocates General and Judges whose cumulative impact, whilst not easily quantified, has nevertheless been considerable. Added to this is the significant contribution

---

[3] Xavier Lewis "A Common law fortress under attack: is English law being Europeanized?" (1995/96) 2 *Columbia Journal of European Law* 1 at 3–4.
[4] T Bingham "The Future of the Common law", The Chatham Lecture, delivered on 30 October 1998.
[5] Later to become President of the Court.
[6] A Dashwood "Tribute to Alexander John, Lord Mackenzie-Stuart" (2000) *European Law Review*.

made by the English Bar—its members are generally recognised as being exceptionally effective at hearings before the ECJ. Consequently, English law has made a significant impact on European jurisprudence in at least the following areas: the style of judgments, the handling of precedent, general principles of substantive law, procedure and remedies. Let me elaborate.

i) The break in the ECJ's style from the syllogistic judgments similar to the French supreme courts has gradually become more marked. ECJ judgments are becoming closer in style to the more discursively reasoned English judgments. A typical ECJ judgment is now more detailed than originally was the case. The judgment responds specifically to arguments of the parties, rather than making pronouncements *ex cathedra*.

ii) Initially the ECJ did not refer to previous case law, although the court might repeat passages verbatim from earlier judgments without giving the citation. This provided little or no indication of whether the ECJ was following, modifying or departing from earlier decisions. Eventually this practice too, yielded to change. By the 1980's references to previous cases became the norm. However, a fundamental difference in principle with the common law tradition still remains—the ECJ does not follow the doctrine of *stare decisis*; it does not regard previous decisions as a binding source of law.[7] Nevertheless, this difference can be over-emphasised. Previous decisions are rarely departed from. In fact, it was not until 1990, in *Hag II*, that the Court expressly departed from an earlier decision. I readily concede that there are differences in high technique between the systems, stemming from their civil law and common law roots respectively. Despite this, the role of case law and the handling of precedent are not as fundamentally and irreconcilably dissimilar as some may contend.

iii) In the application of the Treaty, the ECJ must enforce Community law.[8] Community law is based on written law such as the Treaties. However, the broad skeletal provisions of the Treaties needed to be fleshed out. Accordingly, Community law is "supplemented in its turn by unwritten Community law derived from the general principles of law in force in Member States."[9] This process, of legal transplantation of national law

---

[7] See K Langenbucher "Argument by analogy in European law" [1998] *CLJ* 481 at 508:

"Even if in practice the Court of First Instance is very likely to follow the Court of Justice, instead of risking being quashed on appeal, in theory *stare decisis* does not apply. This is illustrated by the fact that the Court of First Instance is allowed to disregard a precedent in order to induce the Court of Justice to overrule a previous decision."

The footnote (note 111) at the end of this statement reads as follows:

"An ECJ decision is thus only binding after an appeal, Statute of the European Court of Justice, art.54 2nd para., and according to art. 47, 2nd para. of the same Statute. This is not a case of *stare decisis*."

[8] The Treaty requires that "the law is observed" (Art. 164).
[9] Case C–29/69 *Stauder v. Ulm* [1969] ECR 419 at 423.

into the Community, facilitates a dialectic between different legal traditions and norms. The ECJ has become a marketplace for the exchange of legal ideas. It was in this way that the principle of proportionality and, arguably, the doctrine of legitimate expectations, both anchored in German law, were raised to the level of Community law.

iv) A similar development has taken place in relation to the concept of legal professional privilege. As is pointed out by Nial Fennelly[10], the Treaties do not recognise any concept of legal professional privilege: "The Community lived happily without it for 25 years until a Commission 'dawn raid' on a UK company". However, the Court was able to rely on a detailed study of the laws of the Member States, presented by a committee of the European Bar presided over by David Edward who is now the UK member of the Court and the opinions of two Advocates Generals, both of whom were English High Court judges. Not surprisingly the Court came to enshrine legal professional privilege, derived essentially from common law, as a newly established principle of Community Law.[11]

v) Similarly the rule of natural justice and the requirement of a fair hearing,[12] both rooted in English law, were elevated to the status of general principles of Community law.[13]

vi) There are also procedural changes that have occurred at the ECJ which are attributable to the influence of English law. The ECJ is now more concerned to ensure that the parties have an opportunity to comment on a point on which the case might be decided. There is also a greater readiness than was previously the case to put questions, both prior to, and at, the hearing. This is in contrast to the classical role of judges in Continental jurisdictions. They remain silent; the rationale being that judicial questioning might suggest that the judge is inclined to decide the case in a particular way.

vii) One of the traditional distinctions between the common law and the civil law is the former's emphasis on remedies. It has been suggested that the case law of the ECJ has increasingly reflected a greater concern with remedies, in particular, the principle of effective remedies in national courts—now a fundamental principle of Community law.[13A] This arguably reflects a greater common law influence.

---

[10] See N Fennelly "Legal interpenetration—towards freedom of movement of principles" in *English Public Law and the Common Law of Europe* Mads Andenas (ed.) (Key Haven publications PLC, London 1998) at 10.

[11] *AM & S v. Commission* [1982] ECR 1575, para. 18.

[12] The *audi alterem partem* rule, on the advice of Advocate General Warner, was elevated by the ECJ to the status of "a fundamental principle of Community law" (*Hoffmann la Roche v. Commission* [1979] ECR 461, para. 9) in the case of *Transocean Marine Paint v. Commission* [1974] ECR 1063, at p. 1088.

[13] See N Fennelly "Legal interpenetration—towards freedom of movement of principles" *supra* n. 10 especially at paras. 7–8.

[13A] See Tridimas, *General Principles of EC law*, ch. 8; also see J Schwarze, *European Administrative Law* at pp. 1382–1384.

viii) But many of the most important principles applied by the ECJ can be traced back to German sources. This is not surprising, bearing in mind the fact that of the 353 cases referred to the ECJ by national courts up until the end of 1975, no less than 167 were references made by courts from the Federal Republic of Germany. It has been argued that this active dialogue between the German courts and the ECJ accounted for the predominant role that German law played in the development of Community principles. This is a lesson that English lawyers and judges ought to bear in mind.[14]

THE EUROPEAN COURT OF HUMAN RIGHTS

Until recently, the United Kingdom has been heavily criticised for shunning its obligations under the European Convention of Human Rights. This criticism has not been unwarranted. The European Court of Human Rights has found the United Kingdom to be in violation of the Convention in at least fifty cases. This worrying figure does not even include matters that have come before the European Commission on Human Rights and which the United Kingdom has then settled in order to prevent the matter from reaching the Court.

It is possible that the number of Convention violations incurred by the United Kingdom is larger than that of any other state, save perhaps for Italy. The United Kingdom has been found to have violated almost every Article. Bearing this in mind, it is easy to succumb to the suggestion that English contribution to the development of European human rights jurisprudence has been primarily to provide cases which gave the European Court of Human Rights the opportunity to uphold those rights.

This observation may be slightly tongue-in-cheek, but there is nevertheless some kernel of truth to it. It is analogous to apartheid in South Africa contributing to the development of international law through its repeated violations of human rights, rather than through its observance.

However, to confine the contribution of this country to the development of human rights to the violations of the Convention for which it has been responsible would be a travesty of the true picture. The contribution of this country to the development of European human rights jurisprudence has already been significant and, in the future, is likely to be much more substantial. The reasons for making this claim are:

1. The European Convention on Human Rights owes its genesis significantly to British lawyers and politicians. In the earlier stages its main advocates included Churchill, Macmillan and John Foster. It also attracted Liberal and some Labour support. This resulted in many principles of the common law being subsumed and codified in the Articles. To take one example: in 1947

---

[14] JA Usher "The Influence of National Concepts on Decisions of the European Court" (1976) *European Law Review* 359 at 373–4.

in *Christie* v. *Leachinsky*[15] the House of Lords held that an arrest was unlawful because the arrested person had not been told by the police the true reason for his arrest. One of the Law Lords held as follows:

> "Blind unquestioning obedience is the law of tyrants and of slaves: it does not yet flourish in English soil . . . Arrested with or without a warrant, the subject is entitled to know why he is deprived of his freedom if only in order that he may, without a moment's delay, take such steps as will enable him to regain it."

This very important principle of English common law was crystallised in Article 5 of the European Convention of Human Rights. As a result of the major role of English lawyers in its drafting, the Convention fits readily into both the civil law and common law traditions.[16]

2. The United Kingdom effectively 'got the ball rolling', in the sense that on 8 March 1951 it became the first state to ratify the Convention.
3. The procedures of the European Court of Human Rights reflect many of the aspects of English appellate procedure including the acceptance of dissenting judgments.
4. The judges of the Court readily acknowledge that the quality of the English advocates appearing before the Court has contributed to the development of the Court's jurisprudence.
5. Although hitherto, the contribution which could be directly made by English judges through their decisions in our domestic courts has been limited by the inability to apply the Convention directly as it was not part of our domestic law, the contribution has not been negligible. In particular, the Judicial Committee of the Privy Council as the final appellate Court for some Commonwealth countries has been able to exercise a human rights jurisdiction in relation to those countries since human rights are part of the Constitution of those countries. A series of decisions of the Privy Council exercising this jurisdiction have contributed to the development of human rights jurisprudence. The most famous contribution being that of Lord Wilberforce in *Minister of Home Affairs* v. *Fischer* when he described the approach to the interpretation of an international convention on law as requiring:

> "a generous interpretation, avoiding what has been called "the austerity of tabulated legislation", suitable to give to individuals the full measure of the fundamental rights and freedom".[17]

6. The recent coming into force of the Human Rights Act 1998 will undoubtedly change the scale of that contribution.
7. In interpreting and giving effect to the Convention, English judges are now playing an active and constructive role in enriching the constantly evolving

---

[15] [1947] AC 573.
[16] See Lord Steyn "The New Legal Landscape" (2000) *European Human Rights Law Review* 549.
[17] [1980] AC 319 p. 328.

European human rights jurisprudence. The carefully-reasoned decisions of the English courts means that they are ideally structured to contribute to the development of the Strasbourg jurisprudence.

The significance of the role of English law and the contribution of English lawyers and judges cannot be overestimated. There are at least two reasons for this:

(i) The sophisticated proportionality test employed by the European Court of Human Rights seeks to resolve disputes in a manner that achieves integrity with past decisions and yet provides a morally just outcome in light of the constitutional context of the decision and within an articulated theory of democracy. The experience and traditions of the English judiciary mean they are ideally suited to contribute to shaping and interpreting the Convention rights in a manner that fits the theory of democracy painstakingly evolved over a thousand years in England. The judiciary can be relied on to be proactive and positively engage the Convention rights. The disadvantage of our judiciary being excluded from ruling on the Convention is made strikingly clear by Lord Bingham:

"... It is true that judgments on human rights do involve judgments about relations between the individual and the society of which the individual is part ... What I simply do not understand is how it can be sensible to entrust the decision of these questions to an international panel of judges in Strasbourg—some of them drawn from societies markedly unlike our own—but not, in the first instance, to our own judges here.

... I am only suggesting that rights claimed under the Convention should, in the first place, be ruled upon by judges here before, if regrettably necessary, appeal is made to Strasbourg."[18]

(ii) Decisions affecting this country and other countries will undoubtedly be strengthened as British judges exercise the opportunity of contributing to the development of a pan-European human rights jurisprudence. As Lord Hope of Craighead has also explained:

"The jurisprudence on which we depend for guidance as to the progress of European human rights law is soon going to look very different, as the common law systems get to work on it.

...

The judges of our courts are not free to go their own way. The last word on matters of Community law lies with the Luxembourg court, and the last word in matters relating to the Convention rights lies with the court in Strasbourg. Nevertheless there is good reason to think that, now that they are able to engage themselves directly in issues about the application of the Convention rights to our laws and our practices, our judges will have an increasing influence on the development of the jurisprudence

---

[18] Lord Bingham "The European Convention on Human Rights: Time to Incorporate" (1993) *Law Quarterly Review* 390–400.

of these courts. In particular the opportunity now exists for our judges to demonstrate, by means of reasoned judgments based upon established Convention law principles, how the basic human rights which are enshrined in the Convention can be respected without risk to the rule of law or to the established values of our democracy."[19]

DIFFERENCES IN FORM: THE ADVANTAGE OF ENGLISH LAW

As a result of the common law tradition in relation to procedure a number of important changes have occurred in civil law systems. Reference has already been made to the difference of judgment styles. The judgments of English courts, being comprehensively reasoned, are in stark contrast to decisions of the courts in Continental jurisdictions which are relatively terse and devoted in the main part to statements or restatements of principle. Therefore, our common law jurisprudence should be more accessible, and as a result more influential in other European jurisdictions, including the courts in Strasbourg and Luxembourg. Indeed, Lord Goff has already commented that the House of Lords is the only court that is cited as authority across Europe.[20] As Professor Basil Markesinsis has also commented in the context of the potential influence of English law on German law:

"In the analytical and inductive techniques of the English judge one may find one of the (many) areas where English law can make a particular contribution to German legal science; and this is not to mention the refreshing flavour which the literary style of the English judgment can bring to the often abstract law of the German jurist."[21]

This however, does not mean that we close our eyes to the strengths of the civil law tradition. One of the hallmarks of the civil law tradition is that it is largely based on extensive codification of law. This has at least two advantages. First, it allows the law to be more easily ascertained; it permits, in a sense, an enhanced accessibility to the law (a different sense of accessibility to that of English judgments as described above). Secondly, and perhaps more significantly, it allows countries based on a similar legal system to update their system, both procedurally and substantively, by simply being provided with the amendments to the Codes.[22] The relationship between the codified French legal system and that of its former colonies exemplifies this. French law is easily and effectively exported to the former colonies by providing them with amendments to Codes, thereby bringing their legal systems 'up to speed'.[23] In the same manner,

---

[19] Lord Hope of Craighead "Human Rights—Where are we now?" (2000) 5 *European Human Rights Law Review* 439–451.
[20] Lord Goff "The Future of the Common law" (1997) 46 *International and Comparative Law Quarterly* 747 at 757.
[21] B Markesinis "The study and use of foreign law" (1993) 109 *Law Quarterly Review* 622 at 624, see also at 632–3.
[22] See Lord Goff above n. 20 at 750–1.
[23] See Lord Goff above n. 20.

the influence of the English common law on other countries would be far greater were the law codified in one central body. Otherwise, how does a developing country, particularly one that is steeped in a civil law tradition, which wishes to adopt English law wholesale in a particular area proceed? What does that area of law consist of? Where do they find the law?[24] Codification of the law would overcome these hurdles most effectively.

CHANGES IN FORM—THE COMMON LAW CODIFIED AND THE POTENTIAL FOR INFLUENCE

Much to the chagrin of some common law "purists", the imperative of codification is gaining momentum. In certain areas, due to practical concerns, such as that of collating a plethora of legal principles diffusely located in a multitude of cases into a more readily accessible code, English common law has been, and is in the process of being, codified. I mention a few examples.

First, one of the most radical changes in civil law (by which in this context I mean all non-criminal law) over the past few years has been the development of and introduction of the Civil Procedure Rules in 1999. These reforms are still referred to by a number of English lawyers as the Rules of the Supreme Court.

The new Civil Procedure Rules, or CPR as they are called, are a complete code covering all matters of civil procedure, from pre-action behaviour (including alternative dispute resolution), through to the conduct of cases that go to trial, to the orders and costs that are awarded post-trial. Before the development of this code our civil procedure rules were fragmented. There was no clear organisation of them as they had been the subject of numerous amendments and were encrusted heavily by previous decisions of the courts in a variety of cases stretching back over a great many years. The previous sets of rules encouraged litigation that was often too costly, in that costs often exceeded the value of the claim; too slow; resulted in inequality in that they favoured the powerful, wealthy litigant to the disadvantage of the litigant who lacked resources; too uncertain in forecasting what litigation will cost and how long it will last; and insufficiently comprehensible to litigants. Added to these problems the system was too adversarial as cases were run by the parties, not the courts.

The CPR are expressed in understandable language. They are based on a number of principles designed to improve access to justice and achieve results that are just and fair to the parties. I think it is fair to say that the result has been the creation of a system that is generally accepted as being far better organised, more proportionate and cost effective, and fair, not only for lawyers, but for unrepresented and represented litigants as well.

While the CPR are designed to provide a comprehensive code of procedure for the English and Welsh courts, they were heavily influenced by the practices

---

[24] See Lord Goff above n. 20.

The Tides of Change 11

in jurisdictions on the mainland of Europe. They have been described as being positioned mid-Channel.

So far very limited progress has been made in harmonising the civil procedural law within the different Member States except in the area of execution. However, there are now real efforts being made to achieve a common procedural code which can be used both in common law and civil jurisdictions. Most of the Member States suffer from similar problems to those which blighted the English civil justice scene prior to the reforms. In consequence, there has been considerable interest by other Member States in the reforms which have taken place within this jurisdiction. What happens in this country has already had a substantial influence on European arbitration practice. The CPR could have a similar influence on the procedure of other Member States.

So far the development of alternative dispute resolution has been slower on the continent then here. The development here has been facilitated by the fact that the CPR are ADR friendly. This could prove to be a valuable example for other Member States to follow.

Secondly, the organisation of the criminal courts in the UK is the next area to face substantial reform. The Lord Chancellor commissioned a major independent review, which was conducted by Lord Justice Auld, of how the criminal courts work at every level in England and Wales. The Government wishes to provide criminal courts which are modern, in touch with their communities, efficient, fair and responsive to the needs of all their users. They should also work in good co-operation with other criminal justice agencies and use modern and effective case management to cut delays from the system. Lord Justice Auld has just published his review and recommendations as to the practices and procedures of, and the rules of evidence applied in the criminal justice system. In a nutshell, the report recommends that the criminal law should be codified under the general oversight of a new Criminal Justice Council and by or with the support as necessary of the Law Commission. There should be codes of offences, procedure, evidence and sentencing. Thus, when enacted, these codes will amalgamate the various common-law legal rules and principles into one centralised and comprehensive body very much in the civil law style. The problems in relation to the criminal justice system in this country are echoed by those in other Member States and it can be expected that the implementation of the Auld reforms will be followed with interest in other European countries.

Thus we see the threads of various common law rules developed over time being woven together into one codified tapestry. What are and will be the implications of this? I allude to at least three.

i) The CPR reforms and the intended criminal law overhaul epitomise legal reforms aimed at ensuring that the law responds efficiently and rationally to society's needs in the allocation of the courts' resources and the administration of justice. These codes are based on existing common law principles that have been distilled and developed through much consultation and consideration. In essence, the common law principles have emerged well polished, crystallised into a code.

ii) This notion of codification is clearly borrowed from the Continental (civil law) legal tradition. Therefore, it appears as if this is an incoming tide; the English common law tradition is being influenced in a significant way by the civil law tradition, at least insofar as the form of our law is concerned.

iii) However, most significantly, it is by no means all one-way traffic. Again let us not forget about the outgoing tide. These codes could become instrumental in exporting our common law jurisprudence to other jurisdictions. They serve as convenient vehicles which facilitate the export of English common law principles. They enable this country to be a bridge between other common law systems of the United States and the Commonwealth and Europe. In some instances, our body of common law has adopted the *form* of the civil law tradition. In this form, the *substantive* English common law principles will be more readily accessible, and capable of a deeper penetration and a more sustained influence on other legal systems, including those premised on civil law traditions.

THE LEGAL PROFESSION

Both sides of the legal profession in this country have also been subject to extensive reform. In court eighteenth-century wigs may be worn but the wigs deceive. In fact the restrictive practices which used to "protect" the profession have been stripped away. Especially in the commercial arena, the profession is organised in a way which enables it to provide the highly skilled services now required by international corporate clients. This is not, in general, so in the Continent and this means that English lawyers have a considerable advantage when competing with lawyers in other European jurisdictions.

The scale and power of the Anglo-Saxon law firms are causing the European counterparts to change their practices. English firms of solicitors, primarily from the City of London, are becoming established in most of the major commercial centres on the Continent. Alternatively they are amalgamating with and transforming local firms. Countries such as France in particular are concerned as to this trend and if their lawyers are going to compete they will have to provide the same favourable climate as that available to the English commercial lawyers. The example and influence of the commercial approach of the English lawyers cannot be ignored.

JUDICIAL EXCHANGES

One of the greatest changes over the last two decades is the remarkable increase in dialogue between the judiciary of almost all the Member States. Conferences and seminars in different parts of Europe are now filling the diaries of the judiciary. The meetings are transforming the understanding of each other's legal systems.

The meetings between the judiciary are mirrored by those between representatives of the legal professions. The influence of these interchanges should not be underestimated. Over time they are bound to promote the process of harmonisation.

CONCLUSION

The change in the flow of tides is constant and relentless. The gravitational pull one way, and then the other is incessant. English common law and the European civil law tradition have always enriched each other. The strength of the tides is increasing. As Professor Markesinis comments:

> "Convergence is taking place. The convergence is gradual and, indeed, patchy (i.e. more obvious in some areas than in others despite the dynamics of the case law of the European Court which, I believe, has accelerated the convergence process)."[25]

The potential of our common law to extend its influence is enormous. The ongoing dialectic will increase as a result of the reforms that have taken place and are taking place within this jurisdiction. We are grateful for the contribution which we have received already from across the Channel. If we are not now, we shall be soon in a position to make a greater contribution in return.

---

[25] B Markesinis, *The Gradual Convergence: Foreign Ideas, Foreign Influences, and English Law on the eve of the 21st Century*, B. Markesinis (ed.) (Oxford, Clarendon, 1994) at 30.

2
Europe and English Commercial Law

ROY GOODE

INTRODUCTION

The British are great borrowers. Our language draws freely on Greek, Latin, Old and Modern French, German, Arabic, indeed any source providing useful offerings. We are less concerned with our linguistic purity than with having at our disposal the fine gradations of expression that have made English a world language. This is become true of our law. Since we joined what is now the European Union we have become increasingly receptive to ideas from the civil law tradition and our doctrine and even, in some degree, our jurisprudence have been enriched. Our legal system is not based on codes but we too can draw inspiration from the elegant drafting and law-making philosophies of the great code draftsmen of the past, such as Portalis, chief draftsman of the French Code Civil, and Huber, who prepared the Swiss Civil Code

It is, moreover, exhilarating to see the return of the days of the wandering scholar. The modern law student is comfortably at home graduating in one European country, taking a master's course in another and research for a doctorate in a third. So also with law teachers, who travel around Europe giving lectures and seminars and, in their own institutions, receive colleagues from other European law schools who come to impart their knowledge and ideas.

Historically, much of our commercial law was borrowed from others. The English mediaeval law merchant was primarily procedural in nature and made little contribution to the evolution of the European *lex mercatoria*. That honour belongs to the civilians, in particular Italy, with its development of the bill of exchange, the bill of lading, insurance and the concept of agency, and in the field of maritime law France, with its Laws of Oléron, and Spain, with the promulgation of the Consulate of the Sea. Lord Mansfield, who is generally accepted as the founder of English commercial law and who maintained close contacts with members of the business community, whom he regularly consulted, nevertheless did not hesitate to draw on his profound knowledge of the civil law in developing a coherent set of principles from a mass of undigested and often conflicting case law. As late as the nineteenth century the works of the great French jurist Pothier continued to hold sway. Pothier was not infrequently cited by English judges as possessing the highest authority on questions of English commercial law and his writings profoundly influenced Sir Mackenzie Chalmers in his preparation of the Sale of Goods Act 1893.

English commercial law did not come into its own until the end of the nineteenth and the first half of the twentieth century, and characteristically, evolved through case law, though part of this was eventually embodied in two great codifying statutes, the Bills of Exchange Act 1882 and the Sale of Goods Act 1893, now the Sale of Goods Act 1979.

THE CHARACTERISTICS OF ENGLISH COMMERCIAL LAW

1 It is Judge-Made

One of the more remarkable features of English commercial law is that almost all the principles and rules governing commercial transactions are judge-made. Trusts, equitable ownership, fixed and floating security, and extra-judicial remedies, all are creatures of the common law. In fact, the two enactments mentioned above and certain property statutes remain the only major pieces of legislation governing private rights in commercial transactions, and as between the parties most of their provisions may be varied or excluded by agreement. With some minor exceptions the common law continues to hold sway. One consequence of this is that commercial law is not considered a distinct corpus of law. There is no formal status of merchant and no concept of *actes de commerce* except to the extent that business transactions are excluded from the scope of consumer protection legislation. Rather, commercial transactions are governed by the general law, but with certain rules particular to commercial contracts, such as the implication of terms from usage or a course of dealing, the distinctive treatment of floating charges given by companies and the institution of administrative receivership as a default remedy, described briefly below. Up to the present time this dearth of statute law has on the whole proved beneficial. It has enabled the courts to respond flexibly to changing commercial needs and to accommodate new instruments and contractual techniques which Parliament might not have been able to foresee. The doctrine of judicial precedent, which binds courts at each level below the House of Lords to follow the rulings of higher courts, and the Court of Appeal to follow its own earlier rulings, makes for a degree of consistency and stability. The problems created by the inaccessibility of case law and its lack of integration have in large measure been overcome by textbooks and periodic literature, which organise the assembled decisions into statements of principle and rule that give coherence to the law and provide a conceptual framework fully comparable to that provided by civil and commercial codes in civil law jurisdictions. However, as I shall suggest later, the time has now come for a major review of the law governing key commercial transactions with a view to its being codified, simplified and brought up to date.

2 Most Contracts Require no Formality

Another characteristic of English commercial law is that with a few exceptions—for example, contracts relating to land, and suretyship guarantees—the law imposes no formal requirements whatever. There is no need for a signed writing or, indeed, any writing at all. Commercial contracts may readily be created by word of mouth, whether between parties at a meeting or on the telephone, or even by implication from conduct. Such informality greatly facilitates business dealings, and if now and then there is a dispute about the existence of a contract, its terms or the time of its making, the courts usually have no great difficulty in evaluating the evidence and determining where the truth lies.

3 Commercial Law is Based on Freedom of Contract

While both judicial and legislative safeguards exist for the consumer, the courts have taken the view that in dealings between merchants they themselves are the best judge of what serves their respective interests. It may be objected that this exposes one party to the superior bargaining power of the other, but that is a fact of business life and no reason to interfere with the bargain made by the parties, in the absence of bargaining misbehaviour, such as misrepresentation or economic duress. The principle of freedom of contract has other aspects. The parties may choose the form of legal instrument which bests suits their requirements even if the effect is to avoid legal requirements or restrictions that would otherwise have applied. So a company wishing to acquire goods on credit against the security of the goods but having only limited borrowing powers and desiring in any event to avoid having a purchase-money mortgage registered against is free to acquire the goods under a conditional sale or hire-purchase agreement, thus avoiding the legal obstacles to the transaction. Moreover, parties may grant and divide up property rights in almost any way they choose, give security over present and future property and, with a few limits, make any agreement they choose on remedies for default.

4 The Principle *Pacta Sunt Servanda* is Rigorously Applied

Predictability is the essence of commercial transactions, particularly in international trade. English courts are therefore very reluctant to recognise adverse change of circumstances as relieving a party of its obligations or entitling it to an adjustment of the contract terms. It is arguable that this principle of *pacta sunt servanda*, which is also an important principle of international law, needs some alleviation to cater for a major disturbance of the contract equilibrium in long-term contractual relationships. But the general principle adopted by the courts is that it is for the parties to make provision for such events, not for the court to refashion their contracts. Moreover, where it is clear from the terms of the contract that strict adherence to the contract terms is required, whether in regard to the manner or the time of performance, a party may terminate the contract if it is not strictly performed, even if the deviation is of no commercial significance. It is for the parties, not the court, to decide what is to be considered important. Stipulations as to time provide particularly stark examples. In one cases the court upheld the termination of a charterparty where the charterer, who had been warned of the importance of punctual payment, paid 20 minutes late; in another, a vendor of property was held entitled to terminate the contract where the buyer's solicitor arrived a mere 10 minutes after the time fixed for completion. The decisions may seem harsh but they rest on a strong perception of the need for predictability of decision-making in commercial transactions. There is an equitable jurisdiction to grant relief against forfeiture of proprietary or possessory rights but it is exercised sparingly and is not available for the loss of purely personal contractual rights. In a world financial centre nothing is seen as more inimical to the smooth functioning of commercial markets than judicial intervention to adjust, in the name of equity or fairness, the terms of freely negotiated bargains between business enterprises. This insistence on holding the parties to their bargain is thought to be one of the reasons why foreign parties so often subject their contracts to English law, and submit to the jurisdiction of the English court, even where the parties and the transaction in dispute have no connection with England.

5 The Law Provides a Ready Facility for the Creation of Security Interests

Secured financing has always been a significant feature of commercial credit and its importance has increased with the move from planned to market economies, the advent of privatisation and the consequent shift from State to enterprise risk. English law has long had a liberal attitude towards the creation of security interests. Indeed, nowhere is freedom of contract more strikingly illustrated than in the field of corporate secured lending. By a single instrument which may be perfected by a single filing in the Companies Registry, a company can give security over any kind of asset or class of asset, or the entirety of its assets, present and future, to secure all types of existing and future obligation. Nor is this all. That peculiarly English institution, the floating charge, confers on the creditor a security interest not in specific assets but in the floating fund of assets from time to time held by the company, which thus has liberty to deal with its assets in the ordinary course of business free from the charge until such time as the charge crystallises and becomes fixed (usually by reason of the initiation of some insolvency proceeding), in which case it ranks above the claims of general creditors in the insolvency of the company. Moreover, except in relation to land all these rights can be created with the minimum of formality. The security agreement need not be in any particular form and there is no requirement of individual specification of the items constituting the collateral and no restriction on security over after-acquired property. Debts, present and future, may be freely assigned by way of sale under factoring agreements or by way of security for bank loans, again without individual specification, and while notice to the debtors is necessary to preserve the assignee's priority it is not a prerequisite of the validity of the assignment, which binds the assignor's insolvency creditors whether or not such notice has been given. This is of particular importance in modern receivables financing, where the trend has been away from old-style notification to new-style non-notification assignment. Again, flexibility has been the hallmark. Even the fact that there are only four types of consensual security known to English law—the contractual lien, the pledge, the mortgage and the equitable charge—is due not to any formal *numerus clausus* but to the fact that these four types appear to cover every security situation.

6 English Commercial Law has a Liberal Attitude Towards Self-help

A further striking contrast between English law and civil law systems is the degree to which the parties are given the freedom to select their own default remedies without the need to have recourse to the court. Thus contracts and security instruments can provide for acceleration of payment, contractual netting, set-off, rescission and termination of agreements, repossession and sale of security, and, in certain conditions, the appointment of an administrative receiver to take control of the debtor company and its assets and run it, or sell off the assets or the business, for the benefit of the appointing creditor though notionally as agent of the company. None of these remedies requires application to the court or any prescribed period of notice beyond that which may be specified in the contract.

7 The Commercial Trust is Widely Used

The institution of the trust, by which ownership and management are separated, so that the trustee can manage the trust fund on behalf of the beneficiaries but not so as to make it available to the claims of the trustee's personal creditors, originated in the context of wills and family settlements. Today, however, the trust is widely used as a commercial device and has attracted much interest in continental Europe and internationally. Used in a commercial setting the trust fulfils two different purposes. The first is the traditional one of ensuring that assets coming into the hands of one party for the benefit of another are protected against the first party's bankruptcy creditors. Very often the trust is a bare trust not involving management powers and established as a subsidiary element of a commercial transaction. For example, an invoice discounting agreement may provide for a trade supplier to sell its accounts to a factoring company but collect the accounts as agent of the company and hold the proceeds on trust until these have been paid over. The second purpose for which the commercial trust is used is to co-ordinate fractional interests, as by empowering trustees for bondholders to negotiate deferment of repayments or pursue default remedies on behalf of the bondholders as a class, instead of leaving individual bondholders to pursue their own separate claims. The trust is one of the most powerful devices in modern commerce. It is true that the underlying idea is not unique to England or to common law systems; civil law countries also have trust-like devices designed to insulate the beneficiary from the claims of the trustee's insolvency creditors. But our civilian colleagues would be the first to agree that these devices, though useful, do not approach the power and flexibility of the common law trust.

THE IMPORTANCE OF THE INSTITUTIONAL INFRASTRUCTURE

Sympathetic as it has been to the legitimate needs of business, the law by itself would not have sufficed to make London one of the world's leading financial centres. Also necessary was the commercial and financial infrastructure: the highly developed commodity, money, foreign exchange and capital markets; the banking system, which remarkably operated with no legislative underpinnings whatsoever until 1979 and was controlled only by the exercise of moral suasion by the Governor of the Bank of England; the clearing houses and settlement systems, and the facilities which these provided for reduction of risk through system controls and contractual techniques such as novation of trades to the clearing house, multilateral netting and, more recently, real time gross settlement. Another modern development, borrowed from the United States, is the conversion of non-tradeable into tradeable assets by securitisation, a process by which receivables of a particular class are packaged, transferred to a special purpose vehicle and then converted into securities issued on the market in unitised form or provided as security for bond and loan note issues. Of course, such systems and techniques are not an Anglo-American duopoly; they are to be found in all developed financial markets, both within and outside Europe. But what is distinctive to London and New York is the flexibility of the legal regime in accommodating new financial and security instruments. Though the operation of the securities markets is now highly regulated, the regulation is directed more to the control of procedures for bringing securities to the market and for mergers and takeovers than it is to the underlying instruments themselves.

This is not to say that commercial transactions are free from legal constraints. In addition to public law regulation of the securities markets private law exercises a restraining influence on business behaviour. In particular, rules of the common law and equity are applied to ensure fairness in contractual procedures, standards of care in performance, and good faith and loyalty in fiduciary relationships. Our courts allow liberty but not licence; the market is not a free-for-all but a contract-based community which nevertheless operates within certain boundaries which are not set exclusively by the market itself but are also imposed by law. Yet English commercial law remains firmly rooted in concepts of party autonomy, the strict adherence to the terms of freely negotiated bargains and responsiveness to the legitimate needs of the business community.

The richness and variety of contractual techniques are directly related to the volume and diversity of business transactions. The more developed the markets, the more diverse and sophisticated the range of transactions and of instruments used to implement them, and the greater the importance of a legal regime which is responsive to innovation. This applies with particular force in an era of global markets and a huge growth in cross-border dealings and delivery and payment systems.

THE INFLUENCE OF ENGLISH COMMERCIAL LAW WITHIN EUROPE

What contribution has English commercial law made to legal developments in continental Europe? No answer can readily be given in quantitative terms. It is hard to point to any legislative act or judicial decision which bears a specifically English law imprint; it would, perhaps, be surprising if there was. What can be said is, that just as we have borrowed from our civil law colleagues, so also we have had some influence on their own thinking and legal systems. Two motive forces are at work. The first is the process of harmonisation of contract and commercial law, both by international conventions and by non-binding "restatements" such as the Principles of European Contract Law, prepared by the Commission on European Contract Law, and the UNIDROIT Principles of International Commercial Contracts. Both types of harmonising instruments involve collaboration among scholars from different countries and, in the case of conventions, governments. These have led the common lawyers to a better understanding of the concepts and constraints of other legal systems, and, within Europe, have led the civil lawyers to greater receptiveness to the importance of removing impediments to legitimate business transactions. The second is the competition for international business, which tends to gravitate to those jurisdictions—in particular, England and the United States—whose laws are seen as allowing the business community the maximum freedom and flexibility to develop new business products and to utilise forms of universal security.

The impact of these two motive forces has been to initiate a gradual convergence of doctrine, jurisprudence and legislation. One area in which this is happening relates to the assignment of debts, which represent a vital form of collateral in secured financing. The ability to take security over future debts, without the need for specificity or for a new act of transfer after the debts come into existence, is enshrined in the UNIDROIT Convention on International Factoring, the UN Convention on the Assignment of Receivables in International Trade and the chapter on assignment in the forthcoming final part of the Principles of European Contract Law, all of which also recognize the efficacy of an assignment of debts as between the assignor and the assignee and its bankruptcy creditors even if notice of assignment has not been given to the debtors. Italy passed new legislation a few years ago making it easier to assign future claims. German, Swiss and Scandinavian courts, which at one time experienced difficulties in reconciling the assignment of rights under future contracts with concerns over encouraging improvidence and also with the requirement that assets given in security be determined or determinable, overcame their hesitations. In the words of one leading scholar:

"Most of these difficulties have now been swept away by the growing need of the business community to have a workable system of receivables financing".[1]

Another line of convergence relates to demand guarantees, which, after some initial hesitation, are now widely accepted in mainland Europe, as in England, as abstract payment undertakings which do not require to be supported by the normal legal underpinnings of a bilateral contract but, by international banking usage, take effect by virtue of their issue, without need of acceptance, reliance, consideration or the traditional form of *cause*. The concept of party autonomy is now a common feature of private law conventions relating to cross-border transactions. It is to be found in the instruments referred to above and in many others, for example, the UNIDROIT Convention on International Financial Leasing, the UNCITRAL Convention on Independent Guarantees and Standby Letters of Credit, and the Cape Town Convention on International Interests in Mobile Equipment, which was concluded at a Diplomatic Conference in November 2001 held under the auspices of UNIDROIT and the International Civil Aviation Organisation.

The forces of competition are also at work. Thus France, whose legal system is among the most formalistic (though the courts do their best to mitigate the rigour of the provisions of the Code Civil), is about to review its Code de Commerce with a view to facilitating business activity and becoming more competitive on the international scene. The French have already proved adept at adjusting long-established concepts to new situations. Thus, virtually all French securities are now dematerialised, but most are nevertheless categorised as bearer securities. One cannot but admire this neat technique for protecting the issuer from the need to record dealings in the securities.

THE NEED FOR REVIEW

I have sought to highlight the strengths of English commercial law, the role it has played in facilitating the growth of domestic and international business in

---

[1] H Kötz, "Rights of Third Parties. Third Party Beneficiaries and Assignment", *International Encyclopaedia of Comparative Law*, vol. VII, ch. 13, p. 71.

London, and the flexibility provided by reliance on common law rules rather than legislation. But I believe the time has come to take stock of our law and to engage in work on a commercial code. The Bills of Exchange Act 1882 and the Sale of Goods Act 1893, which are in substance codifications in a limited field, have shown the great advantages of reducing a mass of case law to an ordered statement of principle and rule prepared by experts in the field. Such statute law as we have in the commercial field is for the most part, in form or substance, over a century old and has long since been overtaken by commercial developments and kept alive only by the ingenuity of the courts. We cannot operate in the twenty-first century with legislation enacted in the nineteenth. A code covering a limited number of transactions—sale of goods, security in movables, electronic funds transfers, investment securities (and particularly those held indirectly through custodians or other intermediaries) and perhaps suretyship guarantees would suffice, linked by a small number of general provisions. A code of this kind, restricted in scope to areas in which modernisation and simplification are long overdue, is currently under consideration by the government which I hope will give such a project its blessing. It is desirable that the code should not be confined to England but should cover the United Kingdom, including in particular Scotland, whose own distinctive legal system provides a bridge between the English common and the civil law systems of continental Europe.

In the preparation of any such code it is essential that we inform ourselves of developments elsewhere, not only in common law but in non-common law systems, particularly in Europe, and that we have due regard to European-wide initiatives designed to accelerate convergence, in particular, the Lando Commission's work on Principles of European Contract Law, the even broader project by Professor Christian von Bar's Study Group on a European Civil Code, and the recent Communication on European Contract Law from the European Commission. If we have played a role in the development of European commercial law we have also drawn inspiration from our civil law colleagues. A good example is the decision of our courts in the 1970s to jettison our long-established doctrine of absolute state immunity and to follow the trend in other countries to restrict immunity to *acta jure imperii* and abolish it for *acta jura gestionis*.

In recent times we have come to see that exclusive dependence on national law does not always best serve the interests of the international business community and that there is a role for principles of transnational commercial law which cut across national legal boundaries and respond to the distinctive needs of cross-border commerce. As Professor Reinhard Zimmerman has percipiently observed:

> "The age of more or less autonomous systems of national law is drawing to its close. The directives enacted by the Council of the European Union, the case law emanating from the European Court of Justice, the legal problems arising from the application of the United Nations Convention on Contracts for the International Sale of Goods,

these all increasingly affect the legal situation in most West European countries. Private law in Europe is in the process of acquiring a transnational character".[2]

At the same time we need to be cautious in selecting the form of any harmonising instrument. The fact that the Principles of European Contract and the UNIDROIT Principles of International Commercial Contracts have proved so influential is precisely because they are not legally binding instruments and are therefore no threat to national legal traditions, but rather a resource for legislators, courts and arbitrators, and all the more persuasive for having been agreed by experts from all Member States and, in the case of the UNIDROIT Principles, from all over the world without the distortion that can result from political considerations where governments are involved. The dangers of a legally binding European-wide code have been admirably depicted by Professor Basil Markesinis,[3] and we would do well to heed his warnings.

National law is another matter. A United Kingdom Commercial Code needs a statutory base. But it should not be prepared from an isolationist standpoint; it must be responsive to developments in transnational commercial law. In particular, it has the potential both to be influenced by and to influence developments in European commercial law. The Code should reflect the legitimate needs of the market, set out key principles clearly and succinctly, "show its reason on its face" (to quote from the words of Karl Llewellyn, the principal architect of the American Uniform Commercial Code), and, through an open texture and incorporation of reference to trade usage, provide its own internal mechanism for adjustment to change. In short, it should be a living code which can be of service not only to us but to our partners in Europe from whom we ourselves have learned so much.

---

[2] *Roman Law, Contemporary Law, European Law* (Oxford, Oxford University Press, 2001) pp. 107–8.

[3] "Why a Code is not the Best Way to Advance the Cause of European Legal Unity" in BS Markesinis, *Always on the Same Path* (Oxford, Hart, 2001) ch. 5.

3

The British Contribution to the Development of Law and Legal Process in the European Union

DAVID EDWARD

This paper assesses the British contribution to law and legal process in the European Union since British accession to the European Community in 1973. Although the European Community has been subsumed within the European Union since the Treaty of Maastricht, the Court of Justice remains the "Court of Justice of the European Communities" and "Community law" remains the conventional description of this field of law. So, at the risk of some terminological imprecision, the expressions "European Community" and "Community law" are used throughout. The paper does not seek to address other areas of law and law making in Europe, notably the work of the Council of Europe in the field of human rights, where Britain has made and will continue to make a significant contribution.

All the original Six member states of the European Community belonged to the civil law tradition. The structures and procedures of the Community and Community law were put in place when Britain remained outside. Even today, the question most frequently put to me by visitors to the Court of Justice is whether I do not find it difficult, as a lawyer from the common law tradition, to come to terms with the Community system and to work with judges from the civil law tradition. It is assumed that there are two (and only two) very different and incompatible traditions which are subjected to enforced cohabitation. Some lawyers on both sides of the divide go further, contending that enforced cohabitation will, in the longer term, undermine the essential characteristics and strength of both traditions.

In spite of these preconceptions, British lawyers do not, in practice, seem to have found it difficult to adapt to the requirements of Community law. They have, on the whole, contributed as positively to the development of Community law as the lawyers of any other country, including those of the original Six. In certain respects, they have done so in ways that would not readily have been predicted.

There are perhaps four reasons why this has been so. First, there are many more than two legal traditions in Europe. Second, the historic differences between the common law and civil law traditions are only marginally relevant to the primary concerns of Community law. Third, British law, like the law of other countries, has itself undergone a significant culture shift since at least the 1960s. Fourth, the day-to-day operation of the Community system places a premium on co-operation rather than confrontation and, as Jean Monnet observed, "The British . . . are at their best if you firmly offer to work with them on an equal footing".[1] (This is sometimes called British pragmatism.)

(1) There are well-known and well-defined differences between the systems of the Anglo-Irish-American common law tradition and the systems that drew their inspiration from Roman law and the Napoleonic reforms. These differences lie in the traditional fields of civil law—the law of persons, property and obligations (contract, delict and tort)—and civil procedure; criminal law and procedure; and the domain of public law. Within these fields, a lawyer bred in one tradition would expect to go into a law library in another country of the same tradition and find the way around: the books will be arranged under the same categories with the same titles, and a problem will be discussed in broadly the same terms. Exploring a law library in a country of the other tradition is more of an adventure.

Beyond that, the notion that there are two, and only two, traditions is misleading. National systems which originally drew their inspiration from the same source have since gone their own ways. Germany and France belong to the civil law tradition but their legal systems are very different, both substantively and procedurally. They are in turn very different from the systems of Scandinavia which are themselves far from uniform. Irish law retains many characteristics of the English common law, including some that have disappeared in England, but its recent development has been strongly influenced by the existence of a written constitution and this has been true also of Canada and Australia. Amongst countries that have a written constitution, there are significant differences, both in content and structure. Some constitutions contain a bill of rights: others do not. Some countries have a separate constitutional court: others do not.

So, whatever may have been the situation (or the perceived situation) when Britain entered the Community in 1973, the reality now is that there can be as many divergences on a given point between lawyers of the same tradition as there are between those of different traditions.

(2) Apart from public law, the areas of law with which Community law is primarily concerned are not the areas of law where the civil law/common law divide is most marked. Community law exists, first and foremost, to solve the economic and social problems of the twentieth and twenty-first centuries whose effects spill over the jurisdictional frontiers of national legal systems. These problems are not amenable to solutions at the level of purely national law, even

---

[1] J Monnet, *Memoirs*, translated by Richard Mayne (London, Collins, 1978), 308.

with the help of public and private international law and the processes of intergovernmental co-operation.

Moreover, the economic and social attitudes and preoccupations of today are very different from those that prevailed even fifty years ago and would hardly have been recognised by the great jurists of the civil law or common law traditions. Competition law, consumer law, employment law and the law of public procurement have invaded the traditional domains of contract, delict and tort, while changed attitudes to the sanctity (and indeed the necessity) of marriage have profoundly affected the law of persons, property and status.

(3) Over the last 50 years there has been a culture change in British law. The extent of the change can be judged by recalling that in the late 1950s, administrative law covered little more than the law of local government and public utilities, the concept of a separate domain of *droit administratif* having been condemned by Dicey.[2] Judicial review (as such) was unknown. Employment law was at least as much about the contractual rights of employers as those of employees, and there were no Employment Tribunals. Human rights law and the concept of unlawful discrimination were unheard of. The House of Lords was bound by its own precedents. Statutes were interpreted strictly without reference to their legislative history or regard to the spirit of the legislation.

These features of the British legal scene were regarded by earlier generations as quintessential characteristics of the common law tradition. To a law student today, they would seem quaint. Yet British lawyers who have lived through the period of change, and probably most law students as well, would stoutly maintain that the common law tradition remains alive and well.

Britain is not unique in this respect. Other European legal systems have undergone comparable changes because, although their cultures were very different, the economic and social pressures have been the same. Facing up to common problems, including the challenge presented by Community law, has brought about a "gradual convergence" of outlook and attitudes.[3] Although the convergence is far from complete—and is indeed unlikely ever to be complete, the process of legal integration in Europe has been less confrontational than it might have been expected to be. To quote Jean Monnet again, "When you take people from different backgrounds, put them in front of the same problem, and ask them to solve it, they're no longer the same people. They're no longer there to defend their separate interests, and so they automatically take a common view".[4]

(4) Convergence has been helped by the nature of the Community system which puts a premium on co-operation in both the legislative and the judicial

---

[2] Dicey's change of heart about this has gone largely unnoticed—see GJ Hand, "AV Dicey's Unpublished Materials on the Comparative Study of Constitutions", in Hand & McBride (eds.) *Droit Sans Frontières: Essays in Honour of L. Neville Brown* (Birmingham, Holdsworth Club, 1991), 90, and other commentaries there cited.

[3] See Markesinis (ed.), *The Gradual Convergence: Foreign Ideas, Foreign Influences and English Law on the Eve of the 21st Century* (Oxford, Oxford University Press, 1994).

[4] Op. cit., n. 1 *supra*, 248.

process. Although politicians and the media tend, after summits and major negotiations, to claim victory for their national positions, the reality is that the Community's legislative process involves so many actors and takes so long that the end result rarely reflects the position from which any national negotiator started out. Similarly, the absence of dissenting opinions in the Court of Justice makes it impossible to tell whether, or to what extent, any particular judge influenced, or even agreed with, the Court's judgment.

Particularly in the field of public or administrative law, there has been an osmosis between Community law and national law, including British law. Concepts from national systems, such as proportionality and legitimate expectation, have been adopted in Community law and thence into other national systems. This process is going on continuously and it is rarely possible to identify the moment in time when a particular concept formally entered Community law or national law.

For all these reasons, it is not easy to identify particular points on which the British contribution to law and legal process in the European Union can be said to have been decisive one way or another. It is possible to identify some important individual contributions but, on the whole, the most that can be said is that there are areas where, without British participation, things would probably be different from the way they are today. These can be focussed under the following broad headings: legislation and the legislative process; the Court of Justice and legal process; the legal profession; and teaching and writing about Community law.

I. LEGISLATION AND THE LEGISLATIVE PROCESS

Two specifically British contributions stand out. First, as an individual contribution, there was Lord Cockfield's programme of legislation for completion of the internal market (the 1992 programme) which, in large part, is now the core of substantive Community law. Second, as a collective contribution, there is the continuing work of the House of Lords Select Committee on the European Communities.

(1) The importance of completing the internal market had been recognised in the Single European Act and was an essential element in the platform of the Delors Commission which took office in 1985. Up to that time, although there were many proposals on the table, they were uncoordinated and there was no comprehensive programme for legislative action. This was supplied by Lord Cockfield, one of the two British Commissioners, whose White Paper[5] identified the remaining barriers to trade within the Community and proposed a timetable for their elimination over the lifetime of two Commissions (i.e. by 1992).

---

[5] *Completing the Internal Market*, COM(85), 310.

Several characteristics of the Cockfield White Paper are typical of British administrative method and reflect the fact that Lord Cockfield had started his professional life as a civil servant in the Inland Revenue. In Britain, a proposal for legislation does not emerge from the department promoting it until other interested departments have been consulted. They may, of course, disagree with what is proposed but, if so, their objections and the reasons for them are known.

This was not true of the European Commission which tended to operate "vertically", each Directorate pursuing its own legislative projects without finding out how they might be viewed by others. Many of the matters raised in the White Paper were the primary responsibility of Directorates other than those for which Lord Cockfield was responsible, but his careful "horizontal" preparation ensured that the White Paper was produced and approved by the Commission as a whole with remarkable speed.

In addition, the Cockfield White Paper contained a detailed and specific analysis of the problem and the proposed solution: what were the barriers to trade and why, and what type of legislation was required in each case to remove the barrier—harmonisation or mutual recognition? The proposals were made objectively and without regard to their political popularity. Indeed, Lord Cockfield's insistence that some degree of fiscal harmonisation was a necessary condition of a complete internal market seems to have led Mrs Thatcher to believe that he had "gone native" and withdraw her support.[6]

While the President of the Commission, Jacques Delors, led the political drive for the 1992 programme, it is very doubtful whether, without Lord Cockfield, it would have succeeded in the way it did.

(2) The House of Lords Select Committee has, over the years since accession, produced hundreds of reports on proposed Community legislation which are widely read and jealously guarded as indispensable quarries of information that cannot readily be found elsewhere. Some other Parliaments, particularly in Scandinavia, conduct similar enquiries through committees. But the reports of the House of Lords Committee are unique in bringing together in a single volume the relevant written documents together with the oral evidence of politicians, Community and national officials, academics and interested individuals and groups. They also contain a succinct description of the proposed legislation, its purpose and advantages, and any problems it seems to present. A person with considerable experience of appearing before parliamentary committees in Britain and elsewhere remarked to me that he would normally study the papers in the taxi on the way to the meeting; for the House of Lords he would set aside two days for preparation.

(3) As regards form and content, British influence can probably be detected in the greater degree of detail that has tended to characterise Community

---

[6] For an amusing description of their divergent views and a useful description of the Single Market programme, see Lord Cockfield, *The European Union: Creating the Single Market* (Chichester, Wiley Chancery Law, 1994), especially at pp. 55–7.

legislation since the 1970s, particularly in the case of directives. It is sometimes forgotten that the common law doctrine of the sovereignty of Parliament had as its corollary the principle that common law rights are overridden only by express legislation. This has led to a preoccupation—some would say an obsession—in Westminster and Whitehall that legislation, both primary and secondary, must cover all eventualities and leave nothing to chance.

By contrast, the continental tradition, reflected in most of the Community legislation before British accession, has been to legislate in terms of principles. A good example is Regulation 1612 of 1968[7] which, with few amendments, has stood the test of time. Following this tradition, directives were intended to set out the result to be achieved, leaving detailed implementation to the member states according to their own legislative traditions and methods.

If hearsay is to be believed, British negotiators called for greater detail and precision in Community legislation. Whatever the cause,[8] some directives have become so detailed as to be indistinguishable from regulations, and to leave little for the national legislator to do. There are indications that this trend has, to some extent, gone into reverse, and this may be an example of the gradual convergence of approach.

II. THE COURT OF JUSTICE AND LEGAL PROCESS

(1) Notable individual contributions have been made by the three British Advocates General (Jean-Pierre Warner, Gordon Slynn and Francis Jacobs). They have demonstrated that common lawyers have no difficulty whatever in coming to terms with, and contributing to, the Community legal system. The extent of their influence can be judged by the frequency with which their opinions are cited by other Advocates General and in academic writing. Notable examples are the opinion of Jean-Pierre Warner in *Transocean Marine Paint*,[9] the opinions of Jean-Pierre Warner and Gordon Slynn in *A M & S*,[10] and the opinion of Francis Jacobs in *Hag II*.[11]

Lord Mackenzie Stuart as President of the Court made a major contribution in improving the productivity of the Court and in requiring the member states to take seriously their responsibility for appointing the members of the Court in good time and providing it with the resources necessary to do what they expected of it.

---

[7] Regulation (EEC) no 1612/68 of the Council of 15 Oct. 1968 on Freedom of Movement for Workers within the Community, OJ Sp.Ed.1968, No. L257/2, p. 475 (now amended by Reg. 312/76).

[8] German negotiators may also have demanded greater precision, being concerned that the *Rechtsstaat* requires an explicit legal basis for legislative or administrative action.

[9] Case 17/74 *Transocean Marine Paint Association* v. *Commission* [1974] ECR 1063.

[10] Case 155/79 *A M & S Europe* v. *Commission* [1982] ECR 1575.

[11] Case C–10/89, *SA-CNL Sucal NV* v. *HAG GV AG* [1990] ECR I–3711.

(2) Some characteristics of the British approach to law and litigation can be found in the current practice of the Court of Justice and the Court of First Instance. Before British accession, it was virtually unknown for the members of the Court to put any questions to the advocates appearing before them. Now this is common in hearings before Chambers of the Court of Justice and, more particularly, in hearings before the Court of First Instance.

Otherwise, the common law tradition of oral advocacy has found relatively little place in the practice of the Court of Justice. The reason lies largely in the problem of language. Although the rules are somewhat more complicated, the practice basically is that advocates plead in their own language and the judges speak whatever language they find most easy. What is said by the judges and advocates must be interpreted into the other languages being used in the case. This makes it virtually impossible—particularly in plenary hearings of the Court—for judges and advocates to engage in the active dialogue between bench and bar that is so characteristic of British procedure.

Some British advocates have found it difficult to adapt to a system where the main lines of argument have to be set out in written papers and a time limit is imposed on oral submissions. But their difficulties have been matched by those of advocates from other countries where there is no tradition of oral pleading in civil and administrative cases or where the advocates' arguments are never tested by questions from the bench. Moreover, part of the culture shift in Britain has been towards greater reliance on written argument and a stricter limitation of the time allowed for oral submissions. If pleading in Luxembourg still involves a culture shock for British lawyers, it is certainly less extreme than it used to be.

The oral submissions of British advocates are, in general, much appreciated by the Court for their clarity and relevance, though advocates from other countries can display the same qualities in equal measure. What has become more noticeable in recent years is the very high quality of British written pleadings, particularly those submitted by the United Kingdom government. More than one member of the Court has remarked that the quickest way to find out what a case is really about is to read the submissions of the UK government.

There appear to be two reasons for this. First, as would be the situation at home, the UK government is represented before the Court, not by departmental civil servants, but by independent advocates with experience in court work. Second, as has been mentioned above in connection with the Cockfield White Paper, the British civil service works horizontally. The position taken by the UK government before the Court is established after consultation between all the relevant departments and then presented by an advocate, part of whose function when preparing the case is to test the soundness of the arguments being advanced and to suggest how they can be presented in a way that will catch the attention of the Court.

(3) It can also be argued that Britain has brought to the Court a greater awareness of the help that judges can derive from good advocacy, both in defining the

factual context of the case and in arguing the law. It is alleged that in some countries judges regard the facts as unimportant and advocates are happy to leave the law to the judge. If so, the British system may have gone too far in the opposite direction, allowing an inordinate amount of court time to be devoted to witness evidence and discouraging judges from researching the law for themselves. At its best, however, the British system ensures that the case will not be decided on a factual basis that is erroneous or incomplete or on a view of the law on which the parties have never had an opportunity to comment or contest.

The caseload of the Court of Justice is now such that the Court needs all the help it can get in focussing the issues and identifying the points of law that need to be decided. Although the Court is often called upon to decide issues of principle that go beyond the scope of the instant case, clear definition of the factual context in which the problem arises helps to identify the issues that need to be decided for disposal of the case and can frequently illuminate the practical consequences of preferring one view of the law to another.

(4) In so far as British influence can be detected in the judgments of the Court, it may be significant that it was only after British accession that the Court began explicitly to refer to previous judgments as precedents. Before that, it was possible to infer "established case law" only from repeated use of the same formula in a succession of judgments. The practice of citing previous case law is more transparent and easier for busy lawyers to follow. In either case, however, there is a risk that repeated use of the same formula will invest it with almost biblical sanctity, making it more difficult to develop or modify the case law. Rather surprisingly, given the importance that used to be attached in British law schools to finding the *ratio decidendi* of a case, few British commentators have used these techniques in analysing the case law of the Court.

(5) The English courts have been very active in making references for preliminary rulings to the Court of Justice, sometimes in circumstances which amounted to a challenge to conventional wisdom. Thus, the Vice-Chancellor's reference in *Van Duyn*[12] was the first suggestion from a judicial source that a directive might have direct effect. The House of Lords' reference in *Factortame I*[13] put in issue both the doctrine of parliamentary sovereignty and the rule that an injunction could not be granted against the Crown. And, very recently, the reference in *Courage*[14] puts in issue the doctrine that a contracting party cannot invoke the illegality of a contract to which he is a party as a defence to a claim for payment or in order to claim damages from the other contracting party.

By making these references, the English courts have contributed greatly to the development of Community law.

---

[12] Case 41/74 *Van Duyn* v. *Home Office* [1974] ECR 1337.

[13] Case C–213/89 R. v. *Secretary of State for Transport, ex parte Factortame* [1990] ECR I–2433, and [1990] 2 AC 55.

[14] Case 453/99 *Courage* v. *Crehan*, judgment of 20 Sept. 2001.

III. THE LEGAL PROFESSION

At the time of British accession, there were very few organised law firms in the original six member states. At most there were groupings of advocates who shared chambers and overheads in the same way as English barristers. Indeed, it was seriously questioned in some quarters whether British solicitors could properly be regarded as members of the same profession for the purposes of the directive on lawyers' services. Nowadays one need only look at lawyers' letterheads and read the professional journals to see the extent to which the law firm on the Anglo-American model has become the norm in continental Europe, at least in the major centres of commerce and population.

The change has been due mainly to the demands of the corporate client, which have become ever more insistent, and the cost of the professional infrastructure necessary to service them. It has also been due as much to competition from American firms established in Europe as to British influence. The specifically British contribution seems to lie in promoting alliances between firms in different countries without destroying their individual national identity as opposed to the incorporating union preferred by American firms where the European firm is subsumed in the corporate identity of the world-wide American firm.

However, this is a field in which it is dangerous to generalise. There seems to be a global tendency towards a legal environment in which a few very large firms service the multi-national corporate market and somewhat smaller firms service niche markets (including the needs of high net worth individuals), while SMEs and ordinary individuals are serviced by lawyers working alone or in much smaller local groupings.

IV. LAW TEACHING AND WRITING

Perhaps the most significant contribution of Britain to Community law has been in the production of books and periodicals and the teaching of Community law at undergraduate and postgraduate level. This is surprising for two reasons. First, many (perhaps most) British lawyers, both practitioners and academics, are at least mild Eurosceptics and some are active Europhobes. Second, with some important exceptions, law teaching and writing used to hold a secondary place in the British legal scene.

Traditionally, textbooks could not be cited in British courts until the author was dead, and *doctrine* played little part in the development of the law. For the exposition of the law which, in the civil law tradition, would be found in the writings of professors, the common lawyer would look to the judgments of the most respected judges. The purpose of British legal textbooks was either to assist the practitioner in finding the law in the primary sources (statutes and cases) or for use by law students. There were always some books in which an academic writer would take a fresh look at a particular area of the law and reduce the statutes and precedents to a coherent system, but these were exceptional and not always highly regarded by judges and practitioners. Law teaching tended to consist in an uncritical survey of the principal statutes and cases, the aim being to ensure that the student, when eventually let loose on the public as a member of the legal profession, knew the elements of the law.

Here again, there has been a major cultural change in Britain over the past fifty years. But it would hardly have been predicted that Britain would effectively take the lead in teaching Community law and in producing a range of systematic studies both of Community law as a whole and of particular subject areas. The current output of books and periodicals is vast and many of the courses offered by the universities, particularly LL.M. courses, could be filled several times over.

Of course, publication in English ensures a wider market than in any other language so that scholars from other countries frequently write or publish translations of their books in English.[15] Also, many of those who have taken the lead in teaching and writing in British universities hail from other countries. Nevertheless, the phenomenon is interesting and the reasons for it deserve some discussion.

One reason seems to be that in many other countries—particularly those of the original Six—Community law was perceived, not as a subject in its own right, but as an aspect of one of the classical domains of law teaching and writing. Thus, the institutional law of the EC was treated as an aspect of public international law or constitutional law, while the various areas of substantive Community law, in so far as they were discussed at all, were treated as aspects of the corresponding domains of national law (such as business law or intellectual property). This is still the case to some extent.

Also, following the civil law tradition, most of the writings on Community law were commentaries, article by article, on the Treaties or, case by case, on the leading judgments of the Court of Justice. With very few exceptions, there were no books for students or practitioners which presented Community law as a whole, showing the interdependence between the historical context, the institutional structure and the substantive law. There were also very few books on the commercially most important topics—competition law and free movement of goods.

In Britain, by contrast, public international lawyers or constitutional lawyers did not regard the institutions of the Community as particularly relevant to their

---

[15] Notable examples are Kapteyn and Verloren van Themaat, *Introduction to the Law of the European Communities*, first published (London, Graham & Trotman, 1973); Schwarze, *European Administrative Law* (London and Luxembourg, Sweet & Maxwell, Office for Official Publications of the European Communities, 1992); and Lenaerts and Van Nuffel (ed. Bray), *Constitutional Law of the European Union*, and Lenaerts and Arts (ed. Bray) *Procedural Law of the European Union*, both (London, Sweet & Maxwell, 1999).

studies.[16] Those who took an interest in Community law tended, if academics, to be comparative lawyers who were interested in substantive law or administrative law or, if practitioners, to be commercial lawyers who were already concerned with restrictive practices, intellectual property or trade law.

In either case, since Community law was entirely novel from a British perspective, an understanding of the historical and institutional context was seen as essential to a proper understanding of the substantive law and *vice versa*. This approach was reflected in teaching and writing.[17] From a relatively early stage in comparison with other countries, professorial chairs and lectureships specifically for Community law were established and courses were organised, and as the popularity of self-financing Masters' degrees increased during the 1980s, Community law became a natural component of the LL.M. syllabus.

All generalisations are dangerous, but it is legitimate to argue that British lawyers and British universities were the first to teach and write about Community law *as a system*. This is paradoxical since one of the defining characteristics of the civil law tradition is often said to lie in the systematic exegesis and codification of the law: the common law is thought to be rather untidy.

Systematic teaching and writing about Community law is necessary to make sense of the claim that it constitutes a "new legal order"[18] and, in the long term, this may prove to have been the most significant contribution Britain has made.

---

[16] The exception was the late Professor JDB Mitchell, Professor of Constitutional Law at the University of Edinburgh, who instituted regular seminars on Community developments in 1962, and created a Centre of European Governmental Studies (now the Europa Institute) in 1968. Professor Mitchell's interest in Community law stemmed from his early interest in the control of public utilities and nationalised industries which led him to study the mechanisms of the Coal and Steel Community.

[17] Bellamy and Child, *Common Market Law of Competition*, first published in 1973 (London, Sweet & Maxwell), and Oliver, *Free Movement of Goods in the European Community*, first published in 1982 (London, Sweet & Maxwell), illustrate this approach in specific subject areas, while Wyatt and Dashwood, *European Community Law*, first published in 1980 (London, Sweet & Maxwell), is a typically British basic textbook for students and practitioners.

[18] See Case 26/62 *Van Gend en Loos v. Nederlandse Administratie der Belastingen* [1963] ECR 1 at p. 12.

4

The British Contribution to Italian Legal Thinking

GUIDO ALPA

1 FOREWORD

A few years ago Professor AW Simpson published the findings of his painstaking research on the history of the common law of contract and challenged the prevailing view that "English law is to be presented as capable of standing alone".[1] Professor Markesinis has, likewise, dwelled on the inter-relationship—old and modern—between Common and Civil law[2] and either stressed similarities or noted a certain degree of convergence between the legal systems. It is thus no longer easy to argue that the "insularity" and "uniqueness" of the Common law is a universally accepted proposition. In other words, when we speak of the British contribution (and, from now on, I shall refer mainly to England) to intellectual developments in Europe we must proceed on the understanding that these influences have been exerted in a reciprocal manner and are not one-sided.

Relativeness in evaluations is *de rigeur*; and in our case the caution must be even greater. For when we refer to "legal" contribution, we tend to think of the contribution made by the English common law, of which we must first have a clear picture before we can then begin to discuss and evaluate it. This is not as easy as it may seem. For some scholars have drawn our attention to the fact that it is not possible to give a clear definition of the Common law not least because the English, themselves, see it in a complicated way.[3] The idea of the Common law thus changes depending on the periods which are being considered; and its

---

[1] Simpson, "Innovation in Nineteen Century Contract Law", in *Legal Theory and Legal History* (London and Ronceverte, The Hambledon Press, 1987), at p. 171.

[2] Markesinis, "Our Debt to Europe: Past, Present and Future", in Markesinis (ed.), *The Clifford Chance Millennium Lectures. The Coming Together of the Common Law and the Civil Law* (Oxford, Hart Publishing, 2000) at p. 37.

[3] A collection of opinions is referred by the essays collected by Galgano (ed.), *Atlante di diritto privato comparato*(Bologna, Zanichelli, 1992); Alpa (ed.), *Corso di sistemi giuridici comparati* (Torino, Giappichelli, 1996), at p. 121 ff.; Sacco and Gambaro, *Sistemi giuridici comparati* (Torino, Utet, 1996); Losano, *I grandi sistemi giuridici* (Roma-Bari, Laterza, 2000) at p. 257 ff.; Alpa, Bonell, Corapi, Moccia, Zeno-Zencovich, *Diritto privato comparato* (Roma-Bari, Laterza, 1999); Lupoi, *Sistemi giuridici comparati* (Napoli, ESI, 2001).

meaning may also be affected if we are looking at it in isolation or in juxtaposition with its natural "counterpart": the Civil law.

The idea of Common law also changes according to the cultural context in which it is placed. Thus, today we note among English authors differing opinions as to the main features of the Common law. Professor Watson, for instance, believes that the differences between Civil law and Common law reside not in the Germanic customs absorbed by the latter, nor in the influx of Canon law in the rules of equity. For both these sources have exercised great influence in the formation of the Civil law of Continental countries as well. Nor is the difference to be found in the different *degree* of adoption of the principles of Roman law recorded in the two worlds. What differentiates these worlds, always according to Watson, is determined by two different factors: historical tradition for Common law, and the choice of Justinian's *Corpus juris* as an instrument for the organisation of the law for Civil law.[4] Professor Honoré, on the other hand, has stressed temporal distances that he believes explain the differences in the two systems in the history of law.[5] Given the above, Christopher Dawson's warning,[6] shared by the late Paul Koschacker[7] is still valid: "Europe is not a spontaneous fruit, a geographical and natural fact, but a product of history". And as legal organization is an integral part of the history of a people, a nation, or a State it, too, is subject to the same laws of history.[8]

We are, therefore, faced with a deep-seated prejudice though a different reading of the documents and the evidence may allow us nowadays to challenge it.

If we try to view the situation from the other side of the Channel we are faced with a similar landscape. The "lawyer's spectacles" may be different, as Arturo Carlo Jemolo put it so aptly,[9] but not the substance of the matter.

For the Continental jurist has been raised with the same conviction and tends to believe, almost as a "natural" reflex, that the Common law has been coated by an impermeable "otherness" that has guaranteed both its identity and purity. This too, however, is a prejudice, shared by many Continental jurists.

The prejudice fought against by authors such as Simpson and Markesinis is a two-faced Janus. Continental jurists, like traditional English historians, believe that the English system, like Victorian England, is attached to the notion of "splendid isolation". But the history of Continental legal history in general—and Italian legal history in particular—belies this symmetrical prejudice.

Eradicating prejudices is not easy. We have to be armed with historical awareness in order to take stock, even by abridgement and by samples, of the contri-

---

[4] Watson, *Roman Law & Comparative Law* (Athens and London, The University of Georgia Press, 1991), at p. 139 ff.

[5] Honoré, *About Law* (Oxford, Oxford University Press, 1995).

[6] Dawson, *The Making of Europe. An Introduction to the History of European Unity* (London, Sheed & Ward, 1935).

[7] Koschacker, *L'Europa e il diritto romano* (Firenze, Sansoni, 1970), at p. 8.

[8] Alpa (ed.), *Corso di stistemi giuridici comparati* (Torino, Giappichelli, 1996), p. 6 ss. 000.

[9] That was the title of the column written by Jemolo, a master of Church Law, during the Fifties and the Sixties on *Rivista di diritto civile*.

bution that the legal culture, the institutions, the practices from across the Channel, have registered in the individual legal systems of Europe. It is even more difficult to imagine the flow on the basis of the dynamics that govern the construction of EC law. My paper will, therefore, in essence be divided into two segments: one dedicated to the past, the other to the present and the future.

Historical perspective makes us particularly cautious, because we are moving in a linguistic and conceptual environment which is burdened with stereotypes, myths, and simplifications which have become stratified through the centuries. When the Continental jurist reflects about the English legal system he somehow ends up by thinking of a body of rules created by the courts. Thus, the possibility that the relationships established by private individuals, which come under the heading of private law, could be affected by other sources of law—such as statutes, rules and regulations imposed by an authority different from a Judge— somehow does not easily enter his mind. When thinking of the Common law we, therefore, think of a law born from time to time from actual, empirical, casual reality, and shaped by the courts or by the practices and customs that apply to commercial relations. Case law and lex mercatoria are thus the first references that spring to our mind. We, on the Continent, further think that the other sources of law, which have become noteworthy only in recent times, are largely the result of the United Kingdom becoming part of the European Union. This, too, is a stereotype, or an actual prejudice, which contemporary historical analysis takes it upon itself to demolish. Likewise, Continental lawyers tend to treat the English model as standing on its own compared to the other models— French, German, Italian—which are more akin to their own and which they tend to consult more willingly whenever the need for confirmation or inspiration arises. This is another prejudice which scholarship must disprove, or at least try to weaken.

2. THE TRANSLATIONS OF THE NINETEENTH CENTURY AND THE CIRCULATION OF LIBERAL IDEAS

Already during the first decades of the nineteenth century Italian literature is beginning to take note of English thinking and weighing its impact on European legal culture.

The season of translations—a period which extends from the beginning of the nineteenth century to the beginning of the twentieth—offers a delightful landscape for those interested in understanding how cultural models travel. It also helps show how the image of foreign legal systems is constructed and how the techniques for the solution of problems, which are by and large common to all the experiences of Western Europe, are developed.[10] Those who believe that England's geographical distance and natural isolation may have prevented, or at

---

[10] Alpa, *La cultura delle regole. Storia del diritto civile italiano* (Roma-Bari, Laterza, 2000).

least limited, the intellectual contacts between our two worlds, will be surprised if they consult this little-known literature.

Among the hundreds of translations of foreign works prepared by various professionals in the different Italian States, and subsequently in unified Italy,[11] the prize goes to the clear, lively, geometrical books of our French cousins and to the weighty, well-thought out, architectural tomes of revered German colleagues. But the translations of English books is also significant. Translations are a reliable gauge of the tastes, of the needs and curiosities of the readers. We find ourselves—at that time—facing a select, restricted, homogeneous readership, if we bear in mind that in the nineteenth century a very modest percentage of Italians could read and write fluently and had the qualification to exercise voting rights. Apart from those living off incomes, the higher social classes were engaged in the liberal professions, and therefore consisted of lawyers, doctors, engineers, university professors, industrialists, bankers, and high-ranking merchants. Whatever their profession, these people made up a homogeneous cultural *milieu* which was also fairly similar from a political point of view since most of its members professed liberal ideas (albeit tainted by a strong Catholic hue). The works coming from England provided formative reading for them, as well as material useful for their professional lives.

But let us proceed in an orderly manner. The researches of legal historians provide us with interesting data in this respect. It appears, in fact, that over the entire nineteenth century translations of French books number more than a thousand. Those of German books are slightly less than half that number; and those of English books are 160: a fifth of the former and a third of the latter.[12] I think this last figure is extraordinary high given that French was the language spoken by the cultured classes, in some regions even prevailing over Italian! The result is even more amazing if one takes into account the distance between the two countries, the different structure of their political and legal systems, their institutions in general, and the language problems raised by a very different vocabulary and grammar. Seen in this light, the gap between England and Italy is quite substantial. And yet it was bridged in a manner of speaking.

The places of more frequent publications also give interesting clues that must not to be missed. They correspond to the great capital cities: in decreasing order of publications, we find Turin, with more than a third, Milan with one fifth, Florence, Naples and Rome for the remaining part.

The years of publication are also of interest. Thus, in Turin, translations from English are prevalent in the period prior to national Unification. These are the years during which the Savoy State aims to assume the leadership of the peninsula. These are the golden years of the Count of Cavour (1851–1855)—a great admirer of British political institutions (not to mention farming techniques).

---

[11] The political unification dates back to 1861, the legal to 1865.
[12] See Napoli, *La cultura giuridica europea in Italia. Repertorio delle opere tradotte nel secolo XIX, vol.3,* (Napoli, Jovene, 1987).

There is a second wave of translations towards the latter part of the century, when Turin provides a now united Italy with its free, open, and combative spirit, sensitive to class struggles and to the social effects of the industrialisation of the country. In Naples on the other hand, translations cover the years that precede Garibaldi's venture, sustained by Piedmont and by British capital. In Milan, until 1859 an Austrian province, they appear only in the years following the unification of Italy. And in Florence, in the years of consolidation of the new powers (1871–1875).

What could English literature offer the Italian lawyer, judge, notary, university professor and, generally, learned person?

Prior to political union, and then up to the end of the nineteenth century, the boundaries of law, as a science and technique, were quite blurred, and therefore we can freely include in our list, also books of a political and philosophical content. Indeed, numerically these prevail over books of a strictly legal content. The matters dealt with regard the organisation of power, the distribution of goods, the placing of individuals in their social contexts. The British contribution to the construction of foundational values of Italian culture is thus varied and considerable.

In this scheme of things public law is mixed with political philosophy and with universal values, and hence proceeds at full speed towards economics and sociology. Criminal law goes alongside psychology and anthropology. At the beginning of the nineteenth century, books on the idea of the republic and on morals by David Hume and John Locke, those on aphorisms by John Harrington, on social organisation by John Brown, on civil society by Richard Price and Adam Ferguson, are published and read in Italy. Translations, obviously, do not exhaust the cultural horizons of jurists. Locke's thinking, for instance, had been introduced in France with the translations of 1724, and was also known through the works of Rousseau, especially the "Social Contract" which was brought to Italy by Cesare Beccaria and Pietro Verri at the end of the eighteenth century.

But let us return to translations. Thomas Moore's *Utopia* is translated in Milan in 1821, Francis Bacon's universal law, in Turin in 1824; James Mill's *Political Economy* in Naples in 1826. Again Bacon, this time alongside the populariser André Marie (nick-named Aîné) Dupin, in Naples in 1831. Dupin had in those same years edited a very popular manual for students of law and young lawyers, which was to become an instrument and a bridge of ideas with foreign cultures.[13] In the Neapolitan edition of Bacon, the translator inserted the *Aphorisms* and excerpts of *De Dignitate et Augmentis Scientiarum*. The principles of political economy by William Nassau Senior, based on his lectures at Oxford University, are rendered into Italian by the translator of James Mill in Lugano in 1836.

---

[13] *Manuale degli Studenti di Diritto e de' Giovani Avvocati* (Napoli, Ateneo, 1831).

James Mill is one of the ideal partners in the political unrest that flares up in Milan in 1848. Borroni and Scotti's "Tipografia Patriottica" (Patriotic Press), with headquarters in Lugano, publishes his work on reality as opposed to utopia. Lugano was home to the refugees from Lombardy—under Austrian domination at the time—that nourished ideas of liberty, universal suffrage, and struggle against tyranny. At the end of the century it will have become a haven to anarchist exiles.

As regards Richard Phillips, our interest lies in his work on the Jury, which appeared in Florence in 1849. Lord Henry Peter Brougham's *Political Philosophy* appeared in Florence in 1850. A year later Italians could read in their own language John Stuart Mill's *Principles of Political Economy,* which was published in Turin in 1851. The publisher who secured the book, Pomba (who will subsequently adopt the acronym U.T.E. and thus the current UTET), inaugurates a collection which is still renown for its prestigious list. In the same year, the same publisher produces the translation of Adam Smith's *Inquiry*, already translated into Italian in Naples, in 1790. Only a few years later the same collection will contain Italian translations of Bentham's Manual of Political Economy (1854), the principles of Malthus, the works of James Mill, Scrope, Ricardo, Wately and Dupont-White appear. The market is growing and so are the sales. All this represents a healthy injection of utilitarianism and individualism and serves a dual purpose: to reinforce individual rights against an obtuse and tyrannical authority, and to limit the interference of the community in personal choices.

The incipient capitalism (subsequently corrected at the end of the century in its expression of brutal exploitation of the workforce) needed this nourishment. Even this aspect denotes the natural traits of Common law which, as Bertrand Russell teaches, materialises in the dialectical relationship between "Authority and the individual".[14]

There is no lack of interest, either, for the history of *The British Constitution* by Henry Hallam (Turin, 1854), whilst in the Neapolitan State, the studies on the interpretation of the law, in particular the works of Bacon, are appreciated. Bacon's *"Aphorisms"* are greatly successful everywhere, also published in Urbino, in 1855. Sir William Blackstone is admired for his views on the penal code, translated in Milan in 1813.

Only private law, Roman in its roots, French in its codified structure, and then German in its conceptual framework is, apparently, impervious to the influence of the Common law. And yet it is not rash to believe that the views of Blackstone on the Common law, even if not frequently quoted in the Italian literature of the nineteenth century, were known to Italian jurists. In Paris, in fact, many editions of his *Commentaries* appeared. In 1776, four years before the author's death, a French version had already been published in Brussels, based on his fourth English edition; and this was followed by another version in 1801.

---

[14] *Autorità e individuo* (Milano, Longanesi, 1962).

The reasons for this cultural operation are explained in great detail by Councilor Compré: the development of trade between France and Britain, cultural, scientific and industrial exchanges, family relations and friendships, contractual relations, in addition to successions, was a powerful incentive to bring the two worlds closer together. The Italians must have known of all this, in French if not in Italian.

But what are mostly underlined are the divergences more than the similarities. The French system (interchangeable at the time with that of the pre-Unification Italian States) and the English system, seem to rotate around distinct orbits, planets that may, occasionally, come close to each other, but bound never to meet. On private law matters, this view prevails at the time.

3 BLACKSTONE'S SYSTEMATIC OPERATION

In the nineteenth century in France custom was replaced by codes. In England, by contrast, we have general and local customs, the rules of Roman law and Canon law, acts of Parliament and of the Monarch, and last but not least, decisions emanating from judges from time immemorial, gathered in voluminous collections.

Against this backdrop of massive legislative or quasi-legislative material, difficult to decipher for the Common lawyer, and even more so for the Civilian, stands Blackstone and his work, remarkable says the Italian translator of his work, because of its clarity. Blackstone illustrates the history of the laws of his country, their evolution, and their weaknesses. There must be a lesson in such a great work.

Both the translator of the Italian edition and its commentator (Christian), while appreciating Blackstone's effort in the systematic reconstruction of the subject matter, are not always sympathetic towards his aims. Undoubtedly, they have a great respect for English public law. For that unwritten Constitution, which traces its roots way back to medieval times and make it probably the best Constitution among those existing at that time, is not to be ignored. This makes great sense in 1822 when very few liberal constitutions have managed to survive the anti-Napoleonic reaction. By contrast, the Continental commentators reserve lesser praise for the pages on "private law". Indeed they have little doubt that the latter sections are worthy of less attention than the former.

It is difficult to ascertain whether the scant interest shown by the translators towards private law as described by Blackstone is due to the conviction that the Common law on relations between individuals is something so "different" to Civilian law that does not merit discussion. Alternatively, the belief may have been that the evolution of the Common law had led to the stratification of a medieval and mercantile law in categories and structures which were of little use to Continental lawyers. And yet Blackstone's systematic order follows closely that of Justinian's Institutions.[15] Conversely, the roots of Blackstone's thinking, the richness of values which it incorporates, the profound culture which shines through many pages, do not make the book that alien to Continental structures and cultural ideals. In the syllabuses laid down by Napoleon for the students of the Lyceums and Universities of the Kingdom of Italy (1806), Roman law and its sources were, in fact, a compulsory subject; and the *Code Civil* was commented with references to Roman law.[16]

At the beginning of the nineteenth century one of the reasons for the lack of interest in English Common law must be traced to the image which the English legal writers were, themselves, cultivating abroad about their system. Thus, a review published in Naples at the beginning of the century (*Il Giurista. Giornale di legislazione e giurisprudenza—The Jurist. Journal of legislation and jurisprudence*) contains several interesting essays, which substantiate the image of the Common law in Italy.

Take, for instance, an article by Rathery, published in issue N. 25 of the 4 September 1836 of the above-mentioned Journal. It deals with the "study of law and the advocate's profession in England". It contains a concise yet comprehensive account of the history of English law, from the Middle Ages to the beginning of the nineteenth century, an analysis of the legal profession, including the role of the Inns of Court, a concise description of the methods of teaching of the law. The picture is drawn in grim and sarcastic terms. The opening sections of the article are significant since the author warns the reader not to have false expectations. The author begins with a drastic assumption: "Let us say it out loud" he tells us, "the French can be rightly proud when they compare the magnificent monument of their codes with the intricate labyrinth of English laws. Except as regards certain issues on the subject of criminal procedure, we have nothing that will cause our neighbours' envy". After this, our author recalls Hale's assumption that the source of Common law "is as difficult to trace as that of the Nile" and then contrasts statute law with Common law and regrets that a "science of the law" has never developed in England. But if that is how the English present their law, why should the Italians become interested in it? But then not everything in the Common law is to deprecated. What can be saved is "the spirit of practical wisdom that the English nation possesses so pre-eminently, corrects the flaws of a literal interpretation of the law, and sometimes the sublime intent of its judges makes up for the inadequacies of the law". Such saving graces contain interesting thoughts; but they come too late—after statements that have already caused harm by putting the foreign reader off further study.

---

[15] The discussion is open: see Kennedy, "The Struction of Blackstone's Commentaries", in Hutchinson (ed.), *Critical Legal Studies* (Totowa, NJ, Rowman & Littlefield Publ. Inc., 1989), at pp. 139 ff. and (from an opposite view) Watson, *Roman Law & Comparative Law*, cit. (n. 5), at pp.166 ff.; and also Boorstin, *The Mysterious Science of Law. An Essay on Blackstone's Commentaries* (Cambridge Mass., Harvard University Press, 1941–1996).

[16] Alpa, *La cultura delle regole*, cit. (n. 14).

Unfortunately, such critical pieces abound raising doubts as to the English talent in public relations. Even the English judicial system falls under the commentator's axe. Thus, an article published anonymously in issue n. 29 of the 18 February, 1837 on "judicial centralisation in England" criticises the number of cases pending before the Courts of Westminster, and lists the frustrated attempts to introduce a legislative reform of the system. The "Insolvency Court", set up in 1813 is also met with barbs in another anonymous article published in the same year. The rules on *defamation*, on the other hand, and the organisation of the penal colonies meet with great favour, as can be seen from the articles published on several occasions in the Neapolitan review in 1836 and 1838.

Given the time they were written, these pieces may be right to criticize the weaknesses of the English system. But they do not excite interest in English law. To put it differently, the ones that do are the ones that cry out for reform in an articulate manner (whether one agrees or not with their content). I believe that this is one of the many reasons why Jeremy Bentham was welcomed with such warmth by Continental jurists in general, and Italians in particular.

4 BENTHAM AND THE CODIFICATION OF LAW

A curious destiny was Bentham's, to be criticised at home and appreciated on the Continent. So much so, that his works were published in their entirety or in instalments or as extracts without intervals. Thus, his work on civil and criminal legislation is translated into Italian from the French text edited by Etienne Dumont in Geneva, on the basis of the manuscripts entrusted to him by the author. Naples is the first Italian town to bestow this honour upon him in the year 1818. Two years later his works on parliament and on political sophisms are published in Naples from the French edition. In 1830, in Forlì, his writings on codes follow suit. Other editions are printed elsewhere in Italy, such as Venice in 1836. Bentham's volume on the theory of judicial evidence is printed in Bergamo in 1824 and in Brussels, in Italian, in 1842 and 1843.

Bentham's position on codes was of particular interest for Italian jurists, above all those who lived and worked in the States in which the choice of codification had not yet been effected. The discussion centred on whether it was preferable to align with the codifications of the Kingdom of the Two Sicilies, the Duchy of Parma, the Sardinian-Piedmontese Kingdom, or to maintain the traditional sources, which did not record rules in an orderly and structured way in a unitary *corpus*. In the Grand Duchy of Tuscany, the sources brought by tradition were in force. And I believe this is the reason that urged the Grand-ducal Press in Florence to print Bentham's pages on the compilation of codes. In Florence, a brilliant and acute legal writer, Enrico Forti, who was an admirer of conceptually systemised law but opposed to codification, wrote a treatise on Civil law. Those were the years in which the diatribe between Savigny and

Thibaut on codification was closely followed in Italy and its echoes were to take years before they would be subdued. It was an ancient diatribe, which in Italian culture was rooted in Enlightenment thinking. Ludovico Antonio Muratori, in describing the failings of case law, had already shown how the resolution of disputes by recourse to the opinions of legal writers, to methodological fashions (the *mos italicus* was prevailing at the time), to the contradictions of precedents, entailed uncertainty in the application of legal rules. It also earned lawyers little respect from ordinary people. But was it possible to renounce tradition and change course? Had the Italian States, which had opted for codification simply imitated the *Code Napoléon*, or were they convinced by the political reasons underlying codification?

Bentham's thinking as set out in *Law and Legislation* is crystal clear. The law must be made knowable in the entire system to all those who have the power to preserve and apply it and for the part which relates to them, to those who must obey it. The order of exposition is the *natural* order, which Bentham does not make to coincide with that of Domat because it has nothing superhuman. The natural order is the practical order imposed by utility. And thus, in addition to the rules for the drafting of a penal code, Bentham dictates also the rules for civil codification, arranging in sequence things, places, time, services, obligations, rights, contracts, persons capable of acquiring, and so forth.

The conclusions of his work are in one sense touching. Touching because in their clarity they condense the dictates of a legal positivism before its time, and precisely for this reason they are modern, perspective and genial. The composition of a "corpus juris" must be characterised by *purity*. Laws must be cleansed of any extraneous element, to be able to express fully the *intention of the legislator*. "Leges non decet esse disputantes sed iubentes", was Bacon's saying, and Bentham adds: *et docentes*.

Here is a courageous and innovative position (especially for an Englishman) similar in many respects to that of Beccaria. Bentham does not appreciate the Codex Fredericianus prepared by Coccejus because it exalts uncertainty and the triumph of legal scholars but depresses the resolution of disputes. He cautions that one cannot transform the intention of the legislator into the intention of others nor can one think of a natural law that remains obscure. One cannot put veils over the intention of the *positive legislator*. We must not do as the Romans did for the sole purpose of copying them. "La grande utilité d'un corps de droit c'est de faire oublier le debats des jurisconsultes et les mauvaises lois des temps anterieurs".[17]

Clarity and brevity must be the features of the law. The law must not lend itself to differing and conflicting interpretations; its clarity depends on logic and grammar. Brevity is essential so as not to lose sight of the purpose of the law, as is the case (says Bentham) with English *statutes*. But Bentham's recommenda-

---

[17] Bentham–Dumont, *Trattato di Legislazione Civile e Penale* (Napoli, Marotta, 1818), vol.1, p. 45.

tions go well beyond a political evaluation on the procedures for the creation of rules. He also deals with drafting, with enviable competence, offering suggestions that even nowadays maintain their effectiveness.

In Bentham's convincing reasoning, there are signs of a complete and precise legislative programme. Legislators must use terms with which the people are familiar; technical terms must be defined; definitions must be written using common expressions; and these expressions must always be used with the same meaning. It is sad to realise that these words of warning have gone with the wind. Only Eugen Huber, the Swiss legislator, tried to put them into practice. But in the other systems, the growing complexity of legal science and technique have ended up making them vain. Only now that we are faced with harmonisation of the rules of private law in the EC context, do we realise that uniform terminology and definitions are the only means to give actual binding force and greater certainty to regulations.

Bentham the empiricist, the practical man, the astute politician fights against the concept of law as a science. This is not due to a particular aversion to robes, or to knowledge *per se*. What, instead, is feared is the perversion of the purposes of the law which may come from the professors who comment on laws, from compilers of glossaries who obscure their meaning, from petty litigators who fill them with useless quibbles.

Bentham's may have been an ideal model, perhaps unattainable. But it is precisely these models which the legislator sometimes needs; and so does the legal scholar in general to orient his work. The illusion that the legislator does not require mediation to reach the people is frustrated by the irrepressible need for a technical exactitude, which distances the language of the law from the commonly spoken language. This is belied by the necessary interpretation of the text, which enriches, manipulates, alters, bends it to practical needs, and renders it live.

5 JOHN STUART MILL AND HERBERT SPENCER AT THE TIME OF THE INDUSTRIALISATION OF THE COUNTRY

John Stuart Mill has also had a prominent place in the library of many Italian lawyers.[18]

The interest towards Mill increased after the unification of Italy. In Turin his works on political representation, on the interference of the State in the Church's properties and corporations, on liberties and on utilitarianism, were widely discussed. Lawyers did the translations. This was a sign not only of the intellectual exchange that took place between legal and other cultures. It also demonstrated the liveliness and versatility of the legal profession (the

---

[18] *Principii di Economia politica con alcune delle sue applicazioni alla Filosofia sociale* (Cugini Pomba e C., Torino, 1851).

"corporation" as it was known at the time) which, together with that of doctors, formed the country's ruling class.

These works existed alongside those on economics and helped build the Italian economic thinking of the time. It is not by chance that in 1905 it was Luigi Einaudi, the great economist, Governor of the Bank of Italy and, finally, the second President of the Republic after World War II, who translated Bagehot's work on the government's monetary policy and on the role of the Bank of England.[19] Bagehot's book has a sub-title that illustrates its contents. Indeed the work deals with the British money market, but the title is highly evocative for Italians because it recalls the trade and entrepreneurship of the medieval merchants who used to have their place of business in "Lombard Street".

Industrialisation and trade make great steps forward in Italy, so there is a need also for works of a practical nature. Here we find manuals of English maritime cases,[20] of the theory and practice of banks by H. D. Macleod,[21] or works on Company law.[22] But also a collection of model letters of correspondence and sample contracts, such as those proposed by Hugh Darley[23] as well as manuals on copyright with the relative international agreements attached to them, such as the one by Hawkridge.[24]

During this period Herbert Spencer also attracted great attention. His sociological philosophy—very close to reality—his analysis of social needs, of household and ceremonial institutions, constituted one of the pillars of the new concept of social sciences. They also provide ideas for renewal, also from the point of view of methodology, of legal studies that took hold in the country at the time. Socialism advanced together with the affirmation of women's rights. Workers' rights and Labour law, were studied thanks to T W Thorton's book.[25]

6 BRITISH POLITICAL LIBERTIES AND HOSPITALITY

But there are also translations of works on the Church of Rome and the Anglican Church. This, too, is a sign of the lack of prejudice, indeed another sign for this unending quest for knowledge on the part of Italian scholars. Britain is seen as the home of liberty, of freedom of opinion, and freedom of

---

[19] Bagehot, *La moneta*, (Turin, Utet, 1907).
[20] By W A Oliver, *Manuale Pratico della Giurisprudenza Marittima Inglese, ovvero le leggi mercantili in Inghilterra*, in Leghorn (Fiori, 1872).
[21] *La Teoria e la Pratica delle Banche* (Turin, Utet, 1879) (Macleod was Fellow of Trinity College, Cambridge and Master of Inner Temple).
[22] Bruce, *Revisione delle Leggi Inglesi regolanti le Società a responsabilità limitata* (Bologna, Fava e Garagnani, 1896).
[23] *Lettere moderne di corrispondenza commerciale con fatture, ecc.* (Napoli, Marghieri, 1863).
[24] *La Proprietà Industriale e l'unione industriale* (Rome, Artero, 1884).
[25] *Del Lavoro, delle sue pretese e dei suoi diritti* (Florence, Barbera, 1875).

criticism. In fact, precisely through the works of British authors (including Gladstone), the Italians are anxious to learn—in an environment still marked by the Napoleonic influence—of what is said and done across the Channel. After Unification, Italians wished to know what Britain thought of the position of the Church and of the Papacy.

These were the anxieties of a culture that wished to preserve its secular features, which longed for the free circulation of ideas, which saw in comparative studies and in the contributions of foreign scholars the way towards maturity, not an escape from reality. It is thus no coincidence that London is the place where many of the "Founding Fathers" of the Italian State would seek refuge in moments of personal or political crisis. These were lawyers, doctors, "carbonari", free-masons, free thinkers—all of whom had fought against the obscurantism and tyranny of the post-Napoleonic monarchs and had set the foundations of a new society, not only from a political, but also from an economic and social point of view. Giuseppe Mazzini was among these refugees. But there was nothing new in this "escape" as is shown by the personal history of Alberico Gentili, who had sought refuge with his brother in England in order to escape from religious persecution at home. And it was in England that he had laid the foundations of international law, ahead of the more famous Grotius, and had offered his services to a Queen—Elizabeth I—who welcomed him to her court.

Saffi too was a patriot, a follower of Mazzini, who graduated in Ferrara in 1841. Being under the Church Dominions, his aspirations to civil liberties had been frustrated by the disappointing policy of Pius IX. He had actively participated in the Roman revolution of 1849, had become a member of the triumvirate of the Roman Republic and, after its collapse, had sought refuge in England where, having married a Scottish woman, he had lived for a time, teaching Italian literature at Oxford University.

The role of British political science and public law (I shall not dwell on the works of criminal law and forensic medicine though they were equally appreciated in my country) is underlined also by the interest raised by the British Constitution. This is witnessed, among others, by the volume by Thomas Erskine May on democracy in Europe, published in UTET's valuable collection.[26] The idea of Europe is already circulating at that time; it circulates also thanks to the historical studies on medieval Europe by Henry Hallam and William Smith.[27]

The British Government and Parliament are well known through the works of Charles Knight,[28] Henry Latchford,[29] George Lewis Cornerwall,[30] Alpheus Todd.[31]

---

[26] *La democrazia in Europa* (Turin, Utet, 1884).
[27] *L'Europa nel medioevo* (Florence, Barbera, 1874).
[28] *Società e governo di Inghilterra negli ultimi tempi* (Milan, Corona e Caimi, 1867).
[29] *Senno e brio del parlamento inglese* (Milan, Dumolard, 1885 end Naples, 1885).
[30] *Qual è la miglior forma di governo* (Padova, 1868).
[31] *Il governo parlamentare in Inghilterra* (Turin, Utet, 1886).

Even the text that carries the reform of the regulations of the House of Commons will end up being translated into Italian.[32]

But the dialogue is very close between intellectuals on both sides of the Channel. At Edinburgh University, Count Andrea Finocchietti, a Senator of the Realm, will translate the work on Giambattista Vico by Robert Flint.[33] And the major Italian scholar of public law at the end of the century, Vittorio Emanuele Orlando, will edit the translation of the work by Francis Montague on the limits to individual freedom.[34]

7 POLLOCK, MAINE AND HOLMES: THEIR CONTRIBUTION

At the end of the nineteenth century an eclectic fervour grips Italian legal culture. The French model, descriptive and linear, tied to the readings of the *Code civil*, no longer satisfied the needs of Italian legal scholars. Alongside the impressive dogmatic construction of the Pandectists, which entered in full pomp and circumstance the treatises and training manuals of students and lawyers, we find studies by those who believe that law is a social science, and therefore cannot exclude from its purview economics, sociology, and anthropology. Two opposing concepts of the law square up face to face: one is found in the geometric purity of the system, the other in the practical function of the rules and their social effects. Hence, the interest in the method for the study of the law.[35] The two schools of thought, though they confront each other, also manage to establish a debating symbiosis; another sign of Italian eclecticism.

One of the most important reviews of the time, the *Archivio giuridico*—"The legal archive"—published in Pisa under the editorship of a Master of Roman law and a supporter of the Pandectist school in Italy, does not hesitate to publish texts inspired by the opposite school. In the collection of 1886, the *Archivio giuridico* carries a long article by Frederick Pollock on the "methods of jurisprudence" (*jurisprudentia, Rechtwissenschaft*). This, in fact, is his inaugural lecture given at a University Conference in London on the 31 October 1882. Again the translation is edited by a lawyer, Salvatore Sacerdote.

Pollock expresses a modern concept of the law, which should be considered as a *science* and as an *art*. The legal scholar's is a multiform art: "as a consultant he is called upon to form a concept on the legal effects of the facts placed before him; as a lawyer, to present in the most effective and persuasive manner the points in the case which are more favourable to the interests of his client; as a writer, to express in adequate and sufficient words the intentions of the parties who consult him". But precisely because law is a science and an art, the terms

---

[32] May and Reynart, *Leggi, privilegi, procedura e consuetudine del parlamento inglese* (Turin, Utet, 1888).
[33] Giovan Battista Vico (Florence, Coppini Bocconi, 1888).
[34] *I limiti della libertà individuale* (Turin, Utet, 1890).
[35] Alpa, *La cultura delle regole, cit.* (n.10).

and concepts, which the lawyer uses, are technical and practical terms. "English lawyers"—observes Pollock—"for a variety of reasons anxiously avoid verbal definitions". But there is more. In the lecture he explains the salient features of the English model, which differs from the Continental method. It is immediately clear that the comparison between the English method and the Continental one must be placed in historical perspective. As the geometric and ideal study of the Digest was prevailing at the time, Pollock emphasised differences rather than brought to light similarities. It is not only the terminology which strikes the observer of the two worlds: "there is a radical difference of concept and development". This difference is concentrated at the heart of the law, that is the concept of "just and unjust". To understand the differences, Pollock appeals to history and logic. History teaches us that one thing is the aspiration to ideal laws, quite another is the analysis of positive law. "Ethical Jurisprudence", however necessary, crosses into metaphysics, into *Naturrecht*, which is totally alien to the British mentality. The British concept of law concerns "something to be achieved, or to be approached as closely as possible in a current State for the modern citizens by the effective promulgation of legislation". Rules are formed through the decisions of the courts and through the principles and practices of Chancery. But what brings out the spirit of English law is legal practice. This, according to Pollock, is the reason why Bentham's and Austin's models were unsuccessful. At the same time, he heartily promoted the study of comparative law, because both the knowledge of Roman law, and the knowledge of Civil law, are useful for the lawyer's formation. He was convinced that comparative studies and critique will improve the standard of English lawyers, who should behave like "prudent travellers", who never follow all the winding bends of the roads, nor do they cut across unknown ground, in order to avoid being confronted with impracticable precipices.

The appeal to history and anthropology is the impressive and intriguing message of Henry Sumner Maine. *Ancient Law* was a successful book also in Italy, because it showed how rules of law are not the creation of an ideal mind, but rather are rooted in the culture of a people, in the tradition, in the behavioural models spontaneously observed. And the same respect was accorded to Oliver Wendell Holmes whose *Common Law*, as with Bentham, was translated wholly, then in part, and was then finally published in instalments: in chapters and according to topics. In 1889, again in *Archivio giuridico*, the chapter on the "primitive forms of responsibilities" was reproduced, translated by the lawyer Francesco Lambertenghi. This was an accurate reconstruction of the rules of civil liability, which set out from Moses's law, pass on to Greek law, Roman law, Germanic and Anglo-Saxon law, finally ending with English Common law.

8 COMMERCIAL AND MARITIME LAW

Even Italian Commercial law and Maritime law are marked by the important influence of the English experience.

One of the founders of modern Commercial law, Cesare Vivante, included among the major references in his *Treatise on Commercial Law*, published in 1893, in addition to German jurists such as Goldschmidt and French jurists such as Lyon-Caen and Renault, also the tenth edition of John William Smith, *A compendium of mercantile law* published in London in 1890. Thanks to *lex mercatoria*, the image of the "merchant" takes shape. The rules followed by merchants turn from subjective law to objective law, on the basis of the fiction that "anyone should be held to be a merchant when instituting proceedings for a commercial affair".[36] Vivante avails himself of Smith's opinion, in addition to those of authors from older times, such as Stracchia and Ansaldo, to document this important landmark in the world of law. It is, in fact, the quotation of Smith's opinion that consolidates his conviction, where he underlines that when *lex mercatoria* ceased to be a separate branch of the law compulsory for a single class of persons, whoever made any transaction regulated by that same law was held to be a merchant *quoad* such transaction.[37]

This is something that in the Continental experiences was codified that is, it was transformed into an enforceable general rule. But even in the English experience the *lex mercatoria*—in relation to acts of trade—was made mandatory for all. Smith, himself, underlined how at the end of the nineteenth century mercantile customs were incorporated into the Common law, and became mandatory for all citizens, whether they were merchants or not.[38] But this initial unity does not imply an identity of systems. Vivante highlighted the different concepts of Mercantile law in Continental Europe and in England. In the Continental systems, there is a tendency to build a system of Commercial law separate from the general system of Civil law, whilst in English law there are no general theories of commercial obligations, because these are subject to the principles of Common law.

Learned and innovative, Vivante extended his analysis to the main models of comparative studies, including the English experience. Among the sources of his studies, he listed both the principles deriving from the Common law and the institutes regulated by statute law. Again availing himself of Smith's work, he listed the laws of major interest for the scholar and the lawyer who practiced Commercial law. He, therefore, reviewed the Bankruptcy Act of 1883 and its subsequent amendments,[39] the Bills of Exchange Act of 1882,[40] the sale of Goods Act of 1893,

---

[36] Vivante, *Trattato di diritto commerciale* (Torino, Fratelli Bocca Editori, 1902) 2nd ed., vol. I, at p.6.
[37] Vivante, *op. loc. cit.,* at p. 11.
[38] *A Compendium of Mercantile Law,* (London, Macdonnell, 1890).
[39] Translated into Italian by two of the major scholars of the time: Bensa, *Legge sui fallimenti,* Genoa (1882) and Sacerdote, *Rassegna di diritto commerciale—Commercial Law Review*, Vol II, 1902.
[40] Translated again by Sacerdote (Review, ivi, Vol. I, 1901).

the Merchant Shipping Act of 1894, the legislation on commercial companies, and commented on them all in the *Zeitschrift für das gesamte Handelsrecht* of 1901.[41] And more. Among the foreign literature taken into consideration for his *Treatise on Commercial Law*, precisely by virtue of the conceptual unity of Commercial law and private law absorbed in the Common law, Vivante mentioned the works of Anson,[42] Pollock,[43] Duncan,[44] in addition to works by foreign authors published in French such as those of Colfavru,[45] and Lehr.[46] The same conclusions were reached through the analysis and circulation of the institutes and terminology of Maritime law in which we find traces of Roman law, the framework of French law,[47] the collection of usages, laws, and instructions of the Consolato del mare,[48] as well as some "evidence" of the English experience, such as *utmost despatch*, *dispatch money*, *mortgage*, *detention*, etc. clauses.

9 ROMAN LAW AND PRIVATE LAW

The British contribution to the formation of the law and the circulation of ideas in Italy does not stop here. To return to the legal works closest to our subject, it may be surprising how in the nineteenth century, already emerges the refinement and the reliability of the studies on Roman law conducted in Britain. Studies which are all the more remarkable precisely because they were so greatly appreciated in the home country of Roman law.

At the beginning of the century the book by Alexander Adam on the *Roman Antiquities and Civilisation* was translated (Naples, 1820). The book was a great success, and was re-printed several times. At the end of the century, in the fervour over the dogmatic works on the Digest, even scholars who were most receptive to the German doctrine did not hesitate to lend their talent to the translation of an introduction to the study of Justinian's law by Henry John Roby.[49] Two of the major scholars of Civil law and Roman law, Pietro Cogliolo and Giovanni Pacchioni, were called upon to accomplish the task. Cogliolo also wrote the foreword to the translation of the book on the XII tables by Frederick Goodwin and the foreword to the translation of the book by James Muirhead on the history of Roman law.[50]

---

[41] Vol. L, p. 526.
[42] *Principles of the English law of Contract and Agency* (Oxford, Clarendon Press, 1888).
[43] *Principles of Contract* (London, Stevens, 1889).
[44] *The Annual Review of Mercantile Cases*, from 1886.
[45] *Le droit commercial de la France et de l'Angleterre* (Paris, 1863).
[46] *Elements de droit civil anglais* (Paris 1885).
[47] The Ordonnace de la marine of 1681.
[48] In which pre-eminent are the Genoese Targa, *Ponderazioni sopra la contrattatione marittima* (Reflections on maritime dealings (1682) and Casaregi: see the 1707 edition of the *Discursus legales de commercio*.
[49] *Introduzione allo studio del Digesto Giustinianeo, Regole e notizie per l'uso delle Pandette nella scienza e nella pratica. Vita e opere dei giuristi romani* (Florence, Cammelli, 1886).
[50] *Storia del diritto romano dalle origini a Giustiniano* (Milan, Vallardi, 1888).

Italian advocates were interested in the law of property in England, translating the work by Joshua Williams of Lincoln's Inn.[51] They were interested in marriage and divorce, thanks to the writings of William Harris[52] and then the unification of the laws on Bills of Exchange of J D Wilson.[53]

In contrast, John Austin remained unknown in Italy. His contribution was appreciated only recently when his intelligence, his modernity in conceiving the law and the method for studying it become, so to speak, a "literary case". His exclusion was due to two main factors. The first was the aversion with which his lectures were greeted in Britain. On the other hand, the fact that their publication by his wife at the beginning of the 1860s took place at a time in which legal scholars were distracted by other problems also did not help. Thus, in Italy this was the time of unified codification and of social unrest whilst in Britain the practical concept of law was far removed from the speculations of *jurisprudence* as Pollock was keen to point out.

The works of British scholars, read in the original language, or consulted through the French, Italian, or German translations left deep marks in the formation of my country's legal culture for the whole of the nineteenth century. They also ended up breaking out of the restricted circle of intellectually inquisitive persons, and enter manuals, treatises and other miscellaneous works. We already noted Vivante's *Trattato*. But it is worth looking at other examples, as well.

Pietro Cogliolo, in his *Filosofia del diritto privato* (Philosophy of Private Law)[54] quoted extensively from the works of Mill, Darwin, Spencer, and Maine. Of the English method, he praised the interpretation of facts, the legal institutions based on reality, the aversion to concepts formulated "a priori". In the image he had of English law, law was seen as a *social phenomenon,* which required a flexible and changeable structure. Instead "codes stand still, while life moves on",[55] almost as if to say that codes bridle reality, instead of encouraging its evolution. And he depicts the English system based on the precedents of court decisions as "a sort of code but in another form".

But the interest for the English model is not only due to the longing for techniques and solutions to new or hitherto unknown problems. It is also determined by the awareness by many that codification, though appreciated, must not constitute a screen for comparing problems and their solutions, nor an alternative way of producing laws. At the beginning of the twentieth century, Biagio Brugi recalled the controversy on codification. He recalled Meijer's observations"[56] and underlined how codes have, first of all, a political value,[57] and that

---

[51] *Principii del diritto di proprietà reale* (Florence, Pellas, 1873).
[52] *Celibato, matrimonio, divorzio, prostituzione* (Milan, Cesarini Cioffi, 1885).
[53] *L'unificazione delle leggi cambiarie nel congresso internazionale di diritto commerciale in Anversa* (Turin, Utet, 1888).
[54] Cogliolo, *Filosofia del diritto privato* (Firenze, Barbera, 1891), at p. 18.
[55] Cogliolo, *Filosofia del diritto privato, cit.* (n.25), at p. 65.
[56] Meijer, *De la codification en générale* (Amsterdam and London, 1830).
[57] Brugi, *Introduzione enciclopedica alle scienze giuridiche* (Milano, 4th ed., 1907).

it is wrong to consider codes as durable, necessarily perfect monuments. Codes cannot be completely systematic, because "systematic unity is in the mind of the legal scholar". And he added : "if codes should become in future a repertoire of general principles surrounding each legal relation, it might be worthwhile to leave them better placed in a scientific manual".[58]

Through the analysis, even though fragmented and not systematic, of the contacts between the two cultures, we can see how the two cultures achieve, if not a rapprochement, certainly a growing awareness of its each other's thought. This is certainly true of Italy where the basic elements of English law flow through Italian books and the translations into Italian. The definition of the law, its attitudes, its manifestations, its fictions, its imitations, its evolution, its progress and its withdrawal, the phases or sectors more sensitive to social issues, the phases of its indifference to all that is meta-legal.

One must conclude by noting that most of the books translated from English into Italian deal with works relating to public law, not private law. It is clear that the rules of Common law are viewed, by those who have the good fortune of knowing them, as belonging to an "other" model: different, non-repeatable, and not transplantable. But it is also common opinion that "England and France did not lay great stock with the philosophy of private law, but rather developed the doctrine of public law".[59]

10 THE COSMOPOLITANISM OF THE FIRST POST-WAR PERIOD

English law becomes the constant point of reference in the cosmopolitan climate that spread over Europe after World War I.

One of the essays still nowadays read and considered on the subject of common law is due to one of the past masters of Italian civil law, Giacomo Venezian. In 1918 his *Studies on obligations*[60] were posthumously published in Rome. Here was an elegant analysis of the concept of *causa*, the "heart", so to speak, of obligations and contracts. Venezian criticised the concept of *causa* tied to the will of the individual, as put forward by the Pandectist school, and placed it among the anthropological roots of any social aggregation. He used Spencer's criticism of Maine and the works of Morgan and MacLennan, to demonstrate that it is the interest of the group that dominates the collective interest, and that it is the cooperation of activities which renders the will of the individual worthy of protection. And it is in the notion of *consideration*, as described in Pollock's masterpiece *On Contract*, that Venezian found the explanation of the reason for the binding nature of the promise. Thus we see how one of the classical institutions of the theory of obligations is stripped of the frills of German culture and filled with more plausible contents deriving from English culture.

---

[58] Brugi, *op. cit.*, p. 25.
[59] Ahrens, *Corso di diritto naturale* (Milano, 1857), at p. 64.
[60] *Studi sulle obbligazioni* (Rome, 1918).

But this is not the only novelty of the landscape that opens up to our research.

These are fruitful years in which Italy looks to the English system as to a "corpus" of modern rules, which govern economic relations in a particularly effective way, or offer instruments so far unknown to our experience. The task is taken on again by great scholars, such as Ascarelli,[61] Sarfatti,[62] and Grassetti.[63]

The law reviews are once again the chief medium for the circulation of ideas.

Among the instruments for the spreading of culture and techniques applied to the law, we find the *Rivista di diritto commerciale* founded by Vivante at the beginning of the century, and, in particular, the *Annuario di diritto comparato*, founded by Salvatore Galgano in 1925. Here we find not only bibliographical references and debates on individual aspects of English law, but also digests of case law, with the discussion of notable cases. This Sir Percy Winfield contributes regularly to the *Yearbook*, illustrating cases of conflict of laws, matrimonial law, law of contract and torts. For instance, the case of *Hirji Mulji* v. *Cheong Yue Steamship Co. Ltd.*[64] raised particular interest when it was translated and commented upon by Mario Allara. It is one of the cases of *frustration* of the contract, determined by supervening circumstances outside the will of the parties, which disrupt the economic transaction which the parties had set in place. The case is presented as similar to those, well known to the Italian experience, where the rule *pacta sunt servanda, rebus sic stantibus* is applied, drawn both from Common law and from the German law of *Geschaeftsgrundlage*. In *war cases*, Allara observes, the rule of *implied condition* is applied, already experimented in English Maritime law on the subject of contracts of carriage. Not to impose upon the parties the performance of an obligation which is still possible, but has become exceedingly onerous, responds to a requirement of fairness but also to the need for a rational treatment of the interests at stake. Here we find the difference in perspectives between English and Italian law. The English judge relies upon the fiction, openly admitted, of an interpretation of the contract, which introduces in the text a clause which the parties had never thought of, and gives an objective appraisal of the situation. The legal fiction of *implied condition* does not depend on the intention of the parties at the time of entering the contract, nor on their opinions, but on the occurrence of circumstances which prove that the event which caused the frustration of the contract is incompatible with the subsequent performance of the obligation envisaged in the contract itself. The Italian commentators—still enmeshed in the Pandectist theory of the will of the parties—think in terms of the subjective evaluations of the parties. They thus take refuge in the will of the parties: "it is a problem of

---

[61] Ascarelli, *Il diritto comparato e lo studio del diritto anglo-amercano*, "Annuario di diritto comparato", 1930, at p. 493 ff.

[62] Sarfatti, "La nozione del torto nella dottrina e nella giurisprudenza inglese" (Milano, 1903); ID., Il contratto nel diritto inglese, in *Rivista italiana per le scienze giuridiche*, 1912; ID., Le obbligazioni nel diritto inglese (Milano, 1924); ID., Legislazione inglese sulle assicurazioni (Roma, 1938).

[63] Grassetti, *Il trust nel diritto inglese*, in "Rivista di diritto comparato", 1936, 543.

[64] [1926] AC 497.

wills, that is if the parties wanted the contract in relation to a state of affairs, that subsequently ceases to be, due to supervening unforeseen circumstances".[65] History will witness the success of the English perspective, objective, concrete, functional. With the end of the collapse of the dogmatic approach which is centred on the will of the individual, even Italian judges, on the basis of more modern legal thinking, will follow the reasoning of English judges. In the end they will admit that supervening unforeseen circumstances entail the objective termination of the contract due to the modification of the economy of the deal.

To contradict the idea that the English experience is solely founded on Common law, the *Annuario di diritto comparato*, again thanks to Winfield, contains the statutes that were enacted in the first decades of the century. From 1914 to 1926 all the major statutes are reviewed, from those on farming to those on the electoral process, from the organisation of the civil service to family relations, to the Law of Property Act, and also to the reform of the Universities, on the basis of the recommendations by Lord Haldane and of the Tomlin Commission.

Gradually, therefore, we have an outline of an idea of Common law—an outline which is increasingly distancing itself from stereotypes and coming closer to actual reality.

11 THE RENEWAL OF THE METHOD OF LEGAL STUDIES AND GORLA'S WORK

For political reasons, the English model is ignored by the fascist reform, which leads up to the civil code of 1942. The prevailing cultural models are still the French, corrected occasionally by German concepts. But the case method, which constitutes one of the factors of the richness of the English experience, continues to be appreciated.

In the second post-war period, the work that stands out for its absolute novelty of method, for the wealth of cases considered and for talent of its author, is that of Gino Gorla, at the time Professor of Institutions of Private law at Pavia University and of Comparative Private law at the University of Alexandria in Egypt. The work is *Il contratto. Problemi fondamentali trattati con il metodo comparativo e casistico*.[66]

As can be seen from the title, and as the author himself points out in his preface, the innovation of method is determined by the need for concreteness, for control of abstract methods, for emancipation from the theories of natural law. Comparison is used in order to explain the reasons for similarities and differences among legal systems. "Comparison is nothing but history"; it is a way to escape from abstractions and generalisation. For Gorla, comparison means not

---

[65] Allara, *op. loc. cit.*, at p. 758. A complete discussion of these problems is offered by Bessone, *Adempimento e rischio contrattuale* (Milano, Giuffrè, 1975).

[66] *Contract. Fundamental issues treated on the basis of the comparative method with cases and materials* (Milan, Giuffrè, 1955).

only analysis of the French and German experiences, but above all analysis of the Common law, of its contents and method. Cases are useful because they help show the "mental process which brings judges and legislators (...) to formulate abstractions of rules and principles, to come back, in a continuous exchange or circle, to the issue of the actual case. We have to see how rules and principles (or rather the men who use them) adapt and change, faced with this problem, which is none other than that of justice, influenced by history". The case method used is not a mere imitation of the English and US experiences. There it is used in comparative law only to gain knowledge of foreign legal systems. In Gorla's work it is used to understand the Italian system as well, to ascertain the ancient roots of the institutions and the models of reasoning, to verify law in action, as it results from the manipulations of its interpreters. A method, therefore, that does not disregard the merits of systematic logic, but sets them alongside those of historical and comparative analysis. The cultural environment of the time is so hostile or biased against methods other than the analytical and formalistic ones that Gorla feels the need to justify himself. Order, arrangement, the logic of the thought process, and its discipline, are not neglected. But they are no longer considered as the *sole method* for the study and representation of the law. In this way, we avoid the risk of turning into a sort of "natural law" the generalisations and abstractions which hypostatise the law into general theory, almost as if the law were nothing but a general theory and the Common law were not law at all. The consequence of the application of the formalistic method is the sagging of studies, the concept of a law, which is uprooted from its history and from reality, which leads to the chasm between theory and practice. From the point of view of teaching, the work is *extra ordinem* also for another reason. For it manages to give the student a fundamental key to interpretation, that is that the rules we have to deal with are not an "unfailing datum"; it gives the student "the meaning of the problem and of its varied historical development, rather than the solution".

Thus the structure of the book reveals it as a masterpiece. The development of contractual obligations in Civil law sets out from Roman law, moves through the intermediate law, arrives at Domat and Pothier, at Canon law, at Grotius and the theorisation of the principle of consent. It deals with the obligations of giving, with transfers *cum onere*, with *causa praeterita*, with promises, with *nudum pactum*, with just cause, with form; the criticism of the concept of "causa", as an economic-social function of a contract is rigorous and persuasive. In comparison with the evolution of the doctrines and cases of *Civil law*, Gorla illustrates the evolution of Common law, especially with regard to *consideration*.

Already in these terms the subject matter collected in the first volume would be sufficient to unsettle the theory of obligations and contract as taught up to then in Universities. But the second volume, on the case method, is even more surprising. This volume deals with donation as a formal contract in relation to other contracts, sufficient *"causa"*, promise and sale for a *"causa praeterita"*, gratuitous obligations, intent to create legal relations, in cases and decisions of both Civil law and Common law systems. The work ends with a masterly comparison of judicial styles. It is flattering to note that Gorla's work has gone beyond national boundaries, and those who follow methods similar to his, such as Professor Markesinis, do not fail to remember him in their works.

12 MODELS OF LEGISLATION

We have talked a great deal about legal theory and method in these pages. It is now necessary to give some examples of the legislative models which Italian scholars have considered as guidelines to propose the renewal of our national law.

We have to wait until the 1970s to find the first debate on consumer protection in Italy. Legal scholars look to the more advanced experiences: to the United States, first of all, but also to France, Germany, and certainly Britain. On the subject of standard contracts, the Unfair Contract Terms Act of 1977, whatever its flaws, is considered as a model for legislation to bring back reasonableness and fairness in consumer contracts.

With mass production and contracting, the traditional tenets of the law of contract can no longer be deemed satisfactory. We are no longer concerned with guaranteeing freedom of contract, but rather to redress the balance in the "inequality of bargaining power". Professor Atiyah's pages are a veritable source of ideas if one is to understand why it is legitimate to restrict the freedom of the stronger contracting party, the enterprise, and equitable to ensure the protection of the weaker party. Lord Denning's dictum, pronounced in 1956—"*we do not allow printed terms to be made a trap for the unwary*"— becomes a warning for all legislators and for the judges who are forced to apply ancient rules. Again Lord Denning, in 1973, signals a break with the past: "*When a clause is reasonable, and is reasonably applied, it should be given effect according to its terms. I know that the judges hitherto have never confided openly to the test of reasonableness. But it has been the driving force behind many decisions*".[67]

In an environment which is now well versed in the study of comparative law, anything significant that happens in Britain will no longer go unnoticed in Italy. The words of Professor Collins have thus been noted: "... *under the influence of the EC harmonisation programme, UK contract law will eventually be pushed towards a fundamental division between consumer contracts and business contracts with radically different regimes applicable to both ... the assimilation of social values embodied in the European directive will lead the common law of contract, which Kahn-Freund once described as "designed for a*

---

[67] *J Spurling Ltd.* v. *Bradshaw* [1956] 1 WLR 461,466; *Gillespie Bros. & Co.Ltd.* v. *Roy Bowles Transport Ltd.* [1973] QB400, 416 (a quotation of the two sentences is in Alpa e Delfino, *Il contratto nel diritto inglese*, Padova, Cedam, p. 81 ff.).

nation of shopkeepers", to succumb to a more communitarian ideal which balances the interests of consumers against those of shopkeepers".[68]

But the influence of comparison has not been so decisive as to persuade Parliament to anticipate the EC's intervention. The reform of consumer contracts reaches Italy not from London, Paris, or Bonn, but from Brussels. The civil code is amended only in 1996, following the implementation of EC Directive n.13 of 1993.

Again to remain within the subject matters ascribed to private law, I would not wish to forget the interest raised by the Crowther Report of 1974 on consumer credit. And, to move on to an entirely different subject, the Warnock Report on artificial insemination, a topic which still divides Italian legal scholars for its religious and political implications. Biotechnology, whose legal aspects are so delicate, is one of the most controversial aspects of private law; and the English experience in this respect is one of the models to which the more sensitive scholars, such as Stefano Rodotà, do not fail to give adequate attention.[69]

13 THE INDIRECT INFLUENCE OF ENGLISH LAW ON EC LAW AND THEREFORE ON ITALIAN LAW

Going through two centuries of legal history in a few pages we have finally reached the present. And the present projects a picture of Italy increasingly following the pulse of the Common law. A whole book would be inadequate to list the manuals, the treatises, the monographs, and the essays which Italian scholars have devoted, and continue to devote, to English legal culture. Every "school" of comparative law proudly presents its standard bearers well-versed in English law. And translations, in spite of the fact that English is the most widely spoken foreign language in Italy, abound. It is not only the older "classics"—such as Maitland who are being translated. The more modern ones are attracting just as much attention: Sir William Wade monumental Administrative Law; Herbert Hart's work; William Twining's, not to mention Lord Wedderburn's manual on employment law. Historical analyses such those by Professors Peter Stein and Alan Watson also attract attention; and Sir Roy Goode's masterly Hamlyn Lectures on commercial law in the new millennium will soon be inspiring the few Italians who have not yet read them in the original.

Beyond this tangible outline of the debt of our legal culture to the British contribution, we should bear in mind another occurrence, which is taking shape in terms of the "Europeanisation" of the law. Here the English influence is not direct, but indirect, because it is filtered through the texts of the European Regulations and Directives.

---

[68] Collins, "Good Faith in European Contract Law", in *OJLS*, 1994, at p. 229.
[69] *Tecnologie e diritto* (Roma-Bari, Laterza, 1996).

I shall only make a brief reference. The use of the expression "reasonable", which we cannot find in any of the provisions of codes or special statutes, is gradually penetrating our terminology, and also our legislation. We already find an example in Article 1783, c.2, n. 3 of the civil code, on the liability of hoteliers for personal property brought into the hotel. Here the text derives from the Paris Convention, 17 December 1962, ratified by statute 10 June 1978, n. 316, and enacted on 12 August 1979. And it is well known that international conventions tend to condense the various contributions from the legal models taken into account, and that the British representatives are always held in high esteem for their good sense and knowledge of their subject. And, again, Article 5 of D.P.R. 24 May 1988, N. 224, on the definition of defective products, which derives from EC Directive n. 85/374, in which the British contribution, as everyone knows, was decisive. If more examples were needed one could find them in the rules of guarantees in the sale of goods, or the drafting techniques now widely used in the legal profession in Italy.

14 THE PROCESS OF CONVERGENCE BETWEEN COMMON LAW AND CIVIL LAW

The cultural exchanges, the loans, the transplants, stimulate convergence, rather than the differences. Lord Bingham underlined this fact very persuasively during a recent meeting of Italian Judges and Law Lords. To quote his words: "we are right to continue to worry away at the unnecessary divergences which continue to divide us. But the things which unite us are greater than the things which divide us".

The law consists also of myths. We have been reminded of this fact in recent months by Christian Atias and Paolo Grossi.[70] We must find the courage to destroy them and be rid of them forever. Consider, for instance the myth that the Common law consists only of a body of precedents with no relevant legislation or, conversely, that the Civil law consists only of statutes, without any attention paid to the work of the courts. Or ponder, for instance, over the Continental belief that in England statutes are only interpreted in accordance with the literal meaning. Think, finally, of the myth that sees in the law the image of a nation, and therefore appeals to history to justify divergences and oppose convergences.

History cannot be wished away; but the future can only be built in a collaborative manner. Convergence is achieved not only in written rules, but also in those that are interpreted. It is for this reason that Professor Markesinis speaks about the "Europeanisation" of the English *Common law*, especially thanks to the decisions of the Court of Justice in Luxembourg and that of the Court of Human Rights in Strasbourg. The same can be said for Italian law, and other

---

[70] Atias, *Philosophie du droit*, (Paris, Dalloz 2000); Grossi, *Mitologie giuridiche della modernità* (Milano, Giuffrè, 2001).

systems of the Member States. And it is for this reason that the efforts of those—such as the Commission coordinated by Ole Lando and Hugh Beale on the subject of contracts and the Commission coordinated by Christian von Bar on the other sources of obligations—promote harmonisation as a bridge for the unification of private law.[71]

The era of stockades is over. And we must remember that freedom of movement of individuals, of goods, of services and capital was *preceded*, not *followed* by the free circulation of ideas and models in the legal world.

The teachings of history and the consideration for the current political, economic and social needs, lead us to believe that the movement that proceeds at great speed towards the convergence of systems and cultures is by now irreversible. It has also become one of the factors that make Europe stronger and ennoble its mission in the new Millennium. What this essay tried to show an English audience and remind Italian readers was how much we, in Italy, have learned from England. In the light of what I have said it is truly an irony that some in England seem to fear Europe so much. My essay showed how much interest in things English my part of the Continent has shown even at times when communications were difficult, language barriers were almost insurmountable, and conditions of life were truly different. Given increased urbanisation, industrialisation and travel, my prediction is that this interest in your system and ideas will grow. And my hope is that it will be matched by a corresponding curiosity on your part. For as a comparative lawyer I have been trained to believe that comparative law is not a one-way street.

---

[71] See Hartkamp, Hesselink, Hondius, Joustra, du Perron, *Towards a European Civil Code*, Nijmegen, Ars aequi Libri (The Hague, London, Boston, Kluwer, 1998); Lando and Beale, *Principles of European Contract Law* (The Hague, London, Kluwer, 2000). The discussion about a European civil code is reported in Alpa e Buccico, (eds.) *Il codice civile europeo* (Milano, Giuffré, 2001); for a different view see Markesinis, "Why a Code is not the Best Way to Advance the Cause of European Unity", in *Always in the Same Path* (Oxford, Hart Publishing, 2001), 103 ff.

5

Tutorial and Repetitorium: Parallel and different techniques of teaching law in England and Germany[1]

BASIL S MARKESINIS

1 GENERAL BACKGROUND

German Universities like most Continental European Universities and unlike their Anglo-American counterparts, are plagued by two ills which are tolerated in the name of democratic principles but little else. The first is the large number of students they admit every year in all their faculties, including the Faculty of Law which is the subject of discussion in this paper. The second is their relative inability to choose whom they take on the basis of clearly meritocratic criteria. Thirty years of professional contacts with many German law colleagues and even more German law students have left me with the clear impression that among these two constituencies the prevailing system, and especially its two features just mentioned, does not have many friends. All of the above, however, recognise these ills as being irremediable given the general political climate that has existed on the Continent of Europe, especially since the mid-1960s. It would be of little use for an outside observer to dwell more (and critically) on this subject, not least since this underlying philosophy of "downward equalisation" may slowly be spreading to his own environment removing all cause for gloating. But this observer can remark from first hand experience on how this background has affected the size of classes and the ability (or, often, inability) of the law libraries to cope properly in terms of space and material. The ability of many faculties to keep up to date with plant and electronic material is also under question[2]

---

[1] I am grateful to Miss Verena Fricke (Munich), Miss Maria Schuster (Regensburg), Dr. Stephan Enchelmaier (Bonn and Edinburgh) and Dr. Hannes Unberath (Erlangen and Oxford) for sharing with me their experiences as law students in Germany, England, Scotland, and the United States.

[2] Though this piece is about German institutions, the wider remarks made above are backed by fifteen years of experience as a (part time) Ordinarius at the Law Faculty of Leiden, and a one year's (or one term's) teaching stints as Visiting Professor at the Universities of Paris I and II, Ghent, Rome (la Sapienza—a name derived from the Church of Holy Wisdom that exists in the centre of the

though, of course, one finds substantial differences from one Law Faculty to another.[3] These characteristics stand out even more sharply if the Continental institutions are compared with the top half a dozen English academic centres of learning. The comparison becomes positively painful (for all of us in Europe) if it is made with the top fifteen or twenty American Law Schools and their law libraries.[4]

These comments should in no way be seen as containing even implicitly any statement to the effect that German lawyers or German law are in any shape or form inferior to the best one can find in the Anglo-American world. My whole academic career has been spent extolling the strengths of German legal science so I do not feel I have to labour this point further. Indeed, I have always remarked on the excellence of the German (and French and Dutch) students whom I have been privileged to teach in my Anglo-American Universities and who—often—have "topped" our examination lists. But I cannot help thinking that such excellence is invariable achieved *despite* and *not because* of its current environment. So what I am willing to suggest is that German and, indeed European Universities,[5] will somehow soon have to address this problem of numbers, admissions, and sources of funding. In Germany, the slow emergence (of the as yet untested) private law faculties, is a response, though I fear only a partial one, to this phenomenon. For, if the more senior and well-established European institutions of higher learning do not address these problems, they will slip behind the best of the Anglo-*American* world; and I deliberately stress the word American. For I see the strength of American institutions growing even further and surpassing the British (if, on balance, they have not done so already)[6] despite the difficult challenge that "race" and "political correctness" is presenting for them all.

complex of buildings which once house the University) Siena and successive summer courses given at the Law Faculty of the Ludwigs-Maximilians University of Munich.

[3] One feature, I believe peculiar to the German University system, deserves to be mentioned here. When German Professors get a "call" from another University it is customary for some financial "haggling" to take place between him and the Ministry of Education of his existing University. If his University and Land are anxious to prevent him from moving to another University, they will often offer him additional funds which are often used to increase the number of Assistants that are attached to his Chair as well as the library holdings of his sub-department or Institute. These extra funds often account for richer book holdings in one place rather than another. Prestigious awards, such as the Leibniz Prize, also have the same effect for the Institute of the recipient. This is as close as German academics will ever get to the routine haggling that takes place in American Law Schools and encourages the culture of "poaching".

[4] The author's personal experience (in the form of visits for a series of lectures or prolonged courses) covers, in alphabetical order, the Law Schools of Cornell, California at Berkeley, Harvard, Michigan, Texas (at Austin) and Tulane.

[5] For fifteen years I had the privilege of serving as a part time but tenured chair holder of the Leiden Law Faculty and feel the same pessimism about the fate of the great Dutch law faculties.

[6] This assertion is, in my view, supported by the fact that most Continental European lawyers invariably put down American Law Schools as the first choices for study abroad and this even though the fees they charge are considerably higher that those charged by English Universities. The primacy of the top American Law Schools over their British counterparts is, of course, invariably denied by the latter. But having spent over twenty years of my teaching life in Cambridge and Oxford I retain the gravest doubts about the validity of such English claims.

This essay, however, is not about the challenges that confront European Universities in general and law faculties in particular at the dawn of the twenty-first century great though they may be. Its purpose is to pursue a much more modest aim. This is to discuss an 'outgrowth' of the German system—the repetitorium—which, among the German highbrow academic establishment, attracts almost universal condemnation. For me, however, this maligned yet long-surviving institution has (a) a rational reason behind its existence; (b) presents some similarities with the English tutorial system and (c) could be improved if it were willing to learn from its remote English cousin. Reason (a) but, mainly reasons (b) and (c) thus make the institution of repetitorium a perfect candidate for a study in parallel with the English tutorial system. This because where there is scope for learning, the one from the other, there is always a need for comparative studies but also because such studies can provide us with new insights into the legal mind and legal system of our neighbours.

2 UNIVERSITY AND PARA-UNIVERSITY

The size of the German law faculty and its typical classes create the need for smaller gatherings of teachers and students.[7] But why is not this need catered for by the University, itself? Three reasons suggest themselves to me, though others could be considered. The first is historical, the second financial, the third cultural.

The historical reason can in part be traced to Alexander von Humboldt, that great German educational reformer of the first half of the nineteenth century. One of his central ideas was that students should, themselves, be free and responsible to pace their studies in law. This "freedom" contrasts quite sharply with the strictures of the Oxbridge tutorial system; but my impression is that it is profitably used by the "above average" German student who thus learns how to organise his time. But for the average (and lower) type of student, this "freedom" contributes to the uncertainty of the duration of the University phase of the study that will culminate with the sitting of the First State Exam—Erstes juristisches Staatsexamen—which is administered by the geographically relevant Court of Appeal.[8] Thus, to this day, there is no fixed date when a German law student has to present himself for this all-important examination which, undoubtedly, represents a physically gruelling test and brings to a close his university studies. In this sense (and this sense only) the First State Exam can be regarded as the equivalent of our BA or LL.B. course. For, as the name suggests, the exam is organised by the relevant State and not by the University attended

---

[7] I have, myself, given lectures in the le Grand Amphitheatre of Paris II, which can seat 1,500 and the main auditorium of la Sapienza in Rome which can accommodate over 2,500 students. The larger classes in Munich are in the order of 300.

[8] The Court of Appeal is charged with the "administrative" side of the exam. Its academic content, on the other hand, is determined by a specialist department of the local Ministry of Justice—the Landesjustizprüfungsamt. Germanic structures will always defy the English mind!

by the candidate. Further, though the tests set for this "degree" revolve around a certain core of examinable subjects which broadly correspond to the major codifications or branches of the law, there is in practice a certain divergence between what has been taught at the University and what is examined. This separation between what has been done at the University phase—in practice during anything between seven and nine semesters[9]—and this all-important exam is further marked by the fact that whatever written tests[10] the students have sat during their University phase will in no way affect their grade in the State exam. The failure rate in these State Exams is considerable, partly because the exams are both difficult and concentrated in time—invariably students sit eight five-hour tests during a period of just under two weeks—and partly because no weeding out process has taken place previously. The Law Faculty's inability or un-willingness (or both) to prepare students specifically for this exam is thus the first need for the emergence of an institution that does just that. To the extent that it has, by necessity, the attributes of a "crammer" which, in turn, inevitable attracts the scorn of the more highbrow academics. Yet without these schools, the vast majority of German law students would—arguably—not be in a position to pass the kind of test given to them at the State exam level and for which the University has prepared them only in the most general and abstract of terms. Indeed, the repetitoria Schools play on and exploit, sometimes by means of "cheap" advertising techniques,[11] the fact that what the students have learned at the law faculty may not be relevant (Examensrelevanz) to what they will be examined in the First State Exam.

The financial reason is that smaller University classes need more teachers, even of a lower level than the prima donnas that dominate the top German Law Faculties and give them their individual flavour.[12] Given that German students

---

[9] The period of University study (at tax payers' cost) varies widely between (former) East and West Germany Länder and from subject to subject. The average seems to be around 13.5 semesters, or six and a half years. In 1997 one State—Baden-Württenburg—introduced a charge of DM 1,000 (approximately £330) for every semester over this average (plus a grace period of four extra semesters) in order to cut the number of "perpetual students" (who, in that State and at that time, exceeded 37,000 out of a total of about 190,000). The decision was immediately challenged in court (by three students who had studied between nineteen and forty semesters each) on the ground that it violated their right to choose their occupation freely. The challenge was turned down on the 25 July 2001 by the Federal Administrative Court which accepted the State's argument that it had a right to reduce the burden on its taxpayers. As a result, other States, starting with the Saarland, are currently contemplating introducing similar legislation. On this see, Frankfurter Allgemeine Zeitung, 28 July 2001.

[10] I am referring here to the so-called Seminarschein; and I call them tests rather than exams since they take the form of a twenty-page written paper. Writing them—often with some guidance from University Assistants—teaches the students how to approach a problem and develop their ability to argue a legal point. Anything between four to seven of these papers (dealing with civil, criminal, public law and one "general" subject) have to be completed during the University phase of the training; but the grades obtained in these tests do not count towards the final ranking in the State Exam test.

[11] The account given in the Spiegel of 3 June 2001 is, in fact, quite frightening.

[12] The Germans themselves sometimes use the colloquial but colourful term Platzhirsch to describe their top stars.

pay derisory fees for their education, the funds for these extra posts are obviously missing. The Repetitoria Schools, which function as private enterprises outside the University system, can and do charge fees, modest as we shall see by our standards, but sufficient to make them financially viable concerns.[13] These enable them to teach students in sizes, which, though large by our standards, are still smaller than the numbers filling the University amphitheatres. As will be explained below, students taking repetitoria usually pay for a chunk of hours per subject and this could mean anything between DM 1,000 and 3,000 (approximately £1,000) per course on, say, civil law or procedural law etc. Even for those students who follow repetitoria in many courses, the overall cost is still low by comparison to British fees and infinitesimally low by comparison to American ones (though it does not seem so to the German takers). But it is more than what appears to be the norm of free, higher education, which is a key feature of higher education across the Continent of Europe. So most students who wish to pass their First State Exams[14] with high grades have—at least since the days of the great Goethe—been forced to resort to this para-University to remedy the perceived deficiencies of the University proper.

The cultural reason for the repetitorium is immediately obvious to a Common lawyer looking at the German civil law but would be hotly disputed by German academic purists. One must, therefore, proceed to the next section with caution.

3 CASE LAW V. THEORY

German legal teaching is strongly geared towards doctrine, principle, logic and symmetry. Amongst the most immediate and obvious reasons for this is the Pandectist School of the nineteenth century which left its marks just as strongly on the Civil Code as on the successive schools that have dominated German legal exegesis since 1900.[15] On the educational front what, it seems to me, they all have in common is the belief that if the general principle is well defined and the reasoning skills of the student well shaped, the student of today and the lawyer of tomorrow will always be able to apply these principles to any new factual configuration that practice may throw at him in the future. In this world, though there are signs that it is changing, decisional law appears to be accorded secondary importance. For since the practice of *Aktenversendung* was born in

---

[13] The Spiegel, above n. 10, suggested that some 10,000 students a year go through the Hemmer Repetitoria up and down the country generating a 300 million-mark business.

[14] This covers the academic component of their instruction, typically takes four years to complete, and gives them a degree roughly equivalent to our own BA or LL.B. It is followed by a vocational course, again of about two years duration, which includes training periods in lower courts and law offices and leads to the Second State Exam.

[15] For a sketch in English (and how this school affected the German law of contract, see Markesinis, Lorenz and Dannemann, *The German Law of Contract and Restitution*, (Oxford, Oxford University Press, 1997), ch. 1 (henceforth, Markesinis, GLC).

the sixteenth century, universities and not the courts have been the oracles of the law in Germany.[16] Even today, many law Professors often see judicial decisions as providing illustrations of how a rule or principle works in a particular factual configuration. Alternatively, they are used as material that an illustrious Professor employs to back his own theory about how a set of codal provisions should be understood. Thus, the major and most learned textbooks will use case law much more sparingly than their Anglo-American counterparts. Treatises such as Palandt, written for practitioners in Delphic language, will refer to judicial decisions a plenty but again will show few signs of the *light motif* of the Common law viz. the attempt to reconcile them and weave them into a workable whole. They are treated as illustrations rather than as building blocks. Worshipping, as Lord Goff put it so felicitously,[17] at "the shrine of the untested hypothesis" is not part of the local religion. The bulk of the professorial teaching is also *ex cathedra* with little personal exchange with students. Teacher-student contacts are thus maintained through university assistants who do much of their masters' routine jobs, including taking a leading part in seminars, *Arbeitsgemeinschaften*, and *Übungen*[18] attended by anything between 10 and 50 students. The number of assistants assigned to a particular chair can also be seen as evidence of the high standing of its holder (as well as his literary output).

This highly generalised picture is, with all its faults, necessary in order to suggest some of the weaknesses of the German system as seen by an outsider, even of the admiring variety. Four further observations seem worth making.

First, the true reason for a particular result reached by a judicial decision is often either concealed in the judgment or under-stressed in its exegesis, the emphasis being on the legal or legalistic side of the reasoning that produced it. Any examination of the non-recoverability of pure economic loss in tort actions in both German and Anglo-American law can reveal the truth of this statement; and the reader who has not thought of the problem in such terms has only to glance at the comparative juxtaposition of the Anglo-American-German cases that I have assembled in my book to see how much more informative the Anglo-American judgments are about the real reasons for not allowing compensation.[19] The same can be said of the cases that Professor Dagmar Coester-

---

[16] For a brief account in English see J P Dawson, *The Oracles of The Law* (Ann Arbor, University of Michigan Law School, 1968), pp. 200 ff.

[17] "The Future of the Common Law", 1997 Wilberforce Lecture, [1997] 46 *ICLQ* 745.

[18] All these types of classes and sessions are largely entrusted to the Professor's Assistants and are supposed to prepare students to obtain their Seminarschein mentioned above. In many respects, the kind of questions asked and the methodology imparted is that which will be needed to pass the State Exam. So when the average student later attends a Repetitorium for the first time he will have some basic knowledge about the law and also how to solve "problem questions". Without this preparation, the repetitors task would be almost impossible given the constraints on time. But the preceding observations should also alert one to the question: why do not the law faculties take on more of this task thus making the institution of repetitorium redundant?

[19] Compare, for instance, BGH 9 Dec. 1958, BGHZ 29, 65 with *Spartan Steel v. Martin and Co.* [1973] 1 QB 27. See, more generally, Markesinis, *The German Law of Torts. A Comparative Introduction* (Oxford, Oxford University Press, 1994 and 1997), pp 173–194. (Henceforth, Markesinis, GLT). This statement must be tempered by the observation that the policy decisions

Waltjen and I assembled for our book *Tortious Liability for Statutory Bodies*.[20] This is not to say that German jurists have never considered some of the reasons. Nonetheless, it is true to say that the policy consideration of these reasons are scattered among many texts, many rarely if ever consulted by students and, perhaps, even by practising lawyers. Thus, those who do not "search" will not find the true reasons for a decision in its text and rarely will find them fully explored in the kind of books that they will use for most of their lives.

Secondly, with the growing importance of decisional law there is both a practical need to reconcile it if one is to give reliable advice as well as an intellectual necessity to impart the kind of analytical talents that come with the teaching through cases. This need is, to my eyes at least, even greater in Germany where one increasingly has to reconcile decisional law which emanates from different jurisdictional orders—e.g. the constitutional courts and the ordinary courts. This is by no means an easy task. For, first, these decisions emanate from judges that are recruited in different ways and have different backgrounds. Secondly, their reasoning process is not the same. This, at any rate, is the feeling of an outside observer comparing the material that comes out of the Constitutional Court on the one hand and the "ordinary" courts on the other. Thirdly, the Constitutional Court itself, for historical reasons, is not one court but, essentially, two courts, with its two sections not infrequently giving conflicting views on the same issue. These difficulties are clearly revealed by looking at the contradictory views of the Constitutional Court on wrongful life claims. These philosophical or mentality differences are sometimes carried forward to those who cultivate in the Universities these two disciplines—public and private law—even though at this level the training and career background is very similar among these two groups. Thus, to give but one illustration, we note that the constitutional theory of Drittwirkung has, on the whole, found supporters among public lawyers and critics among private lawyers.[21] Not infrequently— and this is admittedly something of a generalisation to give the English readers a flavour of the dispute—the former see it as a natural extension of constitutional ideas while the other see as a dangerous intruder on basic principles of private law (such as freedom of contract.)

Let us flesh out this point with the wrongful birth/life claims in mind since the practical test taken from one of Germany's leading Repetitorium Schools given

---

that the Common law judges have to make may have already been taken by the legislator when he drafted the Civil Code. For the importance of this point in the form of judicial reasoning see Markesinis, "Judicial Style and Judicial Reasoning in England and Germany" (2000) *CLJ* 59 294, 298 ff.

[20] Co-authored with Professor J B Auby and Dr S Deakin and published in 1999 (Oxford, Hart).

[21] English speaking readers who would like more details and more references on this subject might wish to consult the following two works: Markesinis, "Privacy, Freedom of Speech and the Horizontality of the Human Rights Bill", 1998 Wilberforce Lecture, (1999) 115 *LQR* 47 ff. and Markesinis and Enchelmaier, "The Applicability of Human Rights Law as Between Individuals under German Constitutional Law" in *Protecting Privacy. The Clifford Chance Lectures*, vol. IV, (Oxford, Oxford University Press, 1998), pp. 191 ff.

in an appendix to this article deals with this problem. But the points made here could be made in the context of other legal problems.

The story, which is worth mentioning for the sake of English lawyers, begins, as far as the Constitutional Court is concerned, in 1993. It was then that an important decision of the Second Division of the Constitutional Court was published.[22] This Division, known for its conservative tendencies, echoed, in some respects, the kind of doubts expressed in the USA by those who sympathise with the pro-life position. Some (lower) courts immediately heeded the advice of the Constitutional Court to reconsider the question of civil damages in wrongful birth actions and took a similar, conservative stance on the issue.[23] In some instances, they were able to do this on the technical argument that the case before them involved maintenance claims for a healthy child whereas a BGH decision, contemporaneous but contradictory to the judgment of the Constitutional Court, had addressed the claims of the parents of an impaired child.[24] But other courts[25] refused to accept this as a valid distinction and abided by the more liberal position which, at least since the mid-1980s, had favoured the award of full maintenance costs to the parents. In this steadfastness with established case law, these courts found an ally in the BGH—the supreme Federal Court of last resort for civil and criminal matters. For this court not only had by-passed skilfully the Constitutional Court's slightly earlier decision of 1993 by drawing a distinction between the "existence of the child" and "the obligation to maintain it". It was also quick to re-affirm its established case law in a quick succession of judgments, thus preventing the creation of a parallel but different jurisprudence.[26] But the clash of the Titans was not over yet. The subsequent and most recent decision of the First Division of the Constitutional Court[27]—which, unlike the

---

[22] BVerfGE 88, 203 = NJW 1993, 1751 "second abortion" case.

[23] Thus, LG Düsseldorf 2 Dec. 1993, NJW 1994, 805, refusing to follow the BGH decision of 16 Nov. 1993, NJW 1994, 788, decided only a fortnight earlier. Likewise, OLG Zweibrücken, 18 Feb. 1997, NJW—RR 1997, 666.

[24] BGH 16 Nov. 1993, NJW 1994, 788.

[25] See, for instance, OLG Düsseldorf, 15 Dec. 1994, NJW 1995, 788.

[26] For instance, BGH 23 Mar. 1995, NJW 1995, 1609. But the wider Germanic world remains divided. Thus, the Austrian Supreme Court, in its subsequent decision of 25 May 1999, JBl 1999, 593–602, followed the German case law in the case of impaired children but refused to award maintenance costs to the parents of a healthy child, The case is discussed by Bernat "Unerwünschtes Leben, unerwünschte Geburt und Arzthaftung: der österreichische 'case of first impression' vor dem Hintergrund der anglo-amerikanischen Rechtsentwicklung" in *Festschrift Heinz Krejci zum 60. Geburtstag* (Wien, Verlag Österreich, 2001) 1041.

[27] BVerfG, 12 Nov. 1997, BVerfGE 96, 375 = NJW 1998, 519. There is a techincal (and historically explicable reason) for the fact that two different Divisions of this Court were seized of essentially the same kind of dispute (and were given the chance to come to different conclusions). The first dispute (of 1993) reached the Constitutional Court by means of a "review of legislation" (Normenkontrolle) which are handled by the Second Division of the Court whereas as the second case came as a "constitutional complaint" (Verfassungsbeschwerde) and these are heard by the First Division of the Court. An attempt to resolve dispute by having the plennum of the Court decide the controversy was effectively foiled by the First Division on the ground that the pronouncments of the Second Division were "mere obiter" and thus not binding on the First Division. This saga, discussed in 2 *Eur R Priv L*, 241, offers a further illustration of the difficulties that have to be surmounted by foreign observers if they are ever to appreciate the full richness of the German law.

Second Division, is known for its liberal tendencies—has broadly followed the line of the BGH and ignored the views of its sister Division. The decision not to refer[28] to the Plenum of the Court the dispute between its two rivalling Divisions suggests that the status quo is unlikely to be disturbed in the near future. Now such conflicts, and real or apparent contradictions in the case law of supreme courts, is the stuff that makes English legal education and legal practice what they are: analytical, inventive, and immensely challenging. I deliberately chose to include in Appendix Two the wrongful life/birth problem from the German repetitorium. For the model answer provided, illustrates my point elaborated later on[29] viz., that the main purpose of the German exercise is to teach the student how to go through all the steps in the right order and less so to reconcile or interpret creatively the growing and often contradictory case law.

The above shortcomings are not removed by the attempt made by some German jurists to point out that some English cases and some English jurists are showing parallel doctrinal tendencies in contemporary English law.[30] For, as I tried to explain elsewhere,[31] this is not the best feature of German law that we should be trying to copy; and, in any event, those who have attempted to introduce excess systematisation in English law have, thus far, met with little praise from the courts.

Finally, the emphasis on Codes, concepts, and principles is not particularly useful from the point of view of comparative law and the wider purpose of drawing inspiration from other systems. For it means that the comparative movement of ideas from one system to another is impeded by the obvious differences in conceptualism and cannot profit by the underlying similarity that exists at the core of the issues that a court is asked to resolve.[32]

4 THE GERMAN REPETITORIUM

It is, in my view, some of these deficiencies that the repetitorium tries to resolve. Whether it succeeds in doing so can only be answered in two phases. In the first phase, which we shall discuss in this subsection, we shall describe some of the

[28] BVerfG 22 Nov. 1997, NJW 1998, 523.
[29] See, 5 (c), below.
[30] As Professor Dr Werner Lorenz, a comparative restitution lawyer of international reputation, reminded me recently of cases such as *Westdeutsche Landesbank Girozentrale* v. *Islington London Borough Council* [1996] AC 669 and *Kleinwort Benson Ltd.* v. *Lincoln City Council* [1998] 3 WLR 1095 which are dealing with "interest swap transactions." Their lordships' debates about the difference (if any) between "no consideration", "absence of consideration" and "failure of consideration" reveal a preoccupation with dogma which is both Germanic in character and, arguably, dubious in value.
[31] "Zur Lehre des Rechts anhand von Fällen: Einige bescheidene Vorschläge zur Verbesserung der deutschen Juristenausbildung" in *Festschrift für Peter Schlechtriem zum 70. Geburtstag* (Mohr, Tübingen, 2002).
[32] I have made this point on many different occasions, most recently in France in "Réflexions d'un comparatiste anglais sur et à partir de l'arrêt Perruche" (2001) Jan–Mar. *Revue trimestrielle de droit civil* 77–102.

main features of the German institution. In the second phase, discussed in the next sub-section, we shall draw a balance sheet and suggest how the German institution could be improved by copying some of the features of its English cousin.

(a) Repetitoria in General

Comparative lawyers must always be ready to overcome the hurdles of classification which historical accident or human design, have erected over the centuries. In this paper we are only going to deal with civil law—i.e. the section of private law that deals with the material found in the civil codes. In Europe in general and even more so in Germany this has, traditionally, been regarded as the core subject of the legal curriculum. This is due not only to the importance the subjects treated in the Code present to daily life but also because, as Otto von Gierke observed over one hundred years ago, ". . . the general law is the native soil out of which the special laws also grow. By contact with the general law our youth learn legal thinking. The judges take their nourishment from it."[33] This is reflected in the repetitoria in two ways.

First, *Zivilrecht* invariable takes something in the region of fifteen months to cover whereas the so-called *Zivilrechtliche Nebengebiete* (akin) subjects—e.g. Labour law, commercial law and procedural law—together require approximately five. Secondly, of those students who do follow repetitoria—and the impression that I get is that all but the purists who scorn them and the impecunious who cannot afford them do—all take the first but significantly fewer take the second. To make meaningful comparisons one must thus try and find the Common, especially English Common law parallels, and then compare details in terms of time and method of teaching.

The problems of classification, however, are not yet over and must be addressed before meaningful comparisons can be attempted. For, first, whereas all German students will study all the five parts (or books) of the Civil Code—general part, obligations, property, family, and succession law—their English counterparts will, more likely than not, read only part of this material. Thus, they cover only part of the material that is found in book 1, (typically legal capacity and formation of contracts) and parts of books 2 and 3, rarely cover the material of book 4 (family law), and almost never study (at University) the material of book 5 (testate and intestate succession). Secondly, even the apparently recognisable topic of obligations—book 2 of the BGB—must be explained for here, too, we find the German desire for thoroughness and neatness in classification. Thus, the repetitoria on obligations will typical be divided into two

---

[33] Die soziale Aufgabe des Privatrechts (1889) 16 ff., translated by von Mehren and Gordley, *The Civil Law System* (2nd ed. Boston, Little, Brown, 1977), 693. Gierke, a famous 19th century Germanist, was making the point as part of his wider complaint that the BGB was too heavily based on Roman law texts and ignored the more Germanic contribution to modern law.

parts: the *Schuldrecht Allgemeiner Teil* (which follows §§ 241–432 BGB) and the *Schuldrecht Besonderer Teil*, which cover almost all of the remaining material of book two of the BGB. The latter would thus include sales, contract of labour and materials, mandate, *negotiorum gestio* and unjust enrichment whereas, as all English law students know, many of these topics are in English Universities either covered by specific subjects, advanced courses in contract and tort, or not covered at all at an undergraduate level. Unjustified enrichment would fall into this last category (even though things are slowly changing). Since this paper is more interested in the teaching techniques of the repetitorium compared to the tutorial, the comparison will focus on a narrow topic of *Deliktsrecht*, which in our tort tutorial finds a meaningful (though again not exact[34]) parallel.

(b) Length of Course, Size of Classes, Mode of Teaching, Personnel, Costs

The time spent on the various topics tends to be the same irrespective of which repetitorium one joins. The Alpman Schmidt School, for instance, spends about five and a half months (out of the total fifteen allocated to civil law to contractual obligations (*vertragliche Schuldverhältnisse*) and one and a half months to tort (*gesetzliche Schuldverhältnisse*). Kern & Friedel, another such school, will devote the same time to tort (though they will call the subject *Delikts- und Schadensrecht*). The latter, will devote one session per week (over six weeks) to this subject, each of them lasting four and half-hours. From Kern and Friedel's syllabus on tort—given as Appendix One—the way this branch of the law is dealt with is clear under the headings of fourteen practical questions. Appendix Two reproduces one of these practical questions from the same School, dealing with wrongful life and birth claims. More about this later.

The size of a repetitorium class will differ from school to school and subject to subject. Kern & Friedel will typically have up to 80 students in a *Zivilrecht* repetitorium and around 30 in the *Zivilrechtliche Nebengebiete* classes. Other subjects may drop to around 20. Others schools—e.g. Alpmann Schmidt stress that their rooms will take no more than fifty. In some schools, for instance the "Hemmer-repetitorium", the number may go up to, and occasionally over, 100. The above-mentioned Spiegel article suggested even more.

Such sizes are, of course, astonishing to an English audience. In England, very few (main course) lectures will attract more than 100 students on a sustained basis; and that is true of Oxbridge as it is of new Universities in England. Even in the United States, very few classes, even of first year core subjects, are allowed to go much beyond the one hundred mark (in my experience 120 is the usual cut off mark). Where the "freshers" class is larger, they end up divided into sections

---

[34] That is again because some topics—e.g. comparative negligence—and certain defences, tend to be discussed primarily in Book 1 of the Code. The reason why these subjects and others (such as legal capacity) are placed here, at the beginning of the Code is because they are relevant not only to the law of torts but also to other parts of private law.

and taught by two or more professors. But by German standards, the figures given above for repetitoria classes are thus an improvement to what students are accustomed to find at their University—at any rate for the core courses. They definitely represent a significant improvement when compared with main class numbers in such Universities as Paris II, *la Sapienza* (in Rome), or *la Compultense* (in Madrid). I have lectured in two out of these three and found the experience—from a teaching/learning point of view—horrific.

The size of the repetitorium class, though an improvement upon daily University life, is not its main advantage (unless we are talking of the less popular subjects). What brings it closer to our tutorial is three things. First, is its reduced formality. Second is its focus on the presentation of material around a hypothetical problem made up from actually litigated cases. Finally, comes the effort it represents not only to give students information but also to teach them how to grapple with a practical problem and marshal their thoughts. So, the work started in the University *Arbeitsgemeinschafen* is now taken to a more detailed level taking into account the most recent decisions. An incidental advantage of the above is that it forces German students to take more into account the decisional law of their country, especially the most recent judgments, since they can often affect the content of the exam questions in the State examination.

Where the real difference with the tutorial lies is in the fact that the repetitor does most of the talking in class, analyses the problem and then, at the end, hands out a summary of what the model answer should be. The peculiarities of this model answer can be noted by glancing at the model given in Appendix Two; and more will be said about its content and style further down. This student passivity in the repetitorium is somewhat made up by the parallel institution of *Klausuren*. These take place once a week and give students the chance to handle under examination-like conditions (which last for an inhuman five hours) a similar kind of problem as those given to them in the repetitoria to handle on their own. The work produced for these *Klausuren* is, eventually, corrected and the class as a whole is given a one and a half-hour session during which the right answer (and how it should have been set out) is given by the repetitor.

Finally, who are the teachers? Typically, a repetitor is a young or middle aged lawyer who has completed his Second State Exam with good (sometimes excellent) grades and may have a small or part time practice as a Rechtsanwalt. So far as I have been able to judge (and have been also told by students and colleagues) the post does not often attract the academic high flyer that aims to pursue an academic career by writing a doctorate and then a habilitation.[35] Those who have a full and successful practice as attorneys also find it impossible to

---

[35] The higher doctorate that carries with it the venia legendi. I have, however, served as a member of the DAAD examining Committee that selects their Fachlektoren that will eventually teach abroad for periods of two to five years and many of the best candidates that I have encountered have spent some time teaching in repetitoria schools.

practice as repetitors, except, perhaps in the early stages of their career. The different career pattern of the average repetitor may have contributed to the low esteem in which they are, as a class, held by their academic brethren at the pre or immediately post doctoral level. But, in the light of observations made above about their grades in the two State exams, their academic credentials should not, in my view, be held against them. Many German students—high flyers I hasten to add—to whom I have spoken about the subject have almost uniformly praised their repetitors for their ability to analyse their topics thoroughly and to engage the attention of their students.[36] Finally, one should mention that the papers given to the students are either set by individual repetitors or by the schools in question with various repetitors taking a hand in the drafting of the question and the model answers. The ones translated in the appendices of this essay come from Kern and Friedel to whom I gratefully express my thanks for allowing me to use them in this essay.

What does all this very intensive teaching actually cost? The cost of a shared repetitorium class is around 150 marks per month lasting, as stated, between 3 and five hours. Kern & Friedel, for instance, will charge DM 2,225 for their fifteen-month *Zivilrecht* course, which means less than DM 40 per 3–5 hour session. In hourly terms that translates to the paltry DM 10 per hour. (approximately)—a figure that is economically viable for the school only because this is then multiplied by, an average of, say fifty students per session making the gross hourly return to an approximate DM 500 per hour or (again approximate) DM 2,000 per session. The briefer *Nebengebiete* option would, by contrast, cost a student the pound equivalent of DM 750. For those students who also join the criminal and public law options, the rate, per session, drops to DM 140. Students have to book entire courses and not just sections thereof; but payment is expected on a monthly basis.

To a foreign observer these figures invite at least two comments. The first is that they are minuscule given what is attempted by a repetitor and is, actually, imparted on the student. The second is that, to the German students, however, they are expensive, especially in so far as they are all so lucky (or spoilt) by a virtually free higher education. It is impossible, certainly for an outsider, to calculate whether it might be better if this money were given to the Universities in return to them being expected to expand their smaller group tuition that had a less theoretical slant and, instead, approached problem-kind situations from a practical angle. Whatever, the answer, it is unlikely that any of the German States responsible for higher education could ever come up with significantly improved grants to allow a change in teaching that would make the repetitoria redundant. That is why, attempts made by some Universities to "internalise" the

---

[36] This student praise must, however, be weighed carefully for what the students may be really praising is the repetitorium's ability to act as a "crammer" for the First State Exam. It is the "crammer" purpose that attracts the scorn of academic teachers but in levying such accusations my German academic colleagues underestimate, I think, the drawbacks that flow from their large class contacts with their students.

repetitorium techniques can only go so far but not far enough to make the institution redundant.

5 THE COMPARISON WITH THE ENGLISH TUTORIAL

The English lawyer reading the above sketch may be interested in and will certainly be horrified by some of the features of the German repctitorium. A session that may last as long as five hours sounds educationally unsound if not downright cruel. The size of a classroom that contains one hundred or, even fifty, tutees is positively unattractive. The prospect of a student being spoon-fed by a teacher, even if experienced and stimulating as many of these repetitors are, will be seen as an intellectually unattractive endeavour (though even Oxford once used such people to prepare students for their exams!). If to these, rather obvious criticisms, one adds the fact that German academics, themselves, are very snooty about the institution, one is left with one conclusion: the institution is a failure and one can only marvel at its long survival. On closer examination, I think the assessment must be much more nuanced; and I have tried to make it so in my heavily qualified presentation. This is for two reasons.

The first is that the validity of an institution must not be judged by reference to our criteria but to the conditions that prevail in the German higher educational scene and which have sustained it over centuries. For the purposes of comparative law, the moral is, of course wider. Institutions must be evaluated in their own, wider background and not condemned outright by outsiders simply because they appear to them to be odd or imperfectly designed. This kind of thinking should make us reflect about foreign institutions in conjunction to ours and, perhaps, make us think twice before we contemplate changing our own ways of doing things. Such reasoning process is likely to make us feel proud and lucky with what we have. It should.

But there is a second way on which the differences between the foreign institution (here, the repetitorium) can be compared with the indigenous real or apparent counterpart—in this case the tutorial. This second approach may lead one to look at one's native institutions through less rosy spectacles and, perhaps, question their apparent strengths. Are they really as good as we think they are? And is the model of the heyday of the Oxbridge tutorial—probably the first half of the twentieth century—still viable in the conditions of today? And has the Oxbridge model exacted from its teachers a very heavy price in terms of writing and research? This exercise, sometimes humbling, is just as valuable to the observer as the earlier one that instilled great pride. For national lawyers have an in-built tendency to think that their way of doing things is the only one available. And when it is compared with "foreign" institutions, and chauvinism also enters the equation, then "foreign" is easily translated into "bad". So let us conclude by reviewing some of the strengths and weaknesses of our own tutorial system in comparative juxtaposition with the repetitorium.

(a) Total hours/Coverage

The twenty-seven odd hours devoted by Kern and Friedel to tort repetitoria is much more—close to the three times more—the hours an English student would get in his tutorials. But the advantage derived from the larger number of contact hours in Germany is greatly reduced—arguably, even extinguished—by the considerable size of the classes.

In terms of topics covered, both systems in this amorphous corner of the law of obligations seem quite similar. If there is a difference, it lies in the quite complete absence in Germany of an economic or policy-oriented approach to law. But if that is a gap (defect?) in the repetitorium it can—with few exceptions—also be found both in the German University teaching and academic writings as well as the instruction provided in repetitoria where an economic and interdisciplinary analysis of the law is the exception rather than the rule.

(b) Numbers

It was stated at the outset and it is by now more obvious than ever that the great weakness of the German system lies in the impossibly high numbers with which the law faculties have to cope. Large numbers, again, blight the repetitorium, even if in absolute terms they tend to be lower, sometimes much lower, than those in University class rooms. But, having said this, one must add two qualifications. The repetitorium still manages to impart some legal knowledge in smaller and more manageable settings. And the low numbers in an English tutorial must not be judged by reference to the Oxford "ideal" of one to one in mind but with the kind of numbers one finds in the majority of the English law faculties. Thus, in most English law faculties the figures can rise to 12 or even more 20 or 30 (when the tutorial is transformed into a large seminar). Though this is still less than the forty or fifty average we find in Germany, the difference is less significant than the ratio of "one to one or two" that one gets if the comparison is made with the Oxbridge model. One should also bear in mind that the English tutorial system is not known in all Common law systems and that the numbers found in German repetitoria come close to the size of the average class in an American Law School.

(c) Way of Teaching/Marking

Here lies a difference, which in my view is even more significant than that found in the numbers. For the English tutorial, at any rate the best of the kind, depends upon making the student think, provoking him into asking the right questions, familiarising him on how to find the material he needs and, above all expecting him to come to the teaching session prepared in advance. The German repetitorium, as indeed, the kind of answers expected in exams, places a huge premium on memory, completeness, and discussion of *all* relevant points *in the right order*. The kind of attributes—strengths and weaknesses—that the average Englishman ascribes to the German character and mind are thus perfectly mirrored in the repetitorium. Coupled with the instruction given at a German law faculty, it helps inculcate a kind of thinking and writing which, despite its many merits, is not known for its light touch or instant appeal. In a world where the travel of ideas is not only important in an intellectual sense but also a powerful medium for exporting one's culture and ideology, the German legal writing does little justice to the richness of ideas found in the German legal culture. But, again, to the extent that the weaknesses I am identifying are real and not the product of my misconception of the system, they cannot be laid at the door of the repetitorium. I think the latter merely reflects the prevailing legal and educational ethos and, if anything, by focusing on problems minimises the effect of theorising which the doctoral dissertation—in many respects the pinnacle of the German educational process—does so much to encourage. The search for flashes of inspiration and originality is a strong feature of the best type of English tutorial; and the so inexplicable Oxford grade of Alpha/Gama exemplifies this predilection for the effortless success instead of the hard-sweated triumph.

(d) Style of Writing/Approaching a Problem

The above features are also seen in the degree of editorial interference that a good tutor will exercise over the written essay of his pupils. The essay-oriented way of education, a key feature of the English educational system already from the school days, seems doomed to oblivion in a system that (a) expects the repetitor to explain how the problem should be solved (b) expects little or nothing from the student attending the repetitorium and (c) places such premium over completeness and order of presentation at the expense of originality, lightness of touch and even humour. The fact that most German students go to repetitoria unprepared, merely expecting to be spoon-fed, contributes to the weakness of the institution. The *Klausuren*, in which the students do have to write a long and fairly elaborate answer, in my view, do not make up for these absent features. They are merely meant to test whether the student has picked up from the repetitor the right order within which he has to set his answer.

From these specific observations one might even be emboldened to go further and attempt a broader comparison of the English and German law teacher. For the latter, certainly of the archetypal variety, is too conscious of the burdens which come with his progression in the *cursus honorum* ever to admit ignorance let alone error, something which I have repeatedly seen common law luminaries do with real rather than apparent modesty. The German law teachers' sense of occasion also leaves little room for humour, at any rate when the official functions are carried out. Finally, the German law teacher's attachment to logic would seem to allow precious little room for spontaneity and, often, lateral thinking. I submit all these points emerge not only from the reading of the major law treatises or textbooks but also from the more humble exercise of teaching a young lawyer how to write an answer to a legal problem. Certainly, what the model answers reproduced below suggest is that the German law teacher is less interested than the English tutor to write with a sense of form, of drama, and of the possibilities of language. From day one, the German lawyer is thus striving for the perfection which in his eyes comes when what he writes appeals through its completeness and system to his scholarly clique; writing for the educated public is certainly not his goal. From beginning to end the prime aim is thus the discovery of the cause of action and the relentless pursuit of its justification on some codal provision. Neither, it seems to me, does the German University lecture nor the German repetitorium model attach half as much importance on points of style, presentation, and modes of criticising authorities used in the process of justifying a result. Teaching by constantly varying the factual permutations of a problem is thus almost absent.

6 OVERALL ASSESSMENT

In my opinion, those who observe legal systems from without, lack the feel that comes to those who see it from within. Warped though their assessments may be, they are not, however, without some merits principal among which is the fact that they (normally) come to the foreign system without serious preconceptions and untouched by local doctrinal disputes. More importantly, in the instant case these reactions, even when critical, come from an overall admirer of the German system's strong points. So, with these caveats in mind, what are my preliminary assessments? Three may deserve special emphasis.

First, my impression is that the condemnation that the repetitorium receives among German academic purists is too harsh. With all its deficiencies, it fulfils a need that the German Universities are not at present able to meet. If it is a crammer, it is because the German law faculties do not prepare their students fully and specifically for the type of exam, which they will get and which really matters to them. Moreover, the emphasis that the repetitoria place on problems, the prominence they give to cases, and the considerable efforts they make to teach some way of writing are all, in different ways, useful additions to the more doctrinal instruction imparted in the Universities great amphitheatres. The fact that these schools also prosper must also indicate that the market has a need for them whatever highbrow academics may think.

Secondly, as this essay tried to show, these schools perform functions that in some respects come close to those fulfilled by our own tutorial system. The fact that in my own overall assessment, the English tutorial wins over the German repetitorium, especially in matters of style, is not a reason to condemn outright let alone eliminate from the legal scene the German institution. This would only come if German law faculties were prepared to take some of its best features and combined them with those of the English tutorial. One might then witness a considerable improvement of the German educational system bringing together its own traditional strengths as well as those found in the English setting. These may sound as bold suggestions; indeed, they may be little more than euphoric dreams. But the current soul-searching in German educational circles about the appropriateness of the shape and form and duration and cost of higher education is such that almost every bona fide suggestion merits, in my view, some consideration. The *Arbeitsgemeinschaften* run by some Professors and their staff seem to me to be doing just that so that a shift towards what I am advocating is already taking place. On the other hand, the admirers of the classical, Oxbridge model must not forget the price it entails in terms of academic productivity. I have experienced enough of it both in Cambridge and Oxford to be in a position to attest how its exhaustive dedication to labour-intensive teaching has destroyed many a promising research career and pushed many a promising scholar to seek sanctuary in the United States.

Finally, for the reasons given in another piece,[37] I do not think that the contribution that English law can and will make to the future of European legal education is going to be in the area of legal dogma. For to every Treitel, Birks, Glanville Williams, or Baker that we can produce, they can counter with many more. Larenz, Esser, Medicus, Flume, von Caemmerer, Canaris, Schlechtriem, Roxin, Wieacker, Coing, or Koschacker—the list is endless even without having to turn to the golden era of the German professoriat at the beginning of the last century! Nor, I think, will English law, make great strides forward by turning its efforts and energy inwardly and attempting the kind of systematisation which reached its peak in Germany during the late nineteenth century and in many ways affected adversely the system's ability to serve as a model for exportation. But, for a country such as ours, which for centuries ignored a University-based legal education, it would be a paradox and a source of pride if it could one day inspire its foreign friends on how to *teach* law. Over thirty years of teaching in numerous Continental European Universities gives me the feeling that in this area of University instruction we may have something useful to offer. For this is the area where, in my view, we score heavily over Continental Universities. And it will be interesting to see if we ever make a serious offer to help our foreign friends and whether such an offer is ever taken up. In my view, this could certainly be one of the areas where English law could make a useful contribution to the Europe of the twenty-first century.

---

[37] "Zur Lehre des Rechts anhand von Fällen: Einige bescheidene Vorschläge zur Verbesserung der deutschen Juristenausbildung" in *Festschrift für Peter Schlechtriem zum 70 Geburstag* (Mohr, Tübingen, 2002).

Appendix I

Tort law and damages
General syllabus

Part 1: Torts

A. LIABILITY FOR CAUSING DAMAGE

I. Liability under § 823 I BGB
The requirements under § 823 I

Violation of an interest protected under § 823 I
aa) Interference with life, bodily integrity, and health: Case 1 *(Accident with serious consequences)*.
bb) Interference with Property: Case 2 *(Blocking access to a business concern)*
cc) Other rights under § 823 I
Property protection under tort law: Case 3 *(Elevator)*
Right of an established and operating commercial business: See Case 2
General right of personality *(Allgemeines Persönlichkeitsrecht)*: Case 4 *(Panorama)*

Causation *(haftungsbegründende Kausalität)*
Case 1 *(Accident with serious consequences)*
Case 5 *(Jump from a window)*

Unlawfulness, illegality.
Self-defence; necessity.
Fault.

II. Violation of a protective law, § 823 II BGB: Case 2 (Blocking access to a business)
III. Interference with one's credit and earnings, § 824 BGB : See Case 4
IV. Intentionally causing harm *contra bonos mores*: § 826 BGB

B. LIABILITY FOR PRESUMED FAULT

I. Liability for the conduct of one's helpers § 831: Case 6 *(Copper roof)*
II. Liability of persons charged with the care and supervision of others: § 832
Case 7 *(Field glasses)*
III. Owner's liability for harm caused by a working animal, § 833: See Case 15
IV. Liability of the person responsible to take care of a building, §§ 836–838

C. RISK LIABILITY

I. Risk liability for owning an animal, § 833: See Case 15
II. Risk liability under the StVG (Traffic Law): Case 8 (Multiple collision)
III. Liability for defective products under the ProdHaftG (Products Liability Law): Case 9 (Gasoline train)

D. MULTIPLE TORTFEASORS: § 830

Case 8 (Multiple collision)

E. SPECIAL PROVISIONS IN TORT LAW

§§ 842–851: See Case 8

Part 2: Damages

A. THE DAMAGE

I. *The form of compensation*, §§ 249–253; Difference between Naturalherstellung (restitution in kind) (§ 249) and monetary compensation (§ 251) Case 10 (Damage posts in a traffic accident).
II. Calculating damages on the basis of the difference theory (including normative corrections)
1. *Hypothetical situation without the damaging event*
Case 11 (A better offer)
2. *The actual situation caused by the damaging event*: Case 12 (Evening out advantages)
3. *Difference including normative corrections*
a) Housewife: See case 7
b) Costs for precautions: Case 13 (Shop lifting)
c) The objective worth as the minimal damage: See SAT Case 5
d) Liquidating a third person's damage: See SAT Case 5
e) Unwanted children as damage: Case 14 (Wrongful life)

B. CAUSATION (HAFTUNGSAUSFÜLLENDE KAUSALITÄT)

C. CONTRIBUTION BY THE INJURED, § 254

Case 15 (Dangerous country life)

Appendix II

Case 14 Wrongful life

PROBLEM

Daisy, the daughter of Hubert and Wilma, was born in the spring of 1999 suffering from severe health problems. These were the result of Wilma having contracted German measles during her first weeks of pregnancy. Because of the injuries suffered by the child, its delivery had to take place by means of a Caesarean operation. At the beginning of the pregnancy and in order to avoid these consequences, Wilma underwent medical tests by the said gynaecologist. Despite the presence of many indications, Dr Careless failed to detect the infection and Wilma did not terminate the pregnancy in accordance with 218 StGB. Had Wilma been told of the infection, she would have certainly proceeded to an abortion. On the assumption that Dr Careless is guilty of a severe violation of his medical duties, Hubert and Wilma (and the child represented by her parents) now bring an action for maintenance costs including the considerably increased costs caused by the child's disabilities. They also demand damages for pain and suffering.

Suggested Reading

(BVerfG NJW 98, 519 with comment Stürner JZ 98, 317; Deutsch NJW 98, 510; BGH NJW 97, 1638; BGH NJW 95, 2407 = JuS 96, 71 with comment Roth NJW 95, 2399; BGH NJW 95, 1609 with comment Schöbener JR 96, 89; BGH NJW 94, 788 = JuS 94, 608 with comment Weiß JR 94, 461; Roth NJW 94, 2402; Deutsch NJW 94, 776; Giesen JZ 94, 286; BGH NJW 83, 1371 with comment Fischer JuS 84, 434; Picker AcP 195, 484 ff; Heldrich JuS 69, 455 ff; Boin JA 95, 425; BVerfG NJW 93, 1751 with comment Deutsch NJW 93, 2361; see also BGH NJW 94, 127 = JuS 94, 351 with comment Taupitz JR 95, 22; Schnorbus JuS 94, 830; Rohe JZ 94, 465; Nerderl. BW JZ 97, 893)

SOLUTION OF CASE 14[38]
PART 1: THE CLAIMS OF WILMA AGAINST DR CARELESS

A. Compensation for the Costs of Living Including Increased Expenses

I. Based on *positive Vertragverletzung* (PVV)[39] of the contract for medical treatment
Applicability
The possibility of resorting to (PVV) is subservient to the codified rules on irregularities of performance.
The contract for medical treatment is always a contract of employment and not a contract for work and labour, because the complications in physiological developments do not allow for promising a result in the sense of § 631. (Palandt-Putzo vor 611 number 18).[40]
In accordance with this, (PVV) is applicable in this case, because the issue is neither delay nor impossibility, but rather poor performance and §§ 611 ff do not contain rules on this.
Contract
A contract exists if W and C agreed on the characteristics of a contract of employment in accordance with § 611 BGB[41] and there are no legal reasons to prevent such a contract.
a) Agreement with the content required in § 611 BGB (+)
b) No impediments
In this case § 134 BGB in conjunction with § 218 StGB could be applicable because the contract ultimately is to facilitate the termination of pregnancy.
However, the termination of pregnancy is not unlawful (rechtswidrig) where a medical, embryo-related, or criminological indication justifies it. Then the element of unlawfulness in the sense of § 134 BGB is removed from the outset.
Although some contracts for the termination of pregnancy are not threatened with punishment they remain, nevertheless, unlawful—for example terminations while the mother finds herself in a situation of personal or social emergency. Such contracts are not void under § 134 BGB or under § 138 BGB.

---

[38] All notes in the appendix are by the author of this essay and not by the School that is responsible for the "model answer".

[39] German law does not know a unified notion of breach, its Civil Code, largely for historical reasons, regulating only impossibility of performance and delay. The most typical form of breach—bad performance—thus emerged as a praetorian creation, first known under the heading of Positive Vertragsverletzungen and now more commonly designated by the notion of Forderungsverletzungen (wider in that it accepts that some of these breaches arise not from contracts but, directly, from the law itself.) For fuller details, essential to understand fully the discussion in the notes above, see Markesinis, GLC, pp. 418–434.

[40] In a Werkvertrag the contractor is bound to produce the promised work and the customer to pay for it. The remedies for breach of such a contract are specified by the Code in §§ 632–5 BGB and are subject to a very short period of limitation: six months according to § 638 BGB. In these contracts, unlike sales, the courts have not allowed easily an escape into the PVV theory and thus reliance on the more generous period of contractual limitation provided by § 195 BGB.

[41] The contract envisaged here is a contract of service known as a Dienstvertrag. The dividing line between these two types of contracts is not always easy to draw. Thus, see, BGH 9 Dec. 1974, BGH NJW 1975, 305 which offers an interesting comparison with the factual parallel in *Samuels* v. *Davies* [1943] 1 KB 526.

(BVerfG NJW 93, 1763 with comment Deutsch NJW 93, 2361; Palandt-Heinrichs vor 249 number 48; see also AG Bad Oyenhausen NJW 98, 1799 on the voidness of a contract for termination of pregnancy and surgery if at the conclusion of the contract the pregnant woman was not yet advised in accordance with § 219 StGB)
In accordance with this, unlawfulness in the sense of § 134 can be eliminated in this case, because the contract was concluded in order to find out whether the prerequisites for termination of pregnancy for embryo-related indications exist. A termination on this prerequisite is not illegal.
Result: There is a contract.
Violation of a duty derived from this contract
In this case the existing suspicions put C under a duty to do further examinations. C violated this duty.
Fault, § 276 (+)[42]
Consequence: compensation in accordance with §§ 249 ff BGB
a) Damages
Damages are calculated in accordance with the so-called "theory of difference"[43] through the comparison of two pecuniary situations.
aa) Hypothetical circumstances without the event causing the damage.
If the focus here is the child's birth or existence, § 249 s. 1 BGB would be aimed at the elimination of the child and damage compensation, therefore, is impossible.
(see LG Munich I VersR 1970, 428; but see also Staudinger-Medicus 249 number 14:251)
But, on the hypothetical level, the focal point for comparison can be chosen freely. Damages are thus calculated by looking at the burden caused by the cost of living of the unwanted child.
(BGH NJW 80, 1490; NJW 94, 791)
bb) Real circumstances caused by the damaging event: Burdening with the obligation to maintenance under §§ 1601 ff.
It remains questionable whether the damaging event has, in addition to the disadvantages, also brought benefits, which have to be taken into account when balancing the benefits and harm.
Advantages brought about by the birth of a child can be:
Possible joy derived from the existence of the child. (However, joy as a mere immaterial advantage, cannot be subtracted from material disadvantages and should thus not be taken into account.)
Possible right to inherit from the child (§ 1925); parents' possible right to get maintenance from the child; possible right to services (§ 1619). None can be considered because they are not in existence at the time of the trial. (However, there remains the possibility of a later claim for changing the verdict under § 323 ZPO)

---

[42] Liability for ones own mistakes usually includes liability for intention as well as for negligence. What constitutes negligence differs depending on the situation and is determined objectively, i.e., not geared to the actor's abilities but to the standard that the law expects in such a situation. As with English law, this often provides a vehicle for the introduction of near-strict liability which in theory is (with minor exception) banished from the tort section of the Code.

[43] Two theories exist in German law as to how the damages should be calculated. The Austauschtheorie (exchange theory) allows the creditor to the full value of the performance promised him but only on condition of performing his own promise. In the case of the Differenztheorie, the creditor is absolved from performing his own obligation and can claim the difference in price (if there is any) between his obligation and that of the guilty debtor. For more details about how these theories work in practice see Markesinis, GLC, pp 630 ff.

On the other hand, social security aid for raising a child and possible tax advantages have to be accounted for.

cc) *Difference*: burdening with maintenance costs minus the amount of state aid for raising a child. Thus, § 249 s.1 BGB is aimed at releasing the parents from their maintenance obligation.

The problem remains, whether restitution in kind (Naturalherstellung) under § 249 s. 1 is eliminated under § 251 I 1st case, because of § 1614, the transfer of obligations with a release for the former debtor as far as future maintenance costs are concerned is not possible. However, the establishment of an economically comparative situation is sufficient for § 249 s. 1, in this case through the payment of a corresponding amount of money.

dd) It is debatable, however, whether damages for maintenance costs should be denied on the basis of constitutional principles in the light of Art. 1 I GG and because of the obligation to maintain the child under family law provisions.

Arguments for this could be:

- If Art. 1 I GG[44] prohibits the classification of the child's existence as a damage, then the same must be true for the parents' obligation to maintain the child because otherwise the child's right for life would, indirectly, be put into doubt.
- There is a danger for severe psychological damages for the child when he discovers that he is unwanted and his existence is considered a damaging event.
- The obligation to maintain under family law, with its foundation on the biological relationship between parents and child, does not allow its transfer to third persons. For this would improperly split the symbiosis of reciprocal rights and duties imposed on the family by law.

(BVerfG NJW 93, 1751 with comment Giesen JZ 94, 286; Deutsch NJW 93, 2361; OLG Bamberg NJW 78, 1685 with comment Siegel NJW 78, 2340; OLG Frankfurt NJW 83, 341; LG Düsseldorf NJW 94, 805; Roth NJW 94, 2402)

However, it is correct to agree with the prevailing opinion and award the cost of maintenance as damages.

Arguments:

- Where the difference theory for determining damages focuses only on the burdening with the obligation to maintenance and compares this to the situation without maintenance obligation, then no statement is made on the child's worth and existence and consequently its right out of Art. 1 I GG is not in question.
- A damage award helps to improve the parents' positive attitude towards their child and is thus useful for the child.
- A damage award does not cause the inadmissible split of the special family relationship promoted by law, because the maintenance obligation is still the parents' who merely get the chance to get compensation from a third person. Otherwise there would be a non-justifiable privilege immunising third persons helping in family planning from claims.

(BGH NJW 94, 788 = JuS 94, 608 with comment Deutsch NJW 94, 776: Giesen JZ 94, 286; BGH NJW 80, 1452; Waibl NJW 87, 1515 ff; Staudinger-Medicus 249 number 16; Palandt-Heinrichs vor 249 number 47; also BVerfG NJW 98, 519 for cases of a sterilization gone wrong or for incorrect genetic advice)

---

[44] "The dignity of man shall be inviolable. To respect and protect it shall be the duty of all State authority."

The damage payments could have to be limited at least in their amount and duration through a normative correction of the difference hypothesis because of the peculiarity of the maintenance obligation based on family law principles.

(a) Therefore, the amount of damages must be reduced in the case of a maintenance obligation for a healthy child to a proportionate amount under guidance from the Regelbetragverordnung *(see § 1612a) increased by a reasonable amount for the mother's looking after the child. Additionally, the amount of damages must be limited to the child reaching 18 years of age, because a need beyond this time usually arises from special circumstances in the family, which are beyond the control of the person causing the damage and, therefore, he cannot be burdened with it.*
(BGH NJW 80, 1456; NJW 92, 1558; Staudinger-Schäfer 823 number 15)
(b) Where the question is, however, as in this case, the maintenance costs for a severely handicapped child, the additional costs generally must be compensated because this damage is not based on special circumstances in the family but on the child's disability. Result: In this case the entire maintenance cost can be compensated.
(c) Causation (Haftungsausfüllende Kausalität)
aa) Adequacy (Adäquanz): *The burden from the maintenance obligation for the child was generally foreseeable and therefore adequacy is satisfied.*
bb) However, it is questionable, whether the rule which grants the payment of damages in the first place (haftungsbegründende Norm) *is intended to cover all the damages, i.e., a contract for medical treatment would have to include and aim at the protection from the burden of maintenance costs obligations. Insofar it must be distinguished:*
Where a termination of pregnancy fails which was done based on a personal or social emergency situation, the doctor's employment contract is not intended to cover the maintenance obligation, because the intent of the parties is in this case disapproved of by the legal system and an illegitimate (rechtswidrig, *i.e. not legal*) *act cannot be the basis for an obligation to pay damages.*
(Palandt-Heinrichs vor 249 number 48b)
Where the indication is for medical reasons the burden from the maintenance obligation is also not covered by the intention for the doctor's employment contract under which the woman should merely get protection from dangers for her health arising from the pregnancy, its continuance, and giving birth.
(BGH NJW 85, 2751; Staudinger-Medicus 249 number 17; MüKo-Grunsky vor 249 number 12)
It is questionable, whether under the embryo-related indication—like in this case—the intention of the contract for medical treatment covers the maintenance obligation completely, or whether only the increased costs arising from the child's disability can be compensated.
An argument for a limitation to the increased costs could be that the parents did not want to prevent the birth of a child in general but rather wanted to prevent the birth of a disabled child.
(Schünemann JZ 81, 575; MüKo-Grunsky vor 249 number 12a)
However, the correct solution is to regard the complete maintenance costs as being covered by the contractual intention, because the parents did not wish this disabled child in particular and with it also the complete costs for the child's maintenance.
(BGH NJW 94, 788 = JuS 94, 608; BGH NJW 84, 660; BGH NJW 83, 1371 where the question is left open)

Result: In this case the complete costs for maintenance are covered by the intention for entering the contract for medical treatment.

d) A reduction of the damages under § 254 based on the parents being partly to blame is not applicable. There is especially no duty to mitigate through giving the child for adoption because under § 242 such a request cannot be made.
(see also BGH NJW 92, 2961 on partial blame arising for missing the follow-up examination after a sterilisation)
Result: W has a claim against C for compensation for the maintenance costs under (PVV).

II. Claim under § 823 I BGB[45]
Applicability (+)
Violation of a right granted under the law
The violation of a right granted under the law cannot be seen in the mere burden of being subject to a maintenance obligation because this is a mere violation of ones economic situation and the economic situation is not a protected right under § 823 I.[46]
However, there could be a violation of the body's integrity or a health violation.
aa) Following the prevailing opinion, an unwanted pregnancy is a violation of the body's integrity or health, because the protection of the body's integrity includes the decision whether a pregnancy is desired or not.
(BGH NJW 95, 2408; BGH NJW 80, 1452; MüKo-Mertens 823 number 80)
In this case the situation (pregnancy) exists—in contrast to cases of sterilisation—not because of C's acts but as a result of W's free will.
bb) However, the psychological burden of having a disabled child could be a health violation.
This must, however, be rejected, because there is no basis for believing that this burden is intense enough to cross the line and become a medically recognisable disorder of inner life processes.
(BGH NJW 83, 1371; critically Fischer JuS 84, 435)
cc) But the Caesarian section is a health infringement because it goes beyond a woman's usual impairment in giving birth.
On the other side, there is no violation of an other right (sonstiges Recht) under § 823 I BGB because, following the prevailing opinion, a right to family planning, protected by tort law, is not accepted as part of the general right of personality (allgemeines Persönlichkeitsrecht).
(BGH NJW 83, 1371; OLG Frankfurt NJW 93, 2388; OLG Düsseldorf NJW 92, 1566; MüKo-Mertens 823 number 80; other opinion Heldrich JuS 69, 461; Larenz/Canaris SBT §80 116d)
Causation (haftungsbegründende Kausalität)[47]

---

[45] "A person who wilfully or negligently injures the life, body, health, freedom, property, or other right of another contrary to law is bound to compensate him for any damage arising therefrom."

[46] German law, like English law, is reluctant to authorise the compensation of pure economic loss through a tort action. But both systems recognise many exceptions. For details see Markesinis, GLT.

[47] German tort law distinguishes between haftungsbegründende Kausalität and haftungsausfüllende Kausalität. The difference between the two is that the first deals with the problem whether the defendant is liable for causing the damage while the second answers the question whether the actual amount of damage is a result of the defendant's actions. The analogy here is with causation and remoteness of damage in English law. Such a bifurcated approach to causation is less obvious in other systems e.g. the French. The two meanings of causation appear frequently throughout this answer and must be kept separate—hence I have retained the appropriate German version.

C's failure to do further examinations caused the violation of the body's integrity because the child's disability was the reason for the Caesarean section being done.
Unlawfulness (Rechtswidrigkeit) and fault (Schuld) (+)
Consequence: Claim for damages for the damage caused by the violation of the body's integrity
There is no adequate causation with regard to W's burdening with the maintenance obligation because this damage is not a result of the Caesarean section.
Additionally, the area of protection intended by § 823 I, does not cover the maintenance obligation because this rule is intended only to prevent the violation to the body's integrity and damages resulting from it.
(Heldrich JuS 69, 460)
The additional costs resulting from the Caesarean section can be compensated, but reduced only by the amount of costs for the saved termination of pregnancy (evening out advantages—Vorteilsausgleichung). But these additional costs are not claimed in this case.
Result: W has no claim under § 823 I BGB for compensation of the maintenance costs. Although the prerequisites under § 823 II BGB[48] in conjunction with § 229 StGB are fulfilled, these rules do not aim at compensating maintenance costs.
There is no claim for damages for pain and suffering under (PVV) of the doctor's contract of employment because § 253 does generally not allow compensation for non-economic damage.
Claim under § 847 I BGB[49]
Applicability of § 847 I
Violation of the body's integrity (+), see above through tort, in this case § 823 I and § 823 II BGB in conjunction with § 229 StGB, see above
Consequence: Claim for "reasonable" monetary "compensation"
Damage
Damage under § 847 BGB is only for non-pecuniary losses such as pain and suffering, worries, reduced chances for a marriage, etc.
For the measurement of what constitutes a "reasonable" monetary "compensation" the following factors must be taken into account:
aa) the kind and extent of the handicap (= compensation function of § 847)
bb) and, based on the satisfaction function of § 847 BGB, also the degree of culpability, the economic circumstances of the parties, etc.
Causation (haftungsausfüllende Kausalität) (+)
Subtraction of advantages under § 254 (−)
Result: There is a claim for damages for pain and suffering; the amount must be based on the specific facts.

---

[48] The same obligation [to pay compensation] attaches to a person who infringes a statutory provision intended for the protection of others. If according to the purview of the statute infringement is possible even without fault, the duty to make compensation arises only if some fault can be imputed to the wrongdoer.

[49] "In the case of injury to body or health, or in the case of deprivation of liberty, the injured party may also demand an equitable compensation in money for the damage which is not a pecuniary loss."

PART 2: H'S CLAIMS AGAINST C

A. For Compensation of the Maintenance Costs Including the Increased Costs

I. Claim under (PVV) of the contract for medical treatment (§§ 611 ff)
Applicability
Contract
H himself did not contract with C, but he could have a joint claim arising in accordance with § 1357 BGB through W's actions.

§ 1357 is applicable to buying contraceptives and the usual medical or gynaecological contract for treatment. They are examples for contracts in the usual course of business, which are economically less relevant, and more often contracted for, and for which usually no previous arrangements between the partners are made (Waibl NJW 87, 1514 with further references).

The contract in this case, however, was preparatory for the termination of a pregnancy. For this a prior discussion between the partners is usual and therefore there is no claim under § 1357.

But, H could be included in the sphere of protection of the contract between W and C in a way that the duties for care and protection that C owes W are also valid with regard to H with the result that H has a claim of his own right for damages should C violate these duties.

The dogmatic arguments for a contract with protective effects with regard to third persons (Vertrag mit Schutzwirkung für Dritte) *differ (§ 328, contract created by law in analogy to the cic rules based on § 242, or supplemental interpretation of contracts); however, there is a relatively unified opinion on the prerequisites, i.e.:*

aa) There must be a so-called proximity to the obligation (Leistungsnähe).[50]
This is given in this case, because H by virtue of his obligation to pay for the child's costs of living is exposed to the same dangers as is W herself.
bb) The so-called proximity to the creditor (Gläubigernähe) is also present, because H has, based on the mutuality of family planning, a special interest in being included in the sphere of protection afforded by the contract for medical treatment.
cc) C could see these prerequisites (Erkennbarkeit), because his files show that his patient is married.
dd) The so-called worthiness to get protection (Schutzwürdigkeit) is also given, because H has no claim on his own against C on the same subject matter and with the same contents.
(BGH NJW 83, 1371; NJW 80, 1452)
Culpable violation of duties by C
Consequence: Claim for compensation for the costs of maintenance. What was said above under claim W against C applies also here.[51]

---

[50] For further details, Markesinis, GLT, ch. 2.
[51] Because a Vertrag mit Schutzwirkung zugunsten Dritter is the basis for H's claim and this construction leads to H having the same claim than W has, the extent of the claim must also be the same.

II. Claim under § 823 I BGB (−), because there is no violation of a protected right of H, specifically, H has no tort claim based on family planning as a flow out to the general personality right.

III. For the same reason there is no claim for damages for pain and suffering under § 847 BGB.

PART 3: CLAIMS D AGAINST C

A. For Compensation for the Costs of Living Including the Increased Costs

I. Claim under (PVV) of the contract for medical treatment (§§ 611 ff BGB)
Applicability of (PVV) (+), see above
Contract
There is no direct contractual relationship between C and D. But D could be included in the sphere of protection of the valid contract for medical treatment between W and C. Then, the so-called prerequisites for inclusion must be present, i.e.,
proximity to the obligation (+)
proximity to the creditor (+), because of the mother's special interest in the protection of her child
foreseeability for C (+)
the need for protection (Schutzbedürftigkeit) (+), because D herself has no contractual claim against W as the creditor of the main contract.
However, doubts regarding D's inclusion in the contract's sphere of protection could result from D being not yet able to have rights at the time of the acts causing the tort liability, because D was not yet born at that time, § 1 BGB.
But this does not prevent D's inclusion into the contract's protective sphere.
Arguments:
—It is accepted in other areas of liability that so-called pre-natal damage can lead to damage claims from the child later born alive (BGH NJW 72, 1126).
—A even-more-so conclusion with regard to §§ 331 ff, i.e., if the unborn child can be a third party beneficiary under §§ 328, 331 ff, then he must, as a minus compared to the obligatory claim, also have the ability to be creditor of a protective duty (MüKo-Gitter § 1 number 32).
Result: There is a contractual relationship between D and C.
C's violation of a duty
In this case C's duty was to make further examinations so that, should there be an infection, terminating the pregnancy could prevent the child's birth. This duty, however, existed only in relation to the mother. The child, on the other hand, has no claim to have his living prevented or terminated.
Arguments:
—§ 218a StGB explicitly allows the mother to terminate a pregnancy only in her interest so that an additional duty on the doctor to act owed to the child cannot follow from that.
—Otherwise, the unbearable result would follow that then the child could bring compensatory claims against his parents, if those have procreated a child despite their knowledge about a danger for severe genetic defects.

Result: There is no contractual claim under (PVV) because there is no violation of a duty.

II. Claim under § 823 I BGB
Applicability
Violation of a right through C's causal and tortuous conduct
In this case D's health (disorder of the inner life processes) and bodily integrity are impaired. But this impairment was not caused by C's conduct, because W was already infected at the time of the examination.

But C's conduct (failure to undertake further examinations) caused D being born. Insofar, however, there is no violation of a right because § 823 I requires for a violation not the non-prevention of life but rather its extinction. Our legal system recognises no duty in tort to prevent other's lives, but rather, on the contrary, it sees life itself as the highest of rights under the law (see Art. 1, 2 I GG) worthy to be kept alive under all circumstances.

Result: D has no claim for damages under § 823 I.
B. D also has no claim for damages for pain and suffering under § 847 I.

6

Two-Way Traffic: the Warburg Institute as a Microcosm of Cultural Exchange between Britain and Europe

NICHOLAS MANN

When the opening of the Channel Tunnel was hailed as the end of the isolation of Continental Europe, the press understandably enough chose to ignore all traffic that was not on wheels. Yet the twentieth century provided—as other papers in this volume serve to show—remarkable instances of the flow of ideas quite independent of locomotion, and there is no reason to think that such a flow will diminish in the new century. Indeed in the realm of cultural and intellectual history the channels of communication provided by the Internet may well render the tunnel under the Channel redundant in many respects. It is surely too early to anticipate Britain's potential contribution in the twenty-first century to a Europe that is continuously redefining itself, but the intention of the present paper is to reflect upon a remarkable, and possibly unique, instance of two-way cultural transmission which may however serve as a microcosm of a wider and more general phenomenon.

The case is that of the Warburg Institute, now part of the School of Advanced Study of the University of London, but until 1933 the *Kulturwissenschaftliche Bibliothek Warburg* in Hamburg. The story begins on 12 December of that year, and continues to the present day; if the model is of any value (and it is that of *translatio studii*, of a tradition which has its origins in the classical past), it should certainly not come to an end in the course of the present century. The date just mentioned, ten days before Goebbels took over the Ministry for Propaganda, is that on which two small steamers, the Jessica and the Hermia, slipped out of Hamburg's harbour and down the Elbe, bound for London. Their cargo consisted of five hundred and thirty-one crates containing some sixty thousand books, thousands of slides and photographs, and most of the binding machinery and furniture of the institution that had grown out of the private library of the scholar Aby Warburg, who had died four years earlier.[1]

---

[1] For a succinct account of the move to London, see E M Warburg, "The Transfer of the Warburg Institute to England in 1933", in The Warburg Institute, *Annual Report 1952–1953* (London, The Warburg Institute, 1953), pp. 13–16.

This event might in itself seem unremarkable, though the last-minute escape of a unique library from the threat of destruction at the hand of the Nazis is a tribute to those (notably the Warburg brothers in America, Fritz Saxl in Hamburg, and Lord Lee of Fareham and Samuel Courtauld in London) who engineered it. But it did not pass entirely unnoticed even outside the groves of academe. The *Times Literary Supplement* of 11 January 1936 spoke of it as "the most signal addition to the resources available to English scholarship that has been made for very many years"; when in 1944 the Warburg family transferred the Warburg Institute (as it had become in its British incarnation) to the University of London in perpetuity, the *Observer* of 24 December hailed it as "the nation's greatest Christmas present of the year" from Hamburg, while the *Manchester Guardian* celebrated the event in more measured tones: "an institute created by a German scholar was handed over to a British University by donors most of whom are American citizens, in the hope that it will serve the students of this country and be a worthy member of the family of learned institutions".

That hope was surely not vain. Although in the ten initial years of its London life the Institute underwent several moves: from Thames House on Millbank to the Imperial Institute at South Kensington in 1939, and to the safety of Denham in Buckinghamshire from 1941 until 1945, it was quickly to establish itself as an intellectual centre of the first importance, increasing its library holdings by roughly a half over the decade. And while during those early years the activity of the Institute had largely consisted, in Fritz Saxl's characteristically understated terms, "of a few scholars exploring certain aspects of . . . the history of the classical tradition, making contacts as best they could with other scholars and students working on similar lines",[2] the incorporation in the University of London meant that the future was secure and that a wider range of students and scholars would have ready access to its resources and its ideas.

In 1934, the year in which the Institute reopened its doors in London, Edgar Wind prefaced the first publication of its new incarnation—*A Bibliography on the Survival of the Classics*—with an additional Introduction for an unsuspecting public. "The general theme of this bibliography—the survival of the Greek and Roman tradition—is familiar to English readers. They may feel some misgiving, however, at seeing on the German title page the untranslatable word 'kulturwissenschaftlich' which is meant to indicate the method employed. The word is full of odd connotations. English readers might feel themselves reminded of wartime slogans which succeeded in rendering the word 'Kultur' altogether disreputable. . . ." It was of course not merely the word, but also the concept that was deeply foreign, and Wind went to some lengths to explain in simple terms what it implied, describing its use by Aby Warburg:

> "to designate his attempt to tear down the barriers artificially set up between the various departments of historical research. Historians of science were not to work

[2] The Warburg Institute, *Annual Report 1944–1945* (London, 1945) p. 1.

independently of historians of art and of religion; nor were historians of literature to isolate the study of linguistic forms and literary arts from their setting in the totality of culture. The idea of a comprehensive 'science of civilization' was thus meant to embody the demand for a precise method of interaction and correlation between those diverging scientific interests in the humanities which have shown a tendency to set up their subjects as 'things in themselves' ".[3]

Whatever the antecedents of the term and the concept (and one thinks immediately of Burckhardt and Usener), the concrete reality of the *Kulturwissenschaftliche Bibliothek Warburg* had now been transplanted to London. With the Library and the many thousands of photographs that were swiftly to grow into what is now the Photographic Collection, came a small body of scholars dedicated to the interdisciplinary study of the classical tradition. The challenge that faced them was that of integrating into English intellectual and cultural life, and adapting the values and method for which they stood to their new environment. This was not simply a question of translation.

The first thing that is noteworthy is the speed with which the Institute established itself as a centre of intellectual activity. Barely five months after leaving Hamburg it opened its doors in converted office premises in Thames House, Millbank. Fritz Saxl, director from the time of Warburg's death in 1929, who had overseen the move, observed that the new physical environment was in certain respects more practical than its Hamburg home: the shelves, and therefore the books themselves, were immediately adjacent to the reading room, as were also the rooms of the members of staff. Thus readers had easy access to the books and to the staff, "a desirable feature in a library which serves both educational purposes and purposes of research".[4]

The educational function that Saxl thus identifies was undoubtedly one of the major elements in ensuring that the Institute made its presence felt in London. In the spring and early summer of 1934, some informal lectures were held in German, mostly attended by Germans. That autumn, however, a much more ambitious programme of nineteen lectures was inaugurated, attracting a much larger audience of roughly equal numbers of English and Germans. Those who spoke were Roger Hinks on allegorical representations in ancient art, REW Flower on "Methods of Research in Mediaeval Manuscripts", Jean Seznec on "Renaissance Mythography in Humanism and Art", Fritz Saxl on "Humanism in Venetian Art", Ernst Cassirer on "The new ideal of truth in the seventeenth century" and Edgar Wind on "Doctrines of wit and enthusiasm in eighteenth-century English art and philosophy". In addition, Richard Salomon of Hamburg gave a three-week course on palaeography, and special lectures were delivered to even larger audiences by Father Gabriel Théry OP on the activities of Greek monks in Paris in the ninth century, and by Adolph Goldschmidt of Berlin on the influence of English art on the Continent in the Middle Ages.[5] It is clear from

---

[3] *A Bibliography on the Survival of the Classics*, I (London, The Warburg Institute, 1934), p. v.
[4] The Warburg Institute, *Annual Report 1934–1935* (London, 1935), p. 4.
[5] *Ibid.*, p. 5.

96 Nicholas Mann

such details both that the scholarly agenda of the Institute was faithful to the international and interdisciplinary principles of its founder, and that there was from the start in London a considerable degree of contact between German and British scholars. This was further enhanced by institutional links with the libraries of the British Museum and the Victoria and Albert Museum, with Dr Williams' Library and the Institute of Historical Research, by membership of the loan scheme operated by the National Central Library,[6] and by lectures given by members of the Institute elsewhere in Britain: by Cassirer in the Scottish universities, at All Souls College Oxford, and at Bedford College London; by Klibansky in Manchester, by Saxl and Wittkower at the Courtauld Institute and so on. Equally, the Institute became the regular meeting-place for a group of young British medieval scholars under the chairmanship of Beryl Smalley, inaugurating further fruitful collaboration between disciplines and traditions.[7]

At the end of July 1934 a special photographic exhibition—the first of many—was arranged for the International Congress of Anthropological and Ethnological Sciences, intended to demonstrate the connection between anthropological and historical studies. That year too, under Rudolf Wittkower's direction, great improvements were introduced into the Photographic Collection, which was noted as being "of considerable help in establishing contact with English and foreign students"; cooperation with the British Museum, the Courtauld Institute and the Witt Library enabled the Collection to expand with the new aim of becoming the visual counterpart of the library: "as the books give a picture of the history of the classical tradition in religion, art, literature and science, seen through the medium of words, so the collection of photographs will give a complementary picture through the medium of imagery".[8]

It was during this same first year that the Institute's publications entered a new phase with the appearance of the first volume of the *Bibliography on the Survival of the Classics*.[9] At the same time, ambitious plans for the future were announced, finances permitting: numerous works in hand, including the completion of Warburg's *Gesammmelte Schriften* with the ill-fated *Mnemosyne-Atlas* (finally published only in 2000), new series including Klibansky's *Plato Latinus*, new collaborative ventures such as a book on the *tondo*—the circular form—from Greek art to the end of the baroque period, more volumes in Saxl's *Catalogue of Astrological and Mythological Illuminated Manuscripts*, and an international Festschrift for Cassirer's sixtieth birthday, to be published by the Oxford University Press. Although not all the works planned were completed,

---

[6] The *Times Literary Supplement* of 11 Jan. 1936 noted with pleasure: "If other institutions have given a helping hand to the new guest, the guest has given a return by entering freely into the consortium of English libraries, making its books available to serious students elsewhere through the National Central Library's organization".

[7] *Annual Report 1934–35*, p. 6.

[8] *Ibid.*, p. 11

[9] See n.1 above; edited by H Meier, R Newald and E Wind, it covered the publications of 1931.

by 1940 the Institute had managed to publish no fewer than 11 volumes of its new *Studies*, including such major works as the first volume of Mario Praz's *Studies in Seventeenth-Century Imagery*, Wittkower's first volume of the *Catalogue Raisonné* of Poussin's drawings edited by Walter Friedlaender and Anthony Blunt, and Jean Seznec's *La survivance des dieux antiques*.[10]

Even such a summary list will suffice to suggest the quality and level of activity that the Institute had succeeded in maintaining from the very start of its English existence, and the extent to which it had rapidly become a focal point for collaboration between scholars of different nationalities and disciplines. Further proof may be adduced from a brief paper delivered to the XIVth Conference of the International Federation for Documentation by Anthony Blunt in 1938 under the title "A method of documentation for the Humanities". He describes Warburg's *Kulturwissenschaft* at some length, and concludes that "the ultimate aim of the method here indicated is to bring together material out of which it will be possible to compose a history of culture, on the basis of the history of the fine arts, in which men's ideas reach their most elaborate expression, their works being always interpreted in terms of the evidence supplied by their other activities".[11]

The programme of lectures and courses arranged by the Institute for 1936 and 1937 may serve as a striking indication of the way in which it maintained its momentum. In the first of these years, it combined Niels Bohr on "Some humanistic aspects of natural science" with EA Lowe on "Roman culture before and after the Carolingian Reform, as reflected in Latin Manuscripts" and Ernst Cassirer on "Critical idealism as a philosophy of culture"; in the following year Konrad Lorenz, Henri Focillon, Johan Huizinga, Ernst Kris and WG Constable all spoke on different aspects of the cultural function of play. Informal lectures followed by discussion were given by Jurgis Baltrusaitis, Francis Wormald and Edgar Wind on art-historical subjects in 1936, by Henri Focillon, Otto Brendel, Raymond Klibansky, Alexandre Koyré and Paul Schrecker on a wider range of historical and philosophical topics in 1937. In 1939 a series of eighteen lectures on "Aspects of French Civilization" was given by Otto Pächt, Beryl Smalley, George Clutton, Frances Yates, Anthony Blunt, Rudolf Wittkower, Roger Hinks and Isaiah Berlin (who replaced Edgar Wind, then in America, at the last moment). It is unnecessary to insist: long before the Institute explicitly articulated its teaching function,[12] it had already clearly defined an educational role

---

[10] Although Seznec's celebrated study was published in 1940, it was stranded at the warehouse of the Imprimerie Louis-Jean in Gap; it was only once the war was over, late in 1945, that it was possible to bring the copies to London.

[11] AF Blunt, "A method of documentation for the Humanities", offprint from *International Federation for Documentation (FID), XIVth Conference* (Oxford–London, 1938), CD 025.42:009 (Warburg Institute Archive, *Scrapbook*, 15).

[12] This was to come as a necessary consequence of its incorporation in the University of London in 1944: cf. Saxl in *Annual Report 1946–1947* (London, The Warburg Institute, 1947), p. 1: "research continues to be our main task, but for the members of staff opportunities will more readily present themselves for introducing younger students into their special field of learning and to supervise post-graduate work".

98 *Nicholas Mann*

for itself, and was introducing an English public to scholarship of the highest international standards.

It is also worth noting how the scholarly principles and methodological interests of the Institute could be brought to bear in what might be thought one of the most conventional of academic fields. At the 1939 meeting of the Classical Association, held at the Institute, the programme was firmly focused not on the classics, but on the classical tradition, with Wind speaking on method and Blunt on modern classicism; Pächt and Wittkower organised a photographic exhibition on *The Visual Approach to the Classics* to complement the day's discussions.[13]

Such photographic exhibitions were an important innovation. Indeed the distinguished art-critic Herbert Read wrote of what was probably the most significant of them, *English Art and the Mediterranean*, that it "creates a new technique, a new science, even a new art. Let us call it the art of visual education ... The Warburg method begins with an idea, and is the realisation of that idea in the plastic medium of photography".[14] In the early years of the war, the exhibition on *The Visual Approach to the Classics* originally mounted in 1939 was shown at the Courtauld Institute, and subsequently went on tour throughout England with considerable success.[15] Apparently even more successful was the exhibition on Indian art opened by the Secretary of State for India, Mr LS Amery, on 13 Nov. 1940. The fruit of cooperation with the India Society, the India Office, the Royal Asiatic Society and the Courtauld Institute, it "linked up well with the problems of the Institute in general, and enlarged its field. The photographs were of unusual beauty, and the spectator received, through careful use of headlines and captions, aesthetic impressions and instruction at the same time"; it too went on tour, and attracted over 14,600 visitors in Sunderland alone.[16]

A measure of the extent to which the Warburg Institute had by now become a recognised part of the English establishment is provided by a perhaps somewhat unlikely source: the *Lahore Civil and Military Gazette*. Under the heading "Indian Photographs for London", it announced: "A striking illustration of how the English continue their cultural interests unperturbed by the war is afforded by the Warburg Institute of Art, London, which has asked the Archaeological Department of the Government of India to supply as many photographs as possible of the Ghandara style of sculpture".[17]

---

[13] The programme of the meeting, held on 6 Jan. 1939, is inserted in the *Scrapbook* (see n. 9 above), p. 75; apart from those mentioned above, the speakers were Stephen Gaselee, GC Field and AW Byvanck.

[14] *The Listener*, 18 Dec. 1941; cf. *Scrapbook*, p. 88.

[15] *Warburg Institute Report, September 1939–June 1940* [typescript] (London, 1940) p. 5 (*Scrapbook*, p. 21).

[16] *Warburg Institute Report, June 1940–August 1941* [duplicated typescript] (London, 1941), pp. 1–2 (*Scrapbook*, p. 22).

[17] New Delhi, 11 April 1940, quoted by Saxl in *Report, 1939–1940*, p. 7 (*Scrapbook*, p. 21).

But an even more striking tribute is the success of the exhibition on *English Art and the Mediterranean*: in the depths of war, in December 1941, an international team of scholars, led by Saxl and Wittkower, brought home to an English public the "age-long impact of the Mediterranean tradition on the British mind":[18] the deep artistic roots that bind the island to the continent, and the rich texture of cultural connections over more than two thousand years. The anonymous reviewer in *The Times*, who was pleased to note that "even the type of *The Times*, contrasted with a sixteenth-century Italian fount, is an exhibit at the Warburg Institute", concluded that the exhibition, "which has no political purpose to serve, can give one good cause for satisfaction. To have absorbed through so many centuries so many riches, and to have converted them to things new, individual and intensely characteristic, ready to be sent on to new lands in new continents, is to have played the part of an interpreter which cannot have been in vain".[19] The Institute's role as cultural interpreter had thus reached a new peak in 1941; it was subsequently even to become a guardian of the national architectural heritage. The following year, the *Architectural Review*, mentioning the touring exhibitions and the Institutes campaign, under the auspices of the National Buildings Record, to photograph buildings and works of art particularly susceptible to destruction by bombing, declared that "the Warburg Institute is proving more and more of a blessing to live archaeology and history in England";[20] writing on the Public Building Record's exhibition at the National Gallery in the *Observer* for D Day (11 June 1944), Osbert Lancaster singles out for approval the Institute's undertaking of a complete photographic survey of St Paul's Cathedral.[21]

The transfer of 1933 may have seemed a one-sided affair. But it should be clear from what has already been said that the gift to Britain was already being amply repaid. There is one further outstanding aspect of the early activities of the Warburg Institute which is characteristic of its contribution to English culture, and that is the publication of its *Journal*. The Prospectus which announced it in 1937 did so in terms which evidently echo the organisation of the Institute's library, and are designed to make *Kulturwissenschaft* comprehensible to the English reader: ". . . the new Journal will take the study of Humanism, in the broadest possible sense, for its province. It will supply a common forum for historians of art, religion, science, literature, social and political life, as well as for philosophers and anthropologists. Humanism, viewed from so many different angles, will appear not as an established fact, but as a continuous challenge. To understand its failures and its achievements, it will be necessary to explore the

---

[18] See Saxl and Wittkower's Preface to the fully illustrated published version of the exhibition catalogue: *British Art and the Mediterranean*, by F Saxl and R Wittkower (London–New York–Toronto, Oxford University Press, 1948). The entire edition of 1,000 copies was sold out within a few months; it was reprinted in 1969.
[19] *The Times*, 4 Dec. 1941 (*cf. Scrapbook*, p. 86).
[20] *Architectural Review*, Aug. 1942 (*cf. Scrapbook*, p. 101).
[21] See press-cutting in Warburg Institute files.

working of classical symbols, the signs and images created by ancient and employed by modern generations as instruments of both enlightenment and superstition".[22]

The first volume of the *Journal of the Warburg Institute*, edited by Wittkower and Wind, appeared in 1937–38 and set standards which were hard to match. The first fascicle contained articles on "Sign and symbol" by Jacques Maritain, on Piero di Cosimo by Erwin Panofsky, on the Rood of Bromholm by Francis Wormald, and on "Alkestis in modern dress" by E M Butler, together with notes by Saxl, Wind, Gombrich, Salomon and others; the second had articles on "Rhetoric and politics in Italian humanism" by Delio Cantimori, on Italian teachers in Elizabethan England by Frances Yates, on the *Hypnerotomachia Poliphili* in seventeenth-century France by Anthony Blunt, and two "Studies in allegorical portraiture" by Edgar Wind, with notes by Saxl, Wind, Wittkower, Felix Gilbert, Napoleone Orsini and Alfred Einstein, and so on. Among other contributors to this first volume were Gertrud Bing, WS Heckscher, Adelheid Heimann, Roger Hinks, Ernst Kitzinger, Charles Mitchell and Jean Seznec.

Reviewing this remarkable volume, Roger Hinks (who was as we have seen himself a contributor) used the opportunity to explain to his readers the "aims and achievements of a body whose arrival in London has been universally welcomed, but whose purpose is still appreciated only by a rather restricted number of students who have had the good fortune to come into personal contact with the group of workers who accompanied the library when it migrated from Hamburg". He praised Warburg for resisting the rising tide of specialisation that had afflicted the historical sciences in Germany, and declared that "he perceived that the mere accumulation of facts, however necessary to the historian, must end by overwhelming him unless his research was guided by a clear insight into the meaning and value of history as a whole". The library that Warburg had created was therefore "not a mere instrument of history for history's sake, but an active organ for the discovery, the preservation and the regeneration of the spiritual life of Europe". Likewise, the *Journal* was "humanist in the best sense. Though it is written by specialists, it is refreshingly free from the spiritual provinciality of the average learned publication".[23] What he did not mention, perhaps because it was self-evident, was the fact that all the articles were in English, so that the non-specialist reader had access to the finest fruits of continental scholarship.

The *Journal* has continued to the present day. Anthony Blunt, who had become deputy director of the Courtauld Institute in 1939, and did much to cement relations between the two Institutes, joined the original editors from the second volume, and from the third (for 1939–40) onwards it was renamed the *Journal of the Warburg and Courtauld Institutes*. It continued through the war years to publish articles by the scholars who had first contributed to it, but also

---

[22] Cf. *Scrapbook*, p. 33.
[23] *The Spectator*, 9 Sept. 1938 (*Scrapbook*, p. 37).

by others: TRS Boase, Ernst Kantorowicz, Richard Krautheimer, John Pope-Hennessy, Nikolaus Pevsner, Nicolai Rubinstein, Meyer Schapiro, and Egon Wellesz, to mention but a few. Volume IX, for 1946, was an entirely Italian number with a Preface by Guido Calogero in which he sees the *Journal's* gesture towards Italy as one which has "strengthened the ancient ties between our two countries and reaffirmed once again the consciousness we share of the bond that unites all who study man's painful history and of the hope it gives for the future of humane civilization". The contributors included Giulio Carlo Argan, Augusto Campana, Fausto Ghisalberti and Arnaldo Momigliano, their topics ranging from antique sculpture to nineteenth-century historiography. Today, in its sixty-fourth year, the *Journal* continues to publish articles of the most varied cultural and intellectual interest by members of the Institute and scholars from all over the world.

Already in 1936, Saxl had been able to describe the success of the transfer to London in the following terms: "The Institute, taken as a collection of books, has become a member of the family of English libraries; the Institute's lectures show an increasing number of attendance; the Director and two of the Institute's collaborators have become members of the staff of the Universities of Oxford and London; in short, the Institute's place in the intellectual life of scholars in London and England at large is no longer a matter of dispute".[24]

To understand the impact of the details enumerated above, however, and to grasp the significance of what might be seen as Europe's contribution to Britain, we need to look more closely at the reception of the ideas that came with the books and the scholars who had so dramatically transplanted themselves to English soil. The incorporation of the Institute in the University of London was announced to the public on 12 December 1944, and *The Times* of that day declared that the news would be received "with gratitude and relief by all those interested in the history of art and the humanities", for the transfer to London had proved one of the most successful experiments in international collaboration in those fields. It noted how, "as a result of ten years of friendly and intimate contact with English scholars, [the Institute] has amalgamated its own traditions with English historical thought", and spoke of the opening of a new chapter: "The Institute has come of age, and members of its staff—scholars of British and German origin—will be called upon to put their experience in the methods of two countries at the disposal of the students of London University".[25]

More provocatively, John Russell, writing in *Time and Tide*, declared that "English art history does not exist in the sense that the history of the Cabinet system exists . . . The history of English art badly needs its Acton, its Bagehot, its Trevelyan and its Ensor; and its chance of getting them has been notably

---

[24] In *Appeal on behalf of the Warburg Library and Institute*, II, pp. 2–3 [duplicated typescript] (London, 1936; *cf. Scrapbook*, p. 26).
[25] *The Times*, 12 Dec. 1944; *cf.* press-cutting in Warburg Institute files.

increased by the incorporation . . . of the Warburg Institute within the academic structure of the University of London". He went on to praise the interdisciplinary nature of the Institute's concerns: "It applies its method to the study of the humanities in general, not only to the history of art, and its field is European civilization, not a particular branch of it in any one country. . . . Nor is this a matter of unsupported theory; since 1921 the Institute has published lectures and essays, and in this considerable body of work one may see the method in action not only in the investigation of Italian Renaissance art, but in the study of subjects as diverse as Senecan tragedy, Burgundian gothic and the work of Dante, Montaigne, Plato, Shaftesbury and Inigo Jones. Perusal of these volumes will show to what an extent the study of art is enriched if it is considered, not in isolation, but in relation to the general course of historical studies". The case for *Kulturwissenschaft* could hardly have been put more clearly, and he concludes: "now at last there is in England a research centre for the coordination of art history with the other humanities . . . which requires and can satisfy the highest standards of scholarship".[26]

These observations of more than half a century ago have stood the test of time. If, by the end of the Second World War, Warburg's method and the institution that he had created to further it had effectively become naturalised British citizens while yet remaining profoundly European in origins and outlook, the succeeding fifty-six years have confirmed that equilibrium. The essential institutional continuity is that of the Library. Warburg's fifty thousand books have multiplied more than sixfold. The Photographic Collection, embryonic in its Hamburg days, has likewise grown to over three hundred thousand images, a substantial number of them now forming an electronic database.[27] Now, as then, the Institute exists because it has these extraordinarily rich foundations for the research of those who work there, whether permanently or as visitors.

Lectures, seminars and colloquia continue apace, as do publications, with a focus that is above all scholarly, but with a range that remains, as it has always been, resolutely interdisciplinary. The kind of exchange that took place in the Hamburg library in the 1920s between scholars of different disciplines but of like minds, and that is exemplified by the publications of the Kulturwissenschaftliche Bibliothek Warburg, was immediately recreated by the distinguished series of lectures and publications that marked the Thames House years, and that continue today. A tradition of informal lectures followed by discussion, introduced in 1939 to encourage the exchange of ideas,[28] is maintained to this

---

[26] *Time and Tide*, 16 Dec. 1944; *cf*. press-cutting in Warburg Institute files.

[27] The *Census of Antique Works of Art and Architecture Known to the Renaissance*, containing some 25,000 images and 40,000 documents. It was formally inaugurated at a colloquium at the Warburg Institute on 19–21 Mar. 1992, and is now based at the Humboldt University in Berlin; for a recent account of its progress, *cf*. J B Trapp, "The Census: its Past, its Present and its Future", (1999)(1) *Pegasus. Berliner Beiträge zum Nachleben der Antike* 11–21.

[28] *Cf*. also the note on "Discussions" in the *Report 1939–40*, pp. 4–5: "In addition to these lectures, we started discussions at the beginning of the autumn. Informal lectures were followed by a discussion. The lecturers were glad of an opportunity to talk about the work they were engaged

day in the Institute, in particular in the Director's Work-in-Progress seminar, where the whole intellectual community gathers once a week in term-time to hear and discuss papers given by colleagues and by visitors. In addition, there are important developments that have come from the redefinition of the Institute's role brought about by its integration into the University of London: the creation of courses, principally for postgraduate students, and a thriving and ever expanding programme of visiting fellowships for young scholars of all nationalities. In this sense, the traffic is decidedly no longer one-way.

In attempting to sum up the effects of more than sixty-five years of English existence upon Warburg's original model, we may note that it is a necessary consequence of his and the Institute's interdisciplinary convictions that it has tended not to favour any one branch of study. It is, furthermore, not a shrine to its founder, but a constantly evolving scholarly community sensitive to the diverse interests of its own members. It would not now see itself, for instance, as an art-historical Institute, even though art history continues to be an important element in its teaching, its research and its publications. Instead, it has fostered the interests of those scholars who have been attached to it over the years. Many of these have left important traces in the Library, almost like strata in an archaeological site. The example of Henri Frankfort, director after Saxl from 1949 until 1954, springs to mind: his distinguished collection of books on the religion and social organization of the Ancient Near East has added a new element, as have those on Aristotelian philosophy bequeathed by Charles Schmitt. Figures such as EH Gombrich and Frances Yates have inevitably left their distinctive mark upon the library, the publications, and indeed upon the very image, of the Institute.

By now, "the Warburg" is an established and a familiar figure on the British cultural scene. Revered by many, particularly those who have worked in its collections, and who have loyally supported it by responding to appeals for money or for books; occasionally reviled by others, on account of what they see as its "exclusiveness" or its "positivism", it continues to train young scholars of high calibre, many of them teaching in other universities in England and abroad, and continues to generate and to publish research which might otherwise never see the light of day. That it is able to do so is a tribute to all those who have tended it on foreign soil, but is also a tribute to its continental origins, and its membership of a *République des Lettres* that was alive and well in the Weimar Republic, and that has survived into the twenty-first century.

In the 1930s the Institute's contribution might be described principally as one of intellectual importation, not least in the significant part that it played in the rescue of large numbers of refugee scholars.[29] At the beginning of the twenty-first century the traffic is much more perceptibly two-way. The Institute has

upon, and the audience of having interesting material put before them which they could discuss" (*Scrapbook*, p. 21).

[29] Copious evidence for this is to be found in the Archives of the Warburg Institute and of the Society for the Protection of Science and Learning, now in the Bodleian Library in Oxford.

links, formal and informal, with many institutions in Germany, France and Italy and elsewhere in Europe, and further afield, with which it exchanges publications, shares research projects and even on occasions courses. Scholars at all stages in their careers come to London from abroad to work in the Institute, and return home enriched by their research in Aby Warburg's extraordinary library; in particular, the Institute's annual programme of research fellowships enables some twenty young scholars to come to London to pursue their work at pre- and postdoctoral level, an experience which changes many of their lives, and which again is almost always exported to their countries of origin. The Institute was actively involved in aspects of the restoration of its original domicile in Hamburg, now reborn as the Warburg-Haus, and is even one of the main models being studied by the commission established to develop a new national institute for art history in Paris.

With this, the wheel might be said to have turned almost full circle: the Institute is giving back to Europe what Europe once gave to Britain. But the nature of this particular contribution, vital for the strengthening of a sense of common cultural and intellectual purpose across the old barriers of nation and language, is such that it is both intangible and yet, for all its continental origins, ineffably English in its underfunding and its understated scholarly pragmatism.

7

Freedom of the Press and Intellectual Interchange

ONORA O'NEILL

1 THE END OF CENSORSHIP?

Freedom of expression and freedom of the press are among the most revered and least questioned intellectual and political legacies of the Enlightenment. The documents that first proclaimed their importance remain cultural landmarks: Milton's *Aeraeopagitica,* the First Amendment of the US Constitution and John Stuart Mill's *On Liberty* are peaks in a great tradition. They are still admired and cited, taught and read.

The continuing vitality of these ideals is readily explained. Even today censorship is not a distant memory. For much of the twentieth century, wars and emergencies gave all governments (including democratic governments) reason to restrict freedom of the press and of expression to a greater or lesser extent. Beyond the democracies restrictions on both were ubiquitous, relentless and often frightening. The courage of the intellectuals of the formerly Communist world who collected and transcribed forbidden information and literature, and laboriously transmitted it through samizdat publications, is legendary. They developed demanding views on the responsibilities of intellectuals within oppressive regimes,[1] and risked a lot to live up to those ideals. Their work deserves admiration even if more democratic politics have made it obsolete. The commitment of liberals within democracies who supported these efforts from afar, and worked to end remnants of censorship nearer home, is also still a living memory. Meanwhile censorship or partial censorship still remains a daily practice in many undemocratic or partly democratic regimes.[2] Judged against this background, the recent reduction of censorship in many states is evidence of a continuing, but still quite incomplete transition towards a less oppressive social and political order in which freedom of expression and freedom of the press are increasingly respected.

---

[1] See the essays in *The Political Responsibility of Intellectuals,* I Maclean, A Montefiore and P Winch (eds.), (Cambridge, Cambridge University Press, 1990).
[2] Freedom House provides an *Annual Survey of Press Freedom* in different states. In 2000 it found that only 69 of 186 states had a wholly free press. See www.freedomhouse.org.

These ideals arose in a world in which the censors who prevented free communication could usually be clearly identified. Typically Church and State worked in tandem. They united to censor from the *ancien regime* to Tsarist Russia, from Kant's Prussia to 1950s Ireland. However, many states censored long after they had stopped taking Church instruction on what to censor. Images of the journalist, the writer and the ordinary citizen who speak out against abuse and oppression, who speak truth to power, were formed in a world of religious and secular powers that combined to control and censor. The case for speaking out in defiance of censors, often at great personal risk, was repeatedly stated and argued right through this period, perhaps most recently by Vaclav Havel.[3]

This image of writers and journalists as heroes who speak truth to power often outlasts the censorship that made free speech risky or impossible, and speaking out heroic. We think of Charles Dickens writing against the abuses of the Industrial Revolution, or of IF Stone publishing his weekly round-up of significant news that other journalists and papers failed to publish during the Vietnam War. Although each spoke out on matters that some powerful persons would have preferred not to see published, each was in fact admired rather than punished or censored for doing so. Investigative journalists in democracies still draw on the credit established by past resistance and heroism. On the whole they now face censorship only at second hand—for example, when they report on events abroad that would incur censorship if reported there. They may lose their accreditation but not, on the whole, their lives or reputations. If we still admire such writers and journalists, it is less because we think their defiance heroic than because we think, or hope, that they may report facts or correct falsehoods that might otherwise persist.

2 INFORMATION TECHNOLOGY AND GLOBALISATION

Since the ideals of freedom of expression and press freedom were first promulgated and popularised, the contexts in which they serve and are prized have changed in radical ways. In my view some recent changes are so profound that they provide persuasive reasons for rethinking the role and importance of both ideals, and in particular for rethinking our views on freedom of the press. I shall sketch these changes and then suggest some of their implications for arguments about freedom of expression and freedom of the press.

The changes that I have in mind are both technical and commercial, changes in information technologies and in transnational commerce. The changes bear more deeply on freedom of the press than on self-expression, because some self-expression (and a small range of communication) does not depend on technolo-

---

[3] V Havel, 'The Power of the Powerless' in *Living in Truth*, P Wilson (trans.), J Vladislav (ed.), (London, Faber and Faber, 1986), 36–122.

gies. Face-to-face speech needs nothing beyond the human voice and a shared language. Everything else needs technologies, ranging from the quill pen to the Internet. During the twentieth century new technologies reshaped communication, and especially mass communication, without altering its unidirectional character. Sound broadcasting, film and television all reinforced the one-way communication characteristic of print journalism and publishing. These media allow an active writer or journalist, publisher or producer, and those who pay or control them, to address a largely passive reader, listener or viewer, who cannot answer back. (Letters to the editor, phone-in programmes, rights of reply and the like provide only trivial correctives to the one-sidedness of mediated communication.) Like traditional publishing, the new twentieth century technologies were agreeable for censors, who had only to control a small number of communicators to censor the information and views available to all readers, listeners and viewers, and their opportunities for all forms interchange and discussion. Of the early twentieth century communication technologies, only the telephone provided a new form of two-way communication, but it did not undermine the possibility of censorship. The telephone was (until very recently) suitable only for communication between two individuals; it was expensive; like other early twentieth century communication technologies it was ideal for central control. Telephony could be controlled by making it difficult and expensive to obtain a line and by preventing publication of telephone numbers (as in all former Socialist countries); and it was perfect for covert surveillance.

In the last twenty years of the twentieth century, communication technologies that allow more two-way communication have been widely welcomed for shifting excess power away from editors and publishers, producers and writers, and those who pay and control them. Can we expect the newer communication technologies to defeat the ambitions of would-be censors by dispersing communicative power across entire populations? There are some hopeful signs. Barely a decade ago the project of dominating all mass communication, so controlling all public access to information and all public discussion still seemed feasible. It was widely pursued, particularly by elites in socialist and less developed economies. The fantasy began to crumble with the widespread use of faxed communication to disseminate information about events in Tienamen Square within China. Effective censorship, it seemed, was not compatible with new forms of IT, nor therefore with economic modernisation. A decade later the economic and social costs of doing without the new technologies were huge and obvious: it is increasingly likely that only those so poor that they lack electricity will be effectively excluded.[4]

The new technologies seem to promise a transformation in the power relations that underlie communication because they support a wide range of relatively cheap forms of two-way communication at a distance, from which people can only be excluded at very high cost. Cheaper telephony, the photocopier and

---

[4] Many more will be excluded from the Internet; hence fears about a persisting "digital divide".

the fax machine, the personal computer and e-mail seemingly have the potential to shift the balance of power. Taken together they produce severe problems for would-be censors. Above all the Internet seems to expand possibilities for citizens to gain access to information and to communicate with one another, so also to undermine would-be censors or "gatekeepers", who try to monitor or control, edit or filter.

This enthusiastic view of new technologies as undermining old controls is convincing, as far as it goes. But the picture is incomplete without taking account of the deep ways in which these technologies, and their global reorganisation, also transform communication. In particular, the optimistic picture overlooks the fact that the Internet purveys disinformation and misinformation as readily as it purveys correct information, and that it has no internal disciplines by which false, dangerous or duplicitous content can be removed or discredited. Websites need not provide any apparatus or structure, evidence or credentials by which those who stumble upon them can judge the reliability of their contents. Search engines are not devices for reaching the most important or reputable sites dealing with a topic. Self-selection of mutually reinforcing (mis)information sources can shield people from the challenge of differing views. Favourite websites foster only favourite views. The Internet and the proliferation of specialised TV channels also both permit and even encourage relentlessly monotonous communication—whether of pornography or stock exchange news, of sport or shopping. Of course, the mixed diet offered by newspapers or broadcasters that have to satisfy wider audiences has also always purveyed some misinformation and disinformation, but their readers, listeners and viewers have been more likely to encounter material that goes beyond, even challenges, their favourite topics and views, better able to judge a range of issues, and more likely to hear the news if outrageous misrepresentations are noted and challenged. Too narrow reading, listening and viewing may be damage and discourage intellectual interchange. In the past sectarian censors might have done the damage; now focussed marketing of communication products can do it.

The new information technologies may be anti-authoritarian; but curiously they are often also anti-democratic. I say this because they undermine the ordinary processes by which citizens judge one another's claims, and decide when and whether to accept one another's testimony. Our ordinary processes for judging what we hear or read are immensely complex.[5] In face-to-face communication, and in much traditional written communication, we backtrack and ask questions, demand to know some of the evidence and try to work out the reliability and authority of speakers, writers, and sources. By contrast, websites that post misinformation, or even deliberately falsify, are accessible to millions and can assert their claims unchallenged. They can disrupt and undermine capacities

---

[5] C A J Coady, *Testimony* (Oxford, Oxford University Press, 1992); P Lipton, "The Epistemology of Testimony", (1998) 29 *Studies in the History and Philosophy of Science* 1–31.

to evaluate evidence, to discriminate among sources and to engage in fruitful exchange.[6] This may not matter for members of well-educated and well-informed elites who know how to access more reliable sources of information and how to check and judge differing sorts and sources of information; it can matter for those less well-informed or educated.[7]

One might imagine, and hope, that the deficits in the reliability and assessability of information, misinformation and disinformation available on many websites would be balanced by the fact that print and broadcast media are also available, read, heard and viewed. Cannot these more established modes of mass communication continue to support readers' and viewers' capacities to discriminate sense from rubbish, significance from trivia, whatever their sources?

Unfortunately the new information technologies and global commercial structures that are epitomised in the Internet and the digital revolution are also transforming other print and broadcast media in ways that can burden and disorient readers, listeners and viewers. Newspapers now compete not only for local or regional readers, but also electronically and globally. Media conglomerates own publishing houses, newspapers, TV channels and online services; they can market the same content in differing formats for different audiences; satellite and digital technologies allow them to compete to become global providers.[8] These new technologies and global ambitions favour the manufacture and marketing of communication "products" rather than serious—let alone intellectual!—interchange. Distinctions between news copy and advertising copy are blurred; the commercial interests of media conglomerates may influence editorial policies. Editorial talent can be lavished on the endless packaging and repackaging of content for print and electronic products, rather than on the content itself. Sources may be obscure and repetition of programme content and "messages" may substitute for more convincing sorts of authority. No wonder readers, listeners and viewers are hard pushed to judge what is served up to them.

The new information technologies have so far had rather different effects on print and on broadcasting. Publishers and newspapers have yet to find convincing business models for the electronic age: they produce on-line editions but still depend on newsprint and newsstands, on books and bookshops. The financial pressures on them are acute. Newspapers often struggle to retain readers—all too often by relentlessly increasing lifestyle, gossip and "infotainment" pages, while cutting expensive items like the salaries of overseas and specialist

---

[6] See R Wachbroit "Reliance and Reliability: The Problem of Information on the Internet", (2000) 20 *Report from the Institute for Philosophy and Public Policy*, University of Maryland 9–15, which discusses the consequences of anonymous posting of misinformation and disinformation and the prospects of informational fragmentation.

[7] See G Walden *The New Elites: Making a Career in the Masses* Allen Lane (London, The Penguin Press, 2000).

[8] For a recent survey of concentration of ownership see B H Bagdikian, *The Media Monopoly*, 6th Edition (Boston, Mass, Beacon Press, 2000).

reporters who understand some of the more difficult areas that have to be covered.[9] Globalisation is tough for newspapers: there won't be many winners of the competition to become the first global newspaper. Globalisation is also tough for publishers: failures and mergers are frequent, thinly masked by the retention of familiar names as "imprints". By contrast, globalisation is not so damaging to the standard business model and practices of the broadcast media, although competition among providers may be devastating. Both reach and penetration can be expanded without fundamental changes. Yet from the point of view of listeners and viewers the impact of globalised broadcasting may be more noticeable: a choice between the blandly packaged listening and viewing offered by mass channels, and the narrow focus listening and viewing offered by specialist channels.

The new information order is swirling around us, but it is still very unclear whether it will produce the increase in genuine, important two-way communication for which enthusiasts hope. It may do more to produce greater parity, indeed similarity, in one-way mass communication, particularly of advertising, gossip, sports reporting and "infotainment" copy, as well as of soaps, image making and selection of news "stories". It may simultaneously produce greater disparity as specialist channels and websites fragment audiences. No previous culture or technology has made it possible—indeed easy—to consume a non-stop diet of westerns, or stock market news, or pornography.

If global mass communications develops along these lines, viewers, listeners and readers will escape the censors only at high cost. The great media conglomerates will control the technologies, and the ways in which information, misinformation and disinformation are formatted and disseminated. This will indeed undermine the old forms of censorship, by which states controlled their citizens. The new controllers of communication will not censor: they will simply control the manner and content of communication. They will *of course* support the forms of freedom of expression and freedom of the press that were traditional liberal aspirations. Citizens will find that their sources of information and means of communication are uncensored; but they will also find that both are structured and organised to reflect others' choices and agendas. The demise of censorship may not launch an age of open communication and democracy, or of wider opportunity for intellectual interchange: rather it may mark the emergence of new forms of unaccountable power.

3 THE INFORMATION REVOLUTION AND THE RISE OF SCANDAL

Gossip, in particular gossip about scandals, was traditionally a pursuit of small groups—from the parish to the court. One of the more surprising effects of the

---

[9] M Janeway, *Republic of Denial: Press, Politics, and Public Life* (New Haven, Conn., Yale University Press, 1999).

changes produced by the new media culture is that gossip and scandal have transferred extraordinarily well to the new media technologies and to a global scale. The new technologies may have made state censorship less common and less effective; but they support a growing focus on scandal, that has been matched or manifest in a rising "crisis of trust".

In Britain, in particular, the media (including the "quality" press) is increasingly "tabloidised". It focuses more on scandal and sensation and less on reporting. Much of the scandal-mongering would fit round any parish pump, with the difference that the chances of any reader or listener being able to judge what is and what is not true are less. Scandal and sensation have become genres in their own right: they provide a template for discussion and representation of many issues that can marginalise the traditional disciplines of accurate reporting. A particularly striking instance of the growth of media sensationalism in areas where accurate reporting is quite important was the coverage of GM crops in the summer of 1999. This coverage has been carefully documented and assessed by the *Parliamentary Office of Science and Technology* in a Report[10] showing that a number of newspapers gave up any semblance of objective reporting on the issues, in favour of sensationalised campaigning against GM crops. This is not an isolated finding. A more general survey of the changing content and standards of British newspapers recently showed that they have become more scandal ridden and sensationalising than newspapers elsewhere.[11] More reporting takes the form of "stories", often "stories" that supposedly expose something discreditable or scandalous; and the standards to which writing about scandals aspires are not high.[12] This may be a fair enough approach when there are scandals to report, but misleads in other cases. Surveys of the perceived quality of television production report a similar lowering of standards.[13] Somewhat different problems are reported elsewhere, for example US commentators have noted that the boundary between newspaper and advertising copy is often blurred—as has long been the case in US television programming. Readers, listeners and viewers who note an increase in reported scandal and sensation might reach various conclusions. Perhaps there are in fact more scandals, and the reporting is accurate; perhaps there is no more scandal or sensation, but a greater tendency to format "stories" as scandals. Given that the evidence presented could look very similar in the two cases, it is often not easy to tell what has happened.

For example, some current discussions of the "crisis of public trust" assume that there is a genuine increase in untrustworthy behaviour, especially by

---

[10] *Parliamentary Office of Science and Technology*, 138, 2000, *The "Great GM Food Debate": a survey of media coverage in the first half of 1999.*
[11] H A Semetko, "Great Britain: The End of News at Ten and the Changing News Environment" in *Democracy and the Media: A Comparative Perspective*, R Gunther and A Mugham (eds.), (Cambridge, Cambridge University Press, 2000).
[12] J B Thompson, *Political Scandal* (Cambridge, Polity Press, 2001).
[13] S Dex and E Sheppard, *Perceptions of quality in television production* (Cambridge, Judge Institute for Management Studies, 2000).

professionals and holders of public office. More scandal is reported because there is more scandal to report; mistrust in doctors and scientists is more reported because they are less trustworthy; mistrust in politicians is more reported because they are less trustworthy, and so on. The claims that various office holders and professionals are less trustworthy is supposedly confirmed by numerous MORI polls[14] that have surveyed public trust on one area or another, which show the extent to which the public place trust in politicians, or scientists, or industry, or hospitals. However MORI polls in recent years also show that none of these groups is nearly as widely mistrusted as newspaper journalists are themselves mistrusted, indeed that no group—not even politicians—is more mistrusted than newspaper journalists (television commentators ("news readers") are more trusted). A careful look at numerous public opinion polls also shows that the public is often a great deal more discriminating in placing its trust than the selected highlights typically reported suggest. Given that mistrust in the media is so high, it is difficult to know how far to credit its avid reporting of mistrust of others. Since members of the public can hardly avoiding placing their trust somewhere, for quite practical purposes, the main effect of incessant reports of scandal and mistrust has been less a simple decline in public trust, than an atmosphere in which trust is mingled with suspicion and placed with misgivings, in which reports and allegations are half believed but also readily discounted and brushed aside. This is a dangerous and familiar pattern. The shepherd boy who shouted "Wolf! Wolf!" falsely could not attract help when a real wolf came: in a world in which too much is presented as scandal, it will be hard to convince anybody by reporting real scandal.

RETHINKING FREEDOM OF THE PRESS

I have suggested that new information technologies and processes of globalisation are likely to disrupt and displace old practices of censorship. But I do not think that we can confidently conclude that a global information order will be ethically superior to the older world of state censorship confronted by heroic dissidents and investigators. On the contrary, there are reasons to fear that in the new conditions freedom of expression and freedom of the press may no longer constitute adequate ethical standards for public communication. We may need to rethink the norms appropriate for communication in quite radical ways. Freedom of expression will, I believe retain its ethical importance in the new information age; but freedom of the press will need serious reformulation.

The reason why freedom of expression will remain important is that it provides a profound form of protection for individuals. We know quite well that individuals may use their freedom of expression to say and write things that are false or ludicrous, deranged or irrelevant, badly reasoned or offensive.

---

[14] For summaries of many MORI Polls see http://www.mori.com/polls/index_pl.shtml.

Nevertheless there are powerful reasons for thinking that protection for individual freedom of expression matters, and that only self-expression that risks serious harm to others should be prevented by law (shouting fire in a crowded theatre; libel and slander; hate speech and incitement). However freedom of expression is for individuals, not for institutions. Organisations, media conglomerates included, do not have or need a right to self-expression, let alone to unlimited freedom of self-expression. The case for freedom of the press is not that the press has a right to freedom of expression.

There are two powerful and well-known arguments for freedom of the press. The first of these is that freedom of the press is a mean to truth and discovery; the second is that freedom of the press is necessary for open communication, public debate and interchange. Neither line of argument can establish a case for unlimited freedom of the press.

It is clearly true that some sorts of freedom of the press support the discovery of truth. For example, science could not proceed without freedom to publish experimental results. However the importance of freedom of publication as a means to truth cannot easily be generalised into an argument to freedom of the press for activities that do not aim at truth, let alone for activities that aim to deceive. At best the thought that conjecture and refutation, trial and error may help to test opinions can license the publication of speculation and falsehood with the ultimate aim of testing and disclosing truth. But this of course is not equivalent to a general licence to publish falsehood without any further aim of correction or inquiry. Just as commodity markets fail when vendors are wholly at liberty to falsify product information, so the supposed marketplace of ideas will fail if invention and passing off, deception and falsification are not disciplined. In any case where the media aim to entertain and to make money, to influence or to shock, no argument for freedom of the press as means to truth will reach far enough.

The second (and in my view far the more significant) argument in favour of freedom of the press is that it is essential for communication among members of the public. Freedom of the press is needed not for any range of outcomes or results—truth, justice, or even revelation—but for the very process of communication itself. This argument is the more important because it applies not only to those forms of communication that are mainly aimed at acquiring truth, but also at those that aim at enjoyment or entertainment, at persuasion or mobilisation. However if the basis for freedom of the press is that it contributes to communication, then too there can be no unrestricted right to freedom of the press. In particular there can be no justification of freedom to communicate in ways that undermine or damage the possibility and the standards of communication. Those who aim to communicate—whether their intended audience is large or small, homogeneous or diverse, known or unknown—must meet two standards. They must try to be *accessible* or intelligible to those whom they take to constitute their audience; and they must aim to make what they communicate *assessable* by that audience. These tasks have always been much harder for written than for spoken communication, and much harder for communication with strangers than for communication with the like-minded.

Communication without constraints that make it accessible to and assessable by its intended audiences dims the possibility of discussion and interchange, of debate and inquiry. If it is not readily assessable by its audiences, it fails as communication. Freedom of the press cannot reasonably be construed as including the freedom to undermine possibilities of communication. That thought had a clear interpretation in a past in which censors and oppression undermined communication. The new electronic media in their globalising deployment are cavalier about these elementary requirements in different ways. They increasingly lack conventions and genres, standards and disciplines that enable their audiences to feel not only that they can follow the gist of what is being presented, but that they have some ways of gripping and testing what is presented.

It is not particularly difficult to begin a sketch of what is needed to improve matters. We need to develop some clarity about the minimal standards that must be embodied in communication that is accessible and assessable, and some easier ways of telling when those standards are met. We need to develop ways of refereeing websites and channels, and of questioning self-conferred reputations. This task may not be much easier than the ending of censorship, which has been achieved only by curbing unaccountable powers. The global media—for all their glitz and glamour, for all their wealth and hype—are new unaccountable powers. In the very decades in which many—though not all—office holders and professionals have become more accountable and are more stringently audited, the globalising media have achived a remarkable lack of accountability, which they claim in the name of a usurped and obsolescent conception of press freedom.

These remedies cannot be achieved by any exercise of power. They are I think the tasks of the academy in the broadest sense of the term. That is to say that they are the tasks not only of the literary and scientific communities and the universities, but of serious publishers and producers, of learned societies and—yes—of those who hope to construct worthwhile portals on the Internet. These are the bodies best placed to develop and foster conventions by which audiences can gain, or regain, some grip on the adequacy and inadequacy of different presentations, so that those presentations can be judged. A large question, to my mind, is whether this can be done while maintaining a view of press freedom that is totally permissive about the publication and dissemination of misinformation and disinformation. When everyone and anyone is able to send words fatherless into the world, truth and trust are both endangered.

8

Insiders and Outsiders

JOHN ELLIOTT

Around the year 2050 a team of European historians, working in the now well-established collective tradition of Euro-subsidised scholarly inquiry, will launch yet another of the innumerable surveys periodically required by Brussels into the past, present and future of the humanities, culture and the arts. The team's assignment will be to evaluate the distinctive characteristics of the various national schools of historical writing during the twentieth century, and the degree to which they helped or hindered a proper understanding of the European past. When eventually completed, the report will comment approvingly on the technical advances achieved over the course of the century in many branches of historical scholarship, and on the broadening of its traditional range to include hitherto unexplored areas of social and cultural history. But it will also contain some sharp critical comments on the narrowness of vision imposed by national agendas and national historical traditions. It will deplore the absence of a European dimension to so many of the books and articles examined, and the tendency to study the past of each of the national states—Britain, the Netherlands, France or Spain—as an island unto itself. Some of its harshest words will be devoted to the theme of national exceptionalism and to the intense preoccupation with topics of purely parochial interest. Each society, it will conclude, assiduously cultivated its own backyard, with little or no regard for its neighbours. Such narrow parochialism, although happily diminishing, ought to have no place in the integrated Europe of the mid-twenty-first century.

No doubt many of the strictures passed on twentieth-century historical writing will prove to be well deserved. The evolution of Europe into a society of nation-states had, as its inevitable companion, the evolution of national historiographies. The exploration, understanding, and construction—and sometimes the deconstruction—of the national past provided sustenance, and a *raison d'être,* for generations of historians. Nor, it would seem, did the creation of a European community lead to any sudden and dramatic change. Old practices die hard, and especially hard when it comes to historians, whose gaze is professionally fixed on the past. Yet, as they come to examine the record of British historical writing in the twentieth century, our Euro-historical team may be prepared to introduce a few qualifications. The exceptionalism, they will find, is there in full measure—the assumption of a unique (and until the final decades of the twentieth century uniquely successful) national history. So too is the parochialism, the almost obsessive concern with a number of well-worn topics, like the origins of the English Civil War, studied in an almost exclusively English context. Yet at the same time they will find that there were many important twentieth-century British scholars in the humanities who devoted their careers to the culture and history of continental European societies, rather than to those of their native land.

Looking down the list of deceased Fellows of the British Academy over the past century it is not hard to compile a distinguished roll-call of scholars of continental Europe. Among historians it would include CR Boxer for Portugal and the Netherlands, Michael Roberts for Sweden, EH Carr for Russia, CA Macartney for Hungary, Steven Runciman and RW and Hugh Seton-Watson for south-eastern Europe, James Joll for Germany, Richard Cobb for France . . . A no less distinguished, and considerably longer, list could be compiled of British scholars alive today who have made and are continuing to make an outstanding contribution to the study of the history and culture of one or another continental European society. It is an impressive record, and one that would, I believe, be difficult to parallel among continental scholars. It is sufficient to recall the name of Elie Halévy to appreciate how few foreign scholars have made a comparable contribution to the study of the history of the British Isles. He stands on a pinnacle by himself.

How are we to explain this long-standing determination of a respectable number of British scholars to immerse themselves in the study of a continent traditionally isolated from these islands by fog? Is it possible to characterise the nature of the contribution they found themselves able to make? And can we assume that this contribution will continue to grow over the course of the present century? None of these questions is easily answered, and the best I can do is to approach them by briefly surveying the past and the present of my own area of interest, Hispanic studies, before attempting to examine the crystal ball in the hope of discerning future prospects.

British interest in the Iberian peninsula goes back to the seventeenth and eighteenth centuries, when the first intrepid travellers braved the dangers of Spanish roads and the horrors of Spanish inns to explore a land which they tended to see as both backward and un-European in comparison with the societies of the north. Acquaintance with, and interest in, Spain and Portugal was immeasurably increased by the participation of British armies in the Peninsular War. The more exotic aspects of Spanish life and civilisation held a fascination for the Romantic poets and their generation, whose enthusiasm for the plays of Calderón was to have an enduring impact on the study of Spanish literature in Britain. During the nineteenth century public interest was sustained by the books of Richard Ford, George Borrow and Sir William Stirling Maxwell, the author of *Annals of the Artists of Spain*, while the universities began to make provision for the study of Spanish language and literature, initially by appointing teachers from the Spanish community that settled in England as a result of the Liberal diaspora. It was not, however, until the appointment of a Fellow of this Academy, James Fizmaurice-Kelly, to the Gilmour professorship of Spanish in Liverpool in 1909, and subsequently to the Cervantes Chair at King's College, London, in 1916, that Hispanic Studies can be said to have become a serious university subject in this country.[1]

The study of Spanish literature was to be professionalised in Britain well before the study of Spanish history. In the generation after Fizmaurice-Kelly another Fellow of the Academy, Sir Henry Thomas, principal keeper of printed books at the British Museum, made a notable contribution both as a bibliographer and translator, while departments of Spanish began to proliferate in British universities. An impressive group of Hispanists emerged from these departments, and made a remarkable contribution to the knowledge and understanding of Spanish literature, and especially the literature of the Golden Age, during the second half of the twentieth century.

By contrast, Spanish history remained for much longer the province of romantically-inclined amateurs, like Martin Hume in the early years of the century or Sir Charles Petrie in its middle years, and its development as an academic subject came largely in the period after the end of the Second World War. In an unpublished letter of 1903 Fitzmaurice-Kelly, who himself looks in retrospect more like the last of the gentlemen scholars than the first of the professionals, had some scathing comments to make about Martin Hume, a historian always attracted by the more picturesque aspects of the Spanish past: "Have you read *Queens of Old Spain*? I can't imagine what devil has entered into Hume. Courtships of Queen Elizabeth, love affairs of Mary Queen of Scots, wives of Henry VIII (with scandal about poor Catherine of Aragon), Queens of Old Spain, and now Fashions and Femininity: I don't like the look of all this, and should put it down as senile erotomania. But then the public likes it, and the public can't be made up of erotomaniacs? . . ."[2]

Looking back over the record, it would be fair to say that a powerful dose of romanticism stimulated the rise of British Hispanism, and to some extent helped maintain it well into the twentieth century. Literary and historical studies both felt its influence. Spain looked excitingly colourful and mysterious to those who were tired of the greyness of the British skies, and were growing disillusioned with the increasing drabness and uniformity of western civilisation. For some of them, too, there was the pull of religion. Here was a country that had remained true to its traditional values and beliefs at a time when most of Europe was succumbing to a creeping process of secularisation. At once part of Europe and yet in many ways mysteriously un-European, Spain possessed the combined advantages of proximity and strangeness.

---

[1] For the early history of British Hispanism see A Pastor, "Breve historia del hispanismo inglés", (1948) X *Arbor*, and I Michael, "Afterword: Spanish at Oxford 1595–1998", (1999) LXXVI *Bulletin of Hispanic Studies* 173–193. On the formation of foreign images of Spain, including the British image, see JN Hillgarth, *The Mirror of Spain, 1500–1700* (Ann Arbor, University of Michigan Press, 2000).
[2] King's College London, archive correspondence of J Fitzmaurice-Kelly, ref. 21/10, fol. 2v (letter to David Hannay, 4 Dec. 1903). I owe this reference to the kindness of Professor Barry Ife.

No doubt other parts of southern and eastern Europe offered comparable attractions to nineteenth and early twentieth century British scholars and writers, whether professional or amateur. Instinctive curiosity, a romantic quest for the exotic and the different, the search for one's own, or an alternative, identity—all these can stimulate engagement with a society other than one's own. Whether these were particularly compelling considerations for the inhabitants of these islands, and, if so, why this should have been, remains far from clear. A readiness to explore other cultures and civilisations may simply reflect the resources and opportunities open to amateurs and professionals alike in a society that for long enjoyed the material and psychological benefits of global dominance, and continued to draw on those diminishing assets in the long after-glow of empire. Wealthy societies can afford the luxury of "non-essential" research. The effect, in any event, was to open windows onto foreign worlds.

But what can an outsider do that an insider cannot? If one can extrapolate from the experience of British historians of Spain during the second half of the twentieth century, the impact and effectiveness of an external contribution to the scholarship of another country are likely in large measure to be determined by its political, cultural and economic situation at a given moment. Those of us, like Sir Raymond Carr and myself, who entered the field of Spanish history in the 1950's, turned out to be very fortunate in our timing. This was post-Civil War Spain, an impoverished and isolated country, governed by a regime which suppressed free speech. It did so in order to defend allegedly transcendental Spanish values against the attacks of foreign and internal enemies, and it took special pride in proclaiming that Spain was "different".

The poverty of post-war Spain meant that few historians had the resources or the leisure to undertake sustained archival research in a country rich in archives. At the same time, its isolation meant that native historians lacked the opportunity for foreign travel, and were prevented by censorship from keeping abreast of the latest trends in European culture and historiography, many of which were anathema to the regime because of their Marxist or *marxisant* character. While one or two outstanding native historians succeeded, in spite of these obstacles, in shaping their own agendas, they were working against the grain in a political climate in which the emphasis was relentlessly placed by a triumphalist regime on Spanish exceptionalism.

As outsiders, those of us who decided to embark on research into the history either of early modern, or of modern and contemporary, Spain, arrived in the country bringing with us a very different set of attitudes and assumptions. Influenced, to a greater or lesser extent, by the dominant trends—largely French—in European historiography, although filtering these influences through a strong dose of British empiricism, we found it impossible to accept the thesis of Spanish exceptionalism, whether in its triumphalist form, as purveyed by the regime, or in its fatalist form, as expounded by a liberal tradition obsessed by what it saw as the congenital failure of Spain to follow the rest of Europe and move down the road to modernity. The cult of honour, for instance, or the habit of idleness—both of them traditionally singled out as causes of Spain's decline—were hardly unique to Early Modern Spanish society. For us, viewing Spain from the outside and not the inside, it was the similarities of the Spanish historical experience to that of other parts of Europe, rather than the differences, that impressed. Our task therefore became one of placing the history of Spain in a wider, European, context, showing the analogies but at the same time identifying the differences, and seeking to explain them.

This external vision, sustained and promoted from within by a handful of native historians in so far as their situation allowed, was to have a dramatic impact on the development of Spanish historical writing. As the censorship began to be relaxed, and a new, post-Civil War generation of historians emerged, the agenda of Spanish historiography started to move away from its traditional preoccupations, in response to the new influences from abroad. With Spain's return to democracy in 1975, the process of modernisation and Europeanisation became unstoppable. A quarter of a century later, it can safely be said that professional history in Spain is of the same quality as professional history in the western world as a whole, and reflects the same preoccupations and influences. Its history has become—perhaps indeed now to an excessive degree—the history of one more European state.

It will be clear from this necessarily rapid and schematic survey of half a century of historiography, that, in so far as it was possible for British historians to make a contribution, the opportunities for this were favoured by a set of circumstances that, we may hope, will not repeat themselves in the Europe of the twenty-first century. The combination of political repression and cultural isolation had made it difficult, or impossible, for native scholars and intellectuals to become acquainted with, and assimilate, the new ideas and influences sweeping through the western world, and it was up to outsiders to assist with a process that could not be accomplished single-handed from within. From the standpoint of its historiography, at least, Spain was an under-developed country, with considerable stretches of its history neglected, or under-researched. This created opportunities for foreign scholars of a kind which are now disappearing over most of Europe, although to some extent they may still survive in those parts of the continent that are only now emerging from a long night of cultural isolation.

To judge, however, from my Spanish example, this form of what might be described as foreign aid, will be—and should be—a transient phenomenon. Spain is unusual, and perhaps unique, in having a special word—*hispanista*—to describe a foreign scholar specialising in its culture and history. The existence of this word suggests both a certain sense of inferiority in relation to foreign scholarship, and a belief that Spain's exceptional characteristics require, in addition to the normal methods of scholarship, an additional, almost metaphysical quality, capable of seeing into the very essence of Spanish being. Both assumptions are now outmoded, and the age of the Hispanist has drawn to a close.

At this point it might well be asked how those of us who have grown accustomed to being described as Hispanists are to spend the rest of our lives. Or, to put the question more broadly, what possibilities are open to British scholars to make a worthwhile contribution to the study of the history and culture of continental Europe, once there cease to be empty foreign archives or libraries waiting to be populated, or vast historiographical gaps to be filled? One is bound to wonder if there is there still a role for the outsider, even if it might be argued that in practice we cease to be outsiders once we have been integrated (if indeed we are to be integrated) into the European community.

Before attempting to answer this question, there are a number of practical considerations that need to be addressed. The first concerns language. English is now becoming the lingua franca of the European community. The effect of this process will be to increase the already marked reluctance of university students in this country to make themselves proficient in a language other than their own. According to a recent report, some ten thousand British students took advantage of the Socrates Erasmus student exchange programme in 1999–2000, as compared with nearly twelve thousand in 1994–95. One reason advanced for this declining interest in studying on the continent is the absence of language skills. According to the director of the UK Socrates Erasmus Council the overriding reason for the decline "is essentially cultural and motivational. Students, their families and universities in other European countries recognise that if they want to develop their career prospects they need one or two European languages at a good level and experience in other countries. This climate does not exist in Britain."[3] Unless the climate can be changed, at both school and university level, we may thus find ourselves in the ironical position of distancing ourselves from Europe at the very moment when the politicians are seeking to place us at its heart.

Closely allied to the linguistic question, but no less important in terms of Britain's prospects for producing European-minded scholars, is that of the time and resources available for research. Neither the British Academy when it was responsible for allocating research grants, nor the Arts and Humanities Research Board today, have appeared to recognise that research on, and in, a country other than one's own makes additional, and time-consuming, demands. One such demand is to master one or more foreign languages. Another is to learn the ways of a foreign society sufficiently to be able to negotiate its complexities with a certain degree of confidence. Both processes require time and patience, and would seem to me to justify the extension by a year of the time normally expected for the completion of a thesis, with the allocation of sufficient funds to match. I would expect that, in due course, a significant portion of such funding would come from pooled European, rather than national, resources. But if we are not to skip a generation of potential researchers committed to continental European studies, it would seem to me that due allowance should henceforth be made for the granting of extra time and funding in

---

[3] For the statistics, and also the comments by J Reilly, see *The Times Higher Education Supplement*, no. 1,498 (3 Aug. 2001), 7.

order to reduce the practical and psychological barriers to European-oriented research.

At first sight, in spite of problems I have mentioned, the statistics look reasonably reassuring. Over the last three decades, according to information provided me by the Institute of Historical Research, the relation between the number of theses on British and European history completed in British universities has remained surprisingly constant:

Decade	British History	European History
1970's	2524	575
1980's	2820	657
1990's	2689	785

But on closer inspection, these figures may well prove to be less reassuring than they appear. Over the last decade growing numbers of continental European graduate students have chosen to undertake higher research in this country—largely, it is to be assumed on aspects of continental rather than British history. No statistics exist as to what proportion of the theses completed on continental subjects was written by graduate students from the continent, but their exclusion would surely reveal a significant decline in the number of British graduate students working on European history.[4]

If—and it is a large if—the attitude towards the learning of modern languages can be changed, and greater flexibility can be introduced, both at undergraduate and graduate level, in the arrangements for periods of study on the continent, there is every reason to hope that this country will continue to produce a fair number of research scholars whose primary interest lies in some aspect of continental history and culture. Some of these scholars—probably a growing proportion—are likely to be involved in large collaborative research projects with continental colleagues, which I would expect to become increasingly fashionable. Others, it is to be hoped, will pursue a more solitary path, engaged in the kind of individual research which has yielded such handsome dividends for British, and European, scholarship over the course of the twentieth century. These scholars will bring to their work the vision of the outsider, with all the advantages and disadvantages that this entails. The disadvantages are obvious enough. The outsider may be *in* a country, but in the last analysis will never quite be *of* it, in spite of the most strenuous efforts to achieve a total identification. This means that there are some aspects of its culture that will for ever continue to elude the outsider, some nuances of thought and expression that can never be captured. Closer European union will not change this. For all the

---

[4] I am grateful to the Institute of Historical Research for compiling these figures for me (in a letter of 9 Aug. 2001) and also to the Royal Historical Society for providing me with valuable material on the same topic.

European veneer, national traditions, national languages, national histories, will continue to sustain indefinitely a pluralist Europe, of which each component part will to some extent remain a separate unit of study.

Against the disadvantage arising from a form of comprehension that can never be total, there are certain advantages which the outsider has traditionally enjoyed. While the possibilities of transforming an entire stretch of the historical landscape are probably diminishing, as I have suggested has been happening in Hispanic studies, the opportunities for making a distinctive contribution have far from disappeared. There are perhaps three areas where I believe such a contribution can be especially valuable. Excessive familiarity creates notorious blind spots. Certain aspects of an alien society will immediately catch the attention of a newly arrived visitor—aspects so familiar to its inhabitants that they take them for granted. Styles of political or intellectual discourse, marriage customs and inheritance patterns, the physical layout and use of space in houses—these are the kind of cultural and social features which outsiders are likely to notice, precisely because of the contrast which they present to their own experience. They will therefore be ready to devote to them the close observation and analysis that are unlikely to be forthcoming from those who have always lived with them.

An outsider, too, simply by virtue of being an outsider, can challenge, either directly or indirectly, the predominant assumptions of a society, imposed either by authority or by intellectual fashion. Perhaps I may be allowed to offer an example from my own experience. I chose—I must admit innocently rather than by design—the title of *Imperial Spain* for a survey of Early Modern Spanish history which I published in 1963. In that book, I sought to show how much of the Spanish past had been dictated by a continuing dialogue between the centre of the peninsula, Castile, and its peripheral regions. This approach sprang from my original research into the history of Catalonia and its relations with Madrid—a subject that was politically sensitive at the time I embarked on it. The whole insistence of the Franco regime was on the unity of Spain, and a treatment of Spanish history in terms of disunity and diversity ran counter to accepted doctrine. That this alternative approach to the Spanish past should appear under the official-sounding title of *Imperial Spain* made its contents all the more surprising to a generation of readers continuously subjected to the bombardment of government ideology.

Now, forty years on, the approach to the Spanish past inside Spain itself is affected by the reverse phenomenon. The official recognition of the country's political pluralism in the constitution of the new, democratic Spain has led to the fragmentation of the Spanish past into the history of its distinctive component parts, like Catalonia, Aragon, Valencia, the Basque provinces, Galicia, and Castile itself. There is ceasing to be a history of Spain, just as there may one day cease to be a history of Britain. Here, the opportunity that awaits the outsider is to fly in the face of prevailing fashion and remind national, or nationalist historians, that the history of a composite state—in this instance of Spain—is something more than the history of its distinctive parts.

One further area in which I believe the outside scholar can make a significant contribution, lies in the possibilities for comparison offered by the study of a foreign society. I would expect comparative studies in European history and culture to be one of the major growth areas during the course of this century. We are witnessing the birth of a Europe in which there will be a continuing, and creative, tension between the competing claims of unity and diversity. The pressures towards a centralising uniformity will be met, and resisted, by nations, regions and ethnic groupings determined to preserve their own distinctive identities. Indeed, the insistence on the preservation of distinctive identities will increase, not diminish, in proportion as the pressures for uniformity grow. In order to mediate between the competing demands and help to reconcile the conflicting interests, there will be a greater, not a lesser need, for investigation into distinctive national and regional cultures within a comparative European context.

Comparative history is one of the hardest kinds of history to write. It is too easy to concentrate on the similarities, or presumed similarities, between institutions or societies, and to sweep any awkward differences under the carpet for the sake of establishing a superficial tidiness. But the differences as well as the similarities to be found in a united but pluralist Europe demand investigation. A European community will want to identify the common values and features of European civilisation, and I have no doubt that large pan-European research projects into such subjects as the rise of individualism or the rule of law will be undertaken for this very purpose. But it is no less important, or illuminating, to identify and explain what is distinctive in the different states and societies that have gone into the making of Europe, and why those distinctive characteristics arose and have survived. This will create new opportunities and new challenges for collective research. But it will also provide opportunities for individual research by scholars interested in the development and character of societies other than their own—scholars who can capitalise on the advantages conferred by their status as outsiders. As quintessential outsiders, British scholars can and should be in the forefront of inquiry into the origins and survival of European diversity.

If my reading of future developments is correct, the view from the outside will therefore continue to make an important—and perhaps increasingly important—contribution to the European scholarly enterprise. I would hope, too, that it would lead to more continental scholars devoting their energies to exploring British society and culture, as well as to more British scholars devoting themselves to continental Europe. This seems to me desirable for both parties, not only because of the distinctive angle of vision offered by the view from the outside, but also because of the way in which a scholar who has for long been immersed in the study of an alien society tends on returning home to see his or her own society in a new, and different, light. Anyone, for instance, who has studied the past and present of the German Länder or the autonomous regions of modern Spain is likely to return to this country with a rather different notion of federalism than the one currently envisaged in British political debate.

The opportunities and advantages that accrue to national and international scholarship from looking beyond national boundaries are the monopoly of no one country, and are equally applicable to all participants in an enlarged European community. But, if the European community is to work to the benefit of all, each participant must make its own distinctive contribution and bring its own distinctive viewpoint. Here it would seem to me that Britain has an enormous amount to offer, but all too little awareness of this fact, and very little determination to realise its great potential assets.

The large number of students coming over from the continent to study in British universities is evidence that word has got around that they will find something here—and not just the language—which they cannot find at home. Given the current pressures on British universities, it is all too possible that they will not find it for much longer. But, for the present at least, they come, although there are fears that numbers will decline as United Kingdom postgraduate qualifications fall out of line with European ones.[5] They come because they believe, with good reason, that they will receive a greater degree of personal attention from their teachers than they receive at home, and more interaction with faculty and fellow students in classes, tutorials and seminars, than they can ever hope to obtain in the large and impersonal lecture courses which have been the standard fare of most of them. They come, too, because they know they will be embarking on relatively short and concentrated courses, many of them based on primary sources as well as secondary texts. They also know that they will be expected to produce regular written work.

This type of training will, if anything, have an increasing value in preparing the coming generation of Europeans for the kind of careers, whether academic or non-academic, that they have in mind. At its best, it teaches the skill of rapidly mastering a mass of information in a world that is being bombarded with information on a scale far beyond that experienced by earlier generations of students. It teaches how to weigh up the arguments for and against a case, and how to express conclusions in a concise and accessible form. The British empirical tradition has its enemies and critics. Often, and understandably, it has been the despair of continental scholars dismayed by our apparent reluctance to engage with grand concepts, or enter into metahistorical or metaphysical debate revolving around large abstract issues. British empiricism will, in any event, find itself strongly challenged, and perhaps modified, by the closer engagement with continental styles of discourse that closer intimacy with Europe will in due course bring about. But it has, and will continue to have, a valuable contribution to make, not least in punctuating inflated rhetoric and forcing on the attention of those trained in a different form of discourse the sometimes awkward presence of uncongenial facts.

But pragmatism, like patriotism, is not enough. Indeed, the whole notion of a British contribution to Europe couched in terms of the injection of pragmatism and a dose of British common sense, underscores the dangers inherent in the

---

[5] For statistics of European Union undergraduate and graduate students applying to study in British universities, see the *Times Higher Education Supplement* for 3 Aug. 2001, cited above.

exercise on which we are engaged at this meeting. It would be fatal to assume that we start from a position of natural superiority and come to Europe bearing irresistible gifts. To patronise is to risk the rejection of those very gifts which can genuinely contribute to the enrichment of a common European culture. As Britain contemplates what it can offer, a degree of humility is in order. In fact we have a good deal to be humble about.

All too often in our political relationship with the European community we have sat back and waited for Europe to initiate the dialogue, and then have tried to make up our minds as to how we should respond. As a result, we suddenly find ourselves excluded from the dialogue, which inexplicably appears to have bypassed us in a search for more favourable terrain. As I see it, this country is particularly vulnerable in the area of intellectual and cultural interchange, because of its consistent unwillingness to appreciate and take seriously the role and the importance of culture in modern international relationships. As military confrontation within Europe becomes—or so we may hope—a thing of the past, the relative importance of the cultural influence exercised by its different component parts will do much to determine their ranking within the European community, while also defining its future shape and character. Image will count for much in the new, united, Europe.

Although in Britain we possess many advantages, starting with the language, we are at present ill-equipped to engage in the kind of competitive but creative cultural interchange which will help to determine our image, and which will play an increasingly prominent part in European life in this new century. Anyone who has lived for a time in France or Italy or Spain will be aware of the extent to which this country lags behind its continental partners in the place it allots in national life to cultural matters and the life of the mind. We may at times laugh at the pre-eminence enjoyed by European intellectuals, and at the causes which they serve, but the laughter is likely to be accompanied by a twinge of envy. That pre-eminence reflects at the least a view of national priorities which is far from being our own.

Change, if it is to come, must begin at home. Unless or until we can secure for academic, cultural and intellectual achievement a greater respect from society than they at present enjoy, the United Kingdom will remain poorly positioned to make the contribution to European life that it is capable of making. This is a task that cannot be undertaken by government alone, although government has a part to play. It is also a task for the universities and institutions of learning, and for the scholarly and cultural world as a whole. Essentially it involves a process of national reeducation.

Without this reassessment of our own priorities, we shall find it hard to initiate and sustain the kind of cultural dialogue in which continental Europe wants us to engage. It is a dialogue that will need to take place at both the personal and the institutional level, but be conducted in a more intensive and less haphazard way than at present. It is likely to involve a more extensive and systematic interchange of students and faculty, and consequently a much greater mobility and flexibility than now exist in the world of higher education. It will demand active British participation in the multinational institutes which either have been or will be created in major cities of the states that once formed part of the communist bloc, as instruments for assisting them in their emergence from the long winter of isolation and repression.[6] But participation in such European institutions should not, in my view, preclude the systematic creation of national institutes of higher learning and culture in all the European states, somewhat along the lines of the Schools maintained abroad by this Academy. These will provide a central resource for British students working on the history and culture of their chosen European society, while at the same time fostering in that society a greater awareness of the special qualities and values that British culture has brought, and can continue to bring, to the common European heritage. To talk of national institutes in an internationalised Europe might seem to represent a direct challenge to the trend of the times. But in my view the Europe of the twenty-first century will be operating simultaneously at four different levels—the global, the pan-European, the national and the regional. To function effectively at each of these levels will require different approaches and different strategies, overlapping and complementing each other. Behind this assumption lies my conviction that a Europe that fails to recognise and cherish diversity is a Europe that will not be worth having. Its extraordinary diversity—of law, language, institutions, cultures—has led to innumerable internecine conflicts, but has also been the secret of its dynamism and creativity over the course of the centuries. These should not be jeopardized by a doomed pursuit of homogeneity in the name of unity.

Common European cultural initiatives should therefore not preclude national cultural initiatives, just as they should not preclude regional initiatives where they seem desirable. The United Kingdom may or may not remain a united kingdom, but, irrespective of what happens to its political arrangements, there are historic regional connections that transcend modern national boundaries, like those, for instance, of the Celtic cultures of the British, French and Spanish peripheries, which have enriched European civilisation in the past, and are likely to reassert themselves with renewed vigour in the years to come. The recovery of identity within regional frameworks will be one of the characteristics of twenty-first century Europe, adding one more layer to the lattice-work of a continent cris-crossed by national, trans-national and sub-national ties of shared cultures and interests. As members of a composite state in process of rediscovering and reaffirming the cultural and historical identity of its component parts, I would hope that the British would welcome and play a part in this process, which will add to, rather than subtract from, the multi-cultural Europe that is now reinventing itself.

But I believe that the most distinctive contribution of all that Britain can make derives from what at first sight seems its greatest liability as a participant in the

---

[6] See W Lepenies, "Culture, Politics and the European Intelligentsia", (2001) 9 *European Review* 147–58, at p. 156.

European enterprise—its geographical and historical position on the northwestern fringes of the continent. Over the last three centuries British political and commercial interests have been global, rather than European. As the heir to an imperial and an Atlantic tradition this country has special obligations, and special opportunities. As I see it, one of the great dangers attending the formation of the new Europe is that it will be an inward-looking rather than an outward-looking community, a fortress Europe pulling up the drawbridges to prevent the entry of undesirable foreign influences. I would hope that here British global experience—our engagement over the centuries, for instance, with the world of Islam—will enable us to make sure that the drawbridges remain down. The store of knowledge and understanding of non-European societies that is one of the more positive legacies of Britain's imperial past has an important part to play in the creation of a tolerant European civilisation with its windows open to the world.

But it is particularly in the realm of the transatlantic relationship that British scholarship enjoys the possibility of playing a unique and uniquely constructive role. American cultural, as well as political, predominance is at present overwhelming, and is likely to continue so for the foreseeable future. Half hating, half admiring the United States and what it has to offer, the Europe of the twenty-first century will inevitably spend much time and energy defining itself in relation to the onslaught of cultural influences from across the Atlantic. Much of this process of self-definition will take the form of reflex reactions of a largely hostile character in a bid to preserve the European inheritance and European identity against the tidal waves of Americanisation, which will continue to sweep across the continent even if the United States disengages politically from Europe and enters a period of semi-isolationism.

Here there are at once great dangers and great opportunities. The greatest danger is that the British will be seen, as they are already seen, as an American Trojan horse introduced within the walls of the European citadel. It is no secret that, from the standpoint of some European intellectuals, the "Anglo-Saxons" are the quintessential outsiders, purveying a composite culture and a set of values that are deeply antithetical to the authentic European tradition. While I believe that the image is largely false, it may well undermine British efforts to make a greater contribution to European life and thought, unless effective ways can be found of dispelling it.

One way to dispel it is to learn to speak with a more European voice, and to some extent this will happen as Britain's ties with Europe become more closely drawn. But I do not believe that to turn our backs on our "Anglo-Saxon" heritage is the right way forward, even if it were feasible, and in the long run it would represent an impoverishment both of ourselves and of Europe as a whole. Britain's linguistic, cultural and historical ties with the United States are potentially one of its greatest assets, even if at present they may appear, from a European standpoint, its greatest liability. Europe needs and will continue to need the United States, just as the United States needs Europe, and the geographical and historical position of the United Kingdom makes it ideally placed to keep the lines of creative communication open between them.

British scholars and writers can be, and indeed to some extent already are, at once the mediators between America and Europe, and the interpreters of one culture to the other. This country possesses, as a result of its own massive contribution to the creation of North American civilisation, an instinctive affinity with some of its characteristics, and yet at the same time the capacity to view both their positive and negative features with the clarity that comes from the distancing provided by proximity to Europe. The British stand in relation to both Europe and North America as semi-outsiders, an ambiguous status that allows them to enjoy a number of the advantages that accrue to the insider. We should in my view not jeopardise the opportunities which ambiguity affords.

It is an ambiguity that makes it possible for Britain to bridge the Atlantic divide. One of the essential purposes, for instance, of the newly founded Rothermere Institute of American Studies at Oxford, is to provide a way-station for European, and particularly East European, scholars to make a first acquaintance with the history and culture of the Anglo-American world, just as it will help American scholars to become acquainted with European styles of scholarship. There are many ways in which, by institutional and non-institutional means alike, this country can help to explain one side of the Atlantic to the other.

Take, for instance, as one minor example, the Anglo-American style of academic seminar. At its worst, as all too many will be painfully aware, this is little more than a pooling of misinformation by those whose ignorance is exceeded only by their loquacity. But at its best it can promote an authentic exchange of ideas and can widen horizons in unexpected ways. Anyone who has tried to introduce this style of seminar on the continent will be aware of the difficulties involved. Strongly hierarchical structures in a university system characterized by magisterial discourses and relentless student note-taking, are not conducive to the participation of students with senior academics in free, open, and constructive intellectual debate. Yet British academics, with their experience of this style of teaching, are well placed to illustrate its possibilities, and break down some of the traditional barriers to its effective use as a means of instruction.

By drawing on its dual inheritance, European and transatlantic, Britain can make a far stronger contribution to the Europe of the twenty-first century than by drawing on one alone. It is incumbent upon it to keep open for a Europe all too prone to unthinking anti-Americanism, what might be called the Atlantic option, informed by the styles of scholarship and discourse that have emerged from the creation over the past three centuries of an Anglo-American cultural community. Neither fully European, nor fully transatlantic, Britain will continue, whatever political and economic decisions are made, to straddle two cultural worlds. This is our strength, and our opportunity. In our role as insiders who are also outsiders, and outsiders who are insiders, we can best contribute to Europe by giving and receiving, but remaining true to ourselves.

9

British Art, Art History and Aesthetic Criticism in a European Perspective

STEPHEN BANN

Presenting one's own credentials is an obvious way of beginning a paper in a context of this kind. I am an art historian, and historians generally turn to the past when they are asked to prognosticate for the future. This is what I intend to do. But a note from the present is also order. I am currently acting as president of what must be one of the most long-standing disciplinary organisations of its kind, the Comité international d'histoire de l'art. This is an office which lasts for four years at a time, and the present arrangement is that the country which has hosted the international congresses of the CIHA, in principle every four years, nominates the president for the ensuing period. CIHA has a fascinating history, which is, in a sense, a microcosm of the development of history of art over the century and a half of its gestation. It was founded in Germany in 1873, and from the outset enshrined the mission of an already mature German art historical profession to set appropriate standards for the discipline in a supranational context.

However 1873 was not a particularly propitious date for collaboration between scholars on either side of Alsace-Lorraine, and it is hardly surprising that the first congress of CIHA to be attended by French scholars is the fourth in the series, held at Budapest in 1896. From the late nineteenth century onwards, as you might expect, the development of the CIHA mirrors the cultural and political tensions of Europe. The first international congress to be held in London comes at a particularly disastrous moment, the summer of 1939, and one can imagine the difficulty in ensuring the free selection and passage of the delegations, particular those from Central Europe. One can also imagine a certain surprise, among the latter, when they discovered the small size of the art historical profession in Britain, where apart from the Courtauld Institute (founded at the beginning of the 1930s) there was little to be seen outside the staffing of the major museums. Even on their home ground, the English delegates were probably outnumbered by the Hungarian visitors alone.

By the time of the second London congress, in the year 2000, everything had changed, as you might expect. CIHA now has a mission which reflects the globalisation of cultural policy in the present period. On the one hand, there is a strong residual sense that its role is to diffuse good scholarly practice, and if diffusion is the principle to be followed, it is certain that the trail will lead back, one way or another, to the pioneers of art history in Central Europe in the nineteenth century. On the other hand, there is the view that art history should cover the globe, and the countries most remote from the traditional centres of the discipline therefore require and should receive particular attention. CIHA is not as closely aligned with international organisations as, say, AICA (the International Association of Art Critics) which affiliates with UNESCO. But it cannot, and indeed should not, duck the commitment to world-wide membership. Inevitably, the issues that raise most debate at the periodic members' meetings are not the basic questions of art historical methodology which galvanised the nineteenth century pioneers, but such pragmatic questions as arise from this global commitment—such as the extension of the number of official languages used at its congresses to include Spanish.

I am beginning my paper with this reference to the example of CIHA to make the point that intellectual interchange in art history becomes increasingly bland, or at least increasingly technical, in the process of becoming genuinely global. This may be so in the case of Europe, if we only look at the superficial symptoms of current cultural development. It may well be so, for example, that the cultural role of Britain in Europe is being affected the relentless attrition of the European idea in popular journalistic debate. But the answer, in my view, is not to capitulate to the political pragmatism that oddly passes for wisdom. It is to pay further, deeper attention to the polyphony of different voices that have composed the culture of present-day Europe. My attempt will be, for the most part, to anchor my general points about art, art history and aesthetics in the context of particular cases of exchange between Britain and Europe. It is only when such individual cases are brought to the fore that the extent of what has been possible in the past—and may be possible in the future—comes fully into view.

An exemplary case of what I mean can be found in a recent essay by the art historian Alex Potts, and since it relates directly to the CIHA context which I have been describing, I will summarise his argument, however briefly. Potts is writing generally about "cross-currents in German and British studies", but his chosen example is concerned with a particular kind of complementarity between two art historians of an earlier generation, Edgar Wind and Michael Baxandall. Wind was one of the scholars associated with Aby Warburg's art historical library, formed in Hamburg and later transported to London, where it became the basis of the present Warburg Institute. He left Europe for North America at the time of the Second World War, but returned afterwards and took up the post of Professor of the History of Art at Oxford. Baxandall, who spent much of his career at the Warburg Institute (incorporated after the war into London University), finally took up a post at the University of California (Berkeley). Potts, however, rightly argues that this broad comparison between the two much travelled scholars' achievements, which happened to converge in the area of eighteenth century studies, brings into focus a vital point of interchange between two major intellectual traditions, happily brought together: "a meeting between the larger philosophical and historical ambitions of German *Kunstwissenschaft*, exemplified by the hugely influential analysis of Renaissance art and culture that came out of the Warburg Library, and an Enlightenment tradition of sceptical, concretely empirical enquiry associated with thinkers like David Hume".[1]

I cannot go into the evidence presented for this timely fusion between traditions, which Potts exemplifies by particular references to studies of English and French eighteenth century painting. But the model that he presents is worthy of attention. The geographical movements of both of these scholars followed the broad lines of emigration and translocation that were a frequent feature of the mid-twentieth century. But the fusion of their horizons, so to speak, took place on another, more fundamental level. I can offer a small piece of autobiographical experience to gloss this example, once again involving the Warburg Institute, but in this case concerned with the German scholar who became its director, EH Gombrich. When I was studying history at Cambridge, Gombrich's *Meditations on a hobby horse* (1963) came to me as a revelation. It was one of the first books that I reviewed, as a graduate student, and it seemed to me to cast a flood of light on matters apparently quite unrelated to it, like the assemblages of Rauschenberg, then being shown for the first time in London. It was qualitatively different from any of the other historiographical texts that I was studying. What I was discovering for the first time was indeed the tradition of *Kunstwissenschaft*, not quite domesticated enough in its English context to eliminate its shock value.

This example relates to the intellectual benefit that British art history derived, in the past half century, from refugee German scholars. But one only has to draw the net a little more widely, and extend the period two centuries back, to see that British visual culture was formed in a process of continual interaction with the continent, and in this case especially with the very different traditions of France. Again I want to rely first of all on the using the study of a colleague to convey some of the rich cross-currents at work here in the early part of the nineteenth century. Marcia Pointon published *The Bonington Circle*, sub-titled *English Watercolour and Anglo-French Landscape 1790–1855*, sixteen years ago. But its message is still fresh and challenging. The argument is that, even in a period whose opening years were dominated by Anglo-French armed conflict and a brief British occupation of France, the contribution of British artists to a dynamic French visual culture was considerable. This was not by any means simply a matter of a single "star", as Bonington himself has come to be regarded,

---

[1] A Potts, "Visual Obsessions: Cross-currents in German and British Studies of Eighteenth-Century Art", in S Peters, M Biddiss and I F Roe (eds.), *The Humanities in the New Millennium* (Tübingen and Basel, A. Francke Verlag, 2000), 252.

but of a comprehensive overhaul of the commercial conditions of image-making that an engraver like SW Reynolds, for example, helped to engineer.[2]

Once again, this was a continuous two-way process that involved French artists visiting Britain as well as the reverse. It can be assumed that practitioners of the arts on both sides of the channel had a shrewd sense of what, in the neighbouring culture, would help to foster their special talents and interests. SW Reynolds's pupil George Maile took up residence in Paris in 1824 after conducting some of the first successful experiments in steel engraving. This process vastly increased the number of prints that could be pulled from the plate without deterioration of image quality. Although Maile had to contend with the hostility of French engravers and connoisseurs to the distinctively British medium of mezzotint, he remained there until his death in 1842.[3] Moving in the other direction for a short visit in 1827 was the young French painter, Paul Delaroche, who seems to have soaked up a store of British subjects and pictorial motifs that would sustain him for most of the next decade, and would make him probably the most famous artist in Europe by the end of it. Delaroche could well have seen in the French royal collection the famous prints commissioned for Bowyer's Shakespeare Library, and the fine illustrated history books (sometimes involving French engravers) that British publishers pioneered. He certainly seems to have drawn on such materials, in my view, for such works as his *Lady Jane Grey* (1833). But a much later article in the *Illustrated London News* claims that his 1827 visit involved the commissioning of an antique bed "carved and made in England, from the best authorities" which he apparently used in the preparation of the setting for his *Princes in the Tower* (1830).[4]

What I want to emphasise here is that such issues of cross-cultural interchange are still a good guide to the mechanisms by which national cultures communicate. Indeed their processes have perhaps acquired a special interest today, for two interlinked reasons. The first is that conceptions of the range of art history have themselves deepened and broadened to encompass features like the importance of commercial printmaking, and the link between pictorial iconography and the market for "antiques". This is not to diminish the importance of the Royal Academy or the Paris Salon as premier places of exhibition, but to ensure that such institutions are viewed as having a dynamic relationship to the surrounding visual culture. The second reason—and the one more relevant to the theme of this conference—is that cultural exchange itself may be in the process of becoming a more exciting object of study than the ossified concept of

---

[2] Pointon concludes, after citing the contribution of artists like Reynolds: "Restoration Paris may well present, in essence, some of the conditions of work, the relationships between individuals and institutions, the opportunities for enterprise and for marketing that were a new feature of Paris . . . and which were to become ever more refined and more highly developed during the ensuing century": see M Pointon, *The Bonington Circle* (Brighton, The Hendon Press, 1985), 55.

[3] B Hunnisett, *Engraved on steel: The History of Picture Production using Steel Plates* (London, Ashgate, 1998), 66.

[4] Extract from *Illustrated London News*, 5 Feb. 1848, quoted in S Bann, *Paul Delaroche: History Painted* (London, Reaktion, 1997), 94.

the monolithic national tradition. I am presently involved in the planning stages of an exhibition, "Romantic painting in England and France", which is scheduled to be held at the Tate Britain, and two American museums, in 2003. Here it is explicitly the exchanges and affinities between the two cultures that are the subject of the show, though a further important aspect will be the attempt to show works as they would have appeared in some typical exhibition environments of the period.

This then is an example of my underlying point that, when art history shifts its attention, this move may involve implications for the viewing of art by a wider public. It is challenging to try and bring out the deep mesh of connections, while concentrating at the same time on the material accuracy of the surface manifestations. Britain also has a continuing contribution to make in a further area which involves the interchange between art history and aesthetics. I referred at the outset to the relatively recent arrival of institutionalised art history in Britain. But it is certainly not the case that British writers of earlier periods abstained from critical and philosophical writing on art. In fact, this may well have been one of the most influential contributions that Britain has made, in the realm of European culture, over the past two centuries. Since this strand of writing continues to have a vital connection with the past—and European recognition of its importance is undiminished—the homegrown brand of what is often called "aesthetic criticism" is certainly ready for export.

I would underline this by looking briefly at two nineteenth century figures who played a vital role in an earlier dialogue between Britain and Europe, the first being a Frenchman who looked carefully at visual culture in Britain, and the second an Englishman whose aesthetic writings had a remarkable and sustained impact on Europe, especially after his death. Robert de la Sizeranne happens to be an almost forgotten figure, indeed I would say totally forgotten in France, judging by the first reactions when I proposed him as a lecture topic last year for an enterprising series of lectures given at the Louvre in celebration of the Ruskin centenary. He was nonetheless responsible single-handedly—as much as anyone can be—for the belated but successful introduction of Ruskin's writings into France, from the mid-1890s onwards, and he wrote what must be one of the most glowing testimonies ever written by a Frenchman about a British author: *Ruskin et la religion de la beauté*, which was first published in book form in 1897, but had appeared earlier as articles in that paragon of internationally well informed writing on politics and culture, the *Revue des deux mondes*. La Sizeranne had the immense good luck to be the proprietor of one of the finest wine-producing estates in the Northern Rhône, and "Hermitage La Sizeranne" still ranks high among its peers. But around 1895 he decided to make the ultimate sacrifice a *méridional* can make, and spent several months living in London, in an "intérieur bourgeois et strictement londonien", as we are told in biographical sketch.[5] His splendid book on Ruskin galvanised young French writers—with Proust being

---

[5] See "Fidus", "M. Robert de la Sizeranne", (1920) *Revue des deux mondes* 826.

the most illustrious convert—and set off a chain of fine translations of Ruskin's works into French (including Proust's *Bible of Amiens*).

La Sizeranne's perceptiveness as a commentator on Ruskin—who was certainly not short of British admirers—was handsomely acknowledged when the Countess of Galloway—step-sister of the prime-minister, the Marquess of Salisbury—translated and prefaced his book. However he was certainly no blind anglophile. His book on the subject of contemporary English painting left the French in no doubt that he did not expect, or wish, his fellow citizens to imitate the Pre-Raphaelites. But here, as with Ruskin, he managed to achieve a most perceptive overall estimate of what was special in the neighbouring culture. I have confirmation from a colleague, who has specialised in the British painting of the period, that no contemporary British writer on British art can hold a candle to him.

It is a good justification for cultural and intellectual exchange when we recognise that our neighbours can sometimes see us better than we see ourselves. But there is another aspect to this crossing of frontiers, which I want to relate specially to another late nineteenth century figure, the English aesthetic critic, Walter Pater. My declared interest here is that I am currently commissioning the volume of essays on Pater for the British Academy-supported series on the "Reception of British Authors in Europe". Let me say immediately how important and symptomatic a project this series is already turning out to be, under the excellent guidance of Dr Elinor Shaffer. It is the first time that any sustained attention has been given to the question of what foreigners have thought of our great writers, and in the case of all but the most recent of these, the audience is obviously in the first place a European one.

Without prejudicing the detailed responses which my European contributors are going to provide, I should say that one point at least is very clear from the start. Even an author like Walter Pater, whose writings might be thought to be furthest away from the practical questions of cultural politics, has had his work diffused according to the rhythms and pulses of the various foreign cultures that have welcomed him. These are quite different from the conditions under which he himself was writing. The reason why Pater becomes a contested figure in France in the 1920s—securing passionate support as well as ironic denunciation at a time when his work was largely out of fashion in Britain—is to be sought in the specific cross-currents of French culture at that time. In other words, Pater in French can be understood as a commentary on French cultural identity. Equally the fact that a young scholar such as Wolfgang Iser, working in post-Second World War Germany, chose to devote his doctoral thesis to Pater—at a stage when Pater's star had sunk almost below the horizon in his native land—is indicative of the kind of counterflow that cultural exchange can effect even in the least promising political circumstances.[6]

[6] This is of course a very simplified account of a complex situation, which Professor Iser has himself clarified in the Foreword to the English edition of his work, *Walter Pater: The Aesthetic Moment*, translated from the German by D H Wilson (Cambridge, Cambridge University Press, 1987).

I have been writing primarily about individuals, and their involvement in the flow and counterflow of cultural data. Yet there is clearly a point where such initiatives transcend the necessarily limited scope of a single viewpoint, and take on a more institutionalised significance: a programme of translations, such as the Ruskin translations sparked off by La Sizeranne, or indeed this admirable series of international studies on the "Reception of British Authors in Europe". This makes it quite likely that the British contribution to cultural exchange in the arts will continue to recall the individualistic tradition associated with nineteenth century aesthetic criticism, whilst it draws sustenance at the same time from the institutions of art history. A figure like Adrian Stokes, the centenary of whose birth will be celebrated this year, is surely inconceivable outside the specific tradition of British aesthetic criticism as it developed in the course of the nineteenth century, fuelled by the love affair of writers like Ruskin and Pater with the prime locations of high European art and architecture. In a sense, this critical writing is a kind of prolongation of the ritual of the Grand Tour, which enabled generations of earlier British aristocrats to recreate a certain image of Augustan or Renaissance Rome in their country estates. But, as La Sizeranne well recognised, the tourism to which Ruskin and his successors address themselves is not "Grand". It is the tourism of an industrial age, for whose benefit the aesthetic critic serves as a sometimes passionate, sometimes diffident tour guide.

I want to end by invoking another strand of cultural criticism, no less relevant to this issue of intellectual exchange, which is exemplified by the work of Matthew Arnold. When I was beginning my career as a university teacher, Arnold seemed to epitomise the level-headed consensus on cultural matters, which was fundamental for the ethos of a contemporary, interdisciplinary humanities faculty. Scarcely had we left the 1960s behind, however, when so many of the carefully argued positions that Arnold had developed in the first age of mass education in Britain seemed to collapse of their own accord. They will probably never be revived. I confess, however, that I like to imagine what the resources of his satirical pen might have made of every new, worthy attempt to square the circle as regards public expenditure on the arts and education. I can imagine how corrosively Arnold would have dealt with the Golden Calf which we all now worship under the name of sponsorship.

Arnold's great strength, it still seems to me, was that he viewed Europe as a whole as a repertoire of different ways of fostering cultural and educational goods, with the various models of institutional practice in different nations all displaying both inbuilt advantages and disadvantages. He encouraged the British to look overseas, not because the foreign model could be transplanted to Britain, but because it might serve as a corrective to tendencies that were apt to run riot if his fellow countrymen were left to themselves. The principle is perhaps stated most clearly in his excellent essay on "The Literary Influence of Academies" (included in *Essays in Criticism*, First series, 1865). Arnold writes:

> The right conclusion certainly is that we should try, so far as we can, to make up our shortcomings; and that to this end, instead of always fixing our thoughts upon the points in which our literature, and our intellectual life generally, are strong, we should, from time to time, fix them upon those in which they are weak, and so learn to perceive clearly what we have to amend.

It is easy to mock Arnold, and describe his examples as hopelessly out of date. It is no less easy to miss the point that he was trying to reform a society that had dragged its feet interminably—compared with Prussia and France—in the matter of state education. But I want to argue that, in this respect particularly, Arnold is not just worth crediting with a sound strategy for his times, but actually still serves as a guide to some of the deep structures of European cultural organisation. It is extraordinary how easy it is to transpose his trenchant comparisons into a cartography, which suits the mass society of the present day.

Of course, when Arnold was writing, there was of course no such thing as a British Academy, though there was a well-established Royal Academy of Arts. There was a French Academy, loaded with prestige and lineally descended from the original foundation of Louis XIV, though it had been reformed and redesigned several times in the turbulent course of modern history. For Arnold, this was probably the clearest contemporary emblem of cultural authority residing in a national body, though it exercised this authority in a manner which would have been anathema to most British citizens. No one is going to claim that this *grand siècle* model is still a viable one in the present state of Europe. Indeed the only institutions of the kind that attempted to exercise such authority in the recent period were no doubt the overgrown and bureaucratic academies of the former communist states of Eastern Europe. I remember some productive weeks passed as a guest of a research group in the former East German Academy, not too long after the fall of the Berlin Wall, when the institution was almost visibly fragmenting into smaller and smaller units, and the great overarching structure left no more than a fleeting shadow.

In spite of this, it is surely clear that the attitudes to cultural and artistic patronage which were formerly epitomised in the functions of the great Academies have been to some extent perpetuated in current ways of thinking about culture and the arts. To this extent they form a necessary context for any comparative view of the European scene. This is perhaps particularly so in the case of Anglo-French relations, which offer the rare spectacle of a maximum polarisation between the contrasting styles of cultural policy—today no less than in Arnold's time. If one wanted to make a cheap point, one could say that the British took decades to build a National Library which was hobbled by financial constraints and assailed by vicious architectural criticism, but in the end proves to be rather popular; the French, by contrast, took a few years to construct as a presidential project a building almost universally criticised for its access, its circulation and more or less everything else. To rub salt into the wound, one could also say that the British Academy generously supports (though it does not in fact publish) the current major revision of that indispensable but presently flawed source, the Dictionary of National Biography. The French Academy is well known for standing guard over the language, but the impetus behind the more modestly conceived French Dictionary of National Biography has not been sufficient to advance it much beyond the entry for Robert de la Sizeranne (classed under L). In this respect, at any rate, Arnold's point about the unquestioned superiority of French works of reference rings a hollow note.

Such expressions of British complacency are, however, precisely what I do not want to advocate as signals to Europe. I prefer to emphasise the fact that, for example, Paris is now becoming the home of a new Institut national de l'histoire de l'art (INHA) which will occupy a large part of the old site of the Bibliothèque Nationale in the Rue de Richelieu. This had been discussed inconsequentially for about twenty years. But it is finally taking place, and its mission will be, among other things, to offer excellent facilities to foreign academics and research students at a very moderate cost. By contrast, Britain has no such national institute. It has something which is in one sense very much better, which is the Courtauld Institute, an initially private foundation that has grown in stature over the years and acquired enormous international esteem, but still has to fit as a square peg in the round holes which are on offer from London University. University researchers in Britain are now invited to assess scholarly achievement in terms of "national" and "international excellence". But one might well be tempted to think that, in France, "national" institutions always implicitly have an international vocation, whilst in Britain "international" institutions have to find their feet in a national, not to say very local, context.

In Arnoldian fashion, I might suggest that the answer is always to emphasise the strong points of the cultural systems most unlike one's own, despite the likelihood that these strong points have a historical downside. It seems to me excellent that the official French regional collections of contemporary art (the 'FRAC' collections) always made a point of including the works of foreign (and I must say, especially British) artists. This may well reflect, from a great distance, the ideology that was notoriously exemplified in the cultural policy of Napoleon's commissar, Vivant Denon, who thought it eminently appropriate that all the unquestioned masterpieces of European art should end up in the Louvre. From the other side, Regional Arts Associations in Britain (if they still exist) used to build up their collections with a policy of scarcely straying beyond the region. Like many British municipal collections, their strengths lie in the local, and usually topographical celebration of a particular region. In France, the tell-tale legend "envoi de l'état" on so many labels for masterpieces is still a clear indication that regional capitals were thought worthy to display a full range of European works of high art, even if no one was encouraged to look too scrupulously into their provenance.

I will conclude this paper, if I may, with a few, historically based resolutions. I shall continue to look sympathetically at anglophile French painters of the Romantic period, since there are few enough French scholars looking at them, and those that are doing so, are probably in need of assistance. I shall pay as little attention as possible to Young British Artists, since all that needs to be said about their inextricable confusion between art, commerce and advertising was already being said about the objectives of the Royal Academy in the Victorian period. I shall, by contrast, continue to follow and write about some excellent contemporary French artists, who are not confused in this way, and who have virtually no audience in Britain. It troubles me slightly that the noted French critic, Pierre Restany, remarked decades ago that contemporary art had its new heartland, extending from the Low Countries through West Germany and Switzerland to Northern Italy, but conspicuously avoiding Paris. He called it the Holy Roman Empire. I have never quite worked out whether South-East England, at any rate, deserves to be annexed to this oecumenical grouping. But as one of my next tasks is a monograph about a Greek artist who has built his career in Rome, I may be able to tap into this rich seam by proxy.

10

Political Culture: Renegotiating the Post-War Social Contract

FRANK FIELD

SUMMARY

In 1950 Western Europe's post-war social contract looked settled and fairly uniform. Citizenship had been extended to include a basic income and health cover. Fifty years on this settlement no longer has a uniform appeal across the countries of Western Europe. In mainland Europe government attempts to realign future state pension commitments in line with what might reasonably be asked of future taxpayers have been met with mass demonstrations and even riots. At the same time discussion about what is the best way of organising and delivering health care is so uncontroversial that it has almost dropped out of political debate.

Contrast this political pattern with how the UK electorate agreed to a decimation of the earnings related element to state pensions and to annual cuts in the relative value of the State Retirement Pension. In contrast again to mainland Europe, the UK electorate holds a suspicious attitude to politicians attempting to reform the NHS. Public pensions are the live rail in mainland Europe's politics. The NHS now holds similar dangers for British politicians.

Why is there such a marked difference in voter attitudes to different parts of the post-war settlement in Britain and other EU countries? This essay looks at how health has featured in the politics of the post-war settlement in Britain. As in respect to pensions in mainland Europe, health in Britain only became a major political issue as governments were forced by events to renegotiate the post-war social contract. In Europe the attempt was to contain public pension liabilities. In Britain the task was to move from the early post-war producer-dominated NHS to one which, if not consumer driven, had at least begun the long process of recognising a consumer interest.

In reviewing the emergence of health as the live rail in British politics I hope to raise questions which will stimulate a similar exercise across each of the EU countries. Such an audit on the post-war social contract would help focus on the political restraints to further easy integration in the Single European Market.

INTRODUCTION

One of our most talented historians observes how Britons, shorn of their superpower role, have come to see the NHS "as something peculiar and intrinsic to the British way of life: a sort of utilitarian church, mediating the beliefs and presiding over the rituals of a society incapable of advancing any more metaphysical concepts".[1] The suggestion here is that the NHS's hold on public affections, equal if not greater than that once ascribed to the British Monarchy, came about gradually.

Its establishment was enveloped by almost universal approval by voters. But once established health dropped out of the political debate almost as quickly as Icarus fell from the sky. Voters merely expressed how important the NHS was to their standard of living. When health returned to the political agenda in the 1980s the issue played differently. Instead of greeting the actions of politicians with approbation, voters were critical. The reform programme upon which the Government had embarked offered the Left an opportunity to dub the Conservative Party as the ones who had always been deeply hostile to the whole idea of a national health service and that the reforms were in fact a cover for privatisation.

This ebb and flow of the post-war health debate is here examined from three sources. The first comes from looking at voter preferences for the different parts of the welfare settlement on offer as the Second World War came to an end. Second, the election manifestos of each of the two main parties have been read with a view to highlighting what importance the parties perceived voters attached to health services. The third theme uses polling data to examine the re-emergence of health as a major political issue in the most recent post-war period. The essay concludes with a discussion of why health alone has proved to be the one aspect of Britain's post-war social contract least amenable to reform and most likely to damage the political health of would-be reformers.

INITIAL POST-WAR CHOICES

In America, social security, paid for by insurance contributions, is known as a political live rail. Politicians touch it at great risk. Why health has become an equivalent live rail in British politics is far from obvious. Pre World War Two Britain had a national insurance scheme for the loss of income—unemployment, sickness, widowhood and old age—and similarly national insurance provision of health care for the working population. This insurance cover was extensive but far from universal. Failure to gain adequate insurance cover for either

---

[1] J Harris, "One Nation", *London Review of Books*, 23 June 1988, 9.

income or health left the poor, and many working class families, the unenviable choice between the poor law or charitable provision.

As the war clouds once again swept across Europe it would have been difficult for an observer to choose what would be the voters' top priority. Would the vote go to establishing the right to a universal basic income free of the poor law? Or would there be a greater market amongst working class voters—then by far and away the majority of the electorate—for a free health service—free, of course, only at the point of use?

While national polling was started in Britain on a regular basis by Gallup in 1937 few, if any, politicians bothered to acquaint themselves with the findings, let alone pay any attention to them. From the middle of the war onwards, Gallup recorded a large and sustained swing to the left, predicting a Labour win in 1945 and yet the election result appeared to be as much of a surprise to Attlee as it was to Churchill.[2] The latter, comforted by his wife that the result might be a blessing in disguise, replied, "At the moment it seems quite effectively disguised".[3]

As well as Gallup's regular polling, a body called Mass Opinion (MO) also surveyed what the organisation called "more thoughtful sections of the community" on a regular basis by asking respondents to fill in diaries, while other respondents were asked to return questionnaires on particular topics. Similarly, investigators working for MO would report on what people were saying as they queued, travelled, left work and went about their other activities.

The enterprising G D H Cole, who began conducting the Nuffield College Reconstruction Survey, added a third source of information on what the mass of the people hoped and wanted once peace was declared. It was to this source that Beveridge turned when beginning to draft what became one of the most influential of officially sponsored documents.

It was not the Coalition Government's intention that Beveridge should play the role of tribune for a new social order, or that a blueprint for post-war redevelopment should be produced, particularly when the outcome of the war was so uncertain. Yet as is so often the case, luck played more than a walk-on role in the turn of events. Luck, indeed, left its imprint at two key stages of this story.

The first was in the setting up of what became Beveridge's Committee of Inquiry. Senior politicians and civil servants readily conceded that trade union opinion had to be assuaged once the employers withdrew in wartime from the Royal Commission reviewing workmen's compensation. Departmental officials saw a committee to review social security as a tidying-up operation, but one which would also help smooth ruffled trade union feathers disturbed by the collapse of the Royal Commission. The idea of a review committee had little initial appeal to Ernest Bevin, the Minister of Labour at the time, until he recognised

---

[2] Asked in 1943 how respondents intended to vote, 38% replied Labour and only 31% Conservative, The Gallup International Public Opinion Poll—Great Britain 1937–64 (London, Random House, 1976), 77.

[3] W S Churchill, *The Second World War: Triumph and Tragedy*, Vol 6 (London, Reprint Society, 1956), 536.

that the appointment of the chairman offered him an opportunity to rid himself of Beveridge who he regarded, at best, as a tiresome senior member of his department.

Beveridge's immediate response to his appointment was one of desolation at being so neatly boxed off from a pre-eminent position he believed his talents warranted.[4] Such despondency did not last long for Beveridge quickly turned this near personal defeat into an opportunity to influence decisively the course of post war society. He transformed the minimal task he was given into what we now see as drafter and then exponent of perhaps the most influential government reports ever.

Here luck dealt a second hand to Beveridge. As news leaked out on the scope of Beveridge's work, pressure within Government built up to delay the report. The delay proved fatal to those who wished to prevent any discussion of postwar reconstruction until the peace had been won. Indeed, when the report was finally released, the events could not be more favourable to its reception. Its unveiling to an electorate hungry to know what plans were being made for postwar development was accompanied by a sustained period of what we would now call spinning by Beveridge and his assistant Frank Longford. More important was that the delayed publication of the report now coincided with advances in North Africa which suggested that, at long last, the war would go the Allies' way. It was at this point that the mind of the British voter turned decisively towards the kind of Britain which could arise once hostilities ceased, and it was on the crest of this most powerful of waves that the Beveridge Report rode first to influence events, before taking its place in history. But we are now in danger of running ahead of our story.

When thinking about the scope of his report Beveridge turned to G D H Cole who was working on the Nuffield College Reconstruction Survey. In an extraordinary move for the time Beveridge 'strongly emphasised' his wish to find out, "from the consumer's end", what the priorities were for the post-war period.[5] Workers on the reconstruction survey set about finding the answers to Beveridge's questions.

However, the results from this survey did not influence the first and key paper, drawn up by Beveridge in mid-December 1941. The paper, entitled Basic Problem of Social Security with Heads of a Scheme, was written and circulated to his fellow committee members by Beveridge in mid-December 1941—six months before the final report on consumer views from Cole was submitted to him. One assumption set out in this paper which was in Beveridge's view crucial

---

[4] Beveridge was part of a small dining club, including Keynes and Salter which met regularly in the early war years so that its members could commiserate with each other on their exclusion from the upper echelons of Whitehall. Lord Salter, *Memoirs of a Public Servant* (London, Faber & Faber, 1961), 264.

[5] J Harris, "Did British Workers want the Welfare State? D G H Cole's Survey of 1942", in J Winter, *Working Class in Modern British History* (Cambridge, Cambridge University Press, 1983), 201.

to any successful social security reform was the setting up of a "national health service for prevention and comprehensive treatment available to all members of the community". The service was to be free and universally based "on communist lines provided out of taxation".[6]

This emphasis on a new national health service in preventing and treating ill-health follows almost identically the sentiments expressed by Lloyd George 30 years before. The prime aim of the 1911 National Health Insurance Act was not the establishment of a comprehensive health service. The Act, rather, has to be seen as one of a number of moves by the then Liberal Government to attack the causes of poverty. Loss of work from sickness and then disability could plunge a worker and his family into poverty. Hence the coverage of health insurance to the worker only, not his or her family. As with Lloyd George, so too with Beveridge. Health was a means of achieving the primary objective of abolishing Want. That was not quite how voters saw the choice when presented with an array of post-war reforms.

The first consumer response to his 1942 report came from the work Beveridge commissioned from G D H Cole and it "largely confirmed many of the assumptions about 'popular attitude' that Beveridge held already."[7] How representative the views gathered by Cole were is perhaps open to question.[8] What is of importance for the theme being developed here is that Beveridge met the survey's field workers in 1941 to outline the issues on which he wished them to gain views. He told them that he was "particularly interested" in gaining the information about attitudes to the contributory insurance principle, the need for "co-ordination" between different social services, how best to treat the long-term unemployed and whether the payment of old age pensions should be made conditional upon retirement.[9] Health was not a Beveridge priority.

Despite being given such a clear steer as to the opinions he was most interested in, the shape of the final report, in which the section on national health insurance "was by far the most detailed and thorough", led Beveridge's biographer to concluded that "from the point of view of the working class consumer, it was health that was the first priority for future social reform".[10]

The first findings from the much more scientific opinion poll work was published the year following the Beveridge Report's publication. The survey work was conducted by the British Institute of Public Opinion[11] and its findings confirmed the conclusions to which the Nuffield College's reconstruction survey had come. Looking at which of Beveridge's proposals gained most support, the

---

[6] Quotation comes from J Harris, *William Beveridge: a Biography* (Oxford, Oxford University Press, 1997), 379.
[7] *Ibid*. 417.
[8] "Did British Workers Want the Welfare State", n. 5 above, 201.
[9] *Ibid*. 202.
[10] *Ibid*. 203.
[11] The British Institute of Public Opinion, *Beveridge Report and the Public* (1943).

Institute reported health as the clear winner. Eighty eight per cent of those surveyed saw Beveridge's proposals to include doctor and hospital cover for the whole family as a good idea with 6 per cent holding an opposite opinion and a further 6 per cent giving no opinion at all.[12]

In comparing this finding with the support expressed for Beveridge's social security reform one rider should perhaps be added. In contrast to the simple proposal in the report that a national health service should be established, Beveridge set out in 300 pages the most detailed proposals for social security changes. The extent of this detail gave opinion pollsters ample opportunity for a range of questions which could thereby elicit dissent. Answers were not only invited on whether or not a proposal was supported, but whether, for example, the benefit rates for a particular benefit were set at an adequate level, and whether the means by which funds should pay the benefit were the correct ones or not.

So while there was overwhelming support, for example, for Beveridge's idea for a new retirement pension, this support was divided over the time-scale during which the benefit should be introduced and indeed whether the benefit should be paid immediately at the full rate.[13] The universality of the social security scheme also divided respondents. Fifty-six per cent of those polled agreed with an "everybody in" approach, but 30 per cent disagreed and 14 per cent registered a "don't know".[14]

A National Health Scheme was by a clear margin the first priority of voters in the immediate post-war period. Health today has similarly the same priority attached to it by voters. But was that a priority maintained throughout the post-war period? It is to this question that the discussion now turns.

POLITICALLY WINNING THE POST-WAR SETTLEMENT BONUS

The extent to which the Coalition Government's response to Beveridge's blueprint was less than totally enthusiastic is not an issue to be debated here. In emphasising the Coalition Government's response Labour won a crucial propaganda war. Labour MPs were able to charge the Coalition Government (of which their party was part) of dragging its feet over fully implementing Beveridge's proposals. Politicians as well as some historians see this particular campaign as helping convince voters that they should put clear red water between the post-war world and the "low dishonest decade"[15] of the 1930s. Again this is not the place to question this interpretation of events.

---

[12] The British Institute of Public Opinion, *Beveridge Report and the Public* (1943), 13.
[13] *Ibid.*, 6.
[14] *Ibid.*, 12.
[15] W H Auden's phrase in "September 1, 1939" to describe the 1930s in Britain which he fashioned during the war from the safety of the United States.

Political Culture: Renegotiating the Post-War Social Contract 145

What is at issue is how the social contract part of the post war settlement has played during the last fifty years. How did politicians at the time respond to perceived voter preferences and to what extent did the political class initiate or simply follow the electors? The concern here is specifically how health featured as an election issue between the two main parties during the post-war period once the NHS had been established. Did health maintain its position at the top of voters' preferences or did the voters' love affair with the NHS prove a more intermittent relationship?

Almost six decades after the 1945 election three inter-related political images on health are assumed to have been held over the whole of this period. Labour sees the establishment of the NHS as one of its great achievements—a view shared by many outside the party. The Tories are portrayed as being against the NHS from its inception. And, partly because of the way these interpretations have been deployed, the Tories were kept on the back foot in their attempts to reform health during their period of office after 1979.

As a guide to the importance to which the two main parties have attached to the NHS during the post-war period, I have used each party's election manifesto. These documents, it is true, give only a snapshot of party opinion and do not measure the ebb and flow of debate on health between elections. But elections, to rephrase Dr Johnson, concentrate the mind of politicians wonderfully. Despite the fact that the constitutional importance adduced to a political manifesto has changed during the post-war period[16] they have always been seen as the stall on which political parties set out policies in the hope of winning support. They are therefore a strange combination of what parties regard as their core beliefs and values and what programmes stemming from these beliefs voters are most likely to find attractive.

Reading the party manifestos since the Second World War offers up the following impressions. First, for most of the post-war years, right up until the 1980s, it is difficult to discern any obvious party divide on health. Indeed, given that as I approached these documents I held the preconception already referred to, I had to keep checking that the views expressed by the Conservative Party were theirs, and that I was not mistakenly reading the Labour Party Manifesto.

Second, Labour's claim to be the founder of the NHS appears to have taken a little time to register in the party hierarchy's thinking. No mention at all was made to the NHS in Labour's 1950 or 1951 election manifesto.[17] Nor was it until the 1964 election did Labour claim the NHS as one of the 1945 Labour Government's greatest achievements.[18]

---

[16] They are now definitely viewed as the basis of the mandate on which the winning political party governs.
[17] This may have been because of the internecine warfare, which had been initiated over NHS charges.
[18] This claim may have been a response to how the Tories were presenting the NHS in their manifesto. The scope, coverage and range of health issues would suggest to an unsuspecting reader that the NHS was much more of a Tory than a Labour issue. The Tories, for example, were the first to

Third, given Labour's current emphasis on being both parent and midwife to the NHS it is also surprising that it was not until 1959 that Labour reminded voters that the Tories had voted against establishing the NHS.[19] Fourth, only with the manifestos for the two 1974 elections did the political debate change gear. The proposals presented to the electorate became much more detailed and a clear party division is established. Three issues in particular feature in this interchange.

- Prescription charges assume an almost theological importance. Do they prevent access by the poor? Or should they simply be viewed in terms of opportunity costs with the money raised being more profitably used in extending health provision?
- Parties charge each other over the inadequacies of the other's growth of the NHS budget.
- Private health re-emerges as an issue of importance. Is it a help or a hindrance to the NHS?

How is it that voters and politicians alike now generally hold in their mind's eye a pattern of post-war health politics at variance with the information presented here? Labour is widely now perceived with creating the NHS and that because of this health is seen as a natural Labour issue. The Tories, who opposed the NHS from the word go, are also seen, at best, as covert privatisers. Such polarised views would not have been given much credence by voters in the 1960s or 1970s. It is to how events moved from the early 1980s that we have to turn to see an answer.

THE THATCHER EFFECT

Voters' impressions of what were the big issues of the day were captured by Gallup at regular intervals throughout the post-war period. Like the manifestos, the results have a number of unexpected findings. While the Tories billed the NHS in each of their election addresses, and often at considerable length—ten times or so the size of Labour's entry for the earlier part of the post-war period—health after 1948 ceases to feature as an issue that voters thought should be high on the Government's list of priorities. On the few occasions when it registered it comes low down on the political Richter Scale, and only then because a small percentage of voters recorded their wish to see less not more money spent on it.

Between the various international crises of the post-war era the management of the economy remained the issue that voters thought should be the primary

---

begin the debate on promoting good health policies rather than being exclusively concerned with an ill health service.

[19] The grounds for what is called the reason amendments tabled by the Tories to the Second and Third Readings of the Bill now read as an alternative reform programme.

focus of government energies. However it would be a mistake to infer from this that health was not important to voters. On the contrary the NHS, and the health of one's family, was ranked as about the most important issue. Up until the late 1970s governments were generally felt to be doing fairly well on health. This all changed in the early 1980s. Then health featured again by voters as one of the big political issues.

Why is this? At about this time Mrs Thatcher turns her government's attention to NHS reform. Mrs Thatcher is recorded as having the most deep misapprehension about venturing an NHS reform programme.[20] Does she begin to embrace such a programme because of the growing public disquiet about the fate of the health service? Or does her reform programme itself enlarge the numbers of people who become dissatisfied with the state of the NHS? Whatever the answer, it is clear that very significant voter dissatisfaction with the Government's handling of the NHS is recorded by the early eighties. 72 per cent of those polled in 1982, 81 per cent in 1986, and thereafter a consistent 80 per cent of voters polled recorded their dissatisfaction with the Government's management of the NHS. Health is once again a political issue of the first importance.

It is during the initial attempts at NHS reform that Labour's campaign is honed and becomes politically much more decisive. The assertion is that the Tories have always been hostile to the NHS and that their reform programme is presented by the Opposition as a cover for privatisation.

Looking back on events no serious Labour politician would not now support the effort to begin costing each NHS activity, although such an action then constituted the first plank of the Tories' reform strategy. When this reform was introduced Labour saw matters differently. The programme to cost each NHS activity was presented by Labour as being more concerned with constructing the means by which privatisation could be advanced than simply a means by which a more rational distribution of NHS resources might be achieved. Similarly, the divide between purchaser and supplier, which had existed in the original health scheme established by Lloyd George in 1911, and was reinstated by the establishment of GP budget holders, was again presented as a cover for allowing private providers to come within the NHS orbit. That there is now a consensus between both parties on these reforms should not minimise the permanent political damage inflicted upon the Tories as their governments attempted to build a NHS reform programme. It is not a consensus however into which the electorate has so far willingly joined.

BRITAIN AND EUROPE

Why is it that the NHS rather than pensions, as they have in mainland Europe, has emerged as the live wire of British politics? Differences in the kind of pension

---

[20] N Timmins, *The Five Giants* (London, Harper Collins, 2001), 455.

arrangements in Britain and Europe may help to account for these differences in the political profile on this issue. The state pension in Britain was never set at a level which was equal to, let alone above, the state's own definition of the minimum income level. Here is the first major difference. As German workers, for example, protest on the streets at a proposed cut from 67 to 65 per cent of average earnings for their state pension, the British equivalent languishes at around a quarter of this level, and is set to fall further. Defending a valuable asset is clearly a more appealing activity than trying to summons up enough courage and support to prevent what is already a grossly inadequate pension becoming even more inadequate.

Similarly, in contrast to most of the European Union, Britain has funded assets underpinning company and also personal pensions. These assets are larger than all the similar assets owned within the European Union put together. Only Denmark and Holland make a good showing on this front. The assets for occupational pensions are held by trustees and those for personal pensions by finance houses. Neither of these two bodies are open to the political pressure that awaits a state running its own generous scheme.

The different ownership of pension entitlement, and the parsimoniously low level of state retirement pension on which no one is expected to be totally dependent, may help to explain why European-wide protests in support of state pensions are absent from the politics of this country. That does not explain though why the NHS has the same properties of a live rail here as the pensions in most other European countries.

We have seen that it was voters who viewed the establishment of the NHS as the cornerstone of the post-war social contract in Britain. Probably most of those voters who recorded their priorities then have ceased to exist. Yet while an almost totally different set of voters now holds sway the NHS has not been dislodged from the political affections of this radically different electorate.

Its commitment to the NHS is in some senses surprising. The health service is run along the same lines as were the other nationalised industries. This centrally controlled command structure increasingly lost its appeal to voters and denationalisation—the policy of privatisation—had widespread voter support. Why is it then that Britain's last nationalised industry not only survives but is still held in such high regard by most voters?

CONCLUSION

A part of the early post-war settlement has an equal appeal on the continent. There the state's involvement in delivering a decent retirement pensions is what voters are prepared to defend. And while the issue is different the basis of the appeal is, I believe, the same.

In each of the different European countries there lies in the voter's mind an idea of the good society. As politicians rarely talk now in such terms it would be surprising if voters could without difficulty give a coherent answer to what they mean by this idea. But their defence over different parts of the post-war settlement is based on what voters see as cardinal to their vision of that ideal.

Both sets of appeal—pensions and health—are based on a form of self-interest and altruism. My neighbour's needs are met in part by me because I will need my neighbour one-day to meet my needs. Self-interested altruism is not to be dismissed or despised. The altruism of this public behaviour survives because it is so securely underpinned by individual self-interest. It is this self-interestedness which gives the different aspects of the post-war settlement its enduring appeal and determines its scope. The state pension as it is currently constituted is a lost cause in Britain. It is so minimal that self-interested altruism cannot operate on a wide enough basis to protect let alone improve this benefit. On health self-interested altruism can and does so operate. The vast majority of people still receive their formal health care from the NHS.

The reverse applies on the continent. People's stake in the public provision of an adequate retirement pension is so underpinned by such an obvious self-interest that the individual defence of the public good is easy and successful. The public provision of health offers no similar widespread appeal to self-interest.

It is as politicians come up against the self-interest woven into a defence of the public good that the political live rail operates. As the live rail makes reform hazardous, and possibly politically fatal, so lies the explanation why European governments have approached reform on these different fronts with more than a due sense of political caution.

The NHS is the live rail in British Politics. The British electorate's response on health is comparable to the reaction of voters to state pensions in mainland Europe where the debate is exclusively about cutting future entitlement. The British electorate wants the NHS reformed so that it can perform much more effectively. The debate is therefore easier for politicians in that it is about expanding health resources. But failure to deliver successfully may hold even greater danger for British politicians than European politicians face on the pensions front. The collapse of the one major institution for which voters give almost universal support, after significantly increasing taxpayers' contributions to the service, could result in a political backlash so forceful that a new metaphor for the live rail will need to be invented.

11

Strategic Direction or Tactical Management? Doctrinal Constraints and Political Perceptions of Europe

KENNETH DYSON

> We are with Europe, but not of it. We are linked, but not compromised. We are interested and associated, but not absorbed . . . We belong to no single continent, but to all.[1]
>
> The position of Britain is . . . quite unique, for we are part, and an essential part, of . . . the three great unities of the world. The unity across the Atlantic, the unity within the British Commonwealth and Empire, and the unity with Western Europe.[2]

THE POLITICAL INHERITANCE: FROM DETACHMENT TO SEMI-DETACHMENT IN THE TWENTIETH CENTURY

As Britain entered the twentieth century, indeed well into mid-century, Europe was one—but by no means the central—preoccupation of British politics. In a formulation that was to be of lasting political significance, British policy post-1945 was defined by a perception of a special and indispensable world role based on balancing the "three circles" of the Atlantic, Empire (and later Commonwealth) and Europe. The relationship to Europe was viewed as second order, above all concerned with defence and security—and then mediated through the Atlantic Alliance. To the extent that a British contribution was conceded on trade and economics, it was limited to intergovernmental cooperation. Hence in the period 1945–55, formative years in the postwar reconstruction of Europe, Britain's contribution focused on a leadership role in the creation of the North Atlantic Treaty Organisation (NATO) and the Western European Union (WEU).

---

[1] Winston Churchill's comments in the Briand Plan for a united Europe. See "The United States of Europe" (15 Feb. 1930), in M Wolff (ed.), *The Collected Essays of Sir Winston Churchill, Vol. II* (London, Library of Imperial History, 1976), p. 184.
[2] Speech in the House of Commons by Anthony Nutting, Minister of State in the Foreign Office, outlining the concept of the "three circles" associated with Churchill. See Hansard 494/237 (20 Nov. 1951).

In contrast, the European Defence Community was opposed as too supranational. Similarly, participation in the Council of Europe and in the Organisation for European Economic Cooperation (OEEC) contrasted with rejection of the European Coal and Steel Community (ECSC) and of a role in the negotiations leading to the Treaty of Rome.

The long-term and significant consequence is that Britain is not part of the foundation myth of what is now the European Union (EU). She did not shape its early design in her own image, and did not share the memory of association between the glorious years of postwar economic expansion and Community building. The appeal of the EU—as of any institution—is bound up with its foundation myth. For the EU this myth rests on the Franco-German relationship as the motor of integration. It does not embrace Britain. There is a powerful tacit assumption that agenda-setting is a Franco-German matter. This institutional mythology of the EU adds to the problems of British discomfort with the integration process.

Subsequent economic and political setbacks—notably the Suez episode in 1956 and accumulating evidence of relative economic decline—threw established interpretations of the "three circles" doctrine into question, and led to belated and fractious British entry into the European Economic Community (EEC) in 1973. The controversy that surrounded entry and the subsequent development of relations with the EEC testifies to the grip of history on British debate on Europe. This grip is in part deep-seated and contextual. An ingrained sense that Britain occupies a special position and is fundamentally different is a hangover of earlier maritime prowess and the Imperial role, of traditional geostrategic arguments about not being a continental power.[3] It finds a justification in being geographically set apart as a country with its own "island story". There are, in addition, the cultural connections to the far-flung English-speaking world of the former colonies and arguments about "kith and kin".

But, perhaps above all, historical memory of war took on a different form and yielded different lessons from continental Europe. The Second World War had a different meaning and impact. In Jean Monnet's words:

> I never understood why the British did not join this . . . I came to the conclusion that it must have been because it was the price of victory—the illusion that you could maintain what you had, without change.[4]

To this must be added the history of Britain's membership of the EU and the difficulty of making a convincing connection between membership and domestic economic success. This difficulty was at least in part bound up with timing. Entry coincided with the oil crisis of 1973 and the end of the glorious years of the EEC's economic expansion. Subsequent economic crises and the protracted and politically bruising issue of Britain's EEC budget contribution cast a long

---

[3] For the argument that there is a basic difference of outlook between island and mainland see Lord Beloff, *Britain and the European Union* (London, Macmillan, 1996).

[4] From interview in M Charlton, *The Price of Victory* (London, BBC Publications, 1983), p. 307.

shadow over British membership. No clear economic and political connection was made between EEC membership and tackling of Britain's problems of growth and productivity. Similar problems of timing bedevilled Britain's late, unsuccessful and highly controversial entry into the Exchange-Rate Mechanism (ERM) in 1990.[5] The subsequent humiliation of sterling's ejection from the ERM in September 1992 had formative effects in bolstering anti-integration attitudes, especially within the Conservative Party. A regime of domestic monetary and fiscal stability was attained in the 1990s outside participation in the ERM, diminishing the attractions of entry into the single currency. Unsurprisingly, against this background, Eurobarometer surveys in the 1990s consistently showed British public opinion to be the least positive in the EU about membership, about trust in the European Commission, about support for the euro, and about the common foreign and security policy. British public opinion was also the least well informed about the EU.[6]

Hence both long-term political inheritance and the historical experience of entry into, and membership of, the EU conspired to shape the parameters within which British political leadership considered its options in European policy. However, the parameters of policy were also set by far-reaching changes in the European and the international contexts within which these options had to be considered. Crucial to this contextual change were three developments. There was the question of how Britain's relationship to Europe was affected by globalisation. In addition, from the mid-1980s an acceleration occurred in the pace and scope of European integration, the EU began to take firmer shape as a polity in its own right, and a dynamic process of Europeanisation—especially of public policies—became more transparent. Thirdly, after 1989 the dawn of a new post-Cold War world raised major questions about Britain's future relations with an EU in which a united Germany was playing a more central role.

By the beginning of the twenty-first century British policy was confronted with five main challenges in its European policy. Firstly, there was the issue of how British policy should relate to the process of completing Economic and Monetary Union (EMU). Secondly, there were the issues of just what economic and political costs Britain was prepared to bear for the sake of EU enlargement to the east, where enlargement should stop, and what kind of borders (hard or soft) the EU should have with its neighbours. Thirdly, there was the issue of how British policy should relate to the emerging defence and security dimension of the EU, especially in dealing with the "arc of danger" to the east and south and with the emerging threat from international terrorism.[7] Fourthly, there was the issue of British policy on EU institutional reforms both to make enlargement effective and to better connect Europe's citizens to the EU. Finally, there was the challenge of Europe's role in an emerging global governance to tackle problems

---

[5] On this episode see H Thompson, *The British Conservative Government and the European Exchange Rate Mechanism, 1979–1994* (London, Pinter, 1996).

[6] The Eurobarometer surveys are produced twice annually by the European Commission.

[7] Lord Hurd, "Europe Must Respond to the Arc of Danger", *Financial Times*, 28 Mar., 2001.

of trade, of financial market regulation, of development and poverty, of ecological sustainability, of human rights' violations, and of security, especially in the face of terrorism.

Managing this complexity and the tensions generated by these multiple and interlocking challenges offers in principle an opportunity for British political leadership in the twenty-first century. The combination of such complexity and tensions with the historically rooted nature of state sovereignty and national identities does not intimate a European federal state in the making. An emerging EU federal state would favour German experience, qualities and leadership skills. Contemporary developments suggest that the EU is an evolving experimental union, requiring a high degree of pragmatism, practical inventiveness and skills of learning on the job—qualities that are identified with the British.[8] The connections between this experimental union and wider processes of internationalisation again offer a field in which Britain can disproportionately contribute. But, for historical reasons to be explored in this chapter, it remains unclear whether British elites will engage fully and constructively in this experiment in union. Other qualities of the British political elite—ambivalence, semi-detachment, caution and procrastination on Europe—do not suggest that Britain will whole-heartedly embrace this role.

BRITISH POLITICS AND EUROPE AT THE TURN OF THE CENTURY: SEMI-DETACHMENT, CAUTION AND PROCRASTINATION

The difference as Britain enters the twenty-first century from the situation a century before was that its relations with Europe are now established as the central and defining issue of its domestic politics and the fundamental challenge that its political leadership faces. Underpinning the significance of this issue is the growth of European integration and the progressive Europeanisation of British policies and politics, both in scope and in depth. The increased scope and depth of integration—especially in market regulation and in economic stabilisation—has occurred in a complex, mutually supportive interaction between two factors. First, a sequence of formal Treaty changes (Rome 1957, Single European Act 1987, Maastricht 1991, Amsterdam 1997, Nice 2000) expanded the policy competence of the EU and sought to strengthen its institutions. Secondly, informal economic and social integration produced by market and technological changes reinforced the logic for institutionalising integration.[9] In turn, European integration has become

---

[8] On the EU as an experimental union rather than an incipient federal state see B Laffan, R O'Donnell and M Smith, *Europe's Experimental Union: Rethinking Integration* (London, Routledge, 2000). But *cf.* K Nicolaidis and R Howse (eds.), *The Federal Vision: Legitimacy and Levels of Governance in the US and EU* (Oxford, Oxford University Press, 2001).

[9] On informal integration and how it prepares the way for formal Treaty changes see W Wallace, *The Transformation of Western Europe* (London, RIIA/Pinter, 1990), ch. 4. On the institutionalisation of integration see A Stone Sweet, W Sandholtz and N Fligstein (eds.), *The Institutionalization of Europe* (Oxford, Oxford University Press, 2001).

a key factor in shaping changes affecting policies, structures, discourse, identities and public careers in Britain.[10] There has been a creeping Europeanisation of British politics, most pronounced in Whitehall. The result of this pressure to adapt has been some painful choices in particular policy domains and the question of whether Britain wants to present itself as a "pace-setter", as a "foot-dragger" or as a "fence-sitter".[11] With the notable exception of the single European market, the pattern has been one of reluctance to act as a "pace-setter". Hence Britain has retained a reputation as an "awkward" partner, as semi-detached.[12]

Unlike a century ago, the issue of Britain's relations with Europe touches on fundamental questions about the political order. On the process of European integration there are differences of view about whether it should evolve as voluntary cooperation amongst sovereign states, in effect an intergovernmental process, or as a binding "social contract" amongst their nationals, in effect a constitution-making process. The question of the final aims for Europe's institutional design raises the choice between federation, confederation, a looser association of states picking and choosing areas for cooperation, or some new form of multi-level governance. With this question comes the issue of the precise responsibilities to be assigned to the EU and the contested concept of subsidiarity. There follows in turn the issue of the form of legal authority that the EU requires to discharge these responsibilities both efficiently and accountably.

Above all, the EU represents a basic strategic challenge to the nature of political authority that political leaders—by no means only in Britain—have preferred to fudge. This challenge boils down to a political choice between three options. The first is to defend sovereignty as the basic normative premise of British politics, as the precondition of a constitutionally independent state, and to view the EU as just another international organisation.[13] The challenge is to preserve the traditional values of the equality of the British state under international law and its political freedom to do as it wishes. This option has been influential within the Conservative Party during the 1990s and has long held sway within Old Labour.

A second option is to regard the EU as a potentially new post-sovereign legal order, transcending the modern state as the location of authority. It requires a

---

[10] For definitions of Europeanisation see C Radaelli, "Whither Europeanization? Concept Stretching and Substantive Change", *European Integration online Papers*. 4/8, 2000, http://eop.or.at/eiop/texte/2000-008a.htm; also M Green Cowles, J Caporaso and T Risse (eds.), *Transforming Europe. Europeanization and Domestic Change* (Ithaca, Cornell University Press, 2001) and T Börzel, "Pace-Setting, Foot-Dragging and Fence-Sitting: Member State Responses to Europeanization", Paper prepared for the European Community Studies Association (ECSA) Panel "New Perspectives on EU Member State Relationships", Madison, Wisconsin, 31 May–2 June 2001.
[11] Börzel, *ibid*.
[12] S George, *The Awkward Partner* (Oxford, Oxford University Press, 1994). Also S George (ed.), *Britain and the European Community: the Politics of Semi-Detachment* (Oxford, Clarendon Press, 1992).
[13] Close to this position is R Jackson, "Sovereignty in World Politics: A Glance at the Conceptual and Historical Landscape", *Political Studies*, XLVII, 1999, pp. 431–56. For a more robust statement see W Cash, *Against a Federal Europe: The Battle for Britain* (London, Duckworth, 1991).

new form of British politics anchored around a rights-based European constitutional jurisprudence and a more pluralist and liberal political order based on a civic rather than ethnic identity.[14] This option finds favour with constitutional reformers in the tradition of political Radicalism. But, like Radicalism itself, it has had less resonance within the two main political parties and been marginal rather than central to the British political tradition. A third, more pragmatic option is to view the EU not as the end of the sovereign British state but as a new form of sovereignty "game". The "post-Westphalian" sovereignty "game" is presented as consistent with the new realities of diminished state autonomy over basic policy issues in an age of globalisation. On this reading the challenge to British elites is to master the regulative rules of this post-modern game of multi-level governance in the EU.[15] This option is closer to views within New Labour. Hence, as British policy confronts the Europe of the twenty-first century, the EU as a political order remains deeply contested at a fundamental level.

At another level European integration deeply affects the internal dynamics of British politics. Domestic politics are being "Europeanised". This phenomenon is discernible above all across the range of public policies but is also identifiable in the subtleties of political discourse and in the construction and affirmation of identities. It has, for instance, played a part in lending support to Scottish national identity whilst being interpreted as a threat to English identity. Europeanisation could in this way become implicated in calling into question the future of the British state. Not least, developments within the EU have become critical to the making—and most notably unmaking—of political careers. Thus Europe was intimately bound up with the loss of office by Margaret Thatcher and John Major. Tony Blair identified in the issue of whether and when Britain should join the single European currency the most threatening political problem that he faced and the issue on which his historical reputation would rest.[16] Under the leaderships of William Hague and of Ian Duncan Smith a pro-European attitude did not appear compatible with a successful political career within the Conservative Party. Equally, a Labour government with a second huge Parliamentary majority in 2001 again hesitated to take a firm and consistent line of pro-European political leadership and to grasp the nettle of making the political case for entry into the single currency and tailoring economic policies to that purpose.

Europe was associated with memories of political danger and failure, not least of Britain's short and painful experience of membership of the ERM after 1990, her humiliating exit in September 1992, and the subsequent political travails of

---

[14] See J Weiler, "European Neo-Constitutionalism: In Search of Foundations for the European Constitutional Order", (1996) XLIV *Political Studies* 517–33; N MacCormick, "Liberalism, Nationalism and the Post-Sovereign State", (1996) XLIV *Political Studies* 553–67; T Prosser, "Understanding the British Constitution" (1996) XLIV *Political Studies* 473–87.

[15] G Sorensen, "Sovereignty: Change and Continuity in a Fundamental Institution", (1999) XLVII *Political Studies* 590–604.

[16] See H Young, *This Blessed Plot: Britain and Europe from Churchill to Blair* (London, Macmillan, 1998); A. Rawnsley, *Servants of the People: The Inside Story of New Labour*, 2nd edition (London, Penguin, 2001).

Doctrinal Constraints and Political Perceptions of Europe 157

the Major government and the Conservative Party.[17] To these were added earlier memories of what Europe had done to relations at the heart of Mrs Thatcher's governments, most strikingly with her Chancellor of the Exchequer and her Foreign Secretary.[18] Caution on Europe was further reinforced by a party political structure in which pro- and anti-Europeanism was incorporated within both the main political parties. In contrast, the norm in continental Europe is for anti-Europeanism to be exiled to the political extremes of separate left- and right-wing parties.[19] British political leadership on Europe was consequently subordinated to the tactics of a "balancing act" between the two wings of each party. These wings had the potential to act as veto players. In essence, party leaders were treating Europe as a "nested" game, in which "sub-optimal" European policies might be justified as optimal for the purpose of party unity.[20]

The structural aspect of party balance was less significant for the two Blair governments, both because of the huge size of their majorities and because pro-integration views had taken a stronger hold within the Parliamentary Labour Party.[21] Europe still appeared as a "nested" game, but this time the structural constraint was managing the media, especially the Europhobic sections of the press, and in particular ensuring that they were supportive for electoral purposes. How both press and television reported on EU policy issues and represented the EU's political arrangements acted as a constraint on government policy.[22] Hence caution and procrastination continued to prevail, even with a pro-European prime minister and government.[23] Managing personal relations on Europe at the heart of government was bound up with these structural influences in party and media management. Seen from the angle of European policy, the result was a consistent theme of tactical management displacing strategic direction, of caution and procrastination triumphing over boldness.

Whitehall officials are on the whole comfortable with the process of Europeanisation. Operating the complexity of the Brussels machinery offers new opportunities for practicing their negotiating skills and for displaying their superior skills in the smooth coordination of government business. British ministers are in consequence the beneficiaries of first-rate detailed briefing, the negotiating skills of British officials are highly prized in Brussels, and the British

---

[17] For an account P Stephens, *Politics and the Pound: The Conservatives' Struggle with Sterling* (London, Macmillan, 1996).

[18] See K Dyson and K Featherstone, *The Road to Maastricht: Negotiating Economic and Monetary Union* (Oxford, Oxford University Press, 1999).

[19] M Aspinwall, "Structuring Europe: Powersharing Institutions and British Preferences on European Integration", (2000) 48 *Political Studies* 415–42.

[20] G Tsebelis, *Nested Games: Rational Choice in Comparative Politics* (Berkeley, University of California Press, 1990).

[21] A Gamble, "Britain and EMU", in K Dyson (ed.), *European States and the Euro* (Oxford, Oxford University Press, 2001).

[22] For evidence about the nature of this constraint see N Gavin, "Imagining Europe: Political Identity and British Television Coverage of the European Economy", (2000) 2 *British Journal of Politics and International Relations* 352–73; also P Anderson and A Weymouth, *Insulting the Public? The British Press and the European Union* (London, Longman, 1998).

[23] A Rawnsley, n. 16 above.

system for domestic coordination of EU policy is rated an exemplary model. But the degree of comfort with Europe varies: at its highest in the Foreign and Commonwealth Office, but much more problematic in the case of the Treasury.[24] The subsequent tensions surfaced in relation to EMU.[25] More to the point, even those Whitehall officials who subscribe to constructive engagement in Europe are deeply pragmatic and cautious in intellectual outlook. Whitehall remains a mandarin culture that prizes above all the arts of the possible. They are detached players of European games and fixers of the rules. There is an impatience with the long-term rationalist constructions of European policy typical of French and German approaches and a tendency to underestimate the underlying seriousness of political purpose that animates these constructions. Hence there is a symbiotic relationship between political and official levels in the conduct of European policy. The political level does not challenge the official level to provide the intellectual and policy underpinning for a clear strategic direction on Europe. This challenge would force change on the Whitehall outlook of pragmatism, caution and short-term fixing.

But this symbiotic relationship between Whitehall, the political parties and Parliament cannot disguise an asymmetry caused by differences in the institutional scope and depth of Europeanisation. The process of Europeanisation has asymmetrical political effects that simultaneously empower and disempower the executive. Europeanisation gives an informational and negotiating advantage to Whitehall in conducting policy. Its officials operate the complex, tangled web of European relationships, multilateral and bilateral, conduct the intricacies of treaty negotiations, and are on the whole comfortable in the informal world of EU policy. But the lack of similar levels of direct and detailed involvement with the EU within Parliament and the political parties means that Whitehall has to live in a political context that is remote from, and distrustful, of Europe. Equally seriously, the media—press, radio and television—both downplay the European content of news reporting and sensationalise and personalise that content. In the press news reporting and editorial views about Europe become difficult to differentiate, and editorial views on Europe are generally hostile. The result is a gap between Whitehall elite engagement in Europe and public attitudes that reflect inadequate information and professionally poor standards of news reporting. Hence a Whitehall machine that is professionally sophisticated in dealing with Europe lacks a supportive political and media milieu. It is not put into the service of a clear strategic direction on Europe but trapped within the tactical calculations and manoeuvres of a domestic political leadership preoccupied with internal party management and media management on Europe. Whitehall's Europeanisation contrasts with a lack of engagement of Parliament, parties and media.

[24] See K Dyson, "Europeanization, Whitehall Culture and the Treasury as Institutional Veto Player: A Constructivist Approach to Economic and Monetary Union", (2000) 78 *Public Administration* 897–914. For a more historical view see H Young, n. 16 above.

[25] K Dyson and K Featherstone, n. 18 above; A Rawnsley, n. 16 above.

This brings me to my central theme: that Britain's political contribution to post-1945 and post-Cold War Europe has been defined and constrained by the combination of unresolved strategic dilemma with absorption in tactical party, media and electoral management. The twenty-first century may witness an escape from this situation in one or both of two ways. First, events could precipitate a bolder strategic political leadership on behalf either of disengagement or of firm British leadership in Europe. Such a strategic choice would, however, involve great risks. Secondly, an acceleration of the process of disconnection between EU institutions and public opinion across Europe could offer new opportunities for Britain to apply its practical problem-solving skills to making the EU work better. Such opportunities are, however, likely to be more effectively exploited if Britain is seen to be constructively engaged in the Treaty-mandated process of "ever closer union".

Meanwhile, in three key policy domains Britain takes into its relations with the Europe of the twenty-first century clear distinguishing hallmarks. There is a belated, hesitant and critical engagement on the social dimension, complemented by a "wait-and-see" approach to the single currency. She tends to be seen as an "awkward" partner on institutional reforms, where sovereignty is most visibly at stake. Finally, Britain hankers after a world role to balance its European engagement. A shifting blend of pragmatism, caution and hostility informs European policy positions and leads to a disposition to "fence-sitting" and "foot-dragging". Underpinning these features are three doctrines that shape and circumscribe British policies. The doctrine of the continuing and absolute sovereignty of Crown in Parliament supports a consensus around an intergovernmental view of the EU and hostility to supranational integration. An ideological commitment to 'market' capitalism makes for a combination of discomfort with, and rejection of, both the social dimension and the single currency and a preference for seeing the EU as a free-trading partnership. The doctrine of the "three circles" legitimates a semi-detached attitude to the EU. These three doctrines—in combination with a sense of "Britishness"—need closer examination in an assessment of how Britain might contribute to the Europe of the twenty-first century.

THE PARAMETERS OF BRITAIN'S RELATIONS WITH EUROPE IN THE TWENTY-FIRST CENTURY: AN ANALYSIS OF THE COMPLEX DYNAMICS

The central difficulty is how to address the question of Britain's contribution to the Europe of the twenty-first century whilst eschewing predictions that in days and weeks, never mind years and decades, can look foolish. Scholars are at their best when confining themselves to addressing the past and its relationship to the present. They can offer more value in identifying where we start out on our journey into the twenty-first century. They are less secure in spotting the main issues that confront us, and frankly useless on the question of where we shall be in

2100. Too much complexity of, and interactive changes in, structures and agents—in short, contingency and indeterminacy—are involved for the scholar to presume that he/she can guide judgement and prompt action. Hence the aim is to offer an analytical and critical inquiry into the where we are now and into some of the key issues that we can identify in 2001. Both editors and readers are, I suspect, hopeful that these contributions can offer some guidance to judgement. However, practical judgement needs to be grounded in a firm sense of reality and of the objective constraints facing Britain's relations with Europe. Hence this chapter seeks—however futile the task may seem when confronting so controversial a topic—to stay as close as possible to the firmer ground of providing a detached and dispassionate account of what is going on in this complex relationship. In this way—if only by drawing out the genuine difficulties in Britain's relations with Europe—scholarship can best contribute to practical judgement.

There are some serious problems in tackling this question. The question of Britain's contribution to Europe identifies Britain as the key independent variable with which we are concerned. However, five main difficulties arise in assessing this contribution. They point to the complexity of the dynamics at work and the contingency and indeterminacy associated with the British contribution.

Contextualising Britain as an Independent Variable

First, it is necessary to contextualise Britain as an independent variable. Even where Britain is pushing for a particular direction of change in Europe (e.g. towards a market capitalism model of flexible labour markets), it may be no more than a mediating variable. Far more important may be that Britain acts as agent for a deeper structural change like globalisation (pursuing the logic of freedom of movement of capital) or technological change (the logic of transition from Fordist to post-Fordist production system). In particular, British policies are shaped and conditioned by the important role of inward investment in the British economy and its role as a site for multinational corporations. The City of London appears to be a particularly important British variable. But on closer examination the Big Bang of the 1980s turned the City into a place in which financial transactions were increasingly handled by non-British players. In its wake the big City names fell into foreign ownership.[26] Hence in speaking of the City as driving British policy one is handling a British contribution in only a formal sense, its old club atmosphere having vanished. Similarly, European receptiveness to Britain's role in pushing an agenda of private-sector pension provision may be bound up with underlying demographic pressures affecting all European states.

---

[26] D Kynaston, *The City of London, Volume IV: A Club No More, 1945–2000* (London, Chatto and Windus, 2001).

Britain as a Changing Variable

Secondly, Britain is likely to be a changing variable over the next decades and more, never mind the century. Hence its contribution may change. Indicators of the potential for domestic political change include the effects of devolution to Scotland and Wales, a growing resort to proportional representation at the levels of European and subnational elections, and the incorporation of the European Convention on Human Rights into domestic law. In particular, devolution has made more visible the Scottish anomaly as one of the two founder kingdoms of the first United Kingdom (an asymmetrical state). It raises questions about whether the quasi-federal settlement in the 1998 Scotland Act (with its division of legislative powers between Edinburgh and Westminster) is stable. Devolution may have released forces of pluralism and decentralization that will reinvigorate the British state or—consequent on the Scottish sense of nationhood—lead to separation.[27] Whatever the outcome, Britain's relations with Europe will be permanently affected. The Scotland Act and membership of the EU—especially following the *Factortame* decision of 1991—show that the doctrine of the sovereignty of Crown in Parliament is less persuasive as an account of the basis of authority.[28] More unclear in 2001 is the prospect for electoral reform. An extension of proportional representation to national elections would be important in altering the structural party political constraints on European policy. More immediately interesting is the incorporation of the European Convention, which strengthens the development of a more conceptual, rights-based process of constructive interpretation based on European materials.[29] Once again the doctrine of the sovereignty of Crown in Parliament is hedged.

Finally, one cannot discount the possibility that the European issue could be a catalyst for party system change, analogous in its impact to the Corn Law issue in nineteenth century politics. In that case the context in which British policy is made could change dramatically. More prosaically, but none the less significant, the contrast between the quality of public-service provision across the main states of the EU and the condition of transport, heath and education provision in Britain offers the potential for the initiation of an informal policy learning process. An acceleration of the process of Europeanisation of British politics could be achieved by the political commitment to achieve European levels of excellence in public services. Policy emulation would involve seeing Europe as offering a logic of political and social appropriateness for Britain that could

---

[27] *Cf.* V Bogdanor, "Devolution: Decentralization or Disintegration?" 70(2) *The Political Quarterly* 185–94, and N MacCormick, "The English Constitution, the British State and the Scottish Anomaly", in *Proceedings of the British Academy 101, 1998 Lectures and Memoirs* (Oxford, Oxford University Press, 1999), pp. 289–306.

[28] See N MacCormick, "Beyond the Sovereign State", (1993) 56 *Modern Law Review* 1–19.

[29] T Prosser, n. 14 above, p. 481.

prove important in overcoming a past obsession with "lesson-drawing" from the US. In the process Britain would become a more 'normal' European country, more at ease in interacting with her EU partners.

The Issue of Bilateral Relations

Thirdly, we should not lose sight of how Britain's effects on Europe will be mediated through its complex bilateral relations with other European states. Anglo-German relations take on a particular—and contested—significance as united Germany emerges as a key player in post-Cold War Europe, especially with EU enlargement to the east and with the relative importance of the German economy.[30] How they are managed is bound up in the view adopted about the relationship of the EU to the Berlin Republic. In one realist view, influential within the Conservative Party, Germany has, or aspires to, a hegemonic position in the EU. Hence strengthening the EU is the route to giving Germany greater power in Europe, and for that reason to be resisted. This view leads to a suspicious, at best ambivalent attitude to cultivating the Anglo-German relationship as a means of influencing EU development. It usually goes along with a perception of Germany as an anti-model of corporatism and rigidity in economic and social policy. In another view, postwar Germany defines its role as a civilian power, pursuing policies of multilateralism and good neighbourliness, and happy to bind its increased power into a European framework. Its ambitions on political union may exceed what British leaders seek. But it is a state with which British governments can comfortably do business, especially on NATO-related security issues and on economic reforms. This view—which finds an echo within New Labour and the Liberal Democrats—may be accompanied by a perception that Germany serves as a model for a more decentralised and pluralist British state in which citizens' rights and public power are given formalised constitutional expression.

A central constraint on British policy remains the power of the EU foundation myth about the special character of the Franco-German relationship as the motor of European integration. This myth may be refashioned in the context of the historic nature of EU enlargement to the east to embrace Poland in a form of triumvirate, based on the "Weimar triangle". British hesitation, caution and procrastination on European integration—in particular a fundamental unwillingness to subscribe to the historic nature of the postwar project of European union—make it impossible for Britain to be absorbed into the foundation myth. In consequence, British governments will tend to prefer to seek out different allies on different issues, in a more or less active manner. Other EU governments do the same. But the difference in the French and German cases is that they also

---

[30] See W Paterson, "Britain and the Berlin Republic: Between Ambivalence and Emulation", (2001) 10 *German Politics* 199–221.

share a foundation myth and sense of ownership of the European project that draws them together in the face of "history-making" decisions in Europe, like the Maastricht Treaty. A shared foundation myth is by no means sufficient to guarantee the weight of their contribution. Much depends on the will and the capability to deliver of individual French and German political leaders and on their capacity to persuade other EU leaders to go along with them. But they have at least been able to give enough substance to this foundation myth of Franco-German collaboration to ensure its continuing credibility. In this context British governments are faced with a choice. They can subscribe—more or less grudgingly—to this myth and follow Franco-German leadership on the "history-making" decisions, whilst remaining semi-detached and essentially tactical in alliance-seeking on specific issues. They can reinvent Britain as a part of the foundation myth (involving a qualitative leap forward). Or they can disengage (whether by negotiating multiple opt-outs or by exit). Historical form (and form can change) suggests that the Franco-German contribution will continue to be central in imparting strategic direction to Europe on the "history-making" decisions. Britain's contribution is likely to depend on how its governments react to a Europe that form indicates will be made by others.

Europe as a Changing Variable

Fourthly, the dependent variable of Europe will itself change, independently of Britain, and face British governments with difficult challenges and painful choices whose consequences will be profound. A key factor will be the impact of processes and events, internal to the expanding EU, close to its expanding borders and in the wider world. These processes and events include what happens to EMU, the scale of the problems consequent on EU enlargement to the east and south, how new security threats like international terrorism develop, and the institutional development of the EU's governance. They suggest that Britain will be dealing with an unsettled Europe and an experimental Europe.[31]

In so far as EMU evolves towards a "harder" coordination of fiscal and possibly of economic and employment policies, the implications for sovereignty of entry into the single currency may deter British entry.[32] It is also by no means clear how well equipped the Euro-Zone is to deal with a problem of contagious deflation as opposed to inflation. A single monetary policy could also prove politically unsustainable against a background of enduring differences in productivity performance and different degrees of external exposure to movements of the euro. Euro economic governance is an experimental process in the making. At the same time this process is constrained by the Treaty-anchored doctrine of central bank independence and the model of "implicit", ex ante rather

[31] B Laffan, R O'Donnell and M Smith, n. 8 above.
[32] See the discussion in K Dyson, "Euro Economic Governance", in K Dyson (ed.), *European States and the Euro* (Oxford, Oxford University Press, 2001).

than "explicit" policy coordination. In consequence the Euro-Zone may prove more effective in delivering economic stability than sustained high growth.[33]

The sheer scale of EU enlargement, the diversity that it will bring, the reconfiguration of borders and of the "insider-outsider" problem, and decision-making problems in a large-scale EU will have powerful political and institutional implications for the EU and for how Britain relates to the EU. In so far as its implications are a wider and looser Europe, many Britons would welcome its as a more intergovernmental and more comfortable Europe. But in so far as the expanded EU proved both ineffective in taking and implementing decisions and unaccountable and lacking in transparency because of its intergovernmental character, it would risk declining legitimacy and marginalisation as an institution safeguarding prosperity and security in Europe. Hence EU enlargement poses unavoidable and urgent questions about how its governance is to be organised and how the balance is to be struck between effectiveness and accountability. These questions were in any case already on the agenda following German unification and the desire to balance economic and monetary union with progress on political union. In consequence, issues about identity and citizenship and about a European constitution had their own dynamic, but one given a new urgency by EU enlargement. With enlargement concern about securing an identity based around common values and respect for the highest standards of human rights and civil society has grown within the EU (hence the Charter of Fundamental Rights approved in December 2000). No less problematic is the issue of whether new entrants will adapt easily to the negotiating culture of the EU, with its package deals and reciprocity.

These issues combine with an increasingly complex voting system and a greater number and diversity of member states to threaten decision-making paralysis.[34] As suggested below, Britain may be able to make an important contribution to showing how more complex institutions can be made to work. More questionable is whether Britain can in the first place contribute much to designing appropriate institutions for this changed context.

Another process with its own dynamics relates to issues of external and internal security. In the post-Cold War world Europe is confronted by an "arc of danger" stretching from the former Soviet Union, through the Balkans to north Africa, in which complex crises involving war, organised crime and violations of human rights create highly complex and difficult challenges to the EU. The EU is drawn into the process of security building and crisis avoidance and management in this area by a combination of fears of spillover effects with humanitarian motives. Difficult issues arise about its relationship to NATO in security policy. In particular, the dual processes of EU and NATO enlargement affect European security, especially as they extend into the former territory of the

---

[33] On these problems see K Dyson, *The Politics of the Euro-Zone: Stability or Breakdown?* (Oxford, Oxford University Press, 2000).

[34] "Nice Try: Should the Treaty of Nice be Ratified?" (London, Centre for Economic Policy Research, 2001).

Soviet Union. Hence the complex relationships between the EU, NATO and Russia will be pivotal to European security and central to British interests.

Even more ominously, the attack on the mainland of the United States on 11 September 2001 revealed the shared vulnerability of liberal democratic states to international terrorist attacks and raised urgent questions about the appropriate form that response should take. This event opened up an opportunity for the EU to develop a distinctive role in helping to create and sustain the conditions for an international coalition against terrorism by exploiting its political, diplomatic and economic instruments. But it also raised potentially complex and difficult issues in coordinating a response, conditional on how far the United States was prepared to engage in multilateral action. Here Britain had a useful and important role to play in building cross-Atlantic bridges. At the same time the fight against terrorism called for stronger coordination of EU action so that Europe could play an effective role to support the United States. Home and justice affairs gained increasing centrality within the EU

The EU's instruments for extending security stretch beyond the promise of enlargement to new migration, visa, asylum and citizenship policies. They also include new approaches to social and economic reconstruction and new mechanisms for peace-keeping, peace enforcement and humanitarian intervention, aimed at protecting citizens.[35] These measures achieve compatibility with the historic nature of the EU's role, and with German sensibilities, by their stress on a broad civilian power conception of defence and security policy.[36] They also complement rather than challenge NATO's role in European security. In short, the EU's role in European security has little to do with the classic state-building implied in creating a European army. It involves developing a rapid-reaction capability designed to minimise casualties rather than fight wars, the capacity to assist social and economic reconstruction, and the extension of the benefits of deeper economic integration, of shared institutional belonging and of the principles of multilateralism and reciprocity.

Here again, in the context of a complex, multi-layered institutional architecture, European security policies will have their own dynamics, potential tensions and risks of failure, which might expose a British government to problems of strategic choice. Such choice would be all the more difficult as a conception of European security as part of the Atlantic Alliance has been a common thread of vital British interest. The dynamics could involve the consolidation of a European defence and security identity less dependent on the United States. The risk of failure is bound up with a "capability-expectations" gap that could well bedevil EU security policy.[37] From the perspective of 2001 it seems likely that

---

[35] M Kaldor, *New and Old Wars: Organized Violence in a Global Era* (Cambridge, Polity Press, 1999).

[36] C Hill, "European Foreign Policy: Power Bloc, Civilian Model—or Flop?", in R Rummel (ed.), *The Evolution of an International Actor: Western Europe's New Self-Assertiveness* (Boulder, Westview Press, 1990), pp. 31–55.

[37] See C Hill, "The Capability-Expectations Gap, or Conceptualizing Europe's International Role", (1993) 31 *Journal of Common Market Studies* 305–28.

strategic choice in this policy domain would be guided by the deep sense of ownership and commitment that British governments have to the paramount role of NATO in European security and by the abiding legacy of the "three-circles" doctrine. The disposition of British governments will be to pursue partnership rather than rivalry with the United States. They are also more politically comfortable with NATO's intergovernmental character and averse to anything like a European army that would strengthen the EU's "state-like" character.

Despite this disposition, British governments will have to contribute to the great problems of strategic choice facing EU security policy. The key choice—or perhaps more appropriately "trade off"—is between building on the EU's "magnet effect" by attracting new members and diffusing its political, economic and cultural practices and constructing the EU as a fortress to exclude problems and conserve the status quo. It is the choice between "soft" or "hard" borders. On the outcome will depend the kind of post-Cold War Europe in which we live and the nature of the role of the EU. In particular, the EU must decide whether it wishes to serve as a regional pacifier, as a mediator, and as a bridge between rich and poor or whether it prefers to opt for a more defensive inward-looking identity as an oasis of peace and prosperity.[38]

The World Arena, Europe and Britain

Finally, Britain's contribution to the Europe of the twenty-first century is embedded in changes in the world political and economic arenas. From one angle, the EU can be seen as a nascent form of international negotiated order with its own institutional characteristics, reigning ideas and material capabilities.[39] Albeit lacking the conventional attributes of statehood, the EU is an international actor that offers a distinctive "civilising" model of how international relations should and can be conducted, on the basis of a community of law, the principle of multilateral action and the practice of good neighbourliness. It specialises in "soft" rather than "hard" power and relies on a combination of moral authority and calculative appeals to economic self-interest rather than coercion. Its role culture as an international actor is, in short, Kantian and Lockeian rather than Hobbesian.[40] In addition, and problematically for Britain with its commitment to market capitalism, the EU seeks to offer a distinctive European "social" model, combining market change and economic reforms with the maintenance of consent and respect for economic and social rights. In these respects the EU provides an alternative to an American-centred world

[38] On these and other international roles for the EU see C Hill, "Closing the Capabilities-Expectations Gap?", in J Peterson and H Sjürsen (eds.), *A Common Foreign Policy for Europe? Competing Visions of the CFSP* (London, Routledge, 1998), pp. 18–38.

[39] See O Elgström and M Smith, "Introduction: Negotiation and Policy-Making in the European Union—Processes, System and Order" (2000) 7 *Journal of European Public Policy* 678.

[40] On these role cultures see A Wendt, *Social Theory of International Politics* (Cambridge, Cambridge University Press, 1999).

order focused around the values of market capitalism and of great power politics. In consequence, British governments remain ambivalent about projecting the EU as the model for global governance. A traditional attachment to great power politics (including the inclination to play Athens to the US Rome), the "three-circles" doctrine, and the structural power of the market capitalism model make British governments unlikely advocates of fashioning global governance on the European model.

Even independently of British reservations, doubts remain about the power of Europe to shape the terms of global economic and security governance. Not least, its internal institutional and political problems of coordinating its activities and the diversity of interests that it contains make the EU a very conservative international actor.[41] These problems have been demonstrated in the attempt of the Euro-Zone to play an international role in global economic and monetary policies. How effective the EU is seen to be will depend on the context that it faces. Its strengths as an actor in international security are likely to be best displayed in averting military crises and in managing post-crisis situations in Europe. But once order has broken down and rapid response is required to crisis—once parts of Europe revert to a Hobbesian condition—its conservative bias and reliance on "soft power" are likely to be seen as weaknesses. The prospect remains that chaos could prevail over order in Europe, that, rather than the twenty-first century exhibiting a clear long-term trend to increasing interdependency and global cooperation, centrifugal tendencies, regime and societal collapse, and human tragedies might dominate the agenda and prove resistant to EU action.[42] Moreover, the EU's crisis management capabilities after the introduction of the single currency have yet to be tested. The institutional architecture of the Euro-Zone is well adapted to tackling inflationary economic shocks, but its strengths are questionable in the face of multiple, contagious financial shocks and deflationary crisis.[43] In such circumstances its conservative bias could deepen rather than help resolve global economic problems, especially if the US ceased to play a locomotive role in global economic expansion. The relatively benign circumstances of the Euro-Zone's birth will not endure.

Britain's relations with Europe will be powerfully shaped by how well the European "civilizing" and "social" models succeed in delivering both security within Europe and economic prosperity. On security the EU faces a serious "capability-expectations" gap, one painfully highlighted by the Bosnian and Kosovo crises of the 1990s. In addition, it confronts the serious challenge of the nature of the relationship between the EU, NATO and Russia in guaranteeing

[41] *Ibid*, p. 681.
[42] See the debate between R Wright, *Nonzero: The Logic of Human Destiny* (New York, Pantheon Books, 2000) and R Kaplan, *The Coming Anarchy: Shattering the Dreams of the Post Cold War* (New York, Vintage Books, 2000).
[43] See K Dyson, *The Politics of the Euro Zone: Stability or Breakdown?* (Oxford, Oxford University Press, 2000).

European security, the difficulties of which were seen in the Chechnya conflict. Three interlinked problems need to be addressed: how Russia is to be involved in some form of European security architecture; how policy towards Russia relates to EU and NATO enlargement; and how to handle the relationship between addressing concerns about human rights in Russia and providing Russia with a framework of security. In this context British policy faces the challenge of the appropriate policy balance between pursuing the European "civilising" model, via EU enlargement and EU framework agreements embracing the former Soviet Union, the former Yugoslavia and the Mediterranean, and extending the umbrella of the NATO deterrence capability.

On the economy the EU has important international strengths that give it the status of a model on a par with the United States. Most notable are the education and skill levels of its workforce; the productivity-per-hour-worked; the higher levels of capital stock per employee in France and Germany than in the US; its record as an exporter; its hard-won reputation for price stability; and the general high quality of the public services that sustain the economy.[44] The EU has been able to avoid both the abject poverty of an "underclass" and the more excessive differentials of income and wealth seen in the United States. Less progressive tax systems and a less generous welfare system compound the effects of these differentials in the US. The emphasis on redistribution, social solidarity and collective provision to increase the quality of life defines in essence the European "social" model of "co-ordinated" capitalism in contrast with the US model of market capitalism. Reliance is placed on the cooperative management of economic change, most notably through "social pacts" involving employers and trade unions.[45] Conversely, the EU has been relatively poor in its record of economic growth, of exploiting the potential of new technologies, of job creation and of employment participation rates. The result is higher levels of structural unemployment in the EU than in the US, a phenomenon that is attributed to labour-market rigidities by advocates of market capitalism. The British position here is one of critical distance to the EU, arguing that the EU has a great deal to learn from US-style deregulation, especially of labour markets, before Britain can safely contemplate entry into the single currency.

Britain's relations with Europe will be shaped by whether international developments favour the "civilising" and "social" models represented by the EU's core states and by whether processes of internationalisation are shaped and influenced by these models through emulation and diffusion. A key factor as far as the European "social" model is concerned is what happens to the US economy. The open question is whether the model of market capitalism will retain its credibility as a mobiliser of "animal spirits" in economic life or whether it will succumb

---

[44] See the figures and argument in A Turner, *Just Capital: The Liberal Economy* (London, Macmillan, 2001).

[45] See K Dyson (ed.), *European States and the Euro*, n. 21 above.

to its casino-like character and fall victim to irrational exuberance, financial panics and crash.[46] Another factor is whether the market capitalism model will prove compatible with realising the improvements in British public services that had by 2001 become the key domestic political issue. The issue of quality of public services drew attention to deficits vis-à-vis other EU states and the prospect that policy emulation and learning might shift from the US (as under the Thatcher, Major and first Blair governments) to Europe. Such questions might then be reopened as whether private pension provision offers as great a security as compulsory social insurance and whether more decentralised methods of delivering public services like education and health offer greater efficiency and accountability. But by 2001 it remained unclear whether Britain was ready to seek policy lessons from other European welfare states.

Whether international developments favour the "civilising" model in European security depends on the nature, scale and timing of crises, on the behaviour of US administrations, and on boldness in the EU's approach to enlargement and to defining its role in security. A key factor is whether successive US administrations support rather than undermine efforts to project the EU security system outwards by acting as a partner in strengthening multilateralism. Here much depends on domestic developments within US politics and whether those interests that advocate a strategy of unilateralism come into the ascendancy. In that case the US would be more disposed to disengage from multilateral treaties and organisations (as from the Kyoto global warming treaty in 2001), and treat the EU as a sideshow and Europe as an American protectorate. US commitment to playing a great power role, and an inclination to build a fortress around her national interests, underlines the risk of divergence between US and EU conceptions of European security. Unilateralism could have two adverse consequences for US interests. It could serve to bind Europe together as an adversary and/or to undermine the capability of the EU to extend its "civilising" model beyond its borders. Here there is a potentially important role for Britain as a source of friendly but firm pressure on the US to recognise that its national interest lies in building alliances with the EU.

A second factor is the behaviour of the EU itself. If the approach of the EU to enlargement proves to be slow and hesitant, the US will fill the security vacuum by pressing the case for rapid NATO enlargement. This prospect will in turn make east European states more US- and NATO-oriented than EU-oriented and reduce the magnet effect of the EU as a model of international relations. The post-Cold War world offers an historic opportunity for the EU to shape the security arrangements of Europe in the twenty-first century. Without EU enlargement this ambition will not be realised, US hegemony within Europe reinforced, and the risks of a "fortress" model displacing a "civilising" model of European security enhanced. Within this context there is a serious challenge to

---

[46] *Cf.* S Strange, *Mad Money* (Manchester, Manchester University Press, 1998); also P Coggan, *Easy Money* (London, Profile Books, 2001).

British political leaders to define the kind of model of European security that they seek, to confront the British public with the issues at stake, and to construct an appropriate discourse for framing those issues and convincing the public. This challenge has yet to be addressed.

Last, but not least, the context of crises—both inside and outside Europe—will be critical. The range of possibilities includes new aggressive action by rogue states, the internationalisation of terrorist activity and of organised crime, climate change, crises of modernisation and democratisation, ethnic and cultural clashes, violent youth culture in the context of urbanisation, population increase, deprivation and social exclusion, and crimes against humanity.[47] The prospect for the synchronisation of multiple crises—for instance of international terrorist attacks with global economic crisis—makes for an unpredictable world, with the collapse of the EU under their weight as one feasible outcome. The risk of collapse is increased if the EU finds itself weighted down by cumbersome decision-making processes. Within the context of the threats to British security interests, the "worst-case" scenario to contemplate is the EU's collapse. Contemplation of this scenario should be a stimulus to British governments to become more active in ensuring that the EU has sufficient institutional strengths to be able to absorb the likely strains to which it will be subjected in the twenty-first century.

This section has highlighted the complex dynamics that will shape the context in which Britain contributes to the Europe of the twenty-first century. A brief glance back reinforces the sense that one cannot be cautious enough in trying to predict what is likely to happen in Europe or how Britain's relations with Europe are likely to develop. In 1900 the Imperial venture dominated British politics; by the late 1940s British policy was held fast to the idea of a special role through balancing the "three circles"; whilst, by the close of the century, the Empire was a thing of the past and Europe had emerged as the main fault line in British politics, the key determinant of the fate of her political leaders. Over the past century the historical context of Britain's relationship with Europe was radically transformed under the combined impact of two devastating world wars unleashed within Europe, the more gradual retreat from world power status, and the reality of Britain's increasing trade interdependency with the EU. The result was to underline that Britain's vital interests in peace and prosperity were inextricably linked to stability in Europe.

As we have seen in this section, the dynamics forming Britain's relations with Europe are likely to remain just as complex and unpredictable in the next century. The next section will show how embedded British doctrines are likely to shape this relationship and what kinds of perception of Europe prevail as the century begins.

---

[47] Reviewed in Kaplan, n. 42 above.

DOCTRINAL CONSTRAINTS AND POLITICAL PERCEPTIONS OF EUROPE

Earlier this chapter referred to the need for a closer examination of the doctrines that shape dominant British attitudes to Europe and to the ways in which they have become embedded in British institutions. This embeddedness ensures that these attitudes survive changes of party government and ministers, in effect becoming part of the furniture of office. The doctrines of sovereignty, of the "three circles" and of market capitalism give a very distinctive character to how the British understand Europe, situate themselves within it, and chart their positions on Europe. To them can be added the special sense of "Britishness", which is in turn bound up with the above doctrines. Together, they impart a conservative bias to debate about Europe. There are alternative modes of thinking about Europe, but these alternatives are more the preserve of commentators and academics than an active part of vernacular categories of understanding of Europe.

These dominant doctrines and the sense of "Britishness" do more than just coexist at the political level. In the minds of politicians, officials and commentators they co-habit and merge in the ways that they think about Europe and seek to appeal to the wider public. Three points need emphasis. First, the three doctrines and the sense of "Britishness" have a reasonably long historical pedigree and can be traced back at least into the eighteenth century. They remain the dominant set of ideas on offer to politicians as they seek to construct coherent and convincing accounts of Europe to legitimate their policies. Secondly, politicians have been important in seeking to create, articulate and transform how the British have looked at Europe. In their distinctive ways Winston Churchill and Margaret Thatcher actively sought to shape how we looked at Europe and left an abiding impact, and they have done so by rearranging these parameters.[48] Thirdly, these doctrines are sufficiently flexible to accommodate a range of positions that respect these parameters. Thus one can distinguish between "constructive engagement" and "Euroscepticism" as positions that accord with these parameters. As the 1990s showed, the dominant doctrines are compatible with a tough-minded, even bitter debate about how British interests are best realised with respect to Europe.

The open question is how leaders, beginning with Tony Blair, will attempt to change the way in which the British look at Europe in the twenty-first century. The starting point is strongly entrenched notions about sovereignty, Britain's special role, market capitalism and "Britishness". But what we do not know is when, and in what form, structural developments and events will conspire to foster mounting discontent with Britain's relationship to Europe. Inherited doctrines may lose their credibility with time, offering an opportunity for radical rethinking. Embracing Europe might seem more attractive than the options of

---

[48] See e.g. Young, n. 16 above.

political independence and American leadership. On the other hand, the EU may be overwhelmed by the pressures on it and lose its magnet effect. We simply do not know which political leader—on behalf of which political agenda—will succeed in seizing the moment to transform how the British look at Europe. What does seem clear is that breaking free from the conservative bias in British understanding of Europe would take a particularly bold political act and radical historical vision.

The Doctrine of Sovereignty

> The principle of Parliamentary sovereignty means neither more nor less than this, namely, that Parliament . . . has, under the English constitution, the right to make and unmake any law whatever; and, further, that no person or body is recognised by the law of England as having a right to override or set aside the legislation of Parliament.[49]

The conception of Parliamentary sovereignty outlined by Dicey has profoundly influenced British perceptions of Europe. First, it has given members of Parliament a pronounced institutional self-interest in conserving the notion of their absolute legal authority. The European integration process is, in part, seen as about giving up something that is fundamental and of which they are trustees. What is at ideological stake is the identity of the British Parliament as exercising supreme authority. But, lurking beneath the defence of Parliamentary prerogatives is a sense of threat to the political careers and status of members of Parliament, in short political self-interests. Parliament is not a willing accomplice in the undoing of its unique place in the British political order. This unwillingness is bound up with a deep sense of institutional history and dignity.

Secondly, the doctrine of Parliamentary sovereignty provides the rationale for a view of European integration as a process of voluntary cooperation amongst independent sovereign states. There is, in consequence of Dicey's view, a difficulty in the notion of authority as shared, and of European integration as a process of altering how it is shared. The sovereignty of Parliament is an absolutist doctrine that favours a maximalist position on centralising power. Hence European integration is soon constructed as a matter of all or nothing: of either defending British sovereignty and parliamentary democracy or creating a European "super-state" to rule Britain. In the 1990s the concept of subsidiarity has been borrowed and adapted to shore up the defence of British sovereignty. This doctrine also influences territorial politics within the UK. Thus the dominant interpretation of the Articles of Union of 1707 was as the extension and modification of the English constitution rather than constituting fundamental law. The approach to devolution in the Scotland Act of 1998 insisted that the Westminster Parliament remained sovereign.[50] The principles of the English

---

[49] A Dicey, *The Law of the Constitution* (London, Macmillan, 8th edn., 1915), pp. 3–4.
[50] But see N MacCormick, "The English Constitution, the British State and the Scottish Anomaly", n. 27 above p. 296.

Revolution of 1688 were, in this view, confirmed rather than new constitutional doctrine developed both by union with Scotland and by European integration. Again consistent with this doctrine, subsidiarity was not applied to territorial relations within the UK as a rationale for dividing powers.

Thirdly, the doctrine of Parliamentary sovereignty is hostile to notions of a higher constitutional authority and a rights-based constitutional jurisprudence.[51] The notion of fundamental law, distinct from and superior to ordinary law, is seen as an infringement of the sovereign power of the democratic will as expressed by Parliament. The consequence is political difficulties in accepting the authority of the European Court of Justice and in agreeing to incorporation of the Charter of Fundamental Rights in Treaty law.

This idiosyncratic doctrinal background has been accompanied by a reliance on custom and appeal to common sense rather than formal principles to make the British political system work. Against this background, it is hardly surprising that the British have found it more difficult than the Germans and—though this was less the case after 1990—than the French to contribute coherent constitutional ideas about the political construction of Europe. This situation compares with economic policy, where the model of market capitalism has yielded clear and bold prescriptions for Europe. However, in place of a coherent political model of Europe, what the British can offer is the skills and habits to make democratic institutions work on the basis of appeals to common sense and evolving understandings about political method. These skills, habits and manners will be much needed in the twenty-first century as the EU struggles with the complex and difficult aftermath of enlargement, in particular the risk of decision-making paralysis.

One way in which the British might make a democratic contribution that builds on existing domestic doctrine and potentially extends some of its strengths to Europe is through the proposal for a European second chamber drawn from national parliaments. This proposal—developed by the Blair government in 2000 for the post-Nice process—is a way of engaging Westminster politicians more directly in the process of European integration and of making Europe part of their political careers. In essence, this kind of European second chamber would be a means both of informally Europeanising the Westminster Parliament and of strengthening the checks and balances and the idea of government by consent in the European project.[52] The priority to this proposal makes sense against the doctrinal background of a sovereign Parliament, the difficulties of finding common ground between this doctrine and Europe, and the consequent deep political sensitivities about European integration. It does not, however, address the basic issue of principle—of whether this doctrine of sovereignty can ultimately be reconciled with European union.

[51] T Prosser, n. 14 above.
[52] On the need for a stronger British contribution to the debate about how to secure and deepen democratic values in Europe see L Siedentop, *Democracy in Europe* (Harmondsworth, Penguin Press, 2000).

This issue of principle has become more salient as European integration has gathered momentum and assumed widening scope and greater depth. In the process it has proved divisive. For some, dominant constitutional doctrine points clearly in the direction of disengagement from Europe. The issue is defence of British democracy against Europe.[53] This theme has been actively taken up within the Conservative Party and notably by the European Foundation. For others, principally heirs to the Radical tradition and to be found on the centre-left, the European engagement further puts in question dominant British constitutional understandings and perceptions of Europe. From the 1930s onwards there was a growing sense that Dicey's conception of Parliamentary sovereignty was parting company with political realities.[54] This process seemed to gather momentum in the 1990s. Notably, the *Factortame* ruling suggested that judges may refuse to apply UK legislation that contravenes EC law; whilst the Scottish Act appeared to establish a quasi-federal system, based on a division of legislative powers between Westminster and Edinburgh.[55]

A more enduring theme is that the doctrine of Parliamentary sovereignty is a smokescreen for the realities of a fusion of executive and legislature, for the way in which party government ensures executive supremacy, and for executive superiority over the judiciary.[56] This critique led on to an agenda of constitutional reforms and—notably in the proposals of Charter 88—a conception of Europe as part and parcel of a process of reform of the British state. These reforms would define and delimit the powers of different institutions, specify the rights and responsibilities of citizens, strengthen accountability, and substitute popular sovereignty for executive supremacy.[57] Above all, they are about enshrining the concept of citizenship in British politics. A pluralistic and republican conception of authority and a less majoritarian and confrontational style of politics are in essence about making Britain more European and laying the foundations for making the federal concept meaningful in the British context. Engagement in Europe is seen as vital in this process as a means of introducing the notion of fundamental law and a rights-based jurisprudence.

But though this Radical and centre-left critique professes to engage with the changed political realities of the exercise of authority in Britain, it has failed to make much headway outside its main constituency, the Liberal Democratic Party. In the absence of this critique being taken up by the Labour Party leadership as a coherent project of constitutional reform, the traditional doctrine of Parliamentary sovereignty continues to dominate British constitutional understandings and set constraints on perceptions of Europe. The federal idea remains constitutionally alien.

[53] E.g. N Lamont, *Sovereign Britain* (London, Duckworth, 1995).
[54] E.g. WI Jennings, *The Law and the Constitution* (1933) and I Harden and N Lewis, *The Noble Lie: the British Constitution and the Rule of Law* (London, Hutchinson, 1986).
[55] Bogdanor, n. 27 above, p. 188.
[56] E.g. D Beetham and S Weir, *Political Power and Democratic Control in Britain* (London, Routledge, 1998).
[57] *Ibid.*

The Doctrine of the "Three Circles"

The doctrine of the "three circles" offered a flexible policy formula for the postwar world, enabling those who adhere to it to shift priorities whilst maintaining the formula at least formally intact. Above all, it kept alive an older tradition of standing aloof and detached from Europe as an independent great power and of pursuing a balance of power politics. It was also consistent with an attitude of insularity, symbolised by the Channel, and with the historical memory of resisting Hitler in 1940 and emerging as a victor in 1945.[58] In short, this doctrine brought together a number of strands and acted as the bedrock of a broad consensus in the postwar period, a consensus around the notion of a special role for Britain. This notion was, in turn, well-suited to a particular sense of "Britishness".

But the doctrine of the "three circles" has serious problems and weaknesses. Firstly, its original purpose was to highlight the special nature of Britain's continuing role as world power. As a consequence of the harsh realities of the gap between external commitments and material capabilities and consequent humiliations, it became impossible to sustain this role.[59] The result is that the doctrine of the 'three circles' has lost its animating purpose, conviction and capacity to persuade. Secondly, its credibility depends on others—notably superpowers—recognising this role and the special nature of Britain in balancing the "three circles". This recognition was not forthcoming, not least from the US. Its absence produced in Whitehall and beyond incomprehension of US criticisms of the British failure to play a leading role in postwar European integration. Thirdly, its very generality as a formula—especially once the animating purpose of the world role was gone—is an encouragement to tactical management rather than clear strategic direction in foreign policy.

Events conspired to cast doubt in Whitehall minds about the credibility of the "three-circles" doctrine. The Suez fiasco of 1956, the retreat from east of Suez, the end of the sterling area, and eventual entry into the EEC marked turning points in attitudes to the Commonwealth. The special relationship with the US had substance in military and intelligence matters, and sustained in British minds the pivotal British contribution to Europe through NATO. But in political, diplomatic and economic affairs it had less credibility. Overall, the symbolic importance of the special relationship outweighed its substance, especially in a post-Cold-War world in which Washington began to see Germany as its key partner in managing change in a larger uniting Europe.

---

[58] Note Churchill's Cabinet paper of 29 Nov. 1951 relating to European economic integration: "... we are not merged and do not forfeit our insular or Commonwealth-wide character. I should resist any American pressure to treat Britain on the same footing as the European states, none of whom have the advantages of the Channel and who were consequently conquered." Quoted in P Hennessy, *Never Again: Britain 1945–1951* (London, Jonathan Cape, 1992), p. 401.

[59] See generally P Kennedy, *The Rise and Fall of the Great Powers* (London, Vintage Books, 1989).

Britain enters the Europe of the twenty-first century in the shadow of the doctrine of the "three circles". Its imprint is to be discerned across British policy attitudes. But, though it has lost conviction, the doctrine is given oxygen by the sense of a new age of "globalisation".[60] During the 1980s and 1990s the concept of globalisation served as an inspiration for radical domestic economic reforms under the Thatcher and Major governments and remained the mantra of the Blair government. It gives new support to the idea that Britain has bigger interests at stake outside Europe, that the great economic opportunities lie elsewhere, and that the EU is a dated solution to a past problem.[61] This idea is both symbolised and given material form by the explosive growth of the City of London and by the interactivity between British and American media and entertainment interests in the fast-developing cultural dimension of globalisation. In the financial, media and entertainment sectors Britain once again experiences a sense of a special position that had less to do with Europe and more to do with the privileges offered by the role of the English-language in globalisation.

By acting as a new source of division on Europe, globalisation accentuates the sense of strategic dilemma facing British policy makers. For some globalisation suggests a new incentive to disengage from Europe as an excessively closed regional economy and position Britain as a global player, perhaps to negotiate to join the North American Free Trade Area (NAFTA) or perhaps to become the Hong Kong of Europe. At the other end of the spectrum the EU is seen as offering an opportunity to shape a more civilised form of globalisation, as an experiment in creating a new model of an open, competitive economy with a strong social dimension.[62] More typical, however, is a less radical view of the implications of globalisation. This view holds to a belief in a loosely integrated intergovernmental EU, to which Britain would subscribe only on the basis of a strictly utilitarian, hard-headed calculation of national interest. Globalisation offers a new conviction to those seeing Britain's interests as apart from Europe. Overall, its contribution is to open up division on Europe.

The Model of Market Capitalism

Seen from the vantagepoint of comparative political economy Britain appears to approximate to the model of market capitalism.[63] This model visualises processes of industrial finance, labour-market adjustment and technology transfer as market-driven, a shareholder culture as reigning supreme, and both as supported

---

[60] E.g. D Held, A McGrew, D Goldblatt and J Perraton, *Global Transformations: Politics, Economics and Culture* (Cambridge, Polity Press, 1999).

[61] D Howell, *The Edge of Now* (London, Macmillan, 2000).

[62] W Hutton, *The State We're In* (London, Cape, 1995).

[63] See D Coates, *Models of Capitalism* (Cambridge, Polity Press, 2000); H Kitschelt, P Lange, G Marks and J Stephens (eds.), *Continuity and Change in Contemporary Capitalism* (Cambridge, Cambridge University Press, 1999); and V Schmidt, *European Economies between Integration and Globalization: Policies, Practices, Discourses* (Oxford, Oxford University Press, forthcoming).

by a liberal state that pursues an arms-length approach to the economy, distrusts intervention and opts for light-touch regulation. The entrenched nature of this model has been used to explain the relative failures of postwar national economic planning and public ownership in Britain and the failure to make corporatism work.[64] It can also be used to help understand the political effectiveness of Thatcherism.[65] Laissez-fair, free-trade ideas are seen as deeply ingrained in the institutions of the British state. The ascendancy of this model can also be used to explain why the Blair government insists on economic reform, specifically liberalisation of product, services and labour markets in the EU, as a precondition of British entry into the euro.

This picture of a dominant doctrine needs qualification. There have always been dissenting voices. For instance, Empire Free Traders and national planners from both Left and Right were influential during the high tide of national protectionism in the British and world economy from the 1930s to the 1950s. Later, from the 1980s onwards, more radical centre-left reformers saw in the EU's social model—and especially comparisons with policy performance in its key member states—a benchmark both for reassessing the quality of British public services, especially education, health and transport, and for improving productivity performance.[66] In this respect the EU is seen as a vehicle for spreading good practice in involving workforces as full partners in the production process (e.g. the adoption of the EU directive on information and consultation in 2001).

But three factors ensure that the market capitalist tradition remains dominant in 2001. First, the historical conditions of Britain's early industrialisation had spawned an economic culture based on the high status attached to the self-sufficient firm and the individual entrepreneur.[67] This culture attached itself to the joint-stock company, an early developing equity market and a market-driven conception of industrial relations. State intervention was equated with interference in the legitimate autonomy of the firm. Late industrialisation produced very different forms of economic culture in France and Germany, marked respectively by the greater powers of the state and of the banks vis-à-vis firms.

Secondly, the structural power of the City of London has long and deep roots in the British economy, going back to the seventeenth century. In essence, the City is the chief institutional embodiment of the market capitalism model. It espouses the model of the liberal, limited state, the dominance of a market-driven approach to economic change, the vital importance of an open, competitive economy, and the ascendancy of the values of a shareholder culture. The complete liberalisation of capital movement in 1979, followed by the Big Bang of the 1980s, illustrated the close ideological nexus between Thatcherism and

[64] For an early example see A Shonfield, *Modern Capitalism: The Changing Balance of Public and Private Power* (Oxford: Oxford University Press, 1965).
[65] A Gamble, *The Free Economy and the Strong State: The Politics of Thatcherism* (London, Macmillan, 1994).
[66] Hutton, n. 62 above.
[67] K Dyson, "The Cultural, Ideological and Structural Context", in K Dyson and S Wilks (eds.), *Industrial Crisis: A Comparative Study of State and Industry* (Oxford, Blackwell, 1983).

the City. Strikingly, by 2001 financial services had eclipsed manufacturing as a source of employment in the British economy. At its apex stands a City able to offer glittering financial prizes to the brightest and most ambitious. Furthermore, the City is the financial capital of Europe and the home to multi-national financial companies, notably from the United States, Japan and Germany.[68] The City's political influence is secured through the role of the Bank of England as its spokesperson and through the Treasury. Significantly, only one British sector figures as one of Gordon Brown's tests for euro entry—the likely impacts on the City. This is a measure of the importance attached to the City by a Labour government whose traditional political heartland has been in manu-facturing cities of the North, Scotland and Wales.

Thirdly, the postwar circumstances of a US-dominated world economy, along with the political importance attached to the US relationship within the doctrine of the "three circles", favoured the ascendancy of the model of market capitalism. The US focus of the City as the benchmark for the financial services sector provided an economic underpinning for this ascendancy.

The result is an ingrained tendency to benchmark economic best practice on the United States, notable in the work of the Treasury under Brown, and to reject an "over-regulated" social Europe. The combination of policy emulation of the US with the continuing success of the US in growth and employment through the 1990s—and then with steady reduction of structural unemployment in the British economy—led the British government to adopt a "pace-setter" role on economic reform in the EU. The strident message from London is that British liberalisation of product, service, labour and capital markets should be extended to the EU. There is also the implication that for Britain to join the euro the onus is on the Euro-Zone economies to first adjust their supply-side policies.

Whatever talk there is about convergence around a "Third Way", the harsher reality is a process of tension and conflict between the model of market capital-ism—advocated by British governments—and the models of "managed" capitalism and of "state" capitalism—championed respectively by the German and the French governments.[69] Implicit in this debate are different conceptuali-sations of the European state and, by extension, of the EU: the British "liberal" state, the French "interventionist" state and the German "enabling" state.[70] Globalisation creates powerful common pressures for convergence in the direc-tion of liberalisation. But great differences remain in the manner and timing of adjustment and in policy outcomes notably in labour markets, wages and the welfare state. These differences reflect the continuing distinctiveness of different forms of capitalism in Europe because of the particular direction imparted to their policies by domestic economic and political institutions. By 2001 there is

---

[68] Kynaston, n. 26 above.
[69] See A Giddens, *The Third Way: The Renewal of Social Democracy* (Cambridge, Polity Press, 1998).
[70] Schmidt, n. 63 above.

no clear evidence that Europe is converging around the logic of the market capitalism model. The process of managing economic change focuses more on cooperative management by means of "social pacts", witness the Netherlands, Germany, Ireland, Italy and Spain. Policy outcomes do not suggest a "race to the bottom" either in taxation or in welfare-state spending, with states competing for growth and employment by reducing taxes and public spending.[71]

Clearly policy performance, and in particular failure, will affect the extent to which individual models of capitalism have a persuasive power as best practice. On the test of structural unemployment, job creation and economic growth the "managed" capitalism and "state" capitalism models remain on the defensive. However, these two models fare better in providing public services, in productivity per man hour, in containing unit labour costs, and in exports. Whilst the British bias to the market capitalism model is deeply rooted, a worsening of trade problems, the continuing effects of poor productivity and the lamentable state of public services could make European comparisons a catalyst for domestic political changes that question the ascendancy of this model. It is possible to imagine a political leadership that might seek to construct a new policy programme that is closer to European social models of capitalism. But it would have to contend with deeply entrenched traditions of national economic culture and, not least, the structural power of the City.

The Sense of "Britishness"

National identity has been a powerful animator of the sense of distinctiveness that informs the British doctrines of sovereignty, of a special world role, and of market capitalism. Together they form a powerful and robust set of ideas on which politicians and commentators have been able to draw to sustain and reinvent British political perceptions of Europe and legitimate policy positions. The power of myths of national identity is expressed in a sense of enviable difference from Europe.

But two problems bedevil debate about British national identity. Firstly, British identity has been made complex by its coexistence with a multi-national state and, in particular, by the tendency to confuse "Englishness" and "Britishness". Yet, whatever myth might suggest, England has never been an island nation. It has shared an island with two other nations. Moreover, Great Britain is not an island but an archipelago of four nations. Secondly, though there is a dominant narrative of British identity, identity has become increasingly contested under the impact of a number of developments. These developments include a more secular age, the end of Empire, a more multi-cultural society, the resurgence of Scottish and Welsh nationalism, the new politics of devolution, and the engagement in Europe. As the twenty-first century begins, we are increasingly aware of the

---

[71] For evidence see chapter by M Rhodes in K Dyson (ed.), *European States and the Euro*, n. 21 above.

varieties of Britishness and of the ways in which nationalism has obscured the connections and borrowings in British and European history and nurtured stereotypes with which we are all too familiar.

The dominant narrative of Britishness has three main historical foundations. The first two foundations have been sketched by Linda Colley as a British identity formed during the eighteenth century in war against Catholic Europe and, more positively, around Empire-building. National identity was forged around Protestantism, the rejection of Catholic superstition and the notion of being united as guardians of the British Empire.[72] During this period a British ruling elite defined itself through the new public schools, a new more sober ideal of public service, a style of "clubmanship", and the rise of the great British heroes (Wolfe, Wellington, and above all Nelson).

The third foundation was what Churchill described as Britain's "Finest Hour"—the Dunkirk spirit, the Battle of Britain, and the spirit of the Blitz in 1940, culminating in victory in 1945.[73] Standing alone against Hitler's Europe and the last-ditch, dogged defence of freedom were etched into postwar consciousness of British identity, strengthening its sense of specialness, indeed uniqueness. In this context Churchill was the most powerful exponent of the celebration of Britain's "long island story" and of the symbolism of the Channel. This postwar set of self-beliefs fused with a residual anti-Catholicism and the heritage of Empire to make Britishness an identity set apart from Europe. It was the context in which the doctrine of the "three circles" and the maximalist doctrine of sovereignty could take firm root as the consensus setting the parameters of the debate about Europe. The postwar spirit of triumphalism also created a sense that the onus for change was on others, not on the British.[74]

Several developments have combined to erode and challenge these powerful myths of British identity. First, in an increasingly secular society anti-Catholicism has less resonance as a basis for British identity. The notion of the EU as a Catholic conspiracy lacks credibility. Secondly, the Empire can no longer serve as a unifying myth of national identity. Its demise is linked to a third development: Britain has become a more multi-cultural society. This development makes Britain more like many other EU states and suggests a more liberal interpretation of British identity that accommodates multiple identities. Fourthly, the dominant position and privileged position of the English nation has been challenged by those who speak either of the nations of Britain or of Scottish and Welsh identities that should find their expression in separate statehood. In the wake of devolution and a new political awareness of multiple identities radical ideas of federalism seem to possess a new relevance. The big question is whether the English can be convinced about the value of federalism. Fifthly, years of postwar relative economic and political decline raised critical questions about the dreams

---

[72] L Colley, *Britons: Forging the Nation 1707–1837* (New Haven, Yale University Press, 1992).

[73] Evoked in A Calder, *The People's War, Britain 1939–1945* (London, Cape, 1969).

[74] For a sustained critique of British illusions see C Barnett, *The Audit of War: The Illusion and Reality of Britain as a Great Nation* (London, Macmillan, 1986).

and illusions that were the legacy of the Second World War. It became clear that British identity needed to change radically to match her European and global competitors. The question was how this modernisation was to be achieved—by globalisation or by Europeanisation or by some combination of the two.

The European engagement creates a new dynamic of Europeanisation and the question of just how far and fast this dynamic feeds into redefinitions of British identity. There are some effects from informal integration, for instance from travel and acquisitions of second homes, on cuisine and life styles and from exposure to how much better continental European public services work. But these effects may be more superficial than deep-seated. More questionable still is whether formal integration via the EU is giving a European dimension to British identity. Eurobarometer survey findings on levels of British ignorance of the EU and support for its institutions do not indicate that such an effect has been occurring. In addition, as we have seen, British press and television show little evidence of becoming Europeanised, with the European dimension weak in news reporting. Despite these qualifications, Europe remains important as a source of questions about just how special and enviable British identity is. To those of a more Radical persuasion, it also raises the question of whether a European identity could evolve around a shared liberal nationalism based on allegiance to civic institutions that safeguard individualism and autonomy and that might be extended to incorporate social and economic as well as political rights. This kind of identity would contain and condition rather than replace a British identity forged around a belief in a community of common culture and shared historical belonging.[75] This question remains, however, more in the domain of academic discourse and Radical political commentary and has as yet had less impact on party programmes and policies.

In examining the changing sense of Britishness two apparently contradictory developments deserve emphasis. First, Americanisation of British identity has been at least as potent, and probably more potent, than Europeanisation. Indeed Americanisation of mass culture has been a Europe-wide and global phenomenon. But in the British case Americanisation takes on a different quality because of a shared language and of cultural affinities that bind the US together with Britain as one of Churchill's English-speaking peoples. Shared language creates a greater and wider accessibility of the British public to US and other English-speaking cultures. This development reinforces the point about how globalisation is tying British identity to the continuing sense of an alternative to Europe.

The key historical turning points of 1945 and 1989–90 confirmed the twentieth century as the American century. US cultural, economic and political hegemony is its chief legacy. This legacy has complex implications for Britain's sense of its own identity. Globalisation and the prestige of a market capitalism that has become linked to globalisation have become associated with an Anglo-American lingual dominance (and, as some see it, imperialism). Culturally, and

[75] N MacCormick, "Liberalism, Nationalism and the Post-Sovereign State", n. 14 above.

at a working level, Europe is being united around a complexly evolving Anglo-American language, with in 2001 some 47 per cent of EU citizens speaking it (31 per cent of them as a foreign language). This development has ambivalent consequences for British identity in relation to Europe. On the one hand, it gives Britain both a cultural status in the making of Europe and an economic opportunity in new and expanding media and entertainment markets. It acts as a magnet for ambitious, young Europeans anxious to master English. Europe is not being united around French or German or around a demanding multi-lingual Europe. This emergence of a common European language (though not a single language) could make Britons feel more comfortable with Europe. On the other hand, globalisation is defined by British elites as offering either an alternative, US-centric project to an "over-bureaucratic", "over-regulated" Europe or a project for remaking Europe in the image of Anglo-Saxon market capitalism. In this context British identity retains its troubled relationship with Europe.

Secondly, Europe is potentially a catalyst for conflict within, and breakup of, British identity. Scottish and Welsh nationalisms are much more comfortable with Europe than English nationalism; Europe is an alternative to the metropolitan dominance of London both politically and economically. Earlier, Irish nationalism had travelled a similar route; European integration appealed as a means of distancing Dublin economically and politically from London. In consequence, the attempt to play the nationalist card against Europe is fraught with risk for the Union.

During the 1990s anti-Europeanism became associated with new populist political appeals to English nationalism, principally from within the Conservative Party. These appeals have mixed Englishness and Britishness in invoking the spirit of the Battle of Britain and of a plucky, brave island race standing proud against a German-dominated EU that seeks to rule Britain. The evocation of Englishness in this defensive form has a deep historical resonance. Its appeal at the level of popular sentiment can be traced back at least to the thirteenth century, notably its mobilisation by royalists during the French invasion and occupation of 1216–17 and a projected French invasion in 1264.[76] The continuity of this sense of English identity is assisted by the way in which the English state retained its basic form over time. It was reinforced by recurrent threats of foreign invasion and interference culminating in 1940. The populist attempt to exploit this vein of public sentiment has, however, its limits. A resurgent English anti-European nationalism risks undermining the Union. It does not take account of the realities of a Britain of multiple identities, of devolved power, and of European engagement.

George Orwell, writing during the London Blitz of 1940, offered a more nuanced sense of Englishness.[77] For him it was bound up with: "a rather stuffy

---

[76] See A Harding, *England in the Thirteenth Century* (Cambridge, Cambridge University Press, 1993); M Prestwich, *English Politics in the Thirteenth Century* (Basingstoke, Macmillan, 1990); and P Wormald, "The Making of England", (1995) 45(2) *History Today*.

[77] G Orwell, *The Lion and the Unicorn: Socialism and the English Genius* (London, Secker and Warburg, 1941).

Doctrinal Constraints and Political Perceptions of Europe 183

Victorian family... It has its private language and its common memories, and at the approach of an enemy it closes ranks. A family with the wrong members in control..." What emerges is a portrait of the "privateness of English life", the inwardness of its arguments, the tendency to see foreigners as irrelevant, comical or dangerous, and "the gentleness, the hypocrisy, the thoughtlessness, the reverence for law and the hatred of uniforms". Englishness was, for Orwell, bound up with a country in which these attributes and the emotional unity with which they were invested would remain the same whatever the changing circumstances. This rather conservative picture of Englishness does, however, fit oddly with an early twenty-first century Britain of globalisation, Americanisation and Europeanisation.

Britain's contribution to the Europe of the twenty-first century needs to start from a recognition of the varieties of Britishness that had not existed in the same way in 1900. A resurgent populist English nationalism and a quieter, continuing affection for Orwell's somewhat sentimental and romantic picture of Englishness exist as aspects of this variety. The new questioning of Britishness and a greater openness about its definition go along with a greater acceptance that traditional dominant ideas about British identity have simplified what was in historical reality a much more complicated and intimate relationship between Britain and Europe over the centuries. Because these varieties of Britishness include traditional ideas and Americanisation, they do not point to an unproblematic relationship with Europe in the twenty-first century. To paraphrase the novelist Elizabeth Bowen on the relationship between Ireland and England, Britain's contribution to twenty-first century Europe looks set to continue as "a mixture of showing off and suspicion, nearly as bad as sex."[78] But "who the British think that they are" has become a central, contested issue for British politics and one that will define their relations with Europe.

CONTENDING HISTORICAL NARRATIVES AND THE ROLE OF POLITICIANS AS CREATIVE CRAFTSMEN OF DISCOURSE

Britain had not been conquered or invaded. She felt no need to exorcise history.[79]

This chapter has argued that the British contribution to the Europe of the twenty-first century does not rest on a single monolithic conception of Europe. There are multiple ways in which Britons think about Europe and contradictions in the manner in which individuals have viewed Europe, from Churchill and Ernest Bevin to Thatcher and Blair. But it is possible to identify a set of

---

[78] Quoted in R Foster, *Paddy and Mr Punch: Connections in Irish and English History* (London, Allen Lane, 1994).
[79] J Monnet, *Memoirs* (London, Collins, 1978) p. 306 on why the British succumbed to illusions of grandeur. See also on p. 452: "They had not known the trauma of wartime occupation, they had not been conquered, their system seemed intact. In reality they suffered paradoxically—from not having had their pride broken and their factories destroyed."

interconnected doctrines that has provided a dominant way of thinking about Europe, at once politically defensive on constitutional matters of European union, economically assertive on market capitalism, and ambivalent on foreign, defence and security policies. The result has been a somewhat conservative bias in Britain's contribution. Alternative, more radical ways of thinking about Europe have found a stronger hold amongst academics and commentators than within the two main political parties. They include ideas about Europe as a means of constitutional reform to embed citizenship and secure a pluralistic political order; of strengthening the "social" model of partnership in managing economic change and of high-quality public services; of wedding British foreign, security and defence policies to a "civilising" model of European and international order based on multilateralism; and of inventing a more civic and republican identity.

A key difference in thinking about how Britain might contribute to the Europe of the twenty-first century is the starting point in trying to make historical sense of Britain's role in Europe. Debate tends to polarise around two different historical narratives of Britain and Europe. One historical narrative begins by asking what Britain can contribute based on its very individual experiences and strengths. This narrative tends to work within the parameters of established doctrines, revealing a conservative bias in developing policy on Europe, and displaying a pronounced caution about pace in integrating Europe.[80] Against the background of the earlier triumphalist sense of Britishness imparted by 1940–45, it involves the celebration of the nation state and its contribution to peace. The other historical narrative has its starting point in the question: "what could Europe contribute to Britain?" In this narrative European integration is about the political, economic and social modernisation of Britain. Europe provides an external catalyst and discipline to pursue overdue domestic reforms. The focus is on the dangerous illusions that have bedeviled postwar British policy on Europe and on Europe as an agency of domestic change.[81]

The contest between these historical narratives opens up new questions about the desirable political and constitutional shape of Britain, the kind of capitalism under which it should live, the nature and quality of its public services, Britain's attitudes to its international role in a context of globalisation and Europeanisation, and what kind of identity we seek. This chapter has shown how the process of European integration has played an important role in lending a new contention and uncertainty into British politics, a sense that a fundamental choice is required. It has also stressed that the complex interacting dynamics of a changing Britain, a changing Europe and a changing world make it very difficult to discern the precise shape and outcomes of Britain's contribution to the Europe of the twenty-first century.

---

[80] See notably the interview with Jack Straw in "A Union of Love and Understanding", *Financial Times*, 27 July 2001.
[81] E.g. H Young, n. 16 above.

Despite this uncertainty and indeterminacy, some well-defined, albeit challenged and potentially shifting parameters are provided by deeply entrenched doctrines which impart a conservative bias to European attitudes and policies. The ascendancy of these doctrines suggests a potential for British policy to achieve a strategic direction based on an underlying constitutional, economic, foreign-policy and cultural consensus. In practice, this potential has proved elusive for two reasons. First, structural developments and events have eroded the consensus and made European policy increasingly contested, in ways outlined in this chapter. Secondly, political leaders have found themselves absorbed in the tactics of domestic party, media and electoral management on Europe, of European-level alliance-building on "history-making" treaty decisions, and of playing-off global and European interests. This problem of strategic direction on Europe has its structural roots in the gap between the requirements of playing an active and central role in European "history-making" decisions and established doctrines and a sense of Britishness that are highly uncomfortable with the sacrifices involved in this role. This discomfort comes to a head over the doctrine of sovereignty and the issue of identity.

The open question is whether—and, if so, at what stage and how—a British political leader might seek to try to change the way the British look at Europe in a decisive way. Margaret Thatcher sought to do so with and after her Bruges speech of 1988, arguing against "a European super-state exercising a new dominance from Brussels". There are expectations that Tony Blair might attempt to boldly reinvent Britain's European role from a very different perspective. What is clear is that, the more Europeanised Britain becomes, the more party and electoral politics will be about the reinventing, articulation and transformation of British understandings about Europe rather than just reiterating traditional understandings. In short, British politicians will need to be much more creative craftsmen of European discourse and policy as they face up to the challenges of the twenty-first century. The interesting big historical questions are who will succeed in changing the way we look at Europe, how, when and why.

12

After Keynes

GIORGIO LA MALFA

I

At the end of a long and harsh historical confrontation between the socialist and the capitalist systems during the twentieth century, capitalism has finally prevailed, thanks, as John Kenneth Galbraith noted, to its superior ability to adapt and transform itself. Many bright minds in the twentieth century were pessimistic about the fate of capitalism. Suffice it here to recall Joseph Schumpeter and John Maynard Keynes. Yet, whereas socialist systems ultimately proved impervious to economic reforms as well as to demands for greater individual freedoms, capitalist systems managed to produce and incorporate many important innovations.

Galbraith noted four changes as a result of which present-day market economies bear little, if any, resemblance to their nineteenth-century predecessors: Keynesian economics, the philosophy of the welfare state first systematically embodied in the Beveridge Plan, antitrust legislation, and the strength of trade unions as a countervailing power to unbridled market competition. Of these, antitrust legislation mostly originated in the US at the turn of the nineteenth century and it is, therefore, essentially an American legacy. The growing importance of trade unions was probably the result of universal electoral suffrage, increasing associationism, and participation of the masses in the economic and political life of their countries, and thus should not be associated with any one country or name in particular.

Beveridge and Keynes, however, were uniquely British voices in the debate which helped shape the features of modern day capitalism, and as such represent perhaps Britain's most enduring and important contribution to the evolution and adaptation of capitalism during the twentieth century and beyond.

I suspect that Lord Keynes might not have particularly appreciated seeing his name associated with that of Lord Beveridge; at least this is what one gathers from the third volume of Robert Skidelsky's magnificent biography of Keynes.[1] Their contributions were quite different in domain, scope and influence, and stemmed from different political perspectives and ideas. Beveridge's notion that

---

[1] R Skidelsky, *John Maynard Keynes: a Biography*, III, *Fighting for Britain 1937–1946* (London, Macmillan, 2000).

the state must ensure that the basic needs of all citizens are met under all circumstances was probably a development of socialist and Fabian ideas. It has enjoyed considerable longevity, and still represents in some form a distinguishing feature of "European", as compared to "American", capitalism. Keynes' *General Theory*, a theoretical contribution of the first magnitude, is more in the mould of neo-classicism and liberalism. It opened the way to a more active role of the state in the economy, but says nothing about "caring from the cradle to the grave".

In some sense Keynes' contribution may appear more limited in scope than that of Beveridge, as it pertains in the main only to the economic domain, and within it focuses on how to smooth the economic cycle. More specifically it concentrates on how to get an economy out of under-employment equilibrium. The claim to be "a general theory" may look immodest, especially in retrospect. It is, however, the major refocusing of economic thinking brought about by Keynes, and the new analytical apparatus that he developed to deal with the short-term, but critically important, problem of smoothing the economic cycle in a capitalist economy which created the intellectual conditions and established a broad economic rationale for bold social experiments such as those envisaged by Beveridge.

As I shall argue, there is more in Keynes that is relevant today than just the *General Theory*. For this reason I shall concentrate on Keynes' contribution as representing the most important and enduring legacy of British economic culture to the twenty-first century.

II

In singling out Beveridge and Keynes, one runs the risk of underemphasising the enormous influence wielded by British Universities and economists in the areas of both political economy and economic policy throughout the twentieth century, and especially in the years up to the Second World War. So it is useful to remember that, for most of the century, Cambridge, Oxford and the London School of Economics played a crucial role in the education of economists, not only those from the UK and the Commonwealth but also from Europe at large. Here the names of Alfred Marshall, Dennis Robertson, Alfred Pigou, John Hicks, Roy Harrod, Richard Kahn, Nicholas Kaldor, Joan Robinson, and James Meade spring quickly to mind, as do those of Friedrich Hayek, Abba Lerner and others for as long as they were teaching in the UK.

The importance of English universities diminished, as we know, after the War, when the centre of economic teaching and theorising moved to the United States as a result of the inflow of leading economists from continental European countries in that country and the availability of superior resources. Yet for countries such as Italy, which in the interwar years had been cut off from much of the normal and fruitful intellectual exchange that takes place between

European centres of knowledge, the English universities, especially Cambridge (owing perhaps to the formidable presence of Piero Sraffa) gave the young economists of the post-war generation their chance to make up for the ideological seclusion of the fascist period.

A sizeable number of economists in their fifties and sixties currently teaching in Italian universities, perhaps even the majority, spent time studying at UK academic institutions. My country, therefore, owes a special debt to the UK in this area, even if, perhaps, they were exposed not to the full set of economic theories and policies but to the Keynesian tradition in a somewhat narrow definition of it. Thus, the British Academy Conference is a proper occasion on which to acknowledge this debt. It is probably due to this very special link that Italian economists have more forcefully resisted the anti-Keynesian counter-revolution of the 1970s and 1980s, and have been more willing than many of their continental European colleagues to defend the English economic tradition as compared with the American one.

Intellectual legacies take many forms and are diffused in many ways. For this reason their true importance is so difficult to gauge even in retrospect. Yet one can make the case that Keynes and his legacy exerted a powerful influence in much of continental Europe.

III

Returning more specifically to Keynes' legacy to the twenty-first century, one can say that it was twofold. Firstly there is the *General Theory*, with which I shall deal with in this section.[2] There are also many ideas on the nature and the future of capitalism, developed by Keynes at the end of the 1920s and included in his *Essays in Persuasion,* which have not yet been fully investigated, and appear extremely pertinent to some of the questions we face nowadays.[3] Some of these will be discussed in the following section.

It is well known that for most economists around the world the publication of the *General Theory* in 1936 was an exciting event. At that time, Keynes already enjoyed a huge popularity as the most outstanding Cambridge and English economist. It was widely known that he was working on something important, and due to the conditions of very high unemployment in most industrial countries at that time, there was enormous interest in what he had to say about it. Some of the climate surrounding the event is well captured in a most critical review by Joseph Schumpeter, which appeared soon after the publication of the *General Theory*. "A book by Mr Keynes", he wrote, "on fundamental questions which are right at the heart of the practical discussions of the

[2] JM Keynes, *The General Theory of Employment, Interest and Money* (London, Macmillan, 1936).
[3] JM Keynes, *Essays in Persuasion,* (London, 1931), now in *The Collected Writings of John Maynard Keynes,* IX (London, Macmillan, 1972).

day is no doubt an event. Those who had the opportunity to witness the expectations of the best of our students, the impatience they displayed at the delay in getting hold of their copies, the eagerness with which they devoured them, and the interest manifested by all sectors of Anglo-American communities that are up to this kind of reading (and some that are not) must first of all congratulate the author on a signal personal success."[4]

Paul Samuelson, probably one of the students who had displeased Schumpeter by showing their impatience at the delay in getting the book, wrote in his obituary for Lord Keynes in 1946 that "the *General Theory* caught most economists under the age of thirty-five with the unexpected virulence of a disease first attacking and decimating an isolated tribe of South Sea islanders. Economists beyond fifty turned out to be quite immune to the ailment. With time, most economists in-between began to run the fever, often without knowing or admitting their condition."[5]

The "fever" was also recognised by those who reacted negatively to the *General Theory*, the most outspoken of whom was certainly Schumpeter. They tried to cure it in two ways. The most short-lived solution was the claim that Keynes was simply referring to England. "The advice offered implicitly", wrote Schumpeter, "and the social vision unfolded explicitly, do not concern us here. That advice (everybody knows what it is Mr Keynes advises) may be good. For the England of today it possibly is. That vision may be entitled to the compliment that *it expresses forcefully the attitude of a decaying civilization* [emphasis added]. In these respects, this book invites sociological interpretation in the Marxian sense, and nothing is more certain than that such interpretation will be administered to it before long". Thus, the *General Theory* was at best of local interest. In any case, its impact would be short lived. "Speaking to us from the vantage ground of Cambridge and from its author's unique personal position, defended by a group of ardent and able disciples, the book will undoubtedly dominate talk and thought *for some time* [italics mine]",[6] concluded Schumpeter.

The prediction, and hope, that the impact of the *General Theory* would not be lasting is common to many of those who opposed Keynes' ideas. Ludwig von Mises argued that Keynes was in no way an innovator: he had merely given academic respectability to ill-advised policies which many governments were already following.[7] The success of these ideas, he added, would last *for some time*. For Frank Knight "we must simply 'forget' the revolution in economic theory and read the book as a contribution to the theory of business oscillations." "Even from this point of view", he adds, "I cannot see that it gets very far ... The chief value of the book has seemed to lie in the hard labour involved in reading it."[8]

---

[4] JA Schumpeter, "The General Theory of Employment, Interest and Money" (1936) 31 *Journal of the American Statistical Association* 791–5.

[5] P Samuelson, "Lord Keynes and the General Theory" (1946) 14 *Econometrica* 187.

[6] JASchumpeter, n. 4 above.

[7] L von Mises, "Lord Keynes and Say's Law" (1950) 1(3) *The Freeman* 83–5.

[8] FM Knight, "Unemployment: And Mr Keynes' Revolution in Economic Theory" (1937) 3 *Canadian Journal of Economics* 102–23.

The effort to "contain" Keynes has been going on ever since 1936. His most disturbing claim for many of his critics was to have produced a theory which was general in its applicability. This was the second and major strand of the criticism levelled against it. It was argued that unemployment equilibrium was a special case, essentially due to imperfections in the working of the labour market. It was also argued that the ineffectiveness of monetary policy, the so-called liquidity trap, would be balanced by the working of the "Pigou effect", i.e. the effect on consumption of the increase in value of money balances when prices go down. Even more effective in this attempt to demolish the new theory would later become the hypothesis that expectations are "rational", i.e. that markets can fully anticipate monetary and fiscal actions by authorities, thus voiding them of practical effects. The most devastating objection was perhaps that moved by Schumpeter, who noted how the *General Theory* was constructed on the assumption that production functions remain fixed, and that investments, instead of financing the changes in production function, are just a component of demand. Hence the objection that Keynes' theory was essentially static and short term, "the theory of another world and out of contact with modern industrial fact, unemployment included". A theory, Schumpeter concluded, that did not even come close to the essence of the capitalist economy, where "the process is essentially a process of change, of the type which is assumed away in this book".[9]

Every part of Keynes' argument, one can say, has been subjected to dissecting criticism, but the *General Theory* has proved remarkably resistant to efforts to confine it to being a special case of macroeconomic neoclassical equilibrium. The critical fact is that Keynes' attack on neoclassical economics was multi-pronged, so that if one of his arguments is successfully rejected, others remain which are not so easy to deal with. Many early reviewers of the *General Theory* asked what its central feature was. Was it the propensity to consume, or the fact that interest rates do not make savings and investments coincide? Was it the liquidity trap, or the stickiness of real wages? Or were expectations the crux of the matter?

The academic effort devoted to "undoing" Keynes has been enormous. There was, and there still is, something "political" about it, reflecting in some critical way almost a battle of values concerning the capitalist system and a struggle for their preservation. For Keynes, as we will see more fully in the next section, capitalism was a perfectible system, as well as one which was objectionable on ethical grounds. He did not believe, in other words, that the market economy was perfect and impervious to value judgements in either its assumptions or its outcomes. Yet, he remained a convinced liberal. For his opponents, however, in particular Hayek and his followers, to taint the purity of the capitalist model was to bring in features which would ultimately prove to be its undoing. Schumpeter was, instead, exempt from these worries. He was personally quite

[9] JASchumpeter, n. 4 above.

sceptical about the capacity of capitalism to endure. For him the Keynesian system had no "magnificent" dynamics. It was a still picture, aesthetically unpleasing, aside from being theoretically objectionable.

If there were once legitimate worries about the ability of the capitalist system to survive, the demise of socialism should have put an end to them, and to some of the possible motivations for attacking Keynes' theories. But this is not, curiously, the case. There remains in my view a concern with Keynesian ideas which goes beyond their specific economic policy content to address questions which are fundamentally ideological.

There was a period in the 1970s and 1980s when it seemed that the attempt to remove Keynes from economic debate had almost succeeded. Not only was the teaching of economic theory almost exclusively neoclassical, but governments appeared to have firmly embraced the opinion that fiscal and monetary policies are largely, if not totally, ineffective except for the brief spans of time needed for markets to incorporate them and anticipate their effects, thereby annulling them. It was thought that the possible reasons for malfunctioning markets (product and labour) were being eliminated. Choice rationality was triumphant. Competition was "approaching" the ideal state. The international economy, ever more rapidly integrating markets of all types, was doing the rest. Equilibria seemed again relevant, both as respectable theoretical outcomes and as representations of approaching realities.

In such a climate, Keynes' basic propensity to recognize the importance of, and to deal with, states of disequilibrium continued to be perceived as "heretical". Robert Clover is essentially right when he says that Keynes never made a complete transition from static to dynamic "modes of thought", but laid the grounds for others to do so in his time, and so wrought a fundamental change in intellectual perspective in the space of a few years.[10]

So much for the theory. In reality, there seems to be also a pendulum for and against Keynesianism that fundamentally depends on the nature of the problems that governments and economists have to address. When the concern is with inflation, the pendulum cannot but swing against Keynes. But when, instead, unemployment takes centre stage, the pendulum shifts back towards Keynesian ideas and economic policy tools, no matter what academic economists are teaching at the time in their classrooms, and publishing in their increasingly abstruse academic journals. Reality is hard to ignore. For some it may even be "a special case", but it is certainly a push factor that it is difficult to ignore completely. One can see the close correspondence between the price stability and income growth in the 1950s and a good part of the 1960s, and the prevalence of Keynesian ideas and policy frameworks in much of the industrialised world. Yet one can also note the correlation between rising inflation and then unemployment in the 1970s and parts of the 1980s and the re-emergence of neo-classical

---

[10] RW Clower, "Keynes and the Classics: A Dynamical Perspective", in DA Walker (ed.), *Money and Markets: Essays by Robert W. Clower* (Cambridge, Cambridge University Press, 1984), p. 25.

theories, old and new, and related policy positions. One can also perhaps note a return to the centre in the macro-economic debate during the 1990s, when growth was interrupted by a series of financial crises that affected both the financial systems and the productive sectors of many open economies.

One might argue that the Keynesian revolution, following on from the experience of managing an economy which had been spurred on by the need to mobilise resources during the First World War and by the early fascination with socialism, helped to swing the pendulum too far in the direction of statism and interventionism, and away from reliance on market forces and market outcomes. So, in a sense, a Keynesian counter-revolution was necessary to move the pendulum back from excessive reliance on the state towards a greater role for markets. This period was probably already coming to an end in the second part of the 1990s, but the terrorist acts of 11 September 2001, and their dramatic impact on the world economy, are possibly accelerating the change-over from the seemingly successful new neo-classical restoration towards more Keynesian positions.

Suddenly, the main problem has become how to face a downturn in consumer and investor confidence in the United States and Europe. A downturn that has led to reduced private consumption and investments, and will naturally lead in the short run to reduced aggregate demand, reduced income and increased unemployment of resources throughout the world. The problem is now to deal with a shock wave in the short run and with a cyclical downturn in the world economic system, beginning with its largest components.

The response that is taking shape, particularly in the United States, consists of a mixture of expansionary monetary and fiscal policies which fully belong to the panoply of Keynesian economic policy instruments: interest rate cuts, increased government spending and tax reductions on producers and consumers. Europe is following up with monetary easing and some more "covert" fiscal stimuli. The pendulum is finally getting back to where it ought to be.

Fears of inflation and overexpansion of the state are being pushed into the background in much of the industrialised West, and what were once considered key negative legacies of the Keynesian revolution—expenditure policies—are coming back, at least in the short term, and first in the most politically conservative part of our world: the United States. Perceived urgency in dealing with a serious jolt in producer and consumer confidence has produced the quick turnaround in attitudes, judgements and policy tools that we are witnessing today.

Keynes himself was fully aware of this type of cycle, dictated by history and by big events. In his *How to Pay for the War*, he turned his attention to the problem of avoiding inflation.[11] There and elsewhere, he made it abundantly clear that he was concerned at the excessive expansion of public spending, and that his ideas should not be used to justify excessive interference in the workings of the market. In one sense he still considered his theory to be general, but was ready to admit that use of public expenditure, except in circumstances where

---

[11] JM Keynes, *How to Pay for the War* (London, Macmillan, 1940).

unemployment is high, should be considered carefully. James Meade's plea to Keynes: "Would that he were alive to exercise his ingenious and fertile mind on the problem . . . . of making a high and sustained level of *real* economic activity compatible with a restraint of those inflationary rises in *money* prices and wage rates so naturally demanded and so readily conceded in conditions of a sustained high level of demand . . .",[12] is still very apt when one considers the problems industrial economies have to face at the present time.

As the Keynesian revolution generated excesses, the new neo-classical counter-revolution that has taken hold of economics for much of the past twenty-five years has also led to unwise and excessive positions and decisions. Some of them are reflected in institutions and in their mandates. The new European System of Central Banks (ESCB) is one of them. Given that the UK is now facing the critical decision of whether or not to join the European Monetary Union, it may be worth referring here to the design of the mandate of the ESCB. Such a constitutional mandate constitutes one of the most significant "legacies" of the anti-Keynesian counter-revolution, embedded in the Maastricht treaty and in the Stability and Growth Pact which accompanies it. According to Article 105 of the treaty, "The primary objective of the ESC shall be to maintain price stability". The formulation clearly posits a direct and stable relationship between money and prices, and implies that aggregate demand, i.e. investment, consumption, and employment, can be safely left out of this relationship, either because they are of second order importance or because the objectives subsumed in them can be better achieved by other means. Thus it is a straightforward and simple-minded version of monetarism. Furthermore, Article 107 gives the ECSB a completely free hand in carrying out its policies, so that it does not have to receive or accept instructions from the European Commission, the Council, or any political body in Europe. As for the Stability Pact, it states that the EMU member countries must either keep their budgets in equilibrium or carry a surplus in the medium run, being only allowed to run a deficit under certain circumstances and within a ceiling of 3 per cent of GNP (irrespective of the cycle). Special agreements have been negotiated with certain countries in order to accelerate a reduction in their high outstanding public debt.

Whether all this is reasonable in general terms, and whether it will be maintained in the face of the current economic situation, remains to be seen. What is certain is that it was unwise to adopt a special doctrine and embed its tenets in a treaty which is extremely difficult to amend, as if anything such as this could ever be considered beyond discussion in economic or political terms. Keynes would have argued in favour of discretion and less iron-cast and one-dimensional institutional mandates. He was only too well aware of the evolution of history and fashions, and of the need to guard against the many surprises that might arise from them.

[12] J Meade, "The Keynesian Revolution", in M Keynes (ed.), *Essays on John Maynard Keynes* (Cambridge, Cambridge University Press, 1975), p. 88.

IV

In his *Reflections on the Revolution in Europe,* written soon after the fall of the Berlin Wall in 1990, Ralf Dahrendorf recalls a private exchange with the late François Furet.[13] The great historian argued that, following the momentous events of 1989, for the first time in the last hundred and fifty years, intellectual and political discussions would no longer reflect opposing views on the nature and aims of human societies. The downfall of communism as an ideology, as well as a practical experiment, would mark the fact that capitalism on one side and democracy on the other stood as unchallenged arrangements for human societies.

I would add in passing that, in the wake of 11 September some might be tempted to believe that a new global challenge to western values and societies has emerged, and that Islamic fundamentalism could replace socialism as the alternative to capitalism and western democracy to which Furet was referring. I believe this idea should be resisted. However vast the threat posed by terrorism is, and will probably remain for some time to come, there is a basic difference between fundamentalism and socialism. The threat of fundamentalism comes from outside the world of liberal societies as we have come to know them in the West. It is a threat, not an alternative. Socialism, on the other hand, arose from within the liberal societies of the nineteenth and twentieth centuries. The strength of the challenge of communism to liberal societies stemmed from the fact that its very source came from within their midst, and that its ideas were in a sense one of the possible developments of the path which began with the French Revolution. This challenge bears no similarity to that posed by Islamic fundamentalism, which does not and will not purport to transform Western societies here and now, but rather proposes a model of society for the Islamic world. Islamic fundamentalism does and possibly will put our societies to a severe test. But it is to the Islamic world above all that it is addressed. It threatens to destabilise the political order now reigning in much of this world. It aims to be an alternative to it. In this sense, it is still largely external to us and extraneous to our problems and concerns.

The fact that capitalism is no longer challenged by an alternative model of society such as socialism does not mean that one ought to be blind to its problems and contradictions. Dahrendorf made a fitting remark in this regard: if capitalism is a system, he wrote in his *Letters*, it ought to be resisted to the same extent that communism was.

It is here that some of the ideas developed by Keynes and collected in his *Essays in Persuasion* of 1931 may still be of help to us in what lies ahead. In *A Short View of Russia*, written in 1925 following a brief visit to the country,

---

[13] R Dahrendorf, *Reflections on the Revolution in Europe: in a letter intended to have been sent to a gentleman in Warsaw* (London, Chatto & Windus, 1990).

Keynes argued that the strength of communism was not in "an improved economic technique . . .". "I do not think that it contains, or is likely to contain, any piece of useful economic technique", he suggested, but its novelty was to promote "a real change in the predominant attitude towards money. Modern capitalism is absolutely irreligious, without internal union, without much public spirit, often, though not always, a mere congeries of possessors and pursuers. Such a system has to be immensely . . . successful to survive". "To me it seems clearer every day", he concluded, "that the moral problem of our age is concerned with the love of money."[14]

Keynes returned to this theme in 1926 in a pamphlet entitled *The End of Laissez-faire*. There he argued that capitalism had to be defended as an efficient way of producing wealth, not as an expression of a natural arrangement of societies: "I think that capitalism, wisely managed, can probably be made more efficient for attaining economic ends than any alternative system yet in sight, but that in itself it is in many ways extremely objectionable."[15]

The argument was examined further in another essay written in 1930. There he asked what the conditions of the world would be like in a hundred years' time. He imagined that the growth of productivity would be high enough to yield the increase in income needed to solve the economic problem: "Thus for the first time since his creation man will be faced with his real, his permanent problem—how to use his freedom from pressing economic cares, how to occupy the leisure . . . to live wisely and agreeably and well". Once this point has been reached, there will be changes in the way men consider "the money motive": "We shall be able to rid ourselves of many of the pseudo-moral principles which have hag-ridden us for two hundred years, by which we have exalted some of the most distasteful of human qualities into the position of the highest virtues". But Keynes also cautioned: "The time for all this is not yet. For at least another hundred years we must pretend to ourselves and to everyone that fair is foul and foul is fair; for foul is useful and fair is not".[16]

I believe the legacy of Keynes to the present century is not merely in the technique he proposed to smooth the economic cycle and wisely guide our economies towards the elimination of the economic and social waste that is unemployment; a legacy which has re-emerged since the danger of an economic collapse suddenly materialised before our eyes in the aftermath of 11 September 2001. It is also the idea that, as we move towards societies, productive structures and regimes that are potentially productive enough to supply sufficient goods to free us from the economic problem, we have to devise concrete means of achieving this goal in ways that do not overtly exclude great parts of the world from the fruits of our economic systems, and must strive to reduce inequalities in the

---

[14] JM Keynes, *A Short View of Russia*, in *Essays in Persuasion*, n. 3 above, pp. 253–271.
[15] JM Keynes, *The End of Laissez-faire*, in *Essays in Persuasion*, n. 3 above, pp. 272–294.
[16] JM Keynes, *Economic Possibilities for our Grandchildren*, in *Essays in Persuasion*, n. 3 above, pp. 321–332.

distribution of wealth internally and internationally. We should also attempt systematically to minimize the burden that we leave to future generations in the use of resources and the exploitation of common goods.

If "misery generates hate", a motto that William Beveridge inscribed on the front page of his *Full Employment in a Free Society*, that a good part of humanity should reach prosperity, and be "deprived of its traditional purpose", as Keynes wrote in one of his *Essays in Persuasion*, may not be a great benefit. The legacy of these two great British men includes their emphasis on the relevance of this critical equilibrium.

13

The British Contribution to European Union in the Twentieth Century: The Idea of Responsible Government

VERNON BOGDANOR

"The English must stop despising foreigners. They are Europeans and ought to be aware of it".

(George Orwell, The English People, 1947.)

I

Europe of course comprises much more than the European Union. Yet, politically, the contribution that Britain can make to Europe will almost certainly be through becoming a constructive member of the European Union. For much, perhaps most of the post-war period, however, the British have not felt themselves to be European. It was for this reason that Britain did not join the European Coal and Steel Community in 1951 nor the Common Market in 1957.

Even when Britain did finally join the European Community in 1973, after two failed attempts, she had by no means become fully European, and the relationship between Britain and her Continental neighbours in the European Union remains uneasy. This reflects deep-seated psychological factors which are rooted ultimately in history. Indeed, they flow, in the last resort, from the fact that our historical experience since the Reformation has been so profoundly different from that of our Continental neighbours.

This difference can be summed up by noting that the years 1789, 1848 and 1917, which were years of revolutionary turmoil on the Continent, barely disturbed the basic stability of British society. Avoiding the revolutionary turmoil which followed the French and Russian revolutions, the English believed that they had found a path of constitutional evolution different from and superior to that of their Continental neighbours. The Second World War intensified this feeling. For, unlike the six founding members of the Community, Britain suffered neither fascism nor enemy occupation, secure in what Winston Churchill was fond of calling "our island home".[1] Britain therefore saw no reason to crib or confine herself within the corset of supranational institutions.

After 1746, when the Jacobite revolt, the last major rebellion against the Crown, was defeated, and with it the threat of Continental invasion, Britain's path seemed to lie not with Europe, but with Empire; and no doubt the psychological differences between Britain and the countries of the Continent came to be emphasised during the eighteenth century, reinforced as they were by the French Revolution and the threat from Bonaparte.

1947, however, when India achieved independence, symbolised the voluntary relinquishing of Britain's imperial role, and made possible a new beginning. Some might argue that the two centuries between 1746 and 1947, despite the fact that they have so strongly coloured Britain's sense of national identity, were actually an aberrant period in British history, during most of which the fate of Britain and that of the Continent have been intertwined. If that is so, then the mind-set engendered by this period of two hundred years need not prove permanent. Habits of mind, after all, can and do change. Indeed, psychoanalysts tell us that the first step towards changing deep-seated patterns of behaviour is to recognise them for what they are.

Perhaps future generations will perceive the fundamental conflict in British post-war politics as being not so much between Left and Right, as between those who believed that Britain's experience between the eighteenth and twentieth centuries was a deviation, and those who saw Britain's separation from the Continent as a fundamental axiom of her existence. This profound political conflict has cut across the major parties, and it serves to unite, for example, Harold Macmillan, Edward Heath, Roy Jenkins and Robin Cook against Margaret Thatcher, Enoch Powell, Hugh Gaitskell and Michael Foot. Only if this conflict is resolved in favour of those who believe that Britain's separation from the Continent was an accident, and not a fundamental feature of her existence will Britain be able to make a contribution to European Union in the twenty-first century.

II

When Britain joined the European Community in 1973, she found that she had to make more adjustments to membership than any of the founding six member states—France, Germany, Italy and the Benelux countries. It was not only that the British party and electoral systems, the British taxation system and method of subsidising agriculture were quite different from those of the Continental member states. Most important of all, her whole constitutional structure, and

---

[1] The United Kingdom is of course not an island. Until 1922, it comprised two islands, Great Britain and Ireland. Since then, it has comprised one island, and a portion of another, Northern Ireland. But literalness of this sort would have ruined the impact of Churchill's rhetoric.

indeed her whole understanding of what a constitution was, denied the essential premise on which the Community had been built.

Alexis de Tocqueville, in De La Democratie en Amérique, had famously declared that Britain, or rather England, had no constitution. "En Angleterre, on reconnaît au parlement le droit de modifier la constitution. En Angleterre, la constitution peut donc changer sans cesse, ou plutôt elle n'existe point. Le parlement, en même temps qu'il est corps legislatif, est corps constituant".[2]

The lack of an enacted constitution is the first feature to strike the student of British government. The reason for this is not difficult to find. Constitutions are generally drawn up to symbolise the birth of a nation, a new beginning following war or revolution. A constitution marks the start of a new political order, a new epoch in a nation's development. It is an essential pre-requisite to the legitimation of a new regime, since it lays out the goals which the nation is expected to pursue and the means by which they may be attained. A constitution, therefore, marks a sharp discontinuity in the history of a state, a radical break with previous practice. It is for this reason that, for example, Italy adopted a new constitution in 1948, Germany in 1949, France in 1946, and then again in 1958, and Portugal and Spain after emerging from dictatorship in 1976 and 1978. It is for this same reason of course that the European Community began with a treaty, the Treaty of Rome, which, as amended, is the nearest that the Union has to a constitution, unwieldy though it now is.

England, however, has been spared such discontinuities since the seventeenth century. Her progress has been evolutionary, unpunctuated by revolutionary upheaval or foreign occupation. The English people, if not the British, have not felt the need to ask themselves whether they ought to summarise their historical experience in a fundamental document. England's whole constitutional experience seemed, until recently at least, to show that there was neither any need for, nor any virtue in, an enacted constitution. England, so it appeared, was constructed in a different way from other democracies, and in a more durable way. English exceptionalism seemed providential, a matter for congratulation not regret.

What was true of England was not, of course, necessarily true also of the non-English parts of the United Kingdom, which came into existence as a result of specific and datable Acts of Parliament—the Acts of the English and Scottish Parliaments of 1706, replacing those parliaments by a single Parliament of Great Britain; the Union with Ireland Act of 1800 abolishing the Irish Parliament; and the Irish Free State (Agreement) Act of 1922, removing the 26 counties which formed the Irish Free State from the jurisdiction of the Parliament of the United Kingdom. These measures, so it might be argued, were in the nature of constituent instruments. Yet the courts never accepted them as such, and have always held that issues arising from the Acts of Union are not justiciable.[3] Thus,

---

[2] A de Tocqueville, *De la Democratie en Amérique*, Pt. 1, Ch. 6.
[3] See, for example, *Ex p. Canon Selwyn* (1872) 36 JP54; *MacCormick v. Lord Advocate* (1953) SC 396; *Gibson v. Lord Advocate* (1975) SLT 134.

for practical purposes, the effects of the Acts of Union with Scotland and Ireland were assimilative, and England was able, for many years, to impose her own particular conception of constitutional development upon both Scotland and Northern Ireland.

For the English, therefore, a constitution is the product of long evolutionary development, not something that can be summarised in the form of an enactment. The great nineteenth century constitutional lawyer, A V Dicey, in his unpublished lectures on comparative constitutions, characterised the British Constitution as a "historic" constitution.[4] By this he meant not only that it was very old, but also that it was original and spontaneous, the product of historical development rather than deliberate design.

It may seem at first sight as if a constitution of this sort must be a merely pragmatic instrument, bereft of principles capable of constraining the actions of those who rule. But that need not necessarily be the case. There are in fact principles of the British Constitution, but they are based as much upon procedures, upon tacit understandings, as upon rules. One authority on the constitution insisted at the beginning of the twentieth century that, "British government is based on a system of tacit understandings. But the understandings are not always understood".[5] Thus the principles which lie behind the workings of British government are on the whole conventional rather than statutory or enacted. Prime amongst these principles is the idea of ministerial responsibility to parliament, the central idea of parliamentary government; and this idea has two legs, the first being the collective responsibility of government to parliament, the second being the individual responsibility of ministers to parliament.

The European Union, of course, is based on a quite different idea of what a constitution is. By contrast with the British Constitution which legitimises, through the idea of the sovereignty of parliament, a considerable concentration of power at the centre of government, the fundamental leitmotif of the European Union is that of power sharing. For power in the Union is divided both between its main institutions—the Commission, the Council of Ministers, the Parliament and the Court of Justice—and territorially, between the Community and the member states. The territorial division of powers has been buttressed since the Maastricht Treaty in 1992 by the idea of subsidiarity, the idea that decisions should be taken at the lowest level consistent with effective action.

The European Union is of course far from being a federal political system, and yet, since it exemplifies the principle of the division of powers, it is far easier for a federal state such as Germany to understand its workings than it is for a unitary state such as Britain. In Britain, it has proved difficult to internalise the notion of a division of powers, although the devolution legislation of 1998, and

---

[4] AV Dicey, *Lectures on the Comparative Study of Constitutions*. These lectures are to be found in the Codrington Library, All Souls College, Oxford, MS 323 LR 6 b 13. I am grateful to the Librarian for allowing me to consult them.

[5] S Low, *The Governance of Britain* (London, T. Fisher Unwin, 1904), 12.

in particular, the Scotland Act, is an attempt to divide legislative powers between London and Edinburgh. But the British tradition of parliamentary sovereignty implied that power could not be shared, but had to be located in a specific place—either at Westminster, although this would prevent her joining a body which sought to be more than a mere union of member states—or in Brussels, in which case Europe would have become a super-state, something which would mean, in the words of the leader of the Labour Party, Hugh Gaitskell, in 1962, "the end of a thousand years of history".

At the time when Britain made her first application to join the European Community in 1961, an application doomed to failure thanks to the intransigence of de Gaulle, her political institutions and the stability of her system of government were the envy of her Continental neighbours. Indeed, the "Westminster Model", exported as it was to the newly independent Commonwealth countries of Asia and Africa, was widely admired as a paradigm of constitutional government. "In 1953", the American sociologist, Edward Shils declared, "I heard an eminent man of the Left say, in utter seriousness, at a university dinner, that the British Constitution was 'as nearly perfect as any human institution could be', and no one even thought it amusing".[6]

Since then, of course, not only have intellectual fashions changed, but, in addition, the economic decline of Britain and her retreat from the role of world power, have meant that the "Westminster Model" is now seen as something to be avoided, rather than imitated. Indeed, none of the new democracies of Central and Eastern Europe have even considered adopting a system of government which uses the first past the post method of election and seems to legitimise the concentration of power at the centre of government. They have preferred instead, for obvious reasons, the power-sharing models associated in particular with the German Federal Republic. Thus, whereas in 1945, British ideas of government might have seemed appropriate both to new democracies and to European institutions, the danger today is that, in the reform of the European Union, some of the very real virtues of the British system of government, and in particular the idea of parliamentary government, of a government responsible to parliament, will come to be overlooked. It is, however, in the application of the idea of ministerial responsibility to the constitution of the European Union, so it is suggested, that Britain can make her constitutional contribution to the Europe of the twenty-first century.

III

It has become a commonplace that the European Union is suffering from a democratic deficit, because the European Parliament is unable to hold the executive of

---

[6] E Shils, "British Intellectuals in the Mid-Twentieth Century", *Encounter*, April 1955, reprinted in *The Intellectuals and the Powers* (Chicago, University of Chicago Press, 1972), 135.

the European Union to account. Much of the reform agenda which European leaders are preparing for the next intergovernmental conference in the year 2004 is devoted to the internal relationships between the institutions of the European Union and the appropriate balance between them.

The main problem facing the Union, however, is less an imbalance between its institutions than popular alienation from its objectives. Indeed, this alienation is coming to threaten the very legitimacy of the Union itself. It is a striking fact that turnout for the European Parliament elections has fallen steadily and continuously since 1979, the year of the first European Parliament elections.

Turnout in European Parliament Elections, 1979–1999.

Year	Number of member states	% Turnout
1979	9	63.0
1984	10	61.0
1989	12	58.5
1994	12	56.8
1999	15	49.4

In the last elections in 1999, fewer than half of the eligible electorate voted; and this figure itself overstates the true level of voluntary participation, since voting is compulsory in a number of member states.

In the two countries which are seen as the motor of European Union, France and Germany, turnout was 47.0 per cent and 45.2 per cent respectively. In the three new member states, Austria, Finland and Sweden, which voted for the first time in European elections, turnout was, respectively, 49.0 per cent, 30.1 per cent and 38.3 per cent. Turnout was lowest in Britain at 24 per cent. In parts of Liverpool, turnout was just 8 per cent. Turnout in Britain, it has been pointed out, was lower than the percentage who were prepared to "vote" in a popular television programme called "Big Brother". It is hardly possible for the European Parliament to claim a mandate to represent the opinions of 370 million people of the European Union when fewer than half of its eligible electorate is willing to vote for it.

This fall in turnout is paradoxical, since it has occurred at a time when the power and influence of the European Parliament have greatly increased, largely due to two major amendments of the Treaty of Rome, the Single European Act of 1986 and the Maastricht Treaty of 1992. In 1979, at the time of the first direct elections, many commentators, dismayed by a turnout far lower than they had hoped, claimed that apathy was inevitable at a time when the European Parliament had so few powers. Voters could not, they suggested, be persuaded to turn out to elect what would prove to be little more than a talking shop. However, the increase in powers for the European Parliament has coincided with a steady decrease, not an increase, in the percentage of European electors willing to turn out to vote for it. There is thus a striking contrast between the progressive transfer of competences to the European level and the lack of popular involvement on the part of the European electorate. This failure to mobilise popular consent is now the principal weakness of the European project.

There seems, then, little enthusiasm for the European electoral process. Not only is the European Parliament unable to help create a European consciousness, but, far from being seen as the protector of the citizen against the machinery of European bureaucracy, it has come to be regarded rather as part of that machinery itself. Instead of being a counterweight to the technocratic elements in European Union, it is perceived as an element in that techno-structure, part of an alienated superstructure.

This failing on the part of the European Parliament, so it is suggested, is not contingent, but inherent in the way that European institutions have developed since 1958 and on the "tacit understandings" which underlie them.

Some of these "tacit understandings" bear a striking resemblance to those of Fourth Republic France, a political system in which major decisions were taken by non-elected officials, and the line between politicians and officials was often blurred. One commentator on the Fourth Republic saw it as a house without windows, hermetically sealed from popular involvement, whose preoccupation was with *la politique politicienne*, politics for the political class rather than for the people.[7] The founding fathers of Europe were, however, concerned to avoid the kind of situation that had occurred in the Third and Fourth Republics in France when parliament had insisted on intervening in every detail of government, thereby paralysing executive action. Therefore, they gave the European Parliament only limited powers.

The European Parliament stems from the Common Assembly of the European Coal and Steel Community set up in 1952, which was restricted to the exercise of largely "supervisory" powers. It was not at the time seen as central to the European project, but was tacked on to the other institutions of the Community in a somewhat perfunctory way. In the Treaty of Rome, as ratified in 1958, the powers of the Parliament were described in Article 137 as "advisory" as well as "supervisory". The European Community, then, was to be based not on parliamentary government, but on government by wise men and women situated in the Commission, the European analogue to the French *Commissariat du Plan*.

But the European Union has also been influenced by another ethos, important in parts of the Continent, the ethos of consociational democracy. This is little understood in Britain where the ethos of the Union is often, and in a rather facile manner, compared to that of a federal state. In a consociational state, however, as it existed in the Netherlands, for example, politics operated by elite agreement, and the various groupings forming the consociation—in the Netherlands, Catholics Protestants and Liberals, in the European Union, the peoples of the member states—remain separate. In such a consociational system, the legislature

---

[7] N Leites, *On the Game of Politics in France* (Stanford, Stanford University Press, 1959).

foregoes much of its classical role of scrutinising government and holding it to account. For neither the legislature nor the people dare untie the packages agreed by elites, since it is elite agreement which holds the system together.[8]

What both the French technocratic ethos and the Dutch consociational ethos have in common is their denial of the basic principle of parliamentary government, that government should be responsible to parliament. For the French, parliamentary interference would have ruined the European project, as it had ruined the Third and Fourth Republics. For the Dutch, parliamentary government would have divided Europeans in an unacceptable way, and so hindered the prospect of reaching agreement. Such ideas were, of course more plausible in a period when there was deference to political leaders, when the leaders led and the followers followed. It has become less plausible in an era when the leaders continue to lead but the followers decline to follow.

The consequence, however, was bound to be a restricted role for the European Parliament. Thus, elections to that Parliament do not, as we have seen, fulfil the functions which elections are normally expected to perform. In Britain, and in most other democracies, elections confer legitimacy because they fulfil three interrelated functions. They offer the voter first a choice of government, second a choice of who should lead that government, so providing it with a recognisable human face, and third the choice of a set of policies.

Elections to the European Parliament, however, fulfil none of these functions. They do not determine the political colour of the European Union, nor do they determine how it is to be governed, for the government of the Union is shared between the Council of Ministers and the Commission, and the composition of neither of these bodies is affected by European elections. Therefore European elections do little to help determine the policies followed by the Union; nor do they yield personalised or recognisable leadership for the Union. This has important consequences particularly in foreign policy. Henry Kissinger once complained that if he wanted to telephone the spokesman for Europe, he did not know what number to ring. "Who do I call? Who is Mr Europe? If I wish to consult Europe, and I have a phone in front of me, what number do I dial?" At the time of the Reykjavik summit between Reagan and Gorbachev in 1986, Europe, whose interests were clearly affected, was conspicuous by its absence. "Our old continent is absent from the major negotiations between super powers at which Europe's fate is being sealed", the European Parliament complained. "No single person is in a position to represent it".[9] The situation is hardly different today. The creation in 1999 of the post of Secretary-General and High Representative for Commission Foreign and Security Policy, hardly

---

[8] The idea of consociational democracy was developed by the Dutch political scientist, A Lijphart. See, for example, *Democracy in Plural Societies: A Comparative Exploration*, 2nd ed. (New Haven, Conn., Yale University Press, 1977).

[9] European Parliament: Committee on Institutional Affairs: Draft Report on The Presidency of the European Community. Part B: Explanatory Statement. PE 119.031/B. para. 6.

fills the gap. Indeed, it is doubtful if most Europeans know the name of the current incumbent, Javier Solana, who was not, of course, chosen by anything resembling a democratic process, and is therefore in no sense a political leader.

The Presidency of the European Commission is decided not by the voters but by private dealings between the governments of the member states. In 1994, for example, Jean Dehaene, the Prime Minister of Belgium, who had been proposed as successor to Jacques Delors, was thought to be unsuitable, not by the European Parliament, but by Britain's Prime Minister, John Major, who believed that Dehaene was too "federalist". Europe's leaders then agreed upon Jacques Santer as his replacement. But this whole process took place without any involvement or even consultation on the part of the European Parliament, which, nevertheless, formally approved Santer as President.

Yet, Santer, who was a Christian Democrat from Luxembourg, was approved by a newly-elected Parliament containing a majority from the Left. The European Parliament seemed perfectly prepared to endorse a President who did not represent the majority of its members.

In March 1999, three months before the next round of European Parliament elections, the European Commission resigned en bloc, following allegations of corruption. This led to the replacement of Jacques Santer as President of the Commission by Romano Prodi. It did not seem to have occurred to the leaders of Europe, meeting in private conclave, to await the result of the European Parliament elections before deciding upon Prodi as the next President.

Moreover, the nomination of individual commissioners by the member states bears no necessary relationship to the electoral success of the political parties. In the 1999 European elections in Germany, for example, the CDU/CSU, the German component of the Christian Democrat transnational European Peoples Party, secured the largest number of votes, but the SPD/Green government nevertheless appointed an SPD and a Green commissioner. It would be difficult to find more striking illustrations of the irrelevance of the European Parliament to the governance of Europe, indeed of the irrelevance of the elections themselves.

In elections in the member states of the Union, electors generally sees a connection between their vote and the actual outcome in terms of policy and leadership. Elections to the European Parliament, however, do not lead to the choice of an executive nor of an electoral college which chooses an executive. It is hardly possible, therefore, for electors to perceive any connection between their vote and the policy of the Union.

Thus elections to the European Parliament, although in form transnational, have become in practice a series of national test elections, analysed for their implications upon the domestic policies of the member states, rather than the European Union. They are second-order elections in that their outcome is dependent not on European matters, but on national party allegiances, modified by the popularity or the unpopularity of the incumbent government in each member state.[10] They thus bear some resemblance to transnational opinion polls charting the fortunes of the main domestic forces in the various member states. But this means that they are unable to confer legitimacy on the European project.

This weakness has become particularly striking since, in Europe, from the late 1960s, as in democracies in other parts of the world, the demand for political participation has grown apace. One consequence of this has been that the mismatch between popular expectations and the performance of government widened during the 1980s and 1990s. For the effects of social change—rising living standards, the gradual "embourgeoisement" of the working class, the spreading ownership of property, shares and other assets—all served to diffuse economic power more widely and to erode traditional attitudes towards authority. The development of information technology and the coming of an information society seemed to make possible a radical dispersal of decision-making so that centralised, top-down methods of government came to appear outdated. Many, perhaps most, democracies elected governments which sought to move in the direction of a market economy emphasising the importance of individual choice in both the public and private sectors; one consequence was the development of a consumerist culture so that, in social and economic affairs at least, the individual gained sovereignty. The governments of Margaret Thatcher and John Major, moreover, sought to make public institutions themselves more accountable, both through privatisation, and by encouraging devolution from local authorities to individual institutions such as schools and housing estates. The central theme was the attempt to give individuals more control over institutions providing public services. Britain indeed was a pioneer in the 1990s in a revolution in government and in attitudes to government, a revolution which sought to resolve the paradox that the triumph of liberal democracy, following the collapse of Communism, seemed to be accompanied by growing alienation from government. If one had to sum up this revolution, one could say that its essence consisted in government becoming more consumer and voter-friendly, more concerned with outputs than inputs, more concerned to satisfy the needs of voters and citizens. The "Citizen's Charter", introduced by John Major in 1991 was much mocked at its inception, but its basic principle has been copied in a number of other democratic countries. The reforms, sometimes rather superficially attributed to "Thatcherism" were in fact widely adopted, even in countries ruled by governments of the Left—France, for example, Australia, New Zealand and Sweden.

Nevertheless, the growth of consumer sovereignty was not in general matched by corresponding changes in the political sphere. There was indeed something of a contrast between the return of individualism in economic life and the relatively passive role which individuals were expected to adopt

---

[10] The German political scientist, Karlheinz Reif, was the first to characterise European elections as "second-order elections" in his book, *Ten European Elections* (Aldershot, Gower, 1985).

towards their political institutions. Voters, however, have begun to show a disconcerting insistence on untying the consociational packages that their leaders have agreed. That process was apparent in the referendums on the Maastricht and Nice treaties in Denmark, France and Ireland. It might have been apparent in other member states also had they been required to ratify these treaties by referendum. The packages agreed with much effort by political leaders, therefore, are in danger of being untied as the demand for popular involvement in decisions-making asserts itself. Perhaps indeed the concept of "consociational democracy" is actually a contradiction in terms. Perhaps consociational systems only work by denying democratic participation in what are seen as the wider interests of the stability of the system. What is clear is that it is no longer, as perhaps it may once have been, a satisfactory method of governing a community whose members see themselves as active citizens.

IV

If, then, the constitutional structure of the European Union does not yield accountability to the voters of Europe, how might such accountability be secured? Some of Europe's more far-sighted leaders have come to favour the introduction of an element of direct election in European institutions. Ex-President Giscard of France, for example, has advocated that the President of the European Council be directly elected by universal suffrage, while Jacques Delors has called for the direct election of the President of the Commission, and, as a first step towards that aim, the election of the Commission President by an electoral college comprising members of national parliaments and the European Parliament. Jacques Chirac, also, has shown considerable sympathy with the idea of direct election.

It is, perhaps, not at all surprising that support for direct election comes from France whose Fifth Republic finds so important a place both for direct election of the President and for the referendum. Indeed, it may be argued that if the European Community reflects in part the ethos of the French Fourth Republic, it should now be replaced by a system based on the ethos of the French Fifth Republic, and this is the aim of the French reformers.

Direct election would explicitly recognise the principle of the sovereignty of the people as the foundation stone of a united Europe. It seeks to meet the central challenge facing Europe which is that of discovering some means of bridging the gap between the elite and the people so as to construct a European consciousness without which the whole European idea will remain an empty construct.

Direct election would enable European voters to influence the policy of the European Union and to choose its government. It would provide that democratic base of legitimacy which at present the European Union lacks. There would then be a strong incentive for Europeans to vote in elections genuinely designed to determine the political orientation of the Union. Moreover, direct election would focus popular interest on European issues, giving them glamour and excitement, qualities sadly lacking at present, and it might therefore prove a remedy for falling turnout and electoral apathy.

But there are two obvious objections to the idea of direct election. The first is that European solidarity is probably not yet sufficiently advanced for the nationals of one member state to be willing to support the national of another as in effect leader of Europe. Indeed, it may be argued that the proposal for direct election presupposes the very solidarity which it is intended to help create.

Secondly, any alteration in the method of electing the President of the European Council or the Commission would require an amendment to the Treaty. Such an amendment would need to be carried unanimously by every member state. In two member states, Denmark and Ireland, Treaty amendment requires approval by the people in a referendum. In both countries, referendums have led to rejection—of the Maastricht Treaty in Denmark in 1992, and of the Nice Treaty in Ireland in 2001. In another member state, France, where a referendum was not constitutionally required, the government nevertheless called one on the Maastricht Treaty in 1993, and this led to but a narrow majority for the treaty. The two rejections and the one near-rejection led to major crises in the European Union.

It is highly unlikely that, in the current state of Euro-scepticism, unanimous agreement could be secured for an amendment proposing direct election of the President of the Commission or of the European Council. At least one member-state and possibly more would probably reject such a proposal, not only ensuring its defeat, but causing a further crisis in the Union. This would reawaken the same atavistic sentiments which Maastricht aroused. The proposal for direct election is again seen to presuppose that very European solidarity which it seeks to create.

But, if the French method of democratising the European Union seems too Utopian to work in current circumstances, the same may not be true for the British notion of parliamentary responsibility. Article 158 of the Treaty requires the President of the Commission to secure a vote of confidence before assuming office. This vote is generally a formality, and it would be refused only if someone manifestly unsuitable or corrupt were to be proposed. There is no reason, however, why this should continue to be so. There is no reason why the vote of confidence should remain a mere formality. Instead, it could be used, as of course it is in Britain, to enforce responsibility.

In Britain, as in other parliamentary systems, a government's existence depends upon its ability to secure a majority in the legislature. If it fails to do so, it must resign. Why should not the same principle apply in the European Union? The European Parliament could, if it so wished, and without the need for any treaty amendment, simply insist that the political outlook of the President of the Commission, and indeed of the Commission as a whole, conform to that of the majority in the Parliament. Thus, a Left majority could insist that the President of the Commission and the Commission were taken from the Left, a Right majority, conversely, could insist that the President and the Commission came from the Right.

If the Commission were to be dependent upon the majority in the European Parliament, this would entirely transform the role of the Parliament, for it would become an executive-generating body. There would then be an incentive for electors to turn out to vote in European Parliament elections since they would be helping to determine whether Europe was to be governed in a Leftward or a Rightward direction, something which has become of much greater importance with the development of economic and monetary union; electors would also be helping to determine the political leadership of Europe and the broad direction of public policy in Europe. The elections would become a real analogue of domestic elections rather than, as they are at present, a series of domestic elections conducted simultaneously. Elections to the European Parliament would fulfil the same three functions as domestic elections. They would be helping to determine the broad direction of public policy, choosing a government, to the extent that the Commission is in fact a "government", and helping to determine the political leadership of Europe.

This transformation in the role of the European Parliament would almost certainly lead to further consequential changes. For voters would seek to know who the different transnational parties would nominate as Commission President. The larger political groups would probably nominate candidates for the Presidency before the European elections, thus making the process of choice of President more transparent. This would make the European elections in effect direct elections of the European Commission. The analogy with domestic elections, which, in Britain and many other democracies, have the function of directly electing the leader of the government, would be even more complete. Direct elections would then link voters to the Commission of the European Union through the transnational parties.

The British contribution, then, could be to show how the fundamental principle of parliamentary government, of a government responsible to parliament, can be applied to the European Union so as both to yield accountability and to clarify the purpose of European elections.

v

The idea of responsibility, however, implies not only the responsibility of government to the legislature, collective responsibility, but also the responsibility of individual ministers to the legislature, individual responsibility. This too is an idea which could readily be adapted to the European Union.

The essence of the notion of individual responsibility was well stated by Gladstone who declared that "In every free state, for every public act, some one must be responsible; and the question is, who shall it be?" The British Constitution answers: "the minister and the minister exclusively".[11] Ministerial responsibility in this sense is a fundamental principle of the British Constitution, defining and prescribing as it does the relationships both between ministers and officials and between ministers and Parliament. Indeed, it has the same importance in the British system of government as the concept of the separation of powers in the American.

Under the British system of government, executive powers are, with a few notable exceptions, conferred by Parliament upon ministers and not on officials. It is the concept of ministerial responsibility which buttresses the politically neutral role of civil servants. For it ensures that officials, with very few exceptions, speak and act in the name of ministers. They have no constitutional personality of their own. Everything that they do is, constitutionally, done under the authority of a minister, either express or implied. Thus, civil servants are accountable only to the ministers whom they serve. They have, in general, no direct accountability to Parliament. Ministerial responsibility allows the minister to be both the conduit through which accountability flows, and also the wall protecting officials from Parliament. Thus, the concept of ministerial responsibility sustains a structure of government within which ministers are served by permanent officials who are required to serve governments of any political colour, and who, at senior levels, are debarred from party affiliation. It is in this way that ministerial responsibility helps to sustain a politically neutral civil service.

The sharp separation of ministerial and official roles which characterises Britain and the "old" Commonwealth countries—Canada, Australia and New Zealand—is not, by and large, met with in Europe. On the Continent, by contrast, there are instead the phenomena of the elected official and the un-elected politician. Indeed, one of the reasons why we in Britain find it so difficult to understand the European Union is that in it important decisions are taken by unelected persons. I once heard an MP refer at a meeting to a European Commissioner, the late Finn Gundelach, as an "official". Mr. Gundelach bristled. M Delors would, one suspects, have bristled even more strongly. Yet, M Delors, a European leader of great authority and significance, had never been elected to any position in the European Union, except the European Parliament between 1979 and 1981, when he left on being appointed Economics and Finance Minister in the new government of François Mitterrand. Nor was he ever elected to any domestic position, except in local government. It is little wonder that to British eyes the operation of the European Union often seems to blur responsibility and to confuse lines of accountability.

The concept of responsibility both identifies who is under a duty to respond to questions by Parliament, but it can also be used to attribute blame. Thus, the principle of ministerial responsibility to Parliament prescribes, first, that a minister must answer to Parliament for every power conferred upon him; and second, that a minister is answerable to Parliament for the way in which he uses his

---

[11] WE Gladstone, *Gleanings from Past Years* (John Murray, 1879), vol. 1, 233.

powers. Parliament can, in the last resort, if it is unhappy about the way in which a minister has exercised his or her powers, compel the resignation of the minister.

In 1996, the minister responsible for the civil service, Roger Freeman, Chancellor of the Duchy of Lancaster, listed five areas where ministers could be held to be responsible for the actions of their departments. These five areas were, a) the policies of their departments; b) the framework within which policies were delivered; c) the allocation of resources; d) such implementation decisions as may be required to be referred to ministers or agreed with them; and e) ministerial responses to major failings or expressions of parliamentary or public concern.[12]

The principle of individual responsibility, like that of collective responsibility, is not a statutory one, but a convention of the British Constitution. It depends crucially upon the willingness of Parliament to assert it. It depends also upon Parliament being properly informed. In 1996, the Scott Report on the alleged sale of arms to Iraq, declared that "the obligation of Ministers to give information about the activities of their departments and to give information and explanations for the actions and omissions of their civil servants, lies at the heart of Ministerial accountability".[13] Sir Richard Scott endorsed the view of the Treasury and Civil Service Committee of the House of Commons which, in 1994, held that ministerial responsibility "—depends upon two vital elements: clarity about who can be held to account and held responsible when things go wrong: confidence that Parliament is able to gain the accurate information required to hold the Executive to account and to ascertain where responsibility lies".[14] For Parliament cannot be in a position to enforce responsibility where there has been mismanagement unless it has an accurate account of the circumstances in which that mismanagement occurred. There is thus an intimate connection between ministerial responsibility and freedom of information.

There is a great contrast between the principle of ministerial responsibility as it operates in British government, and the absence of such responsibility in the European context. When, in 1999, various commissioners were accused of mismanagement and corruption, the European Parliament seemed to have no form of redress against the errant Commissioners. The only form of redress was to secure the resignation of the whole Commission en bloc, and that required a two-thirds majority in the European Parliament. At one time, it looked as if an overall, but not a two-thirds majority would be secured. This would have meant that the Commission, despite having lost the confidence of the Parliament, could continue, broken-backed, until the end of its term. But in any case the resignation of the whole Commission would have punished the innocent along with the

---

[12] Hansard, House of Commons, Debates, 12 Feb. 1996, vol. 271, col. 684.
[13] HC 115, 1996, para. K8.2.
[14] HC 27, 1993–4, vol. 1, para. 132.

guilty. It was as if in Britain, the only way to punish a minister who had made a mistake was to require the resignation of the government as a whole.[15]

To introduce the principle of ministerial responsibility into the government of the European Union would not, it seems, require any constitutional amendment to the Treaty. It could be achieved if members of the European Parliament were prepared to use their existing powers to the full. In addition to a vote of no confidence in the Commission as a whole, it would be perfectly possible for the European Parliament to put down a motion of no confidence in a particular commissioner on the grounds of mismanagement, incompetence or corruption, and to insist on securing access to all the documents relevant to the decisions which were being questioned, in order to debate the motion. This would force the commissioner to defend his or her record, and it would act as a powerful incentive to better administration in the European Union. For, where there has been mismanagement, the Commissioner might well be required to demonstrate to the European Parliament that action had been taken to correct the mistake and to prevent any recurrence, and that, of course, could involve calling officials in the Commission to account for their mistakes, perhaps even subjecting them to disciplinary procedures. Certainly, the European Parliament would need to be assured that appropriate remedial measures had been taken. Thus, the principle of individual ministerial responsibility could be a powerful tool of accountability in the affairs of the European Union.

VI

The European Union has, as we have seen, been based on conceptions of government that are outdated in the modern world of assertive democracy. It was much influenced by the ethos of Fourth Republic France, which legitimised technocratic leadership, and sought to insulate this leadership from effective parliamentary scrutiny; and by the ethos of consociational democracy which legitimised decision-making by elites, with the role of the electorate being confined to one of ratifying these decisions. It is time for these outdated conceptions to be replaced by the British ethos of parliamentary government, which entails the collective responsibility of the Commission to the European Parliament, and the individual responsibility of individual Commissioners for mismanagement, incompetence or corruption. But, of course, the European Union will only accept this British ethos if Britain can be persuaded to play a more constructive part in European affairs. It is perhaps worth pondering on the words spoken by Winston Churchill at the Albert Hall in 1947, when he insisted that, "If Europe united is to be a living force, Britain will have to play her full part as a member of the European family". These words remain as true today as they were fifty five years ago.

[15] A lurid account of alleged fraud in the Commission, involving misappropriation of funds, corrupt dealings with contractors and "jobs for the boys", is to be found in a book by P Van Buitenen, formerly assistant auditor in the Financial Control Directorate in Brussels, *Blowing the Whistle; One Man's Fight Against Fraud in the European Commission* (London, Politico's, 2000).

14

The British Contribution to the Europe of the Twenty-First Century

LORD HURD

It is impossible to define the British contribution to the future of Europe in any calm or certain way, since it lies at the heart of the shifting controversy which dominates British politics. The perspective varies from year to year. What follows is a tentative analysis and forecast by one practising British politician who lived close to the centre of the controversy over three decades. It makes no claim to completeness, let alone infallibility.

The General Election of 2001 showed that the British electorate as a whole does not share the quarrelsome preoccupation of politicians with Europe, and may even penalise those who harp on this subject to the exclusion of others. But given the strength of feeling on the subject, both in the House of Commons and in most parts of the British press, it is hard to avoid the conclusion that a noisy and confused debate will continue. This fact makes it difficult to foresee the course of the British contribution to European policy. Those who form policy will inevitably be influenced by the ups and downs of the debate, even though it is notably stronger in volume than in quality. Despite thirty years of more or less continuous discussion, there is a marked lack of understanding in Britain of the fundamentals of the European Union. Or to put it less generously, there is a constant tendency to subordinate fundamental considerations to the ebb and flow of media-driven feeling as one particular aspect of the controversy or another gains attention.

It seems unlikely that this ebb and flow of controversy will lead to British withdrawal from the European Union. It is not inconceivable that the Conservative Party in Britain might drift even further towards a policy which contemplated such withdrawal, and that the Conservatives, perhaps elected to power for quite different domestic reasons, might find themselves rather reluctantly on a slide towards withdrawal. It seems much more likely that in those circumstances the fundamental interests of Britain, reflected perhaps most vividly in the views of the business community, would prevent such a dramatic outcome.

On the other hand, it is also unlikely that the present sullen reluctance of much British opinion when confronted with the prospect of further European integration will be changed within the foreseeable future into anything approaching enthusiasm. If that is correct, then this reluctance will continue to influence heavily the nature of the British contribution. It must, therefore, be worth analysing briefly the reasons for this reluctance, which is considerably more marked now than at the time of British entry into the EEC in 1973.

German students of Britain, including many Germans living here, become preoccupied with a purely anti-German element in this British reluctance towards Europe. For example, they examine painstakingly the time and enthusiasm which the British media spends on contemplating over and over again the Second World War. This anxiety is misplaced. The British will continue, naturally enough, to remember with pride what was for us an extraordinary and noble episode in our history. Dunkirk, the Spitfires and the Hurricanes, Dad's Army, the Dambusters and Arnhem will not be forgotten. But that has nothing to do with the way in which Britons regard modern democratic Germany. There are a few, notably Margaret Thatcher, who continue to worry, as she particularly did at the time of German unification, that the strength of modern Germany in Europe might lead to renewed political and economic (though not military) domination. But this fear, never dominant even when expressed by a Prime Minister, weakens steadily over the years as more and more people in Britain gain experience of the nature, and indeed anxieties, of modern Germany.

More subtle, more long-lasting and deeper-seated is a British distrust of France. This distrust is based not so much on ancient wars, as on a fear that what is regarded as the natural straightforwardness of the Anglo-Saxon character would constantly be outwitted and put at a disadvantage by French subtlety and deviousness. The fact that there is a similar and balancing fear of the British, or at least the English, on the other side of the Channel, is barely perceived in Britain. The points of contact today between these two close neighbours are innumerable, even though the two cultures continue to differ. The British have been less successful than the French in living with the teasing but friendly rivalry which is the natural result of our history and geography. If I can insert a personal and subjective comment based on anecdote, I have the impression that in the last few years this British distrust has begun to dry up as more Britons form their view of their neighbour from their own experience rather than from the newspaper they read. France is a remarkably pleasant and well-organised country, a fact which cannot be indefinitely concealed from the British public.

Yet neither of these sets of prejudices, whether against Germany or France, is really decisive in forming the reluctance with which many British view European integration.

More relevant is the reputation, which the central European institutions have gained or, in the case of the European Parliament, failed to gain for themselves in Britain. The European Parliament has not, contrary to my own expectations in 1977 when the legislation was passed for direct elections, put down roots as an influential force in the British political system. Many British Members of the European Parliament work usefully in their cities or regions, and are respected by policy makers in those areas. But there is no political strength behind them to counter the damaging impression created over the years in Britain by the best known of the central European institutions, namely the Commission. Only once, when President Delors captured the enthusiasm of the British Trade Union movement during the early days of Mrs Thatcher's Government, has the European Commission established a strong bridgehead in Britain. Even that success was achieved at a heavy price in terms of the opinion of Conservative Ministers at the time. For the most part the European Commission has too often damaged itself by a combination of ambitious rhetoric about the future with detailed and unpopular bureaucratic intervention in the nooks and crannies of national life.

The opponents of European integration in Britain feed on a constant diet of utterances from the European Commission, for example concerning the early stages of ill-founded future plans. These impressions are to a large extent caricatures rather than portraits. An important separate study could be made of the influence on public opinion of the wayward reporting from Brussels of the Eurosceptic press. The good work of the Commission, for example in constantly pressing forward with a liberalised single market and now in laying the foundations in aid and trade for a European foreign policy, is largely ignored.

This reluctance of British opinion towards European integration is not immutable. It would be strongly in the interests of all leading British politicians to modify it so that they can work out a British contribution to the future of Europe which actually suits objective British interests. But the existence of this reluctance must be accepted as the background as we turn to examine the likely British contribution, both in terms of institutions and policies, to the future of Europe in this century.

EUROPEAN INSTITUTIONS

It may be convenient at this point to distinguish between the progress of European institutions and the policies which are operated within those institutions. It is a peculiarity of the debate in Britain that most of it is concerned with institutions rather than policies, with what the EU is rather than with what it does. Discussion of the merits of a policy is quickly swallowed up in debating how that policy would affect the institutional balance of the European Union. This concern with institutions, which must be regarded as a weakness, is the direct result of the debate just discussed, which has created the widespread conviction in Britain among otherwise sensible people that the EU is essentially a mechanism for subjecting Britain to alien and damaging pressures and concepts.

The founding doctrine of the European Union stemmed from the experience and teaching of Jean Monnet, imparted to the European statesmen who originated our present EU institutions in the Treaties of Paris and Rome. Winston Churchill gave eloquent encouragement, not to Jean Monnet or to those Treaties, but to the reconciliation of France and Germany within a United Europe. But Winston Churchill's eloquence was that of an enthusiastic observer, rather than of a participant. He never established in his own utterances a priority between the three circles which Britain inhabited, namely of the Empire/Commonwealth, the relationship with the United States, and Europe. Harold Macmillan began to tilt the priority towards Europe, though only to an extent which President de Gaulle found inadequate. The remarkable achievement of Edward Heath in leading the failed negotiations of 1961–3 and the successful negotiation of 1971/2, and later playing a formidable part in the referendum of 1975 was to insert Britain, with popular consent, into a community guided by a founding doctrine which ran counter to many preconceptions about Britain's place in the world.

The doctrine, like most powerful founding doctrines, can be simply stated. According to Jean Monnet the nations of Europe would take a series of practical collective decisions, in each of which a sector of national decision taking would be moved from national governments and entrusted to the institutions of Europe, in particular the European Commission and the European Court of Justice. Each of these steps would have to be justified by practical need, but each would explicitly contribute to an ever closer union between the nations concerned. The exact end state of that union was not defined, but until recently its enthusiasts had no difficulty in talking, as Jean Monnet did himself, about a United States of Europe.

The power of this idea, operating on nations whose self-confidence had been blasted by their experiences in the Second World War, needs no description here. It led from the Coal and Steel Community down the false trail to a European Defence Community, then to Euratom, to the Common Market, then to the Single Market, then to the Single Currency. Edward Heath managed to persuade the original Six that in spite of the different historical perspective experience Britain should join the existing institutions; he then persuaded the British people that this was the right destination for us. The notion that Edward Heath and those who worked with him at that time were simply talking about a European trading area does not survive any reading of his speeches, or of the documents connected with the Referendum of 1975, including for example the speeches on that occasion of the Leader of the Conservative Party, Margaret Thatcher. It was indeed Margaret Thatcher who took the next substantial step by agreeing to the completion of the Single Market and the greatly extended majority voting embodied in the Single European Act of 1986. By comparison, and contrary to a widespread myth, the Treaty of Maastricht in 1991 as far as Britain was concerned was a lesser step, given the opt outs on the Single Currency and the Social Chapter obtained by John Major.

The establishment of the single currency under the Treaty of Maastricht was the last major achievement of the European Union along the path of the original Monnet doctrine. Since then the European Union has altered course without fully realising it. Many European leaders continue to hold and to preach the original doctrine. The phrases characteristic of that doctrine, for example the "ever closer union", continue to recur in speeches and documents. But the balance of the discussion has subtly shifted, as illustrated by the fact no mainstream European leader now talks about a United States of Europe, and most of them tumble over each other to deny the possibility of a European superstate.

For the first time in the history of European treaties, the Treaty of Maastricht envisaged something which was happening in any case in practice, namely that European progress could occur not by transferring the decision making power to central institutions, but by agreement between governments who would then operate such agreement by their own decisions or legislation. Since Maastricht this intergovernmental method has become typical. Indeed, the creation of the single currency at Maastricht ten years ago may turn out to have been the end not the beginning of an era, the era of integration by means of centralisation. Decisions since Maastricht on foreign policy and defence, and on economic policy, have followed the intergovernmental route. For example the economic reform programme sketched at Lisbon in March 2000 was a classic example of governments agreeing in some detail what needed to be done and on what timescale, but assuming the responsibility themselves, with their own continued accountability to national parliaments for carrying out those decisions. The distinction, sometimes mocked, between "harmonisation" and "coordination" is in fact crucial to any understanding of how the EU increasingly operates. Harmonisation fits under the old doctrine of centralisation, coordination under the new doctrine of convergence of partner nations.

This change of direction is on the whole ignored by *eurosceptics* in Britain, because it removes a large part of the reasoning behind the hostility on which they thrive. To use a very English metaphor, their fox has been shot. The *enthusiasts* on the Continent for the traditional doctrine recognise the change away from tidy centralised integration as only too real, and lament it. The enthusiasts are faced, however, with a number of realities which it is hard to gainsay. Of these, perhaps the least important from their point of view is the state of the British debate. Embracing that debate, but going much wider, is the stubborn survival of loyalty to the nation state, both its reality and its symbols, which has persisted and even increased during these decades. It has shown itself in two Danish and an Irish referendum, in the underlying philosophy of the present French, Spanish and now even Italian governments, and in some, though not all, aspects of German thinking. Added to that is the commitment, reluctantly entered into by some but now hard to evade, of enlarging the European Union to include more than a dozen candidates from the east and south of our continent.

The tactical alliance of eurosceptics and enthusiasts against intergovernmentalism is particularly illustrated in the argument about taxation. It is constantly repeated by both these groups that the existence of a single currency must lead inevitably to a European economic government, with the main elements of fiscal and indeed social policy determined by a central institution. Eurosceptics like this argument because it reinforces their hostility to the single currency. The enthusiasts like the same argument because they are keen to see precisely this

European economic government. Yet both the economic and political arguments against this process are formidable. On the economic aspect, given that the convergence of the national economies and labour markets is far from complete even in the existing eurozone, there is a strong argument for allowing national governments to use fiscal measures within the constraints of the Stability and Growth Pact, in order to handle the strains which these objective differences will, from time to time, throw up. One interest rate for all is difficult enough to handle; to add to it one tax rate for all, or to determine variations of tax rates centrally, would be to take an enormous and unjustifiable economic risk.

Politically the wave of enthusiasm for supranational European institutions is no longer running strongly up the beach. This is partly the result, as already stated, of our experience of those institutions, and partly a natural consequence of the fact that for a new generation the lessons of the last War are no longer so vivid and compelling.

As a result there is no longer a majority among the countries of Europe, even within the eurozone, for moving towards a centralised system of taxation, let alone pensions, health or education policy. In all these zones there are grey areas which are constantly under discussion, but the fundamental position was well described in 1999 by Sir Nigel Wicks who, perhaps more than any other Englishman, knows the background and character of the governing Treaty of Maastricht. Sir Nigel wrote in 1999:

> "We will not see a European Economic Government in the sense of an EU Finance Minister presiding over an EU Ministry of Finance in Brussels. Many aspects of economic union will not be decided by some central authority precisely, because of their very national nature. In all the Member States budgetary issues are regarded as a matter for national governments. The Stability and Growth Pact makes it quite clear that 'in stage three of EMU member states remain responsible for their national budgetary policies subject to the provisions of the Treaty, those provisions being the Treaty requirement to avoid an excessive deficit'.
>
> That recognition of member state responsibility was not an ephemeral outcome of the negotiations at Maastricht. It reflects the enduring fact that throughout the EU national parliaments value their role in national budgetary issues.
>
> The same philosophy of member state responsibility applies by and large to most other aspects of economic policy. And it is right that the member states retain responsibility for matters which often reflect deeply entrenched national cultures and ways of doing things, and which go the heart of member state identity. So running the economic union on a decentralised basis is the only way of proceeding efficiently without provoking tensions. That is precisely my view."

If this is right it follows that in all likelihood the European Union will continue institutionally to operate under a mixed system. Some crucial aspects of policy, for example the European role in World Trade negotiations, the European Development Fund, and the growing enforcement of the single market, will continue to be the centralised responsibility of the European Commission, sub-

The British Contribution to the Europe of the Twenty-First Century 221

ject to the powers of the other European institutions. There may be some pressure from both Britain and Germany to renationalise some aspects of one important common policy, namely the Agricultural, but it remains to be seen whether such pressures will have enough strength to prevail. In the opposite direction there are now strong reasons, including British reasons, for working out an integrated common policy for the control of frontiers.

But across another swathe of decision taking, already summarised, the procedures will be essentially intergovernmental.

If only we realised it this mixed system suits British interests and instincts well. It should be the main institutional objective of the British Government to make this mixed system work effectively. In terms of British interests there can be no serious argument, for example, in favour of splitting up Europe again into different national negotiating teams in world trade negotiations. Under Leon Brittan and now under Pascal Lamy the Commission has shown skill and energy to justify the power we have given it to negotiate on our behalf on an agreed mandate. By this act of centralisation we have given ourselves an equal strength with the United States and Japan. And no British interest would be served by splitting up the role of the EU in the Balkans (which includes a substantial part for the Commission) so that once again Britain, France, Germany and Italy had to wrestle with their own rivalries as well as with the stubborn facts of the region. There is a question whether the present negative condition of the British debate on Europe will allow a British Government, even one with a large parliamentary majority, to exert the necessary intelligence and flexibility to make the mixed system work.

Success will depend on skilful handling of the timing and substance of enlargement, and on understanding the place of majority voting in an intergovernmental system. The intergovernmental part of the system will not operate well if there is a general conviction that one of the big European states, namely Britain, looks at each proposition not on its merits for Europe or even for Britain, but with an ingrained hostility to any form of further European coordination. The British Government, like other member states, is taking a gamble in urging that the nature of the mixed system should be more clearly defined. There is a danger that the new European debate undertaken in the Treaty of Nice will eventually sputter out in deadlock and recrimination about institutions. It sometimes happens in diplomacy that progress on the next and necessary step is easier to achieve if there is ambiguity about ultimate objectives. But the time for this constructive ambiguity has passed, and the case for greater clarity is cogent.

The alternative approach would be that of enhanced cooperation. This is the obscure phrase used to describe a simple argument. Under this argument a group of countries should be able to retain the traditional Monnet doctrine and place further decision-taking powers in a European centre, even though other member states are not willing. It is not surprising, given the nature of the debate across Europe, that enhanced cooperation finds its supporters both among sceptics and enthusiasts. Once again the extremes coalesce. Eurosceptics see a way in which Britain can duck out of further European enterprises without sacrificing existing benefits, for example that of the single market. On the other side enthusiasts see it as a way of building a coherent and disciplined European system, for example in taxation and foreign policy, without having to bother with the eccentricities of Britain, Denmark and others. Anyone with a sense of history will understand why the instinct of the British Government should be suspicious of enhanced cooperation. The thrust of British foreign policy for several centuries has been to prevent the growth of a European power on the Continent, whose decisions we would not control or substantially influence, even though we would be compelled to live under the shadow of those decisions. Norway and Switzerland may for a time be content to live in this semi dependency, but it is not a role which could fit a country the size of Britain.

EUROPEAN POLICIES

Once we turn away from the seemingly eternal debate about institutions and consider the policies to be pursued within these institutions, we find three main policy areas in which the British contribution ought to be positive and notable, and one area in which the British will continue, probably with good reason, to act as a brake. The negative area relates to the social dimension of EU policy and legislation. Here there is a genuine difference of opinion between the two main parties in Britain which should be distinguished from the debate already described about institutions. As an extension of the normal battleground between centre left and centre right in Britain, the British Conservative Party is bound to resist on the grounds of competitiveness almost any effort to strengthen through further legislation the European Social Model. In this opposition they are joined by British employers, even those who deplore the general hostility of the Conservative Party to the EU. The British Labour Party under Mr Blair is more favourable to the Social Model; it abandoned the opt out to the Social Chapter of the Treaty of Maastricht which Mr Major obtained with such difficulty in 1991. The Government is well aware of the enthusiasm with which further social legislation would be viewed by the British Trade Union Movement, and would be anxious not to antagonise that Movement more than necessary. Nevertheless it is fairly clear that compared to the real enthusiasts for the Social Model on the Continent, even a British Labour Government will be a laggard on this subject.

That leaves three main policy areas where British policy should be positive and forward looking.

The first is enlargement. All the British political parties have pronounced in favour of enlargement of the EU, ever since Margaret Thatcher as Prime Minister strongly endorsed it in her Bruges speech of 1988. It does not follow from this unanimity that there is widespread enthusiasm on the subject, on which indeed most of the British electorate and Parliament are reasonably apathetic. But there is, in addition to traditional sympathies between Britain and many of the candidate countries, a common sense feeling in Britain that we cannot indefinitely describe the EU as "Europe" if we continue to exclude countries which are certainly European and which qualify for membership, simply on the grounds that the necessary arrangements are too difficult to make. So far at least there are no alarms in Britain to match the German alarm about opening their labour market to the east, or the Spanish alarm about losing their privileged financial position to new entrants poorer than themselves. We can therefore expect, I hope, solid and sustained British support for the admission to the EU over a reasonable timescale of the existing candidates. The particular difficulties arising from the decision to give Turkey candidate status are for the EU as a whole, rather than for Britain in particular.

The second positive area concerns the general thrust of economic policy as defined in the Lisbon Summit and reaffirmed at Stockholm. The present British Government, having turned its back on traditional socialist economic policies, is committed to the concept particularly associated with Margaret Thatcher that prosperity is best achieved through competition and the operation of the market. British diplomacy will therefore continue to encourage those parts of the European Commission which work to complete the liberalisation of the single market, the reduction of state aids and the lowering of trade barriers between Europe and the rest of the world. Although there will be occasional exceptions, since no member of the EU is wholly consistent in all its actions, in general Britain will be found among the present majority of nation states on these subjects rather than with the remaining protectionists. Under this heading I would also include the reform and perhaps partial re-nationalisation of the Common Agricultural Policy in the direction now outlined by the German and British Governments and by Herr Fischler, the Commissioner for Agriculture.

The third positive area covers foreign policy and defence. The experience and natural instincts of Britain, whether the Government or the electorate, point towards a positive foreign policy. Although like all European countries British spending on defence falls well below the prevailing rhetoric on security policy, nevertheless our Armed Forces are structured to enable effective action in the style of humanitarian intervention which has become familiar since the end of the Cold War. British opinion up to now accepts, to an extent which would seem strange in Germany or the US, that intervention may mean casualties among our troops. The examples of such British intervention, Iraq, Bosnia, Kosovo, East Timor, Sierra Leone, are national rather than European, but so long as foreign policy and defence remains essentially on an intergovernmental basis within the EU I would expect the European dimension of British diplomacy to strengthen. Already we are accustomed to operate in the Balkans as Europeans rather than maintaining a British policy alongside separate French, German and Italian policies.

A crucial question here concerns the relationship between the EU and the United States. One still occasionally hears in British polemics about Europe echoes of the old question of General de Gaulle, whether Britain in the last resort chooses Europe or the Atlantic. The concept of a choice in those terms was fairly artificial even in General de Gaulle's time, and is now obsolete. An overwhelming majority in the European Union sees cooperation with the United States as a prerequisite of our security and prosperity. Despite occasional rhetorical outbursts from Paris few Europeans, and none I think of the candidate members, contemplate Europe as a rival superpower, equipped in every aspect of life to match or overtake the United States. On the other hand, neither European governments nor electorates wish to see Europe as simply a collection of satellite countries, waiting obediently to hear a decision from the White House in order that they may copy it. Emerging instead is the concept of the valid partnership, the forwarding of which ought to be a major British concern. The partnership is not at present valid because the disproportion between the United States and European effort is too great. Europe needs to strengthen our component of that partnership so that consultation within the partnership becomes for all partners a matter of self interest as well as courtesy. Mr Blair in his speech last year in Warsaw on the future of Europe described Europe as a potential superpower not a superstate. I doubt if this formulation accurately expresses the direction of British diplomacy. A superpower has the strength and the will to intervene effectively in conflicts and crises in any part of the world. That is not a realistic aim for Europe, but only in the foreseeable future for the United States. Sometimes, as this year in North Korea, there will be moments when European diplomacy can usefully fill a gap left by temporary American inattention or uncertainty.

But it is unrealistic to suppose that on questions of peace and war in, say, the Taiwan Straits, the weight of Europe will ever match that of the United States. It would be foolish to pretend otherwise. Exaggerated rhetoric is the hallmark of feeble policy. Europeans should concentrate on the realities of the map. We Europeans live within an arc of danger stretching from Kaliningrad in the north, south and east through the Caucasus, the Caspian, the Balkans and the Middle East, and west again along the shores of North Africa. The danger arises not so much from threats to our own security from countries living around this arc, but from the virtual certainty that from time to time in these regions upheavals and tragedies will occur which we will regard as unacceptable and which will prompt Europe's diplomatic, economic and perhaps military intervention. Around that arc of danger the effort of the Europeans should be at least as strong and coherent as that of the United States. That is the road along which I would expect British diplomacy to travel.

In thus defining three positive and one negative area for British effort within the EU in coming decades I may give an over optimistic impression. For the strength of that effort in the positive areas will depend on the future of the debate within Britain which I have described, and on resolving in a way acceptable to

Britain the institutional questions discussed above. If this cannot be done then the positive British instincts in those three areas will not be reflected in effective action. British ministers in those circumstances will continue to look behind them at newspapers and opinion polls instead of giving the lead which is required.

Those of us who are now commentators on affairs rather than actors must beware of glibness on this question of leadership. In a democracy the successful leader is two or three steps, not two or three miles, ahead of his followers. Yet, while a leader has to recognise the difficulties of the terrain, he must not see these difficulties as a reason for abandoning the journey. In 1972 Edward Heath as Prime Minister exercised his powers of leadership on this issue to good effect, and Britain entered the EU in the following year. In 1975, less enthusiastically, Harold Wilson presided over a referendum, and the public followed the lead provided by the politicians whom they respected, regardless of party. Between 1991 and 1993 John Major attempted a similar feat of leadership in support of the Maastricht Treaty. This started with successful debates in Parliament and victory after Maastricht in the General Election of 1992. But our effort lost impetus after the first Danish referendum that summer. Although the Treaty of Maastricht was at last ratified, there was no strength left to update and transform the British public's attitude to the EU. No substantial effort in this direction has so far been made by the present Labour Government, perhaps because of wary preoccupation with the related question of Britain and the euro. In this study I have deliberately refrained from analysing this particular question. I do not believe it can be resolved as a matter separate from the general British attitude to Europe.

Whether on the euro, on economic policy in general, on foreign policy and defence, or on any other possible sphere of European action, a successful British role depends on a fuller and more accurate understanding by the British people of the EU than exists at present. To secure that improvement is not an impossible task, as has been shown in the past—simply a difficult one.

POSTSCRIPT

Since 11 September we have lived through a time of genuine solidarity between the peoples of Europe and those of the United States. This solidarity has been expressed in countless public events and declarations which have shown that popular opinion has been moved well beyond the ordinary

It is timely now to consider the long term implications for cooperation across the Atlantic. Inevitably in Britain such discussion begins with the Anglo-American relationship which has once again shown itself to be robust. There are several elements in that relationship, beginning with a particular closeness of feeling between our peoples. But the decision takers in the United States, like the decision takers in any great country, do not base those decisions on sentiment.

The robustness of the Anglo-American relationship is founded on the high usefulness of Britain to the only world superpower. At times, when that usefulness has been in doubt, the decision takers in Washington refused to allow sentiment to dominate their calculation of American interest. Lord Keynes found that when at the end of the Second World War he went to negotiate financial help for Britain. I remember it vividly again at the time of Suez when a massive British error lead to the virtual breakdown of the relationship over several weeks—we had ceased to be useful and become a liability. It follows that those in Britain who rightly believe in the importance of the Anglo-American relationship have to work hard at keeping it strong. Sentiment is not enough.

The different strands of our relationship include the unique cooperation in intelligence, and some particular capabilities of our armed forces. Both these elements are of high value in the present campaign. But crucial to the modern Anglo-American relationship is Britain's role as a European power—not just a country anchored offshore the Continent, but a full partner in the European Union. Those who argue that Britain should weaken its links inside the EU in order to cosy up more intimately with the United States are ignoring the facts of power. Such a shift would actually reduce our importance in the eyes of American decision makers.

It is not easy for our American allies to understand how Europeans work together in foreign policy. They are, after all, familiar with their own system in which many domestic powers are devolved to the states of the Union, but foreign policy and defence are wholly reserved to the centre. They suppose that this must be the European objective too, and that the variations which they see now when they look at Europe have to be regarded as defects of immaturity which time should cure. In this of course they are joined by some of the most enthusiastic integrationists on this side of the Atlantic. But the present state of European decision taking, although certainly imperfect, reflects the realities of the European Union which will not quickly change.

As Europeans we now use a mixed set of instruments in operating foreign policy. Sometimes we still act as *individual nations*. This is not just a result of some insular obstinacy of Britain. Who will live to see the day when France abandons her French deterrent or her French seat on the Security Council? Sometimes we act together *intergovernmentally*, using the new machinery now headed by Xavier Solana. Sometimes we act *supranationally*, for example when using through the European Commission the weapons of trade and aid. Provided (a big proviso) that we consult and coordinate effectively there is positive advantage in this flexibility. What counts is the total effectiveness of what we do, not whether we act as Europe or as Europeans.

Europe cannot realistically aim at the status of a superpower. Nor need we make the attempt. A superpower has the ability and potentially the will to intervene, if necessary with force, in any part of the world. It is hard to foresee a time when the crisis in the Taiwan Straits or between the two Koreas would attract such intervention from Europe. Our immediate aim is to sustain

American leadership in the campaign against terrorism – not just in Afghanistan but elsewhere. This involves grasping the fresh opportunities of a new and more vigorous diplomacy in tackling old disputes, such as those in Palestine, Kashmir and Cyprus. There is no purpose in trying to negotiate with confirmed murderers like Osama bin Laden, since they have no other profession but murder. But we must try again to settle these old disputes before they provide in turn fresh recruiting grounds for terrorists. The Palestinian teenagers who now throw stones at Israeli tanks are not yet suicide bombers; but unless we exert ourselves they may become precisely that.

Since we are not rivals but partners of the United States we can in many of these enterprises accept a supporting role. It is possible for Europeans to probe and try to influence the policies of countries such as Syria and Iran in ways not at present open to the United States.

But Europe has three specific tasks in which our role should be greater than, or at least equal to, that of the Americans. All three tasks arise from the arc of danger which envelops us to the east and south of our Continent.

The first is the enlargement of our European Union to the east. This complex enterprise will come to a head at the end of 2002, with a view to the first wave of new members joining in 2004, after the necessary treaties of accession have been ratified. For twelve years now we have been slowly filling the waiting room with candidates for membership. At the beginning we led some of those concerned to believe that the process would be rapid. I remember vividly, when Foreign Secretary, being embarrassed by the assurances which Chancellor Kohl and President Chirac gave in Warsaw that Poland would be a member by the year 2000. Of course the candidates for membership have to adapt themselves to our existing policies, and negotiate the necessary details with the European Commission. But we too have to show a readiness to understand and to compromise, particularly perhaps in the case of the largest candidate, Poland, where the tasks of adaptation are particularly difficult. If there are further delays in enlargement we shall run the risk of creating the instability in Eastern Europe which can result from hopes too long postponed.

Second, we have to continue the slow process of pacification of the Balkans. At the time of the Kosovo War the immediate need was for advanced military technology, and in particular missiles. The United States filled much the greatest part of that need. Now the need is for diplomacy, economic help and skilled military peacekeeping on the ground—men and money, not missiles. Europe, operating through different institutions, has quietly assumed the main responsibility in ensuring that this part of our Continent does not relapse into violence, but moves steadily towards full integration in the different institutions of Europe.

This is a long and expensive task, in which there will be setbacks. But we have undertaken it, and there can be no drawing back. It is encouraging to see in this context how quickly the

German attitude has changed. I remember Chancellor Kohl saying that regardless of the constitutional niceties in Germany, it would be politically and historically impossible for German troops to be deployed in any part of the former Yugoslavia. Now we see German troops taking over from their British partners the lead in the necessary operation in Macedonia.

Third, we have to tackle once again the whole relationship of Turkey with Europe. There can be no denying the huge importance of Turkey, situated as she is at the meeting place of the Middle East, the Balkans and the Caucasus. We have allowed Turkey to enter the crowded waiting room as a candidate for membership of the EU, but that cannot be an early or easy prospect. The application of Cyprus for membership of the EU could either accelerate the agreed end to the division of that island through a negotiated settlement—or it could provoke a crisis next year, both for our relationship with Turkey and possibly for the whole programme of enlargement of the EU.

Finally, we have to press ahead with the European Security and Defence Policy (ESDP). The partnership between Europe and the United States will only be valid if the effort made by each partner, particularly in military strength, is recognised as substantial by the other. We have some way to go in Europe before we can prove this to most Americans. One main purpose of ESDP is to provide this proof. I recognise the difficulties, particularly for Germany, in reaching the specific objectives set for ESDP by the year 2003. But the German Government is showing admirable courage in allotting sizeable forces to the struggle against terrorism. I hope that the same impetus will carry forward all our contributions to the European defence effort. Unless we use the ESDP as a spur to modernise the quality of our defence spending, many Americans in key positions will not recognise us as valid partners.

That is quite an agenda, and of course it is not complete. We shall only succeed if we tackle these tasks as Europeans, using the flexibility of instruments I have described, welcoming partnership with the Americans, showing them that in the matters of closest concern to us we are ourselves energetic, farseeing and coherent.

15

Great Britain and France, Driving Forces Behind a Benchmark Europe

LAURENT FABIUS

A NEW CENTURY TO BUILD

The violence of our history is such that, as I write this contribution on Europe, the world is reeling from the open wounds inflicted by the terrible World Trade Centre tragedy. Every single one of us senses the dawning of a new era that has as yet revealed neither totally its name nor its form. We all fear that economic globalisation is now being met with the globalisation of threats to society.

This makes our responsibility even greater. Some of the world's post-Cold-War illusions have now been dissipated. No, history is not over and if we don't record it with the words of freedom, dignity and solidarity so close to our hearts, others will record the course of events with intolerance and fanaticism. This proliferation of threats is no time for burying our heads in the sand. Look to the other side of the Atlantic: what are the Americans doing in the face of one of the most violent shocks in their history? They are showing hope, energy and determination. They are working and rebuilding. In this troubled world, a stronger European Union should be able to form the best of responses to all kinds of crises, the most effective shield and a real guarantee of international stability and global development.

This is the task I want to talk about. It could bring together our two nations, Great Britain and France, whose contributions to the European venture have gone a long way to ensuring its success.

EUROPE AS A BENCHMARK

Deepening the European Union could provide a future solution to the unprecedented shockwave hitting us today, because it is flexible and manifold. Power was previously gained purely on the basis of numbers and military strength. Such was the way of a world we have left behind us, where supreme power was measured by borders crossed, lands conquered and spoils gained, where states saw themselves as all the stronger when their neighbours were weak, where the idea of domination was never entirely absent from nations' plans. Yet we now understand that there can be no sustainable political construction without a common concern for the world's future, without a will to see ourselves not only as a "supreme power", but as a reference power: a reference in the concern for freedom, a reference in the defence of global public goods and the promotion of sustainable development, and a reference in the respect of the world's diversity and attentiveness to widely held aspirations. At a time when Asia is emerging, Africa suffering, the Orient flaring up and the Americas wounded, the European Union should become this centre of stability and integration, this benchmark. Because what it has built over the decades, in trial and error, forms an unprecedented model of the free association of nations and peoples working towards a common goal. A benchmark rather than only a power. If we are to make this transition, we need to consolidate a Europe of growth, democracy and security.

A EUROPE MAINTAINING SUSTAINABLE AND UNITED GROWTH IN THE FACE OF GLOBAL ECONOMIC UPS AND DOWNS

Growth: it may seem optimistic to back this particular horse at a time when the economy is showing many signs of weakness. Europe and the United States slowed slightly before the shockwave of the terrorist attacks even hit. This slowdown was associated with the rise in oil prices and problems with the new economy. After some highly buoyant years, our economies started showing signs of flagging in the spring of 2000. After September the 11th, the repercussions of the terrorist attacks with their intrinsic risks of a chain reaction, especially as regards economic player confidence, have exacerbated matters.

Given this uncertain backdrop, it is probably too early to draw any conclusions. Yet there is already positive signs. The European Union has shown its maturity and solidarity, even if we might have wished for a more proactive economic reaction. The European Central Bank co-ordinated with the American Federal Reserve to ward off the spectre of systemic crisis and global recession. As with the Asian and Russian crises, the euro formed a shield and an element of solidarity among European countries. The dangers resulting from separate and even antagonistic monetary policies are fading. The euro zone countries are gaining from this in their capacity to influence the international economy and also in their possibilities for protecting themselves against an unstable international financial system.

The slowdown has moreover come after several years of firm growth, leaving our economies stronger and boding well for a rebound. During these years, our countries grew closer in both their choices and performances. Strong guidelines were favoured: more control of public accounts, lightening the tax burden and making priorities of training, employment and jobs for the unemployed—all without forsaking the demands of solidarity and the government and public service modernisation that make our European growth model unique. Today, all European Union citizens share at least two strong and complementary ambitions:

full employment, in which Great Britain has a lead, and high-quality public services, in which France is not the worst pupil in the European class. This shows that we can combine our experiences.

Given that the EU Member States share common goals and often agree on the ways of reaching these goals, they should now step up the co-ordination of their economic policy. From ECOFIN and Eurogroup to the tax projects, I expect more from the tools and bodies that we have set up in recent years. I am convinced that, united, the European states can go further and, bolstered by each state's assets, can improve employment, innovation and ultimately growth and welfare throughout the EU.

A EUROPE CONSOLIDATING ITS DEMOCRATIC INSTITUTIONS

The tragic events of 11 September 2001 signalled a resolute return of politics and a need for regulation. In the face of these sudden attacks and this challenge to democracy and our values, Europe must more then ever stand firm as a social contract and a political community bonded by values, institutions and projects. The often-abstract debates between "federalists" and advocates of sovereignty, between supranational supporters and defenders of the nation state, miss the point: the uniqueness of European construction as an unprecedented historical form. Europe is neither a repeat nor a copy. It is an invention. Its reality shapes the guidelines for its development. Current events compel that it changes gear to a higher speed.

From the European Commission through the Central Bank to the Court of Justice, Europe has long had institutions that transcend national boundaries. We need to use what we have to improve the way they are run, deepen their responsibilities and rebalance their powers. There is no lack of reforms to be implemented. They must be decided on before the major Berlin summit in 2004. The Commission-Council-Parliament triangle would gain from a better definition of roles and a clarification of the decision-making process. Giving the European Parliament more weight would seem logical, provided it brought the members of the European Parliament closer to the citizens by electing them on a territorial basis and no longer a national basis. Extending the Council of Ministers' voting to a qualified majority would put a stop to the ossifying effect of unanimity. France pushed for this at the last Intergovernmental Conference in Nice and obtained some progress, but clearly it was not enough. A Vice-Prime Minister could be appointed to each government to improve government involvement and co-ordination in European decisions. This Vice-Prime Minister could move the European Union forward on a daily basis. Closer co-operation would help some Member States move forward faster in unison towards a common goal. It doesn't matter whether they are called "avant-garde", "hard core" or "centre of gravity" as long as we make real progress. These improvements would combine to help Europe make useful progress.

There remains the two-pronged question of deepening and enlarging the European Union. I consider these two issues to be inextricably linked. The enlargement being prepared could increase the risks of red tape, complexity and, let's say it, opaqueness. It could create a gulf of inequalities between the Fifteen and the new arrivals. The EU's population and surface area will grow by a third, while its domestic product will only increase by 5 per cent. Whereas our common policies are hitting financing and implementation problems, opening up the EU to thirteen new Member States could dilute the "acquis communautaire" and undermine the EU's institutional operations. Taking this number of countries on board therefore implies first and foremost a successful internal reorganisation. This is why the reform of the European institutions is so decisive and should be implemented rapidly. A more well-defined and rooted Europe will be better placed to receive the newcomers. If we try to operate with 27 in the same way as we have sometimes found it hard to do with 15, Europe will fail.

Does deepening call for a written European constitution? It would be useful, but substantial institutional progress could quickly be made with the tools we already have. The adoption of the Social Charter bears witness to this pragmatic convergence. Civil society could help by building a real European political space. Media and intellectuals, parties and unions, associations and NGOs should all work together on this new level to give European citizenship real meaning.

A EUROPE STEPPING UP VIGILANCE AND SECURITY IN THE FACE OF GLOBAL THREATS

In addition to growth and democracy, the European Union should also help to build a better-governed international society. Only concerted global action by nations will ensure balanced growth and sustainable development for all. The environment, health, food, living organisms, international law and peace are all global public goods. Yet, as we are reminded every day, although they are essential, they are also perishable. It is up to the politicians and economic players to prevent them from being depleted. Europe, as a midway point between the global and the national and a model of successful regional integration, has the wherewithal to meet the current challenges. The European Union has no lack of work to do.

First of all, improving the environment. There are many threats. Two-thirds of the cultivable potential of the developing countries may disappear by 2100. Deforestation is vast in the Southern countries, the Amazon and Africa. Water reserves are drying up. A quarter of the animal species will be extinct by 2025. The volume of greenhouse gas emissions has risen 30 per cent in volume compared with 1990 despite the Tokyo Conference setting a goal for them to fall 5 per cent by 2012. Action is urgently needed to counter these threats that are inflicting the current "offhand" attitude on the planet and future generations. Europe should call for a real World Environmental Agency to be set up. This agency would transcend national players with tripartite regional or national members in the image of the ILO. It would lend consistency and prescriptive strength to many environmental protocols that today have an ambiguous status and limited effectiveness. One of the most important, the Kyoto protocol, is currently in danger of not being applied. Europe managed, at the cost of certain compromises, to win over countries as decisive as Japan and Canada at the Bonn summit in the summer of 2001. This was an important move forward in curbing polluting emissions. It proves that Europe can be effective in regulating globalisation.

Another urgent matter in hand is the introduction of a worldwide health policy, in particular to address the AIDS virus. The hardest hit region is Africa, with 24 million AIDS sufferers. Security and stability at all levels depend on health. Great Britain, like France, is extremely concerned about this geopolitical health situation. What's to be done? Set up an international fund and bilateral treatment mechanisms; mobilise the World Bank's "concessional" and nonconcessional resources; co-ordinate action with UNAIDS, WHO and the NGOs; declare the health situation an emergency and introduce a price control system to deal with pharmaceutical companies that may try to set the prices they want for their drugs; guarantee access to essential molecules in all countries and for all people; distribute prevention tools and appropriate treatment everywhere. Progress is being made with the search for a vaccine and treatment. The funds required, estimated at 10 billion euros, can be assembled. There is reason for hope. Along with the UN, Europe has a duty to mobilise the world in the fight for an ambitious and united health policy.

The third imperative is food security. The recent prion, dioxin and nitrate crises, especially in Great Britain and France, have alerted Europe to the need for caution. Where some countries have balked at restricting or prohibiting GMOs, the European Union made it compulsory a year ago to label organisms with a detailed description when products contain more than 1 per cent GMO. Japan and Mexico, to name but a few, have joined us in this. A European Food Agency will soon be operational to prevent the risks. It will be independent of economic interests and protected from national reluctance and is expected to impose the necessary measures on each state. This is a step in the right direction.

Biosafety is about protecting the living. The recent breakthrough in human genome sequencing gives an idea of the challenges to come: competition between international public research and private interests, rivalry between universal knowledge and market-based patent confidentiality, competition between care for all and preferential treatment for those who pay. Genetic know-how equals economic power and there is a real risk of living information being privatised. Cloning personifies all the promises and all the doubts. In its therapeutic form, it will improve knowledge and treatment. In its reproductive form, it could undermine our ethics and hence what makes us human. We Europeans believe that biosafety should be inextricably linked with bioethics, prohibiting the merchandisation of bodies and living organisms.

From a more directly economic standpoint, Europe's action for a safer world obviously includes combating financial crime, tax havens and money laundering. The events of 11 September 2001 showed just how decisive this challenge is. The first decisions made following the attacks, especially those by the Liege summit of finance ministers, showed a new European determination on this front. We will have to remain determined to win this long battle against the clandestine networks.

This European security policy also calls for more work in two crucial areas: the European legal space and European defence. These two areas are complementary at a time when the nature of the threat of attack is changing and hyper-terrorism can hit at the heart of our towns while barbarity can break out on the other side of our borders, especially in the form of ethnic conflicts. Our Union should move swiftly in this new decade to organise police co-operation and a European warrant for arrest as well as concerted diplomatic action and defence capabilities. France and Great Britain will naturally play a decisive role in the success of this undertaking.

The shared battles, united ambitions and common values of growth and prosperity, democracy and citizenship, vigilance and security all define a strong and responsible Europe. Great Britain and France are more often than not at one on all these issues. This common goal should alone suffice to dispel past misunderstandings between Great Britain and the continent. Yet the fact that Europe will never be entirely whole without the definite participation and commitment of the British citizens calls for a calm look at the reality, the past and future links between our two nations and between Great Britain and Europe.

THE LINK BETWEEN FRANCE AND GREAT BRITAIN

I must admit that it is never easy for any of us to talk about our two nations, let alone the relationship between them. This past millennium was a constant battle between our countries, fought with weapons and minds. However, the last century was one of long-awaited reconciliation. From the Triple Entente through the forming of the Allies to the European undertaking and inevitable co-operation, a new era opened up in our relations. The future should have friendship in store for the French and British in a united and peaceful Europe.

Looking at our history, I think that paradoxically what has distanced and divided us may, at the end of the day, be essentially our similarities. France and Great Britain had the advantage of being sovereign nations early on; one founded on the pre-eminence of the State, its institutions and duties, and the other founded on the primacy of the individual and his freedoms and interests. Both countries, along with Germany, paved the way for modern industrial development at different times and with different structures. Each in its own way combined economic strength with cultural influence: British sensibility as opposed to French rationalism, admittedly, but the Russel paradox is definitely English and Hugo's mystique undeniably French. Without wanting to go too far back in history, from the ascendancy of France in the seventeenth century to the Congress of Vienna, French and English punctuated the old continent with their constantly rekindled conflict, depriving the other countries of power, influence and independence from one decade to the next. Each side had its strategy to contain the other. For the French it was to limit British development to its isles. For the English it was to maintain the balance on the continent by undermining French pre-eminence.

We were basically too similar not to be competitors. Today, we know that we are too close to not be partners. The old imperial reasoning has had its day and our bonds now outweigh our rivalry. The two oldest states in Europe are also two secular democracies, two major economic and cultural powers each with equivalent national wealth of around 1,350 billion euros in GDP in 2001, large armed forces, international sway and a demography that remains upbeat in an ageing Europe. We have constantly developed all sorts of exchanges between us. There are the dynamic, age-old cultural exchanges balancing French philosophers' love for the English language, from Montesquieu and Voltaire on, with interest in the French way of life. And then there is the brisk, growing trade, which has made Great Britain France's number two customer and number four supplier. Over 200,000 French people currently live in London, while France remains the leading point of entry onto the continent and favourite holiday destination for the British.

The cordial dissension between the powers eventually melted happily into alliance and friendship. Two world wars tore the world apart and brought us together. This patiently built and hard-won friendship comes into its own with European integration. In France, we have overcome the reluctance shown by General de Gaulle and certain others. Our French will to build a benchmark Europe and your British determination to no longer be seen as a reluctant partner in the integration process have generated a new order. Great Britain has overcome its reticence about the European Union and is proving it. France has accepted that the European Union will no longer always be built in the French image, but will reflect more the diversity of its members.

GREAT BRITAIN'S COMMITMENT TO EUROPE: A VICTORY OVER PAST DETERMINISM AND AN OPPORTUNITY FOR THE FUTURE

Great Britain's commitment to Europe was not automatic. A long legacy appeared to be opposed to it. Great Britain long remained faithful to its island singularity while France believed in transforming its territory. Although they shared a similar history, these old nation states were geographically different and looked in different directions. Like a true ruler of the waves, Great Britain looked to the

236 *Laurent Fabius*

open sea. Its survival, expansion and empire depended on its control of the major sea routes. France, in the heart of the continent between the Mediterranean, the Alps and the great plains of the north, defined its borders by cultivating and extending its lands. The island mentality made the British look to their future as relying on three overlapping factors: transatlantic, imperial and European. For a while, Great Britain's special relationship with the United States and its privileged links with the Commonwealth relegated European attachment to the rank of poor relation.

Great Britain actually saw political Europe as conflicting with many of its principles. It refused supranationality out of regard for its institutions and national sovereignty. It cultivated a distrust of the treaties out of attentiveness to its own interests and a desire for autonomy. As a traditional free trader, it objected to the Community preferences. And out of loyalty to the Anglo-Saxon culture, it preferred to talk to people overseas in its own language. Yet in just half a century, the British revolutionised their view of Europe. A significant step was taken with the shift from a feeling of incompatibility to support without participation and then political co-operation on ad-hoc issues. The globalisation of concerns, the success of the Community venture and the convergence of the leading European states towards the core issues drew the Isles closer to the continent. Great Britain realised early on that its destiny was also tied up with Europe and finally joined the Community soon after its creation. However, the last four years have seen it enter a new phase by tightening its links with the European family.

A NEW DIRECTION: GREAT BRITAIN AT THE HEART OF EUROPE

Tony Blair and New Labour have achieved a great deal since the 1997 elections. The new labour generation has come down clearly in favour of Europe. It has stated that true patriotism rests in rejecting island isolation, that Great Britain intends to defend its interests wherever these should be, especially within the European Union, and that it has to make a more thorough commitment to Europe if it is to have more influence in the world. Great Britain hence sees Europe as an opportunity and a way of strengthening its power. This was France's view right from the start of European construction and I am pleased that Great Britain is with us on this point.

Today, our two countries share the same point of view on many subjects. The work done by Mr Blair's government has a great deal to do with this: ratification of the Social Charter, commitment to a CAP and structural fund reform, support to Commissioner Kinnock in his drive for a strong, transparent and more accountable Commission, and the will to build a common security and defence policy.

As shown by the progress in the defence arena, we have found a method long wanting to together build the Union of tomorrow. We are moving forward project by project, preferring concrete deadlines to overly generous concepts. We have learnt to work together pragmatically.

I feel that two of the aforementioned arenas, education aside, are priorities for our two countries. These are defence and the euro. Great Britain's commitment to the first is exemplary. And I hope that the British people will make a positive decision about the second.

TOWARDS COMMON DEFENCE AND SECURITY

French and English together have a driving role to play in the EU as regards European defence. We have a long tradition of global diplomacy. We have nuclear capability and powerful conventional forces. We sit on the United Nations Security Council. Our two countries have been committed to an independent European military capability since Saint Malo in December 1998. What some observers call the Saint Malo mindset has stood strong ever since. A year after Saint Malo, at the London summit, our Heads of State and Prime Ministers confirmed our united views on the future of European defence.

The European Councils of Cologne, Helsinki and Nice went one step further by providing for the creation of a European force of 60,000 persons able to be deployed within 60 days. At the same time, the British commitment to the European armament programmes showed that it was serious about greater Europe-wide military autonomy: assembling Meteor air-to-air missiles and Airbus military transport aircraft, participation in the European Organisation for Joint Armament Co-operation (OCCAR), and signing the LoI agreement, which lays the foundations for harmonisation to foster European co-operation in the long run.

All of these accomplishments are commendable, but more still needs to be done. The safety of the Union calls for an independent projection capacity and substantial trained forces with modern "interoperable" equipment and clearly identified command capabilities, despite the fact that our military strategy demands close co-operation with our American allies. This is our game plan for the coming years.

Yet that's not all. The threats in this twenty-first century can have many faces. The classic strategies of confrontation settled between two sworn enemies in keeping with accepted standards have been superseded by the spread of hyperterrorism and cloak-and-dagger warfare. The Union must respond to these mushrooming threats with determined and concerted measures: intelligence service co-operation and a stronger Europol, increasing the Financial Action Task Force's role in combating the financing of terrorism, centralising the fight against terrorism, and creating a real European police force. In early September, the European Parliament laid three important flagstones by coming out in favour of the creation of a European intelligence service, an end to extradition for terrorist acts and the creation of a European warrant for arrest. Some of the goals set to combat the new forms of crime are pooling communication interception methods, stepping up the electronic security of networks and information, consolidating the legislative arsenal to improve co-operation between police forces, closer liaison between judicial authorities and more synchronised penal system provisions. We need to make these goals our own.

Great Britain recently took a new step by deciding to step up the fight against money laundering in the City. As it declared during its presidency of the European Union, France is at the cutting edge of this decisive quest. The British authorities are showing their determination to guarantee security on all sides by deciding to cut off funds to armed Islamic groups, strengthening legislation to tighten the control of financial flows through Britain and hence altering certain traditional rules and interests. We need to act fast and sharp, because an unarmed Europe is a condemned Europe.

THE EURO, AN ASSET FOR THE FUTURE

The second decisive issue in store for us is the physical arrival of the euro. I fear that the single currency could well be incomplete without Great Britain's participation. Although I naturally understand the affection of Her Majesty's subjects for the pound sterling, I can also see the risks of Great Britain remaining by the wayside. A number of studies by British and international institutions state that the overvaluation of the pound may have already cost the country nearly 250,000 jobs and could put millions at risk in the medium run. Large corporations established in Great Britain are threatening to move their factories to the continent where monetary conditions are more attractive. Joining the euro would give the British a considerable asset for their jobs, their industry and their influence in trade. The British government recently catalogued some of the direct, concrete advantages that the euro would give the British: no more transaction costs for holiday-makers, greater price transparency throughout the EU, an end to exchange rate risks in 50 per cent of British industry's trade with the EU, membership of a zone of macroeconomic stability virtually the same size as the United States' area.

Both sides would share in the benefits. The euro zone would benefit from the City, the British experience, the buoyancy of its economy and its reactivity. But Britain also needs the euro, the trade opportunities it brings, the co-ordination it allows and the stability it guarantees.

If we consider the five criteria expressed by Chancellor of the Exchequer Gordon Brown as conditions for membership of the euro in terms of economic flexibility, investment, employment, financial services and the convergence of business cycles, the single currency would definitely benefit the British economy. Then there is the sixth, decisive and political criterion: the population's support. As a staunch euro supportet and a resolute European, I would like to see Tony

Blair win this battle even though I see the difficulties of a decision which somehow, in an important field, changes the concept of sovereignty.

THE EURO, A SHARED VALUE AND A POLITICAL PROJECT

The single currency is not just an instrument for growth or a stabiliser in times of crisis. Its shielding effect against the various Asian, Russian and Latin American crises and the autumn 2000 oil shock is indisputable. As are its function as a financial stabiliser and trade reference, and its dynamic effects on trade and the creation of the Community. Yet the euro is more than this. The pound sterling and French franc's histories have shown that all currencies create a social link. The currency transcends the role of simple object to become an instrument for trade and communication. Like the pound and the franc, the euro will create and is already creating links between all the members of the euro zone. It is an institution that embodies the contract uniting European society, promotes individual mobility and crossovers of wealth, and establishes a common measure for all. Aristotle himself remarked that since its earliest invention, currency "served to maintain the reciprocity of social relations from the point of view of justice." Already a remunerative and distributive tool, the euro will also be a vehicle for redistribution.

Yet the European currency has another, equally important, significance. In the past, monetary unification experiments were all inspired by imperial and even imperialist thinking regardless of whether the power was called Rome, Charlemagne or Napoleon. Today, and this is unique in history, monetary unification is a free choice clearly expressed by many peoples. It shows a shared will to build a peaceful, powerful, innovative and united Europe. Monetary unification has grown from a weapon of war and oppression into a guarantee of peace and shared development. The former instrument of domination has become an instrument of integration. It has changed from a source of rivalry into a vehicle for solidarity. Although the currency still serves a political ambition, this ambition has changed. Europe is at peace, lives in friendship and acts together in solidarity. The euro will ensure that this choice is never challenged again.

BUILDING A BENCHMARK EUROPE TOGETHER

The demise of their empires set Great Britain and France on the same road. There is absolutely no question of our two countries giving up what made them strong for centuries, that is the nation state. But they would do well to extend its prerogatives and its scale via the European institutions. Just as everyone is taken up with critical mass, our European Union has the optimal stature to take on the challenges of the imminent globalised world. Up until the First World War, history was made by the states of the old world in a continental rivalry that sometimes slid into European civil war. The sixteenth century was Spanish, the seventeenth French, the eighteenth French and English, and the nineteenth English. The twentieth century saw the power changing continents to America and triggered a first geographical revolution. If we want, and we will apply ourselves to making it happen, the twenty-first century will be European and worldwide, possibly bringing about a second, this time political, revolution: making Europe a reference for everyone, transcending the old forms of power and working for governance with a human face. I would like to see France and Great Britain contributing to this side by side with the same will and the same hope.

16

The Role of Britain in the Europe of the Twenty-first Century: The International Law Firm Perspective

KEITH CLARK

The second half of the twentieth century provided mixed messages about Britain's contribution to the Europe of the twenty-first century. Was Britain truly ready to accept its modern destiny as a European country? The Prime Minster has said[1] that the "blunt truth" is that British policy towards the rest of Europe over that half-century was marked by:

"gross misjudgements, mistaking what we wanted to be the case with what was the case; hesitation, alienation [and] incomprehension—with the occasional burst of enlightened brilliance which only served to underline the frustration of our partners with what was the norm."

In his book, "The Blessed Plot",[2] Hugo Young has provided a masterly account of Britain's troubled relationship with Europe from Churchill to Blair. He opens with Shakespeare's vision of England as set out in Richard II:[3]—

> This royal throne of kings, this scepter'd isle,
> This earth of majesty, this seat of Mars,
> This other Eden, demi-paradise,
> This fortress built by Nature for herself
> Against infection and the hand of war,
> This happy breed of men, this little world,
> This precious stone set in the silver sea,
> Which serves it in the office of a wall,
> Or as a moat defensive to a house,
> Against the envy of the less happier lands,
> This blessed plot, this earth, this realm, this England.

[1] Speech to the Warsaw Stock Exchange, 6 Oct. 2000.
[2] H Young, *This Blessed Plot—Britain and Europe from Churchill to Blair* (London, Macmillan, 1998).
[3] *Richard II*, Act 2, scene 1.

Contrasted with this idyllic vision of national excellence is Victor Hugo's rather more integrationist approach of 1849:[4]

> "A day will come when you, France; you, Italy; you, England; you, Germany; all you nations of the Continent, without losing your distinct qualities and glorious individuality, will merge into a higher unity and found the European brotherhood."

Although the language and vision of Shakespeare's "demi-paradise" and Victor Hugo's "European brotherland" are full of differences, they are in fact not at all inconsistent. There is no mismatch between a splendid British heritage and a picture of genuine European harmony. This "scepter'd isle" has never been truly insular. From Shakespeare's days to our own, there has been a great inter-change of ideas and a cross fertilisation of cultures. The Palladian style is Italy's enduring contribution to our landscape. At a different but no less important level, Professor Alpa has shown us in his paper, the impact that English thought has had on Italian political and legal thinking. The examples could be multiplied almost ad infinitum. Above all, however, this has been a great trading nation. International trade has been the foundation of British influence abroad and prosperity at home. Total exports are now worth some £254 billion—nearly £4,000 for every British citizen. The pre-eminence of the English language is just one symbol of this internationalist tradition. I stress this with pride and also because I know how important this is in the context of contemporary law and commercial legal transactions and not out of lack of respect for the beauty and strengths of other key languages such as French, Italian, German, or Spanish. For Britain there is nothing new about globalisation—it is only the communications, which have speeded it up as many of the barriers have come down.

We celebrate today the centenary of the British Academy—the country's leading institution in the world of arts and humanities. I know how important continuity and tradition are, as is the imperative of embracing change. The British Academy stands for all this; and so does what is best in the City. My own firm started exactly 200 years ago—in 1802—when a young lawyer (Anthony Brown) began to practice just around the corner from here, at 20 Pudding Lane in the City of London. That firm—described as "highly respectable" by *The Times* newspaper in 1844[5] and "of high esteem" by the *Law Journal* in 1910[6]—developed into what is now Clifford Chance. For many years we were a "City" firm without the need for further national identity. From the outset, international commerce and its financing formed the mainstay of our work. I am proud that we established offices in Paris and in Brussels during the 1960s. I am proud that, during the 1990s, we rapidly became known as the pre-eminent European law firm. We started the twenty-first century—by merging on 1 January 2000 with leading US and German firms—as a truly global firm. We are now a single international firm with more than 3,500 legal advisors spread

---

[4] Quoted in *This Blessed Plot* n. 2 above.
[5] J Slinn, *Clifford Chance—Its origins and development*, (Granta Editions, 1993) at p. 18.
[6] *Ibid.*, at p. 37.

across 29 offices in all the leading business centres of the world. We make no secret of our aspiration to be widely regarded as the world's premier legal firm. Just as important, it is English firms, and not just ours, which have given this lead towards internationalisation. From our vantage point, this is already an English contribution to the world and not just Europe of the twenty-first century.

At Clifford Chance we have a shared vision of where we want to go, and a shared awareness that our combined international efforts achieve far more than we could ever achieve on a merely national basis. I will argue shortly that this same approach—shared vision and collective power—is even more important for the future of the European Union. But let me first say a little about the Clifford Chance approach.

The drive towards high level, international legal services has come from a rapidly changing market. Changes in the legal services market are being driven by the same powerful forces, which are forcing a high level of rationalisation and consolidation in many industry sectors. In the financial sector, the process is already well advanced. But a similar process is well underway in the telecoms, oil and gas, cars and trucks, retail and other markets. The true global players are beginning to emerge.

We had to be quick to recognise that this process would affect the way in which these international players approach the buying of legal services. The scale and complexity of business transactions is increasing, together with the frequency with which they span territorial boundaries and the speed with which they are required to be executed. In addition, the control of legal risk in a large multi-national corporation is becoming more complex and attracting more focus at senior management levels.

A consequence of this is an increasing need for high quality legal service delivered quickly and seamlessly across a range of jurisdictions in a way, which responds to the commercial needs of the client. Our clients tell us that there is now a greater awareness of value, which can be added by a law firm, which can provide these services, at a consistently high level, and on an integrated basis, across the relevant jurisdictions. Certainly, many large corporations are looking for deeper relationships with a smaller number of law firms and are favouring those firms, which have a global perspective.

The challenge for Clifford Chance has thus been to offer consistently high level service, on an integrated basis, and with the necessary depth and breadth of expertise and resource, spanning the world's major economies and markets. This is the challenge of becoming the world's premier legal firm. We have had to raise our game well beyond the aim of being the best at national level. We must be able to demonstrate that we have the depth and breadth of expertise in all the major economies and markets. But we must also show that we can exploit and blend these in ways at the international level, which produce distinctive, high quality service, which is genuinely responsive to the needs of the clients. At the same time, we must retain the authority and confidence, which is to be expected from a firm acting at the very top of its markets. This is the rationale behind the "one firm" approach which we adopted when the three firms merged in January 2001, seeking to achieve the highest levels of integration and coherence across the network. This does not only cover the substance of the work, which we do. It also covers such crucial matters as training, working methods and client relationships. In order to achieve that coherence, we are establishing a single culture and a reputation for quality in all our areas of practice—debt and equity capital markets; banking, derivatives and other financial products; projects; corporate, mergers and acquisitions; litigation and dispute resolution; real estate; tax and so on.

As we gain the benefits from our merger, we recognise that we have built a unique firm. Many of our practice areas have secured top-tier reputations in the principal financial and commercial centres of the world. We have a strong and diverse client base. Relationships with major clients are deepening, and increasingly cross practice areas and geographic boundaries. More than half our top 50 clients in revenue terms are now using the firm across more than three practice areas. The overall depth, quality and maturity of our European practice is particularly strong. World-wide our clients have supported us and, increasingly, recognise and value the unique proposition we can offer. We also made sound progress towards integrating our people, our businesses, our systems and our training and education systems. We understand the challenges, which technological progress is presenting us with and we are making progress in assessing and prioritising the investments we need to make. The demand for high-level legal services of the type we can provide is likely to be sustained by:

- increasing regulation (and complexity of regulation);
- continuing consolidation across most sectors; and
- the pace of change itself, which is unlikely to slow significantly—even during a recession in some parts of the world.

As a result, the forces, which will create the global elite of law of firms are intensifying.

We cannot be complacent. Market conditions in the US were slowing, even before the terrible events of September 2001. How severe the global downturn will be, how long it will last and the implications of this in relation to market activity in Europe and other key regions are all uncertain. A changing marketplace imposes the need, and creates the opportunities, for change. Our clients are becoming more sophisticated, our recruitment market is becoming more difficult and information technology requires us to rethink how we deliver many of our services to clients.

The environment in which we operate is also becoming more competitive. We must sprint in order to keep ahead. Like all successful organisations, we cannot just plan for today and we must plan well ahead. We must also recognise the need for improvement, and identify our weaknesses and see these as opportunities to improve.

Across the world, a client focused law firm requires a new kind of lawyer. We are broadening and intensifying the training and career development we give to all our associates. Our lawyers are becoming more rounded business advisers—financially literate with an understanding of markets and a finger on the pulse of current business events. They must be international in outlook and confident of their ability to operate effectively in different cultures. They need strong commercial understanding and the ability to obtain deep insights into our clients, their businesses and their requirements. We also need "best in class" knowledge management systems and processes that allow all our lawyers to access the collective knowledge and wisdom of the firm and deliver the best of the firm to our clients. The diversity and range of people who make up the firm is one of our greatest strengths and we must encourage that diversity and create an environment where any talented person can build a successful career with us.

Our work is substantially international, but the law remains deeply embedded in national cultures. But, in the modern world national cultures interface continuously one with another by reason of the globalised economy, modern means of communication, travel, and the migration of people. Our daily experience at Clifford Chance tells us that the law is very much part of this phenomenon. In the course of my own career, we have seen the creation of the Euromarket, with credits syndicated among banks from all over the world and denominated first in dollars, then in other currencies, then in units of account. This led to the development of the enormous derivatives market. During the same period, governments agreed to subject banks to one set of prudential rules, and stock exchanges adopted similar regulations. Business practices and the requirements for the spread of risk between parties to contractual arrangements became standardised through the expectations of the markets. Consequently, our daily practice of the law can be said to have become an activity not just of lawyers, but of translators—not of words but of legal concepts developed in one jurisdiction which are to be used in another, quite different, jurisdiction. In these circumstances, our clients rightly demand, and get, a global legal service. We provide this as a single firm from our many offices around the world. We co-ordinate our activities and standards of service and are building a common culture. But these facts mean that we make considerable demands of imagination and initiative of our lawyers. In order to prepare them for this, we have created the "Clifford Chance Academy". One of its roles is to help our lawyers from civil law countries and those from the common law tradition to understand each other by approaching together the elements of their respective legal backgrounds. Similarly, we support the Institute of European and Comparative Law of Oxford in its relations with the University Paris I, Cambridge in connection with the "Double Maîtrise" recently set up with Paris II, and the Institute of Global Law of University College, London. In these circumstances, it is imperative for us to keep a considerable degree of local autonomy. We must continue to be strong wherever we are, with local lawyers of the highest calibre, whether it be in Madrid, Paris, Amsterdam, Frankfurt, Milan, or anywhere else.

Whatever may be the legal system implicated in matters submitted to us, we are, and must continue to be, able to deal with it at the highest level of competence. In introducing these approaches and techniques we have not only modernised the firm; we have significantly assisted the processes of legal education in Britain. More significantly, perhaps, for the purposes of the theme of this lecture we have set a benchmark for others to follow and are showing the way forward to many law firms around the world in general and Europe in particular.

The balance of unity and diversity is the essence of an international partnership. And it is also, on a far grander scale, the essence of what Europe should be all about. The EU must also accommodate unity and diversity at the same time. As with a law firm, it must also aim for *shared vision* and *collective power*. Each Member State must be highly competitive and Europe as a whole must be highly competitive. Participation in a wider community is essential to British and European prosperity and to the economic, social and peaceful wellbeing of future generations.

Britain must, in my view, be at the centre of Europe in spelling out the shared vision for the Europe of the future. We simply cannot afford to be left on the sidelines, reluctant to participate until after the last moment and then complaining that all the rules were made to suit the original members of the club. The power and role of the City of London, in particular, are at risk if Britain is not seen to be permanently and positively at the heart of Europe.

For me the Little Englander mentality is a source of constant surprise since it ignores the stark economic facts about the benefits of British membership of the EU. For example :-

- With 376 million people, the EU is now the largest consumer market in the world. This provides British producers with unrivalled opportunities and gives British consumers more choice and lower prices.
- 57 per cent of British exports now go to other EU countries;
- Up to 3.5 million British jobs depend on exports to the EU;
- Britain receives the largest share of inward investment into the EU. (US firms alone employ about one million people in Britain);
- Britain will receive £10 billion of EU structural funds from 2000 to 2006.
- The EU negotiates as one on international trade, environmental standards and the fight against crime and terrorism. In short, Britain enjoys greater international clout because of its EU membership.

But we must get the politics right as well as the economics. I am not unduly concerned about so-called erosion of sovereignty. Sovereignty is never a fixed or absolute concept. But I do worry about the need for the European Union to achieve full credibility and legitimacy. It must strike deeper roots. Many of the problems currently facing the European Union lie in the obscurity and remoteness of its institutions and procedures. You should not have to be genius to understand how Europe works. The processes and language of EU institutions are as unfamiliar as they are threatening. Most British people have a broad idea of how laws are made by the Westminster Parliament. Very few have any idea at all about law-making at the EU level. We also need greater clarity, and if possible simplicity, about what can and should be done at the European level, and what can and should done at a national level. Europe must be shown to be relevant and important to all citizens, and not just to the political and business elites.

The Inter-governmental Conference in 2004 must address public concerns about the way the European Union works. Enlargement means that—as a matter of some urgency—the issue is not whether to reform, but how to achieve this goal. Like most people, I am not attracted by the extreme models. Europe should not be seen purely as free trade area, like NAFTA. But nor, it seems to me, should it pursue the classic federalist model with an elected President of the Commission, and the European Parliament as a fully-fledged legislative body.

The EU must remain a unique combination of the inter-governmental and the supra-national. The EU can and should project its *collective power* as a combination of independent sovereign states who have chosen to pool some sovereignty in pursuit of their own interests and common good, achieving more together than can be achieved individually. And let us not forget that the problems that confront us today are not just problems of free trade. They are also problems connected with the fight against drugs and terrorism, the maintenance of law and order and peace, the preservation of basic human rights.

There are numerous detailed reform proposals, which might promote the British Prime Minister's vision of Europe as "superpower, but not a superstate." Reforms which I regard as particularly important include:

- a more proactive role for the European Council, setting overall political direction with a clear and coherent programme of policy and legislative goals;
- shared Presidency arrangements;
- a second chamber—involving representatives of national Parliaments—for the European Parliament, mainly with a scrutiny role;
- a reform of the composition and procedures of the European Commission and revised Council voting arrangements;
- greater flexibility within specific areas of competence, but avoiding a multi-tier Europe with a series of "hard-core" groupings;
- enhanced co-operation on foreign and security policy and the fight against terrorism and crime.

The above do not mean or require a single Constitution for Europe. The "constitution" will continue to be found in a number of different treaties, laws and precedents rather than a single legal binding document. But I am attracted to proposals for a Statement of Principles (or Charter of Competences) spelling out what is best done at the European level and what should be done at national level.

But Britain cannot expect to have a decisive role in pushing these—or any other reforms—unless there is full-hearted commitment. Britain has a great deal to contribute as a fully paid-up and fully grown-up European country. We have a powerful economy. We have harnessed the benefits of free markets. We have learned the lessons (positive and negative) of de-regulation and privatisation. We have an obvious role in defence and foreign policy. We have a proud record of respect for human rights and of government according to the rule of law. We are an important bridge between the EU and the US. Our cultural and intellectual credentials are as strong as they are diverse. Even the food in London is now amongst the best in Europe and that is arguably because it is no longer only English!

But Britain in the twenty-first Century—indeed in the first decade of this century—must unreservedly welcome what Europe has to offer in return. The Little Englander mentality must be banished once and for all. We must attack those who deride everything that originates "from Brussels" and demonstrate the tangible benefits of being genuine, full-blooded Europeans. This will involve a great deal more effort to capture hearts and minds. It is no longer "Britain and Europe"—it must be, as in the title of today's conference, "Britain *in* Europe."

Today's conference has explored legal, intellectual, political, economic and constitutional interchanges. It has shown that the idea of interchange and co-operation has a long pedigree and much to show for it. The Conference, however, also showed that much more has to be achieved. I am delighted that Clifford Chance has been able to support this endeavour. I am optimistic that it will contribute to much better mutual understanding. But I will not be satisfied that an enlarged European Union is achieving its full potential—in terms of prosperity, stability and well-being—unless and until Britain *enthusiastically* joins its partners at the centre of influence. As the great Bard put it:

This "happy breed of men" *can no longer live alone* in "this little world".

17

The Impact of European Law in French Law: Lessons for England?

NOELLE LENOIR[1]

1 INTRODUCTORY REMARKS

Is France the land of paradox? The way in which international law, especially European law, has woven itself into French domestic law has given rise to several paradoxes, and I would like to identify two of them.

The first has to do with the apparent contradiction in the French Government's attitude towards international law. France is, throughout the world, one of the main inspirers of major international agreements. But once these agreements are signed, the French Government is not usually in a hurry to bring them into force at the national level. Such was for instance the case of the European Convention of Human Rights (ECHR). One of the main "founding fathers" of this Convention was Pierre-Henri Teitgen, a minister during France's Fourth Republic (1946–1958) and President of "Le Mouvement Européen", an NGO acting in favour of European integration. Nonetheless, it was not until 1974, that is to say 25 years after it had been signed in Rome, that the ECHR was finally ratified by the French Government. This ratification took place well after the Algerian war came to an end in 1962 even though the Algerian crisis had been the main reason why it had been postponed.[2] In the same way, French politicians and top officials played a decisive role in promoting a supranational model of European co-operation. The pooling of Franco-German coal—which resulted in the European Coal and Steel Community treaty (signed in 1951), and later on in the European Economic Community Treaty (signed in 1957 along with Germany, Italy, and the three Benelux countries)—was proposed from the 1950s by Robert Schuman, the then French foreign minister, according to a plan

---

[1] This is the text of the Annual Clifford Chance Lecture delivered at UCL's Institute of Global Law on 1 November 2001 with the Rt Hon the Lord Nicholls of Birkenhead in the Chair. The text reproduced here has been enlarged somewhat as well as adapted in light of the aims of the Centenary conference. I am grateful to Keith Clark, formerly Chairman of Clifford Chance, and to Michael Bray, current CEO of Clifford Chance, for the invitation to give the lecture.

[2] N Lenoir "The Constitutional Council and the European Convention of Human Rights: the Paradox", *in Liber Amicorum in Honour of Lord Slynn of Hadley*, Volume II, French *Judicial Review in International Perspective*, edited by Mads Andenas and Duncan Fairgrieve (London, Kluwer Law International, 2000).

drafted by Jean Monnet, a top French official and committed federalist. However, when De Gaulle came into office in 1958, the French Government showed much less enthusiasm towards European integration than the other member states of the new Community. Instead, he favoured an intergovernmental pattern of Europe which, incidentally, led to durable tensions between the Commission in Brussels and the French Government.[3]

The second paradox concerns France's so-called "monist" system. In theory, this system facilitates the introduction of international law into domestic law. Contrary to German, Irish, Italian, and UK law, French law does not require treaties to be incorporated by means of specific legislation.[4] On the contrary, treaties become applicable as soon as they have been ratified by the Government and published in the "Journal Officiel" of the French Republic. Nonetheless, this system has not really made France more internationalist than the "dualist" countries. France has sometimes even more nationalistic tendencies than these countries.

The third paradox has to do with the unexpected turn of events in the history of the Fifth Republic. The current Constitution of 1958, inspired by General De Gaulle, adopts a less open approach to international law than that of its predecessor (enacted just after the end of World War II). Nevertheless, since 1958, France has been able to adapt remarkably to the European legal systems created by both the ECHR and the European Community. The way things happened, however, is not always the way the creators of the Constitution had in mind.

—For example, De Gaulle's obsession with safeguarding national sovereignty led to new constitutional provisions. First, Article 54 provides for the possibility of constitutional review by the Constitutional Council in order to ensure compatibility of treaties with the Constitution prior to ratification.[5] The purpose of the "founding fathers" of the Constitution was to protect against treaties which could endanger national sovereignty. Such was the case, according to De Gaulle, with the dangerously radical "European Defence Community"! It should be recalled that this treaty, inspired by French politicians, was finally rejected in 1954 by a French National Assembly wary of the re-arming of Germany.[6] Along

---

[3] P Craig and G de Burca, *EU Law, Text, Cases and Materials*, 2nd ed. (Oxford, Oxford University Press, 1998), pp. 7–19.

[4] This system is based on the idea that treaties prevail over domestic statutes as was firmly stated by the Constitution of the Fourth Republic of 1946. Art. 26 of this Constitution provides that "Diplomatic treaties that have been properly ratified and published shall have the force of statute even if they are contrary to French statutes, and their application shall require no further legislative provisions than those whereby they were ratified". Although Art. 55 of the 1958 Constitution is less explicit, it still states that "Treaties and agreements duly ratified or approved shall, upon publication, prevail over Acts of Parliament. . .".

[5] Art. 54 of the 1958 Constitution states that " If the Constitutional Council, upon a referral from the President of the Republic, from the Prime Minister or from the President of one to the other assembly, or from sixty deputies or sixty senators, has declared that the commitment in question contains a clause contrary to the Constitution, authorisation to ratify or approve this commitment may be given only after amendment of the Constitution".

[6] Craig and De Burca, n. 3 above at p. 10.

the same lines, Article 55 of the Constitution, while stating that treaties prevail over statutes, imposes an unprecedented condition for their implementation, namely "reciprocity".[7] This condition was criticised by many jurists at the time, as it seemed to provide French authorities with a flexible means of avoiding their international commitments on opportunistic grounds.[8]

—However, I am speaking of the law. Facts are different. Thanks to the European courts, by which I mean the courts in Strasbourg and Luxembourg, the primacy of international law over domestic law has now become a reality. Nowadays, national courts apply European law. And they thus promote the European idea in various shapes and forms. Undoubtedly European law has markedly increased the powers of the judiciary.[9] This is a revolution in a country such as France in which traditionally, it is a political imperative that the Executive possesses almost untrammelled powers. Let us not forget that during the Republic, the expression "The King Can Do No Wrong" had turned into "The People Can Do No Wrong". And then the balance changed again. There was a jump—from sovereignty of the people to sovereignty of the Executive! This primacy of politics over law is now being challenged by the rule of law. European law had a hand in this.

In my view, European law has had a very positive influence on France. It has forced political authorities to abide by the law and accept the limitation of powers that it involves. It has also given national judges more prestige. Historically, the French—especially the establishment—rather distrusted judges[10]. Even Montesquieu wrote that judges were supposed to be the "mouth of the law" and nothing more. One must admit that this distrust has not disappeared. It is still present today, but the situation has changed since the judiciary has gained greater power and legitimacy. European Law has helped in this process for three distinct reasons.

   I. The supremacy of European law over domestic law has resulted in a new balance between the judiciary and the public powers.
   II. The recognition by French courts of the direct effect of European law has prompted a new culture regarding the rule of law in France.
   III. In changing the content of French law, European Law has enriched French democracy.
So let us look at these points in turn.

---

[7] Art. 55 of the 1958 Constitution provides that "Treaties or agreements duly ratified or approved shall, upon publication, prevail over Acts of Parliament with regard to each agreement or treaty, in its application by the other party."

[8] N Quoc Dinh " La Constitution de 1958 et le droit international", (1959) *Revue de Droit Public* 516.

[9] See for instance O Dubos, *Les Juridictions Nationales, Juge Communautaire*, Nouvelle Bibliothèque des thèses (Paris, Dalloz, 2001) (with regard to the influence of EC law), p. 723.

[10] Two laws dating from the French Revolution (16 and 24 August 1790) famously stated that "The jurisdictions cannot take any part whatsoever in the exercise of the administrative power, neither can it render impossible or suspend the execution of laws regularly promulgated without committing an abuse of its power".

2 THE IMPACT OF EUROPEAN LAW

I The Supremacy of European Law

The French have had more difficulties than other European countries in integrating European law into their own legal system and recognising the supremacy of European law over national law. It was indeed difficult for French society to renounce Rousseau's theory, expressed in "Le Contrat Social"(1762), according to which " *the general will of the people is always right and is always aimed at complying with the public interest*". "Public interest" and "public prerogatives" are two notions, which underpin French administrative Law, justifying the granting of extensive powers and sometimes privileges to public authorities. Those who know about the French law of contract are perfectly aware of this situation. For someone of my generation, the limitation of State prerogatives as a result of European law represents a complete change in our legal culture. This change is recent, but it is significant and tangible. National courts, from both the administrative and ordinary jurisdictions, no longer hesitate to set aside legislation and regulations, which they deem to be contrary to European law. This development has been as much of a sea change for the French as I guess the "Factortame" case, or more recently the Human Rights Act, has been for Britain.

Anyone familiar with the French judicial system knows that the supremacy of European law over later national laws was recognised much sooner by the Cour de Cassation—our superior court in civil, commercial and criminal matters—than by the Conseil d'Etat. Whereas the Cour de Cassation recognised the doctrine of supremacy in 1975 (Café Jacques Vabres[11]), the Conseil d'Etat did not accept this until 1989 (Nicolo[12]). Everyone knows that the Conseil d'Etat, set up by Napoleon to mirror the King's Council, jealously guards its close links with the Executive. Although it plays the role of a superior administrative court, it still advises the Government and has thus traditionally struggled to avoid overshadowing the public authorities in the exercise of their powers. But now both superior courts apply European law in its entirety, namely to protect the rights of individuals, citizens and foreigners alike.

As for the Constitutional Court, although it still refuses to review the compatibility of domestic legislation with European law, it has also contributed to establishing the supremacy of European law.[13] It recognised the tenet of "Pacta

---

[11] "*Administration des Douanes* v. *Société des Café Jacques Vabres*, 24 May 1975, published—along with submissions by A Touffait, General Prosecutor of the Cour de Cassation—in (1975) *revue Dalloz-Sirey*, jurisprudence, 497.

[12] "Nicolo", 20 Oct. 1989, published—along with the submissions of P Frydman, Goverment Commissioner—in (1989) *Revue Française de Droit Administratif* 812. See also M Long, P Weil, G Braibant, P Delvolvé, B Genevois, *Les Grands Arrêts de la Jurisprudence Administrative* (Paris, Dalloz, 2001) p. 715.

[13] N Lenoir "The Response of the French Constitutional Court to the Growing Importance of International Law", in *The Clifford Chance Millenium Lectures: The Coming Together of the Common Law and the Civil Law*, edited by Basil Markesinis (Oxford, Hart Publishing, 2000), p. 163.

servanda",[14] that is to say the obligation to apply treaties in good faith, as a principle of constitutional value. (Decision on the Maastricht treaty, 1992[15]). More notably, the Council decided that the very controversial "reciprocity clause", to which I made allusion earlier, did not apply to European law and European Human Rights Law. Why? First, because there is a specific legal mechanism provided by the EU treaty to ensure the respect of European law (decision of 1998 on the right for all Union citizens to vote in municipal elections[16]), and secondly because humanitarian principles of international law preclude the application of the reciprocity clause to Human Rights' treaties, such as the European Convention of Human Rights (decision of 1999 on the international criminal court[17]). The result of this is that although France still refuses to ratify the Vienna Convention of 1969 on the laws of treaties—since it does not accept giving any effect to the jus cogens[18]—almost all the principles established by this Convention have been introduced through the case law of the Constitutional Council into domestic constitutional law! This is quite a roundabout way to underline the importance of the law of human rights and to encourage national judges to apply it without risking conflict with the Court in Strasbourg.

II European Law contributes to the Reinforcement of the Rule of Law in France by means of the Doctrine of Direct Effect

Today, European law has become an integral part of French domestic law. As stated, the Conseil d'Etat has had more difficulty than the Cour de Cassation in accepting the binding and direct effect of European law.[19] Nevertheless, now

---

[14] This principle refers to Art. 14 of the Preamble to the 1946 Constitution, which is part of the "bloc de constitutionnalité", and solemnly asserts that "France, faithful to its traditions, respects the rule of public international law. . .".

[15] Decision No. 92–308 DC of 9 April 1992, in the Recueil p. 55. According to this judgment, the constitutional rule of "Pacta sunt servanda . . . implies that any treaty in force is binding on the parties and must be executed in good faith".

[16] Decision No. 98–400 of 20 May 1998, in the Recueil p. 251. According to this judgment, "The principle of reciprocity set out [in the Constitution] has been met; should a member state [of the EU] fail to comply with the obligation arising from [the European treaty], France could refer a case to the Court of Justice on the basis of Art. 170 of the Treaty establishing the European Community".

[17] Decision No. 98–408 of 22 Jan. 1999, in Recueil p. 29. This judgment rules that "There is no need for the condition of reciprocity—imposed by Art. 55 of the Constitution—to apply, given the purpose of the international commitments entered into in order to promote peace and security in the world and to secure respect for the general principles of public law".

[18] France is, indeed, reluctant to ratify this treaty since it does not yet accept that jus cogens could have a normative value. Jus cogens is the technical term given to those norms of general international law which are of peremptory force and from which, as a consequence, no derogation may in principle be made. This means that a treaty which conflicts with such a norm is void. These norms are almost common law norms, defined as such by courts, and that is why the French Government is as a matter of principle opposed to their recognition. But all the other provisions of the Treaty of Vienna on the law of treaties have now been recognised by the Constitutional Council as norms of constitutional value.

[19] See Craig and De Burca, n. 3 above, p. 264. See also TC Hartley, *Foundations of European Community law*, 3rd ed. (Oxford, Oxford University Press, 1994) p. 247.

even the Conseil d'Etat refers to European law or applies a preliminary ruling to the European Court in Luxembourg at the drop of a hat. This is a complete turnaround.

Oddly enough European law is much less well-known by the public than ECHR law (except for law firms and multinationals, as one can imagine). This is nevertheless understandable. It took a long time for France to ratify the ECHR. Because of the Algerian war and the accusations of torture committed by the army during this war which lasted about six years, the French Government put off ECHR ratification until 1974. Moreover, it was not until 1981 that the right to individual petition before the Court in Strasbourg was recognised.[20] From then on, French lawyers have systematically invoked the ECHR and the case law of the Strasbourg Court. And believe me, when lawyers threaten to make a claim before the Strasbourg Court, their threat is taken seriously. Since individuals cannot provoke constitutional review of the law—only the President of the Republic, the Prime Minister and parliamentarians, after the vote of an Act and before enactment, have the right to challenge a law before the Constitutional Council[21]—the right of petition before the Strasbourg Court is used as a substitute. Condemnation by the Strasbourg Court is ever present in the mind of the Government and the courts. For instance, in its judgment delivered a few weeks ago concerning the French President's criminal liability under Article 68 of the Constitution, the Cour de Cassation took a slightly different stand from that which could have resulted from the 1999 decision of the Constitutional Court[22] on this subject, just to avoid condemnation by the Strasbourg Court. The Cour de Cassation ruled that for "High Treason" perpetrated during his mandate, the President could only be impeached by the "High Court of Justice", which is made up of members of Parliament. However, it stated that any crimes committed before the President took office were punishable in the ordinary courts after the termination of his tenure, at any time. That is to say, with the limitation period extended.[23] In this way, the Cour de

---

[20] See N Lenoir " The Constitutional Council and the ECHR: The French Paradox" mentioned above.

[21] According to Art. 61 of the 1958 Constitution, "Acts of Parliament, before their promulgation, may only be referred by the President of the Republic, the Prime Minister, the President of the National Assembly, the President of the Senate, or 60 deputies or 60 senators."

[22] In its decision No. 98–408 of 22 Jan. 1999 on the Treaty creating an International Criminal Court to be set up in The Hague, the Constitutional Council ruled that this Treaty's provision, which denies judicial immunity to Heads of States or Government in office, was contrary to Art. 68 of the French Constitution establishing at least partially such an immunity. On this occasion, it interpreted Art. 68 by stating that "by this Art., the President of the Republic may not be held liable for acts performed in the exercise of his duties except in the case of high treason; he may be indicted only by the High Court of Justice pursuant to the procedure set out by that Article". This suggests that even acts perprertrated by a French Head of State or Government before his/her coming into office could lead to a trial before the High Court of Justice during his/her mandate. However, the Cour de Cassation did not abide by this interpretation to which it denied *erga omnes* authority and ruled that such acts could only be dealt with by a procedure before ordinary courts after the termination of the mandate of the person involved.

[23] Decision No. 481 of 10 Oct. 2001, published on the web side of the Cour de Cassation along with the report of the Conseiller Rapporteur, www.courdecassation.fr/agenda/arrets/arrets/01-84922.

Cassation considered that it would be respecting the principle established by Article 7 of the ECHR, which lays down that only a law can define a crime and prescribe a penalty; a principle which cannot be properly applied before the High Court of Justice.

Another point which should be mentioned is that the Cour de Cassation transposed the case law of the Strasbourg Court much more speedily than the Conseil d'Etat. Consider, for instance, the following example. A few months after France had been condemned for having refused to modify the status and first name of a transexual who had become a female, the Cour de Cassation reversed its earlier decision, and accepted the applicant's request for changing his/her entries in the register of births (Marc X V. Procureur général, 1992[24]). By contrast, it took fifteen years for the Conseil d'Etat to abide by the decisions of the ECHR (Le Compte 1981[25]), which hold that Article 6 of the Convention imposed a duty to ensure that hearings of disciplinary courts were open to the public (Maubleu, 1996[26]).

The ECHR, and the case law of the Strasbourg Court, are also very influential on legislation and regulations. It is well known for instance that legislation was adopted to regulate tapping of telephones for reasons of public security, soon after the Strasbourg Court found France to be in breach of the ECHR for having failed to regulate this practice (*Kruslin and Huvig v. France*, 1990[27]). I have been told that in the UK, the Interceptions of Communications Act of 1985 was enacted for similar reasons, that is to say, after the case of *Malone v. UK* in 1984.[28] We did not understand in France at the time that this case law applied to us as well!

However, as I was saying, European law is still more influential than ECHR law. This is for diverse reasons: firstly because France was already accustomed to enforcing Human Rights. French courts have always been used to referring to the Declaration of 1789 on the rights of Citizens and of Man, even before the Constitutional Council granted it constitutional value. France, which likes to call itself "la patrie des droits de l'homme" has long had a superiority complex, considering that it had patented the idea of Human Rights which it naturally claims to have invented at the end of the eighteenth century! The ratification of the ECHR, whose spirit is very close to the 1789 Declaration on Human Rights, has therefore not radically changed French legal thinking. On the contrary, it was European law that brought radical change, transforming "statist" France into a country more oriented toward market economy. More than 80 per cent of

---

[24] Two judgments given on 11 Dec. 1992, in journal Juris-Classeur Périodique, jurisprudence no. 21991, p. 41, with submissions by M Jeol, Advocate General of the Cour de Cassation. These judgments follow the case law of the European Court of Human Rights which had just condemned France in a decision made on 25 Mar. 1992 for having failed to recognise that a transexual had the right to change its name and its sex as mentioned in the register of births.

[25] *Le Compte Van Leuven and De Meyer v. Belgium*, série A, no. 43.

[26] Judgment of 14 Feb. 1996, in Recueil p. 34 with submissions of M Sanson, Government Commissioner of the Conseil d'Etat.

[27] *Kruslin v. France*, 24 Apr. 199à, série A no. 176-A; *Huvig v. France*, 24 Apr. 1990, série A, no. 176-B.

[28] *Malone v. UK*, 2 Aug. 1984, série A, no. 82.

French legislation in economic fields results directly from European Law! I mention in passing that to general consternation, our cheese was at one stage on the verge of being compulsorily pasteurised!

Surprisingly, the French Government is none the less unenthusiastic about some of the changes European law has generated in respect of the management of the nation's economy and the regulation of commercial activity. The Conseil d'Etat itself was slow to give precedence to European directives. Soon after the decision in Nicolo in 1989, the Conseil d'Etat recognised the direct effect of European Regulations at the very moment of their publication in the European Community Journal (Boisdet, 1990[29]). But its views were not in line with the Court in Luxembourg with regard to the effect of directives. The Conseil d'Etat considered that Directives, even if they were detailed and "unconditional", were deprived of legal effect in France until they were transposed. This is exemplified by a decision in 1978, when it ruled on the expulsion of Cohn Bendit, then leader of an extreme left-wing movement in 1968, and now the head of the French Greens in the European Parliament. In this quite colourful case, Cohn Bendit claimed that the administrative measure effecting his expulsion from France should have resulted from a directive of 1964 which had not been implemented in time by the French Government. The Conseil d'Etat's answer was crystal clear: there is no such thing as direct applicability of a non-implemented directive. A sort of nothing from nothing is nothing, if you will. The Conseil d'Etat sharply pointed out that *"no stipulation of the European Community treaty . . . empowers organs of the Community to make regulations concerning public order . . . directly applicable in the member states. . ."*.[30] This decision came as a bombshell to the European cause as it looked decidedly anti-European and contradicted the ECJ's case law, namely the Van Duyn jurisprudence (*Van Duyn* v. *Home Office*, 1974[31]). However, the war between the ECJ and the Conseil d'Etat did not last long. Little by little, the Conseil d'Etat put into effect non-implemented directives. In 1984, the Conseil d'Etat decided that the French administration could not invoke a national regulation, which violates a directive, even if the directive had not yet been transposed (Fédération française des sociétés de protection de la nature et autres[32]). In 1989, it recognised that people had a right to ask their administration to take measures necessary to transpose a directive and to invalidate former ones henceforth contrary to Community text (Alitalia[33]). More recently, the Conseil d'Etat declared a statutory instrument void which was con-

---

[29] Boisdet, 24 Sept. 1990, in Les Petites Affiches of 12 Oct. 1990 along with the submissions of M Laroque, Government Commissioner.

[30] C Bendit, 22 Dec. 1978, in (1979) *revue Dalloz* 155, along with submissions of B Genevois, Government Commissioner.

[31] Case 41/74 [1974] ECR 1337, [1975] 1 CMLR 1. See Craig and De Burca, n. 3 above 187.

[32] Fédération Française des Sociétés de Protection de la Nature, 7 Dec. 1984, in (1985) *Revue Française de Droit Administratif* 303, along with submissions by O Dutheillet de Lamothe, Government Commissioner.

[33] Alitalia, 3 Feb. 1989, in (1989) *Revue Française de Droit Administratif* 391, along with submissions by N Chahid Nouraï, Government Commissioner.

The Impact of European Law in French Law: Lessons for England? 257

trary to the objectives of a directive (Union des transporteurs en commun des voyageurs de Bouches du Rhône, 1994[34]). It has also allowed an applicant to invoke a directive not yet transposed and contrary to national legislation in order to challenge an administrative measure by means of judicial review "recours pour excès de pouvoir". (Revert and Babelon, 1996,[35] concerning a fiscal exemption provided by a directive). Last but not least—I quote this example to stress the impact of European law on French political life—the Conseil d'Etat boldly forced the Government to strictly enforce the very unpopular directive of 1979 on the hunting of migrating birds. Why is this directive so controversial? Because hunting in France is not only a mere sport. It is also regarded as an almost God-given right, or at least a right bestowed by the revolutionaries in 1789. I realise that it is also a sensitive subject in the UK. The right to hunt is not mentioned in our Constitution, unlike in the US Constitution, which explicitly provides for *"the right of the people to keep and bear arms"*. Yet the right to hunt is rooted in French tradition. Consequently, in a country like France whose strong rural traditions have not yet completely disappeared, and which claims to love the "terroir", in other terms the bucolic life, limitations on the right to hunt are considered by hunters as undemocratic. That is why all Governments have had difficulties with the directive in question. In 1999 (Association ornithologique et mammalogique de Saône et Loire et Association France Nature Environnement[36]), the Conseil d'Etat condemned the State for having failed to decide the dates for hunting migrating birds as mentioned in the 1979 Directive. The Government claimed to have grave reservations about this judgment. However, I think it was actually relieved since it could tell the hunters' lobby that it was thus obliged to comply with the Directive. . .[37]

The Conseil d'Etat has not been the only one to accept compromises. Whilst the Conseil d'Etat has increasingly recognised the binding effect of directives, the ECJ has itself deferred to the Conseil d'Etat's approach by not placing an obligation upon a private person in respect of a directive which has not yet been transposed. This means that the Court finally denied horizontal direct effect to non-implemented directives (Marshall, 1986[38]; Paola Faccini Fiori,

---

[34] Union des Transporteurs en commun des Voyageurs des Bouches du Rhône, 11 Mar. 1994, in (1994) *Revue Française du Droit Administratif* 1004, along with submissions by B du Marais, Governement Commissioner.

[35] SA Cabinet Revert and Badelon, 30 Oct. 1996, in (1997) *Revue Française de Droit Administratif* 1056, along with submissions by G Goulard, Government Commissioner.

[36] Association Ornithologique et Mammalogique de Saône et Loire et Association France Nature Environnement, 3 Dec. 1999, in (2000) *Revue Française du Droit Administratif* 59 along with submissions by F Lamy, Government Commissioner.

[37] The ECHR law has also obliged the French Government to revise its legislation on hunting. The Strasbourg Court declared in a judgment given on 29 Apr. 1999, *"Chassagnou and others v. France"* (série A req. 25088/94, 28331/95 et 28443/95) that the so-called "Verdeille Act" on hunting and shooting was contrary to the ECHR since it obliged landowners to authorise hunters to use their land without taking into consideration their right of property.

[38] *Marshall v. Southampton and South West Area Health Authority (Marshall I)* [1986] ECR 723, [1986] 1 CMLR 688, about the effect of the 1976 Equal Treatment Directive on the UK legislation, namely its effect on the retiring age applicable to women and men.

1994[39]). There is thus almost no divergence between the Conseil d'Etat, which is in charge of protecting national identity, and the ECJ, whose mission is to ensure the integration of EC law in the legal systems of member states, which all in all shapes the legal and even political structure of the Community.

Not surprisingly, this integration by the Cour de Cassation has been quite easy since 1975, which is the date of the "Café Jacques Vabre" decision. First, the Cour de Cassation hardly makes any difference between directive and regulations, following in that respect the ECJ's doctrine about the direct effect of directives. More astonishingly, it goes further than the ECJ and recognises non-implemented directives to have such an effect, in the field of criminal law. For instance, it directly applied a non-implemented directive of 1972—regarding civil liability in case of a car accident—in a dispute between two insurance companies, giving thus to this text a horizontal direct effect (judgment of 11 December 1984[40]).

The increasingly open attitude of French courts towards European law explains why the references under Article [177] by courts are not less numerous than in other countries. The number of preliminary rulings in Germany and in France is quite comparable: 1209 in Germany for a population of some 85 million inhabitants, and 617 in France, which has 60 million inhabitants. Figures for the UK are more modest: 317 preliminary rulings in 2000. Is it due to the fact that English judges are more familiar with European law than their colleagues in France and Germany and do not need to turn to the ECJ ?

III European Law Has Changed the Content of French Law and Enriched French Democracy

It is difficult in this respect to separate European law and ECHR law, the Luxembourg and the Strasbourg courts' case law. There are great similarities between them since they have a combined influence on the content of national law. For instance, European law and ECHR law have both helped shape the rights and obligations of foreigners residing in France, and have helped bolster the rights of women based on the principle of equality between men and women (regarding in particular access to employment and prohibiting discrimination at work).

However, European law has also had a major and specific influence on certain fields, mainly the economy. It has thus changed the very conception of the State. Traditionally in France, the concept of the State is very strong. Ever since Louis the Fourteenth proclaimed: "l'Etat, c'est moi", at the end of the seventeenth century, submission to State authority has been a strong dogma

---

[39] *Faccini Dori* v. *Recreb SRl* [1994] ECR I-3325, in which the applicant, P F Dori sought unsuccessfully to rely on a right arising from a non-implemented directive, to resist the enforcement against her of a contract she had entered into with a company.

[40] See comments in J L Sauron, *L'application du Droit de l'Union Européenne en France*, Collection Reflexe Europe, La Documentation Française, Paris, 1995, p. 55.

expressed through the idea that the State represents the general interest of the people, which gives it a privileged role. Only now is this religion losing its believers. Furthermore, State interventionism is still a favoured tool of the French Government. Many State-owned companies still exist, since the nationalisation of industries has been a popular governmental activity in France: during the "Front Populaire", after World War II, during De Gaulle's reign and again in 1982–1983 when Mitterrand came to office. There are still quite a number of important public utilities in the main strategic sectors: not only railways and airlines, but also electricity, gas, defence and telecommunications (France Telecom is still mainly state owned). The State in France has traditionally had a leading role in shaping economic policy. More than in most industrialised countries, it plays a decisive role in the regulation of economic activities. This is based on the idea that the State—that is to say public utilities and public services—can bring about public good much better than the market itself. However, the policy on which the EC is based has a somewhat different focus. It involves the freedom of circulation of goods, services, persons and money and the competitiveness of economic actors. It has thus been important in helping France to adapt to the global economy.

It is now well understood in France that the creation of legal monopolies by national law is prima facie illegal under European law. Privatisations are also well-accepted. The privatisation of "Renault", the famous car company, was for instance welcomed with open arms. The top officials—who have now become CEO's of these privatised companies—enjoy a free hand in managing their company and have been converted by the cult of the market economy. The staunch trade unions were much less keen on privatisation, but compromises were adopted. In particular by allowing the transfer of 49 per cent of the shares of France Telecom, the legislator allowed the civil servants of this former public utility to keep their rank and status. The 1996 Act which transformed France Telecom into a private company has simply entitled civil servants to retire at the age of 55 instead of 60 with immediate payment of their pension.[41] Result: French privatised companies still employ civil servants. I should point out that French bioethics law strictly prohibits the production of hybrids and chimeras, but this is one notable exception!

It was much less easy for French officials and politicians to change their conception of another key concept in French public law: the very notion of "public services" which include the transportation of people, electricity and gas supply etc. Traditionally, the view is that the public authorities know best how to manage

[41] This provision was a key to prevent French trade unions from challenging the decision to privatise France Telecom. And the Constitutional Council, in a judgment given on 23 July 1996 (Decision No. 96–380, in Recueil p. 107) accepted it. It ruled that this provision did not infringe the principle of equality before the law since "the equality principle does not preclude the legislature from departing from equality on grounds of overriding interest where the differences in treatment are directly linked to the attainment of the Act's objectives", that is to say "easing the retirement of France Telecom staff to reflect demographic trends in the structure of overall manpower by means of social measures".

these activities in the interest of the common good. This justifies the prerogatives given to public authorities when they enter into contracts with other public bodies or private companies invested with a mission of public service. The doctrine of the public service was developed by the Conseil d'Etat at the beginning of the twentieth century as an essential means to satisfy the public interest and the right of the people to equal access to the services in question. The 1994 annual report of activity of the Conseil d'Etat expresses a fear that the laissez-faire approach of the EC treaty might prevent citizens from benefiting from this equal access.[42]

These criticisms have been watered down, however. Now everyone realises that the French economy has benefited from the market economy. The issue is also less controversial because the ECJ has softened its approach in allowing legal monopolies if they are justified by a national legitimate objective and if they satisfy the principle of proportionality (*Procureur du Roi* v. *Corbeau*, 1993[43]; Municipality of d'Almeo, 1994[44]). In any event, the French Government is not in a hurry to privatise its biggest and most efficient utilities. All things considered, European law has become closer to French law in giving the concept of "services of general interest" a meaning which is not so different from public service "à la Française".[45] French national identity is thus not really threatened. The cock still crows. The State is just a bit less powerful. This, however, would have happened anyway with globalisation. To finish with the issue of the transformation of the State due to the construction of the EU, let me just mention another interesting change regarding the mode of intervention of the State in the economic sphere. European law has interestingly fostered new forms of regulation by delegating powers of regulation to "independent administrative authorities". They now exist in telecommunication, electricity, data protection, and especially finance. The Conseil d'Etat is not too keen on these new kinds of exotic bodies whose multiplication it considers to be a reflection of the decline in the State's authority.[46] The Constitutional Council is surprisingly not so bothered by this new trend. Indeed, it accepted to confer on these independent authorities the power to determine rules to give effect to

---

[42] Rapport Public of the Conseil d'Etat, Etudes et Documents, 1994, Paris, La Documentation Française.

[43] *Procureur du Roi* v. *Paul Corbeau*, [1993] ECR I–2533 [1995] 4 CMLR 621, concerning the creation of a specific postal service for the City of Liège in Begium. This judgment of the ECJ clearly states that national rules conferring a monopoly or exclusive rights may be justified in certain circumstances.

[44] *Municipality of Almelo* v. *NV Energiebedrijf Ijsselmij (IJM)* [1994] ECR I–1447, concerning exclusive-purchasing agreements provided for by Art. 85 (now 81) of the European Treaty, in which one party agrees to buy all it needs of a particular product from a particular provider. EPA has to be strictly notified.

[45] C Leroy, "L'Intérêt Général comme Régulateur des Marchés", about public interest and the functioning of the European market, concerning two cases of the ECJ: Centro Servizi Spediporto of 5 Oct. 1995 (C–96/94) and Autotrazsporti Librandi of 1 Oct. 1998 (C–38/97), in (2001) *Revue Trimestrielle de Droit Européen* 49.

[46] Public Rapport of the Conseil d'Etat, *Etudes et Documents du Conseil d'Etat* (Paris, La Documentation Française, 2001).

The Impact of European Law in French Law: Lessons for England? 261

a statute, a power which is usually only given to the Prime Minister (Article 21 of the Constitution).[47]

European law is changing the face of the State, its structure, its habits and even the way it exercises regulatory powers. The European Convention of Human Rights along with the Strasbourg Court's case law is reshaping the French judicial system. The judge in France has always had a subordinate role vis-à-vis political power. As rightly stated by Jens Plötner, Professor in law, "it is in the purest French legal tradition to turn to political power for arbitration and not to count on the courts".[48] But nowadays judges are gaining more power and more legitimacy. I think this is due to a dialogue between national and supranational judges, which is a first in French history.

The right of access to an independent and impartial judge lies at the heart of the ECHR, namely Article 6. For the British, who have long recognised that the rule of law is an essential condition of democracy, this right is not novel. But in France, this Article is key since it gives the judge a major mission to construct a European model for Human Rights.[50] Article 6 has had so many applications that it is impossible even to sum them up. Let me just take a few examples of its influence on the judicial system. The principle according to which the State cannot restrict or eliminate judicial review in certain fields (*Golder* v. *UK*, 1975[51]) resulted in strong limitations to the definition of "Actes de Gouvernement", that is to say, sensitive governemental decisions which benefit from judicial immunity. Article 6 has also led the Conseil d'Etat to review disciplinary measures (in prison, at school, in the army, etc) which it had previously considered as "mesures d'ordre intérieure" and, as such, not subject to judicial review (Hardouin and Marie, 1995, regarding punishments of inmates in prison[52]).

My second example concerns the retrospective validation of statutory instruments. It is not unusual in France for the Government to amend surreptitiously the Finance Act to validate illegal administrative measures and thus avoid the consequences of an inconvenient judgment. In general, it is a way to avoid paying back the money that taxpayers for instance have unduly paid to the State. In 1998, in a judgment of the ECHR concerning legislation which had

---

[47] The Constitutional Council considers that although Art. 21 of the Constitution gives the power to implement a statute only to the Prime Minister, such power can also be exerted by an independent administrative authority for measures of limited content and field of application. For instance, it ruled that the powers to implement statutes, bestowed on the Conseil Supérieur de l'Audiovisuel, "to set the minimum programming quotas of European and original French-language production that must be broadcast" are not contrary to the Constitution since " these powers are limited in their field of application" (Decision No. 86–217 of 18 Dec. 1986, in Recueil, p. 141 and Decision No. 91–304 of 15 Jan. 1992, in Recueil p. 18). Other decisions have been made along the same line, namely about the Stock Exchange Commission and the Conseil de la Commerce.

[48] *The European Courts and National Courts: Doctrine and Jurisprudence*, Slaughter, Sweet and Weiler (eds.) (Oxford, Hart Publishing, 1997) p. 41.

[50] See the articles written by judges and professors of law in "Pouvoirs" no. 96, Jan. 2001, Paris, Le Seuil.

[51] *Golder* v. *The UK*, 21 Feb. 1975, série A no. 21.

[52] Hardouin and Marie, 17 Feb. 1995, in Recueil p. 82, along with submissions by P Frydman, Government Commissioner.

been deemed constitutional by the Constitutional Council (*Zelinski and others v. France*[53]), the Strasbourg Court held that legislative provisions which retrospectively validated the interpretation of contracts between the social security and its employees so as to avoid the payment of a bonus, was contrary to the requirement of fair process. There was no justification to deprive those concerned of their right to access to the courts. This decision is all the more striking as it is the first time the Court in Strasbourg condemned the French legislator for having validated retrospectively legislation that the Constitutional Council had previously deemed in accordance with the Constitution. Indeed, in 1994,[54] the Constitutional Council ruled that the disputed provision was constitutional given that it allowed the French Government to avoid financial risk, in other terms to pay its debts. It is hard to say, even as a former Justice on the French Constitutional Council, that the Strasbourg decision is a bad one.

The impact of the ECHR on substantive rights is also very important. For a long time, the French have argued that this Convention did not bring any new rights to those already recognised by French courts. But that was not so. The ECHR has notably enriched the French conception of rights as well as helped generate new rights.

There are so many examples that it is hard to choose which are the most illustrative. I would like to mention freedom of speech, "one of the most precious rights of Man", as stated by the Declaration of 1789. Its conception has been renewed entirely. Freedom, in our modern information society, does not only mean prohibition of censorship. It also involves access by the public to pluralistic sources of information. This idea, clearly expressed in the Strasbourg Court case law, such as Handyside in 1976,[55] which is naturally well-known in the UK, is now part of French jurisprudence, even of the Constitutional Council.

Among the new rights generated by the jurisprudence of the Court in Strasbourg is the right "to lead a normal family life".[56] This quite striking since

---

[53] *Zelinski and Pradal and Gonzalez and others v. France*, 28 Oct. 1999, req. 24846/94, 34165/96 and 34173/96. The severity of this judgment is all the more obvious since two years before the Strasbourg Court refused to condemn the UK in another case regarding a retrospective validation of legislation. Building societies alleged that the validation of 1986 fiscal regulations had deprived them of their right to claim repayment of the sums they had paid under the transitional provisions of these regulations. But the Court in Strasbourg declared that the validation was justified and that the British Government had not violated the ECHR ("*Affaire National and Provincial Building Society*", *Leeds Permanent Building Society and Yorkshire Building Society v. UK*, 23 Oct. 1997).

[54] In its decision No. 93–332 of 13 Jan. 1994, in Recueil p. 21, the French Constitutional Council stated that the cost of reimbursement of the bonus owed to the employees concerned "would be high and could only be covered by increasing employers' contributions", but this reason did not seem sufficiently convincing to the Strasbourg Court!

[55] *Handyside*, 7 Dec. 1976, série A, no. 24.

[56] This right was first established by the Conseil d'Etat in "Groupe d'Information et de Soutien des Travailleurs Immigrés (GISTI) and others", 8 Dec. 1978, in (1979) *Revue Droit Social* 57, along with submissions by Philippe Drudoux, Government Commissioner. It was then recognised as a right of constitutional value by the Constitutional Council in a judgment given on 13 Aug. 1993, No. 93–325, in Recueil p. 224, which states that Immigration Acts "must reconcile the need to preserve

it has facilitated the creation of a protective status of immigrants and refugees in France. It allows, in particular, immigrants to have their family join them in France, and thus obliges the French Government to ensure that these families benefit from the welfare State. By and large, the ECHR has prompted the adoption of less restrictive immigration laws. It has consequently led to the imposition of positive obligations upon the State.

3 WIDER CONCLUSIONS

In this lecture, I was offered the opportunity not only to refer to recent developments in French law but also to suggest what lessons the British can draw from them. However, I have chosen to deviate from my sub-title "lessons for the British". Although the French have a strong reputation of arrogance, I would not wish to provide further ammunition in support of this opinion. Besides, I am one of those who admire the common law and feel that we stand to learn at least as much as we may be able to teach. The development of English administrative law and the writing of such respected jurists as Sir William Wade and Lord Woolf of Barnes have long convinced me of this. So, instead of giving lessons to the English, I wish to draw some wider conclusions and let my audience decide to what extent developments in France offer examples of what to do and what to avoid.

I start, *first*, with a general observation, but one which is backed by the little that I have said thus far. The relationship of law and politics is very close, and certainly decisions in the area of public law (including, of course, human rights) can be best understood if seen in their wider context and approached in an interdisciplinary kind of way. This is indisputably the case of French law.

Secondly, politics in France, and certainly its Constitution, still bear the marks of General De Gaulle. Interestingly enough, however, wider events have also left their mark and often trumped the original intention of the legislator. I certainly do not wish to import into France the kind of constitutional debates about "original intent" that one finds in the USA. On the other hand, it is worth reflecting upon the time-honoured dispute as to what makes history; great men or historical events and societal needs and pressures. The question is not just a theoretical one since European integration or collaboration in some form or another is an undeniable issue that is with us and will not go away easily. Given the many open-ended questions it raises, it seems to me that we can only gain by studying each other's experiences and learning from each other's faults and predicaments. It also suggests that developments in other countries may also exercise an influence on the development of national law. The French experience supports this assertion; so it may be valid for Britain as well.

---

public order, a constitutional objective, with the constraints of individual liberty and the right to a normal family life" of aliens residing in France.

My thesis, *thirdly*, has been that for France, at any rate, the exposure to European law—and by this I mean the law of both Strasbourg and Luxembourg—has resulted in an increase in the transparency of ordinary governmental activity and has promoted accountability in general.[57] An extensive application of the principle of proportionality has also duly contributed to a more balanced role of public authorities. For someone who believes in the rule of law, this must be a welcome phenomenon. But I am also conscious of the increase in judicial power which it has brought in its wake and which may not be to everyone's liking. I say this because I am aware of the current debate in England—apparently between the Lord Chancellor and the Home Secretary—concerning the advantages and disadvantages of enhanced judicial powers. Since the newspapers in my country are always quick to exaggerate problems experienced in England—and I have no doubt the reverse is also true—I say nothing further on this point. I do, however, reiterate my belief that in some of the important cases where our courts—for instance the Conseil d' Etat—were forced to change long-established practices, the skies did not cave in. It is possible that the same might happen in your country as to which, as stated above, beyond raising the issue, I can say no more.

My *fourth* point, inadequately stressed but important nonetheless, ties in with the previous ones. To understand the law, you must not only see it within the wide ambit of the society it is meant to serve, but also study it, knowing something about the background of the judges who make it. I recall Professor Markesinis stressing in one of his papers the need to study more judicial profiles.[58] As France goes, however, I go further and remind my English readers to try to understand the esprit de corps of our highest judiciary or, I should say, judiciaries, for the judges of the Cour de Cassation, the Conseil d' Etat and the Conseil Constitutionnel are not imbued by the same ideas or influenced (or burdened) by the same background. This is a topic worthy of a lecture of its own but here, of course, I can do no more than raise it and hope that someone else takes it a step further.

Fifthly, European law fosters the coming together of Common law and Civil law, a notion on which my friend Professor Markesinis has been working hard to promote throughout his professional career.[59] I find the idea very appealing; and judging from some recent decisions of the plennum of the Cour de Cassation, I think there are other judges who are developing such an interest in

---

[57] I take it that similar developments are taking place in your country where, under the influence of European law, there seems to be a gradual development of State liability. On this, see, inter alia, P Craig and D Fairgrieve, "Barrett, Negligence and Discretionary Powers", in [1999] *Public Law* 626. Cases like "*Z and Others v. UK*", 10 May 2001, [2001] 2 FCR 246, by imposing an extensive duty of care on national social services, seem illustrative of this trend.

[58] "Five Days in the House of Lords. Some Comparative Reflections on *White v. Jones*", reprinted in *Foreign Law and Comparative Methodology: A Subject and a Thesis* (Oxford, Hart Publishing, 1997), Ch. 15.

[59] See his *The Gradual Convergence. Foreign Ideas, Foreign Influences, and English Law on the Eve of the 21st Century* (Oxford, Clarendon Press, 1994), especially ch. 1.

foreign law. Like language, law is a living matter. It evolves and takes into account what is good in other systems. The Perruche decision,[60] to which I have just alluded to, is an example of comparative law practised by the highest court—no doubt, thanks to the influence of open-minded jurists such as its current First President M Guy Canivet and M R Denois de Saint Marc, Vice President of the Conseil d' Etat, who has, likewise remarked on the convergence of common and civil law.[61] Likewise, the principle of fair trial was, originally, more British than French, originally but has now become embedded in French law, as well, largely as a result of European law (see the Act on the presumption of innocence of 15 June 2000[62]). Perhaps the "principle of equality before burdens" which does not exist to my knowledge in British law, could be of some help in your legal system.[63] The list of "gives and takes" could, of course, become endless.

Sixthly, the ECHR law and now European law have enriched human rights as well. I think you are about to discover this yourselves, especially with your new Act beginning to have an impact on your domestic law and even applied—I note with great interest—horizontally as well as vertically. These are important and welcome developments. Nevertheless, I am going to go out on a limb and say something which may sound very French. In the present climate, free speech may have dangerous consequences if allowed to operate in an irresponsible way. I think, in particular, of some representatives of Islam, recently interviewed on the BBC, whose speech struck me as excessively inflammatory. Is it enough to rely on Article 15, which allows restrictions on freedoms "in time of public emergency threatening the life of the nation?" This is a difficult question and I wonder whether some of your practising lawyers may not be tempted to take the human rights culture too far, forgetting that in law—as in everything else in life—striking the right balance between competing interests and rights is the greatest service a judge can offer to society.

Finally, I note on a very abstract plane that European law has all in all been a positive influence since it represents the winds of change that our times seem to welcome. For it has helped us to adapt to the new challenges and to be more rigorous with regard to judicial proceedings. For instance, I am not among those

---

[60] Ass plén. 17 nov. 2000, JCP 13 déc. 2000, no 50, p. 2293.
[61] Le Débat, no 115, mai-août 2001 (Gallimard, Paris).
[62] Act no. 2000–516 published in the Official Journal of the French Republic on 16 June 2000, and commented on in several law journals. For instance, (2001) 14 *Les Petites Affiches* and (2001) 14 *revue Dalloz.*
[63] The famous case of *Burmah Oil* v. *Lord Advocate* [1964] AC 75 about the loss of oil installations which had been destroyed by the British Army during World War II, seems to be the only one in which the House of Lords referred to dicta in an earlier decision that "burdens borne for the good of the nation should be distributed over the whole nation". On the contrary, the principle of equality before burdens has had a very significant influence on French administrative law, to extend State liability without fault, especially in case of damages generated by the due application of international commitments. See, for instance, "Compagnie Générale d'Energie Radio Electrique", 30 Mar. 1966, in (1966) *Revue de Droit Public* 774 with submissions by M Bernard, Government Commissioner.

who are outraged by the Strasbourg judgment handed down last June (*Kress*[64]) which considers that some aspects of the procedure before the Conseil d'Etat violate the fair trial principle. Nonetheless, it is hard for an institution as old and as "sacred" as the French Conseil d'Etat to abandon a long-standing procedure which in practise has been applied in a fair way. This is the kind of thing that can make jurists and not only ordinary people see the European influence as an interference. The dilemma that I am trying to describe is one which judges, more than anyone else in the audience, will best understand.

In view of the above, my enthusiasm for the influence of European law on French law, although obviously favourable, is not unqualified. I, for one, cannot hide my concern about the way the European landscape is changing or, just as worrying, failing to change. The events of 11 September suggest to me that much in Europe will never be the same again. But Europe cannot be led by a dynamic law, lawyers and judges alone. Although they have their role to play, and I think in France it has been positive, they are not enough. Political coherence is needed as well, based on the will of the people of Europe who must be made to feel part of this new and exciting venture. Thus far, politicians across the European political spectrum have often failed to engage the ordinary citizen; and this, more than the attacks periodically launched by eurosceptics—be they French or English—is what is making the progress of the European idea more difficult.

---

[64] In this case law of 7 June 2001, the Strasbourg Court considered that the fact that the submissions of the Government Commissioner (the Advocate General at the Conseil d'Etat) were not communicated in advance to the applicants did not comply with the principle of equality of arms and of fair trial. It also deemed contrary to the fair trial principle the Govermenent Commissioner's participation in the Conseil d'Etat deliberations. See comments on this decision namely in (2001) *Les Petites Affiches*, 3 Oct. p. 13; in (2001) 7–8 *Actualité Juridique du Droit Administratif* 675 and in 3 *Revue de Droit Public* 895.